Queer Theory in Education

✦ ✦ ✦

Edited by
William F. Pinar
Louisiana State University

LEA LAWRENCE ERLBAUM ASSOCIATES, PUBLISHERS
1998 Mahwah, New Jersey   London

Lawrence Erlbaum Associates, Inc., Publishers
10 Industrial Avenue
Mahwah, NJ 07430

Library of Congress Cataloging-in-Publication Data

Queer theory in education / edited by William F. Pinar.
    p. cm. — (Studies in curriculum theory)
    Includes bibliographical references and indexes.
    ISBN 0-8058-2864-8 (hardcover : alk. paper). — ISBN
0-8058-2921-0 (pbk. : alk. paper)
    1. Homosexuality and education. 2. Gays—Identity.
3. Lesbians—Identity. 4. Gay and lesbian studies. I.
Pinar, William. II. Series.
LC192.6.Q84 1998
371.826'64—dc21   98-25271
                                                  CIP

Books published by Lawrence Erlbaum Associates are
printed on acid-free paper, and their bindings are
chosen for strength and durability.

Printed in the United States of America
10 9 8 7 6 5 4 3 2 1

Queer Theory in Education

✦ ✦ ✦

Studies in Curriculum Theory

William F. Pinar, Series Editor

Contents

Introduction

William F. Pinar
Louisiana State University

> *[W]e live the political reality of our identity effects.*
> —Cindy Patton (1993, p. 175)

> *The preference of "queer" represents . . . an aggressive impulse of generalization; it rejects a minoritizing logic of toleration or simple political interest representation in favor of a more thorough resistance to regimes of the normal.*
> —Michael Warner (1993, p. xxvi)

> *In a word, [queer] theory may be described as a post-Marxian left discourse that leans in a postmodern direction yet retains much of the modernist legacy, in particular its millennialism and vanguardism.*
> —Steven Seidman (1993, p. 130)

> *Queer speech is vague, indirect speech.*
> —Hubert Fichte (1996, p. 403)

Queer theory in education is not exactly new, of course. The ancient Greeks—and their successors in Rome—although not using the phrase, did link the two. The most recent visibility of queer theory is hardly an expression of nostalgia for those days of homosexuality coupled with misogyny, slavery, and elitism (Block, 1997; Pinar & Grumet, 1988). In education, it appeared in curriculum theory, that site (within the larger field of education) of intellectual revolution for the past three decades (see Pinar, Reynolds, Slattery, & Taubman, 1995, chaps. 1, 4, & 15). Although this is not the occasion for an official history, it is obligatory to mention

1

several events. Peter Taubman's 1979 doctoral dissertation relied on Foucault to destabilize gender categories generally, and gay/lesbian categories specifically. Taubman's work anticipated much of the work that would follow concerning essentialism and identity (Taubman, 1979; for a genealogical history see Pinar & Reynolds, 1992). In December 1981, merged with Chodorow, in bed with Hocquenghem, I attacked the macho Marxists in our field, insisting that for curriculum to escape reproduction it needed to be degenerate. The piece is reprinted in this collection. About this time Meredith Reiniger (1982, 1989) employed Mary Daly's provocative work to study internalized misogyny in her secondary English students. The next year, Jim Sears appeared. No man has done more to challenge heterosexism and to promote understanding of educational issues associated with homosexuality than James Sears (1983, 1987a, 1987b, 1988, 1989a, 1989b, 1990a, 1990b, 1992). But of course, this is not (only) a man's job. Several women have been prominent in this complicated, arduous, necessary effort, most notably Deborah Britzman, Mary Bryson, and Suzanne de Castell. Britzman's "stop reading straight" essay (which appeared in *Educational Theory* and which I included in the "new identities" collection; see Pinar, 1997) signaled a heightened visibility for scholarship focusing on gay/lesbian/queer concerns, concerns de Castell and Bryson had also articulated (1997; Bryson & de Castell, 1993a, 1993b). Jonathon Silin's (1992, 1995) and Elizabeth Ellsworth's (1986, 1987a, 1987b, 1989, 1992, 1994; Ellsworth & Miller, 1992) work has been influential as well.

Homophobia (not to mention heterosexism) is especially intense in the field of education, a highly conservative and often reactionary field. Still, the closet is being emptied, identities are being declared, practices and theories are being challenged, and, as this book testifies, new ones formulated. *Queer Theory in Education* seeks to heighten the visibility of the issues, complicate and intensify critique and theory, while challenging homophobic and heterosexist nonsense—for the children's sake; for all children's sake, including queer children, who must feel as if they come "from another planet—Planet Queer" (Watney, 1996, p. 24). In memory of those who have been murdered and beaten in gay bashings, those exterminated in the Holocaust, those who struggle(d) to survive in families whose "values" justify sadism, for all those who have died of and are living with AIDS, you are with us here. We acknowledge all those who have come before us, especially those whose courage has now made possible a certain (if slight and problematical) clearing of the public space for us to speak. It is long past time for us to speak. Will our colleagues in education hear us?

Queer theory is not unique to education, of course. In this, as in other areas, we are late. For more than two decades, lesbians and gay men in the profession of language and literature have been engaged in the projects of research, interpretation, and theory development, as well as the popularization of lesbian and gay writers, issues of gay and lesbian textuality, the sexuality of literature, and the literature of sexuality. Writing in the Modern Language Association (MLA) *Gay Studies Newsletter*, Adrian Tinsley notes that the first formal gay-studies seminar at an MLA convention took place in 1973; it was entitled "Gay Literature: Teaching and Research." In 1981, the MLA established the Division on Gay Studies in Language and Literature (Haggerty & Zimmerman, 1995). In 1995, George E. Haggerty and Bonnie Zimmerman edited *Professions of Desire: Lesbian and Gay Studies in Literature*, published by the MLA. Regarding the title they note: "The title *Professions of Desire* is meant to convey just that idea: this is a field that one does not enter so much as come out in" (Haggerty & Zimmerman, 1995, p. 2). This book should be taken less as a "coming out" and more a demand that the field "come to"—come to its senses regarding the presence of gay and lesbian youth in the schools, not a few of whose teachers are also gay and lesbian. It is past time to correct the repression of queers in the curriculum, especially in history and literature and the arts. It is past time to think out loud what queer pedagogy and queer curriculum might be. There is the matter of the canon, for starters. As Terry Castle (1993) wrote in regard to lesbian fiction, we assert in regard to the curriculum generally: "What then is a lesbian fiction? . . . Such a fiction will be, both in the ordinary and in a more elaborate sense, noncanonical. . . . It will exhibit an ambition to displace the so-called canonical works that have preceded it" (p. 90). Queer pedagogy displaces and decenters; queer curriculum is noncanonical, for starters.

Queer is not a neutral term, even though it wants to be a term of coalition between lesbians and gay men. (Stephen Murray, 1996, prefers "lesbigay" [p. 2], a neologism that constructs "us" as a "quasi-ethnic group" [p. 4].) Queer has been criticized, accused of effacing specific subject positions occupied by these two broad and diverse groups. Queer theorists and activists have pointed to the perceived classism, racism, and Eurocentrism (see, i.e., Boykin, 1996, p. 92) of the terms *gay* and *lesbian*, suggesting that *queer* may need the queer position from which to speak. Queer has become the chosen term for many who have come to be dissatisfied with what they perceive to be the assimilationist politics associated with the terms *gay* and *lesbian*. Of course, lesbian and gay have not outlived their usefulness in the struggle for our civil rights. Nor can they be forgotten, given certain nonessential but significant divisions between men and women. During the early 1970s and the mid-1980s, as Steven Seidman (1993) notes, this division became enacted politically. "Gay men and lesbians went their separate ways. The tensions in the early gay liberation days evolved into a full-blown separatism even though some lesbians still identified with an inclusive gay movement. A gay subculture was created largely by and for men. Moreover, many lesbians either identified with the women's movement or with the lesbian separatist project of forging a womansculture" (p. 116).

There remain, of course, compelling reasons for women to be cautious about men, including gay men. So let us think of queer as a very provisional term of perhaps a momentary coalition. Bringing us all into one room may serve important intellectual as well as political and pedagogical purposes. As George Haggerty and Bonnie Zimmerman (1995b) hope for their MLA collection, we might hope for ours: "We hope that this volume, instead of systematically addressing questions of identity, identity politics, and terms of identification, opens all these issues for discussion from various points of view" (p. 4). Let this new discourse in education be profoundly "conversational" (Pinar et al., 1995, p. 848).

IDENTITY POLITICS

In a 1996 *New York Times Magazine* article on the state of queer culture in New York, Daniel Mendelsohn contrasted "Rome," a glitzy but fading nightclub in Chelsea (filled with faux Pompeian frescoes of naked boys) with the increasingly popular Big Cup coffeehouse nearby. This apparent shift in location of male gay culture is not a simple matter of caffeine's ascendancy over alcohol, Mendelsohn thinks. "Things are just as PG-13 half a block away at Barracuda," he writes, "one of the neighborhood's newer gay bars. Like the coffee shop, it is virtually always packed. 'This is 1996,' one man volunteers. 'It's just not about style anymore' " (quoted in Mendelsohn, 1996, p. 26).

Such a statement, Mendelsohn points out, would have sounded odd just a few years ago. He points out that, in male gay culture especially, style has been inextricably linked with the very idea of the homosexual since the concept was first articulated, just about the time Oscar Wilde took center stage. Ever since, male gay urban culture "has played Wilde to the world's London" (p. 26). Style has functioned:

> as a pin to prick the certainties and presumptions of the "normal" universe. You see that sensibility at work from Wilde and Noel Coward to Larry Kramer and Tony Kushner. (The character in Wilde's *The Importance of Being Earnest* who declares, "In matters of grave importance, style, not sincerity, is the vital thing," is really the ancestor of Kushner's ghostly Ethel Rosenberg, saying Kaddish at Roy Cohn's deathbed: Both outrageously force audiences to rethink "seriousness" and justice.) And you see it even in everyday gay life, where the emphasis on stylization made the most banal routines like breakfast into tableaux worthy of Vincente Minnelli. (p. 26)

What has happened? Is Ellen not Oscar our cultural icon? Has the "gay community" simply aged? Has assimilationist politics triumphed? In both style and substance, Mendelsohn believes, gay culture has become increasingly like the straight mainstream. ACT UP's politics-as-theater is now a memory, replaced by what one AIDS writer calls the "more reality-based disease activism" (quoted in Mendelsohn, 1996, p. 26) typified by the Treatment Action Group (TAG), which works closely with the same Establishment public health institutions ACT UP once protested. "Gay culture," Mendelsohn (1996) writes, "has gone from *épater*-ing *les bourgeois* to aping them" (p. 27). He wonders, as might we, whether something valuable has been lost.

It was not a decade ago, Mendelsohn (1996) recalls, that ACT UP, in order to focus attention on the AIDS crisis, employed "outré gay style-consciousness" (p. 27) to advance an important political agenda. This "new, distinctively gay" brand of activism was characterized by one observer as "the politics of style" (quoted in Mendelsohn, 1996, p. 27). Founded by playwright Larry Kramer, ACT UP demonstrations were conceived as theatrical events, as performances for (usually hostile) "audiences." Mark Schoofs, a *Village Voice* AIDS reporter, says: "The moment of ACT UP was really 1987 and 1988. You can be very precise here. That was the floruit of the movement. You had this really wonderful string of attention-grabbing demonstrations: stopping traffic on Wall Street, shutting down the FDA— amazing stuff" (quoted in Mendelsohn, 1996, p. 27).

At its zentih, ACT UP was, in the words of a former member, "fabulous" (quoted in Mendelsohn, 1996, p. 27). It was a vibrant movement, recalls Spencer Cox, a 28-year-old former ACT UPper who is now the director of the antiviral project at TAG. "[A]ll this creative energy was going into it and that was really producing results," he remembers. And ACT UP generated its own style: "Look at the fashion that gay men wore in the mid-to-late eighties," Schoofs says. "The military jackets . . . there was a whole paramilitary thing going on. It was because we were, in fact, fighting" (quoted in Mendelsohn, 1996, p. 27). Today ACT UP is rarely taken into account; occasionally it is not even taken seriously. "For despite its claim to artistic and cultural exceptionalism," Mendelsohn (1996) concludes, "gay culture today is suffering from a classic assimilationist aliment: You can't take away what was most difficult about being gay without losing what made gay culture interesting in the first place" (p. 31). This sounds like Pier Paolo Pasolini, the brilliant Italian filmmaker, novelist, poet, and essayist who resisted gay politics from the beginning, in large part due to his contempt for "normalization" (Greene, 1990).

Certain contemporary intellectuals such as Stephen Murray (1996) decline assimilationism as well. For instance, Murray disagrees with the assimilationist view that "we're the same except for what we do in bed." He argues that those of us who came of age estranged (sexually or otherwise) from the heterosexist culture do in fact experience the world differently from those who (especially from a gender point of view) easily fit into it.

Furthermore, he asserts, what homosexuals do in bed is not so very different from what heterosexuals do—"so that both halves of the claim are wrong" (p. 4). Murray thinks assimilationism represents, in part, a "compensatory hyperconformity" (p. 4). He acknowledges that for some, homosexuality was never a basis for condemnation, and that many others ("queer" as well as "closeted") decline to be defined by their sexuality. Those folks acknowledged, Murray regards "*gay* a state of mind, not of body, so that homosexual apologists for the socio-political status quo are not *gay* (or *lesbian*), i.e. those with gay (/lesbian) identity are only a minority of those who engage in homosexual behavior" (p. 4).

Homosexuality has been regarded not only as not assimilable into mainstream culture, but as exhibiting revolutionary potential. For Herbert Marcuse, homosexuality challenged the very ontological structure of technological society by intervening in the reproduction of competitive, aggressive men and commodified women. Writing in the 1960s from California, a new consciousness seemed possible, one that might support a revolution in the existing technological society (Marcuse, 1966; Murray, 1996). In *Eros and Civilization*, Marcuse (1971) argued that "perversions":

> express rebellion against the subjugation of sexuality under the order of procreation, and against the institutions which guarantee this order. Psychoanalytic theory sees in the practices that exclude or prevent procreation an opposition against continuing the chain of reproduction and thereby of paternal domination—an attempt to prevent the "reappearance of the father." (p. 49)

Are we queers revolutionaries against the patriarchal heteosexist social order? Or are we just plain folks? Many of us in the academy would answer both questions affirmatively. True, there is a separatist moment for many of us now; many of us reject assimilationism while retaining interests in broader alliances and coalitions. Yet, none of us can feel the revolutionary optimism of the heterosexual Marcuse. Still, we work toward a future that is hardly visible, still not on the horizon. Despite the explosion in scholarship and an apparent and slight clearing in the public space, we remain in a defensive position: trying to teach tolerance, trying to teach the truth, trying to find ways to decenter and destablize the heterosexual normalization that so constructs the students we teach, indeed the public world we inhabit.

But queer is not only queer; it is not identical with itself. We are now clear that both what we are and what we are not are implicated in the construction of identity and community. There are, then, at least two forms of group identity. The first is affiliative, characterized by strategies of identification; the second is exclusionary, typified by strategies of disidentification. These two movements of identity formation seem to characterize the movements of that political and pedagogical subject formation called queer in North America at this time. A decade or so ago, only the first movement, employing an essentialist conception of identity, was widely discernible (Patton, 1993).

Contemporary conceptions of identity and their political expression, which Cindy Patton (1993) characterizes as "postmodern" (p. 165), may be more sophisticated, more "true" than previous essentialized ones. Still, there has been a price to pay for this understanding. When we abandoned essentialist positions, Patton (1993) argues, we lost a degree of consensus and mobilization. If she is right, then we have a theoretical frame for understanding New York gay men's move from "Act-Up" to "Cup-Up."

That lost political consensus and mobilization can also be illustrated by Queer Nation's first T-shirt, which extended an earlier graphic produced by Adam Rolston. The shirt read "I Am Out, Therefore I Am." Queer Nation's shirt declared that it was the public space in which the individual Cartesian subject must be enacted, transforming that public terrain to survive privately. The shirt's design mapped a psychic and bodily territory—lavender in color—that threatened to "stain" the entire nation (Berlant & Freeman, 1993).

Then, when we knew who we were (but were less aware of what we were not, that is, of what we had repudiated to become what we affirmed ourselves to be), we were "desire," free-floating in the social field, making liberal hets nervous, right-wing crazies crazier. But, as Patton notes, now that we as the "social" id have been deconstructed and replaced with an identity-specific concept of the "cultural," the discursive and political game is different.

> The crucial battle now for "minorities" and resistant subalterns is not achieving democratic representation but wrestling control over the discourses concerning identity construction. The opponent is not the state as much as it is the other collectivities attempting to set the rules for identity construction in something like a "civil society." (Patton, 1993, p. 173)

Now that the id is loose in the house, the struggle is over the characterization of the new, non-split off, social field. For Patton (1993) it is a matter of "duties" and "alliances." True enough, but probably these cannot be accomplished by old-time street politics or union organizing (ACT UP is now a memory), but by discursive acts of identify formation—by that pedagogical intervention in the complicated social, political, and gendered conversation that is the curriculum. We must teach our students their inextricable relation to those they fantasize as *other*. This relational character of identity is reflected and reconstructed through identity politics:

"[T]he achievement of identities is precisely that staking out of duties and alliances in a field of power. Postmodern mini narratives of individual and collective moral legitimacy are replacing the rational metanarratives—like the social contract, pluralism, and democracy—that characterized state legitimation in modernity" (Patton, 1993, p. 174).

How can we teach others while reconfiguring ourselves? How can we move beyond a simple and defensive self-affirmation toward a more profound social relationality in a new nation-state? How, Patton (1993) asks, can we formulate post-democratic ("democratic" understood, as does, say, Rorty, 1991a, 1991b, as involving sharp distinctions between public and private, politics and ethics, pragmatics and aesthetics) modes of a gendered social and political life? The intellectual/pedagogical labor involved in such formation is complex and long-term, but, it seems, we have no choice. As we see in the essays in this collection, the work is underway.

These are not efforts at (a Sartrean) retotalization, however. The "social" is imaginary as well as material, and like a conversation, we can intervene in it but not control it. No longer do we even imagine we hold the discursive "key" to education. As Steven Seidman (1993) observed more generally, "Totalizing efforts by neo-Marxists such as Althusser or Habermas have not proved compelling. Social criticism has splintered into a myriad of local discourses mirroring the social fracturing of the American left" (p. 108), and, we might add, of the geopolitical world. "Furthermore," he continues:

> [I]n place of the global, millennial politics of Marxism, radical feminism, or gay liberationalism, I view postmodernism as speaking of multiple, local, intersecting struggles whose aim is less "the end of domination" or "human liberation" than the creation of social spaces that encourage the proliferation of pleasures, desires, voices, interests, modes of individuation and democratization. (p. 106)

And yet, as Seidman (1993) points out, appealing to one's sexual, gender, or ethnic identity as the ground of community and politics is of limited use due its essential instabilities and exclusions, an understanding he attributes to Derrida. Fuss describes the Derridean understanding of identity as follows:

> Deconstruction dislocates the understanding of identity as self-presence and offers, instead, a view of identity as difference. To the extent that identity always contains the specter of non-identity within it, the subject is always divided and identity is always purchased at the price of the exclusion of the Other, the repression or repudiation of non-identity. (quoted in Seidman, 1993, p. 130)

Referring to Williams' (1991) use of the phrase *inessentially speaking*, Fuss (1993) explains the double relational character of queer identity:

Inessentiality is a particularly useful figure for describing homosexuality's foundational yet liminal position in psychoanalytic accounts of identity formation. The preposition in "inessential," which here doubles as a prefix, connotes at once a relation of exteriority or nonessentiality (in the sense of incidental, superfluous, peripheral, unimportant, immaterial, lesser, minor, secondary. . .) and a relation of interiority, of being inside essentially (in the sense of indispensable, central, important, fundamental, necessary, inherent, vita, primary. . .). (p. 45)

This sounds like Derrida alright. As James Creech comments: "deconstruction is nothing if not a general economy of queering" (quoted in Dellamora, 1995, p. 136), indicating that "all identity, any sexuality, all presence to self of whatever kind are equally queer in that they are undecidable when—as deconstruction allows us to do—we view them against the ceaseless movements of différance and rhetoricity" (Dellamora, 1995, p. 136). Creech argues that deconstruction has played an important role in contemporary queer theory by demonstrating that supposedly natural norms of gender and sexuality are power-effects produced within the institution of compulsory heterosexuality. Deconstruction is connected with "queering" in yet another way, Dellamora (1995) believes. Perhaps there is something perverse about the very notion of deconstruction. The concept may perform the dynamics of identification and disidentification that characterize (queer) identity formation and collective mobilization.

Repudiating views of identity as essence or its effect, Derrida insisted that the identity of an object or person is always implicated in its apparent opposite. "Heterosexuality" has meaning only in relation to "homosexuality"; the coherence of the former idea is predicated on the exclusion, repression, and repudiation of the latter. The two concepts comprise an interdependent and of course hierarchical relation of signification. Seidman (1993) summarizes: "The logic of identity is a logic of boundary defining which necessarily produces a subordinated other. The social productivity of identity is purchased at the price of a logic of hierarchy, normalization, and exclusion" (p. 130). I insist on this point in my piece.

Because identification is identification with an other it is never identical to itself. This alienation of identity from the self it constructs—a structural recapitulation of a primary psychic self-alienation?—does not mean only that any proclamation of identity is necessarily partial, that it will also be exceeded by other elements of identity. As Douglas Crimp (1993) observes, what we know now is that "identity is always a relation, never simply positivity" (p. 313), an important starting point for Britzman, Sumara, and Davis. Identity politics has most often been misunderstood and now denigrated, in Crimp's (1993) words, as "essentialist (denigrated in certain quarters, in fact, as essentially essentialist; this is what Diane Fuss recognizes as the essentialism of antiessentialism)" (p. 314).

It may be relational and unstable, but Eve Kosofsky Sedgwick (1990) locates the heterosexual–homosexual distinction at the very center of Western culture. She and those influenced by her and by Derrida insist that this distinction structures the core modes of thought and culture of Western societies. It is this thought and culture that queer theory wants to decenter. In this regard, Seidman (1993) declares: "Queers are not united by an unitary identity but only by their opposition to disciplining, normalizing social forces" (p. 133). This poststructuralist view moves, for him, too completely to textuality and discursive locations: "[T]o the extent the poststructualists reduce cultural codes to textual practice and to the extent that these practices are abstracted from institutional contexts, we come up against the limits of poststructuralism as social critique" (Seidman, 1993, p. 135).

Queer theory is, in Seidman's view, simultaneously modernist and postmodernist, structuralist and poststructuralist. It straddles, as it were, the divide. It shares with both defenders of identity politics and its poststructural critics a preoccupation with the self and the politics of its representation. But Seidman (1993) argues that this agenda must change; he predicts that any renewed political vision must taken into account self, subject, and identity as a social positioning, as "marking a social juncture in the institutional, administrative, juridical organization of society, and as an axis of social stratification" (p. 135). Seidman urges a shift away from the preoccupation with self and representations characteristic of identity politics and poststructuralism "to an analysis that embeds the self in institutional and cultural practices. . . . This suggests an oppositional politic that intends institutional and cultural change without, however, being wedded to a millennial vision" (Seidman, 1993, p. 137). To some extent, this is the opposite direction from the one in which queer theory in education (not that it is a monolith, mind you) seems to be moving. Perhaps because we tend to be so preoccupied with institutional issues, our agenda seems to be shifting toward the structure of the self (see, for instance, Carlson, in this vol.), toward certain strands of poststructuralism and psychoanalysis (see Britzman, Luhman, Haver, and Walcott). Although not true of all analyses (see Meiners, in this vol.), this shift does reflect the movement in the field that William Tierney and Patrick Dilley describe in their essay. A queer pedagogy would, presumably, call forth and speak to a restructured self.

POSITIONED BODIES

What are the prospects for a queer pedagogy? Gregory Bredbeck (1995) is not optimistic. He characterizes the prospect of describing a queer pedagogy as a "bleak project" (p. 169), a pessimism several of our contributors do not share (see, for instance, Susanne Luhmann and Rinaldo Walcott). But Bredbeck has a specific (if complicated) idea in mind, not a general concept. He starts with Jane Gallop's (1988) discussion of "the student body" in *Thinking Through the Body*. Discussing the pedagogical techniques of Sade's bedroom philosophers, Gallop observed: "One of Sade's contributions to pedagogy technique may be the . . . examination; they use the verb socratiser (to socratize), meaning to stick a finger in the anus" (p. 43).

This examination, which Pasolini had his libertines perform in *Salo*, may, Gallop suggests, be the basis of all pedagogy. She writes: "A greater man penetrates a lesser man with his knowledge. The student is empty, a receptacle for the phallus; the teacher is the phallic fullness of knowledge" (p. 43). And we thought those deposits made in "banking education" were units of cultural capital.

Bredbeck notes that this argument tends to view the anus as an anterior vagina (is this heterosexism or what?), even though Domancé, the pedagogue in Sade's *Philosophy in the Bedroom*, "refuses on principle 'normal' penile–vaginal intercourse" (Gallop, 1988, p. 43). A man with a dangerous sense of humor, Bredbeck (1995) quips: "If pederasty is, crudely put, an old prick and a young asshole, it here becomes just another dick and his chick" (p. 170). This heterosexist logic follows from Sade's sexual preference, his obsession with a "heterosexual pederasty," which Gallop (1988) calls "a contradiction in terms" (p. 44). Bredbeck (1995) suggests that this "contradiction" is in fact "the condition of meaning in pedagogy, a condition explicit in the theorization of learning (whether in the classroom or in the bedroom) since at least the time of Plato, a condition that always changes (as Gallop does) the sexual *difference* of the pederastic Ur-scene into what Teresa de Lauretis would call sexual *indifference*" (p. 170).

The text that anticipates both Sade's neologism *socratiser* and Western pedagogy generally, Bredbeck (1995) notes, is Plato's *Symposium*. This text has been "marked and remarked" (p. 170) in queer culture. Clive Durham, Bredbeck recalls, tried to start something with the central character of E. M. Forster's *Maurice* by asking, "You've read the *Symposium?*" David Halperin (1990) has. He suggests that what characterizes Plato's text is a supreme indifference to sexual difference. Halperin focuses on Diotima's "education" of Socrates; she tries to teach him that the object of all love, especially pederastic love, must be procreation, "the nearest thing to perpetuity and immortality that a moral being can attain" (quoted passages in Bredbeck, 1995, p. 170). Her pedagogical intervention in the all-male Greek world might be remembered (even as it is forgotten) through Socrates' allegiance to indifference:

> Diotima's feminine presence at the originary scene of philosophy, at one of its founding moments, contributes an essential ingredient to the legitimation of the philosophical enterprise; her presence endows the pedagogical process

by which men reproduce themselves culturally—by which they communicate the secrets of their wisdom and social identity, the "mysteries" of male authority, to one across the generations—with the prestige of female procreativity. Diotima's erotic expertise, on this view, constitutes an acknowledgement by men of the peculiar powers and capacities of women; thus Diotima is a woman because Socratic philosophy must borrow her femininity in order to seem to leave nothing out and thereby to ensure the success of its own procreative enterprises, the continual reproduction of its universalizing discourse in the male culture of classical Athens. (Halperin, 1990, p. 144; quoted in Bredbeck, 1995, p. 171)

Jealous of the procreative powers of women, these boys claimed the creation of culture for themselves (Grumet, 1988; O'Brien, 1981).

Halperin suggests that at the origin of Western philosophy is a profound indifference to difference. Bredbeck characterizes this attitude as "a strategy of solidification" (p. 171). It obscures then erases the difference between pederasty and the "contradiction" of heterosexual pederasty by defining both as expressions of the reproduction of sameness. The move nullifies, Bredbeck (1995) continues, gender difference as well. It defines all gender meanings and functions within the shadow of the male, a male "marked as unified within reproduction, plenitude, and continuance: *like father, like son*" (p. 171, emphasis in original). "In reality," he concludes, "there is no woman in the text, only a man's recollection of a man's retelling of a tale a woman has told to a man" (Bredbeck, 1995, p. 171). Lacan thought he himself discovered that "woman" does not exist. That crime is an ancient one, Jacques.

The woman who questions indifference is not easily tolerated in the male academy, whether that woman be Diotima or Irigaray or Madeleine Grumet. The woman can be tolerated only if the question is somehow consumed "by the (re)productive male project, subsumed or expelled, eaten or defecated." And, Bredbeck (1995) notes:

the Freudian school is as much as boy's club as the orgiastic "boy-dello" that houses Plato's philosophers or the pathologically masculine bedroom that is the center of Sade's Philosophy in the Bedroom is; all are worlds of the same, by the same, and for reproduction of the same (but only insofar as that same is masculine and reproductive). (p. 171)

From the couch it is a short trip to the classroom, where, Bredbeck reminds, homosexuality is erased by hommo-sexuality. It is the presence of one self-reproducing (male) gender who totalizes both gender difference and sexual difference. "As the seemingly deviant ped(erast)agogy," he laments, not without his sense of humor, "becomes a missionary spreading the word of gender, which is always already the word of one gender:

man without end, (a)men" (p. 172). That such orthodoxy and misogyny follow from "the Sadean anus" is unsurprising; the truth is that "heterosexual pederasty is not a contradiction in terms" (p. 172). It is, Bredbeck (1995) understands, the "hommo-sexuality" of the heterosexual that subsumes the different into the same, that reproduces any difference as indifference.

It is precisely this subsumption of difference into the same that we intend to interrupt. In various ways, the essays comprising *Queer Theory* challenge the reproduction of sameness, of indifference, of patriarchy. In different ways we work to teach the same(sexed) as the exemplification, the solidification and mobilization of difference. As Marla Morris will point out, a queered curriculum is one of individuals not of categories. A(wo)men.

THE ESSAYS

Tierney and Dilley introduce their paper by reminding us that few educational issues are as contentious as those surrounding the "queer." New York City's "rainbow curriculum" became a meltdown point of contestation; the school chancellor was fired, in part over the controversy. They recall the Salt Lake City school system's decision to ban all after-school activities rather than sanction a meeting of a lesbian/gay group. Accompanying this public controversy, they note, has been an explosion in research. This has occurred largely outside education; in our field relatively little research and scholarship have appeared. Tierney's (1997) *Academic Outlaws* helps correct that situation as does, one hopes, the appearance of this collection.

To illustrate the homophobic history of the field, Tierney and Dilley cite Willard Waller's (1932) *The Sociology of Teaching*, once a widely taught textbook filled with anti-homosexual stereotypes. The present time is typified, they suggest, by four categories of research. Each of these, they believe, employs an idea of normalcy. In contrast to the Waller book, contemporary educational research acknowledges that homosexuality is not deviant or pathological, but normal. The problem is not homosexuality but rather those organizational constructs and constraints that stifle gay and lesbian life.

The most recent stage of research is queer theory, which, they write, has little interest in normalcy but instead "seeks to disrupt and assert voice and power." Use of the term *queer* is in itself defiant, as it rejects the clinician's use of medical terminology (homosexual) or the assimilationist's less confrontational terms. As we have seen, the queer theorist "[s]eeks to bring even language itself in question." "Unlike the petitions for civil rights," they continue, "queer rebels constitute a kind of activism that attacks the dominant notion of the natural." They assert "Queer activism seeks to break down the traditional notions of 'normal' and 'deviant,' by showing the 'queer' in what is thought of as normal, and the 'normal' in the queer. As such, queer theory is more related to critical theory and cultural studies."

Citing the work of several theorists whose work appears in this collection (Britzman, de Castell/Bryson, Haver, Honeychurch, Sears), they note: "Queer theorists argue that proponents of normalcy and deviance have accepted a sexual binarism—heterosexual/homosexual—that privileges some and silences others." Rather than emphasizing specific institutional issues, such as faculty appointments, queer theorists focus on those fundamental discursive structures that need to be disrupted, structures that make oppressive institutional practices possible. If presently institutionalized structures of knowledge have functioned to define normalized relations that excluded "homosexuality," then these structures—as Suzanne de Castell and Mary Bryson (1997) once declared—must be destroyed.

James Sears tells the story of the gay and lesbian movement since World War II, emphasizing the issue of adult–adolescent relationships as a point of focus and destabilization. Early on, opponents to gay and lesbian rights focused on the issue of youth, insisting that "homosexual" and "child molester" were, in effect, interchangeable terms. The Mattachine Society was founded in 1953 by, among others, Harry Hay; during this Eisenhower–McCarthy period, the group knew "if we were going to get along in society, we were going to have stay in step with the existing and predominant more and customs." This male-led and controlled group was joined by the Daughters of Bilitis in 1955; its publication, *The Ladder*, indicated the movement out of the "well of loneliness," a reference to Radclyffe Hall's 1928 novel. Relying on straight experts such as Donald Webster Cory and Alfred C. Kinsey to defend the normalcy of homosexuality, both women and men struggled to survive during a time when police raids and public condemnation were common. Women tended to be ignored, whereas gay men were in the spotlight—portrayed as molesters of youth. The Boise scandal intensified an already virulent homophobia. In the early 1960s, when activists such as Frank Kameny and Jack Nichols insisted that lesbians and gay men (not psychiatrists and sex researchers) could best speak on behalf of the movement, a shift in movement thinking occurred. There was, of course, opposition to this more aggressive stance from more conservative, assimilation-minded men and women. Much debate centered around the sickness issue. "It would take rebellious hustlers and drag queens," Sears writes, "at a seedy Greenwich Village bar and the radicalism of the student movement to shift the ideological terrain." From this "lumpen" moment, gay liberation became linked to other resistance movements, especially to feminism.

During the 1970s, gay liberationists "separated as the issue of gender defined the homosexual landscape as much as the sickness issue had during the previous era." Many lesbians separated from gay men, in acts of self-protection, self-understanding, and self-affirmation. Many—Sears cites Rita Mae Brown—separated from heterosexual feminists as well. I leave the remainder of the story to Sears—he tells it well—and focus here on the intergenerational issue he emphasizes. This issue—institutionalized in the formation of the North American Man–Boy Love Association—has remained outside mainstream gay and lesbian dialogue. Moving through several sectors of theory and scholarship regarding sexuality, Sears questions this taboo. He quotes Edward Brongersma, who argued that: "a boy is mature for lust, for hedonist sex, from his birth on; sex as an expression of love becomes a possibility from about five years of age; puberty is the best time for the 'oceanic,' the mystic experience and for using sex to unite one with nature." Sears cites a Dutch study of 25 minors who were engaged in sexual relationships with adult men. Researcher Theo Standfort found that these youths had not been recruited into their relationships. In fact, more often than not it had been the boy who had initiated the relationship. Sears reports the testimonies of men who as boys were engaged in intergenerational relationships. He concludes: "[A] strong case could be made that its [intergenerational sex] recurrence across time and culture evidences a predisposition for such behaviors." "The challenge of radical pedagogies," he continues, "is to re-examine the assumptions underlying the perversity of pederasty concept; I've written this essay not to advocate engaging in any illegal act, but with the hope that it will allow us to act in reconceptualizing Eros in relationship to Logos." May it do so.

Dennis Carlson focuses on the "new" multiculturalism, with its visible inclusion of gays and lesbians. Clearly, this idea represents an important advance over earlier "normalizing" conceptions of community. He worries, however, that multiculturalism may prove to be less progressive than it promises, unless it is developed in new directions. What new directions does Carlson have in mind? Dennis argues that multiculturalism and identity politics need to be characterized "by a politics of the self that disrupts the underlying binary logic that govern identity formation in contemporary culture. For it is this binary construction of identity, and with it the representation of the subaltern Other as deficient and inferior, that provides a common threat that runs throughout the histories of class, race, gender, and sexual orientation in the modern era."

In recent years, democratic politics has meant identity politics. Like the other major progressive identity politics movements which originated in the 1960s (i.e., the civil rights and women's movements), gay and lesbian identity politics devised a tripartite agenda. First came the demand for recognition; second was a self-affirmative renaming; the third moment involves re-representation. Separatism emerged in the gay and lesbian movement, as it did in the Black and women's movement.

Separatism can go too far. The risk occurs when "we become so aware of identity categories we no longer see anything in people but their identities." Carlson fears that contemporary versions of identity politics—such as queer theory—may fail to distinguish between the strategic uses of identity categories and their capacity to define and position the self. "For a democratic politics to be progressive," he writes, "it has to provide some basis for building a broad-based democratic movement and power block, and identity politics does not take us far in that direction, despite what some have claimed." In fact, he argues, it largely abandons any concept of a public interest that is more than a sum of the specific agendas of various identity groups. He wonders to what extent separatism is finally illusory; is it really possible to separate from the dominant culture in hopes of creating an autonomous space and language of one's own? "In the end," Carlson declares, "progressive politics must offer more than a collection of seemingly autonomous discourses of liberation or empowerment, and this means taking on the dominant consciousness." The "dominant consciousness" is a form of common sense structured by the logic of binary oppositions.

Like Foucault, Carlson views identity as a historical production implicated in relations of power. If we recognize all major identity categories (including queer) as functioning in like ways, we cannot celebrate uncritically a multiculturalism that reduces the self to these historically contingent identities. What we need, Carlson continues, is a democratic multicultural education that examines critically the process of identity formation, a process, he notes, "that too often establishes borders between self and Other and represents and positions difference as the polar opposite of self." Identity formation at this time still tends toward "alterity identity," he says, "identity that is dependent upon an alter-ego Other to define self, an Other who incorporates all that is excluded and devalued in the self."

Such a politics of the self does not, he is quick to add, signify the end of identity politics. Collective identity remains essential to the political agendas of marginalized groups. As well, it provides an answer to the question, "who am I?" But what we need, Carlson declares, is a politics of the self that takes into account the ultimate goals of identity politics, namely to free the self from the Same–Other binary. Such a self would be free of limitations due to race, class, gender, sexual orientation, or other markers of difference. What Carlson wants is a "self [who] does not lock itself into rigid oppositional identity politics and never mistakes its identities for itself." He concludes:

> It seems to me that such a politics of the self is desperately needed within multicultural education if it is not to become a fragmented field of study that treats various minority and marginalized groups separately, each given its week or month in the curriculum, and if it is not to encourage young people to think about themselves and others according to reductionistic

categories of difference in a new multicultural community. If the promise of multicultural education is to be realized, it must be committed to helping young people learn the technologies of self that will allow them to work together strategically across as well as within various identity boundaries to advance common democratic projects.

In a different way, Erica Meiners is concerned that an identity politics somehow severed from broader political questions risks complicity with macro-economic processes like consumer capitalism. To elucidate this important problem, she thinks about the relations among identity, mobility, and capital. "As an identity marker," she notes, " 'queer' is posted as a way to disrupt and simultaneously expose the construction of the reified binaries of heterosexual and homosexual and the static, constructed gender assignments male and female." Queer theory "questions the foundations and formations of sexual identities or sexual identifications." Although she does not claim to be "the mistress of totality" (Meiner's paper is funny as well as shrewd), she does want to "point to some contradictions and implications that arise from . . . the increased use of mobility or travel metaphors in contemporary deployments of queer theorizing." She asks us to think about whose interests are served by these fluid constructions of queer: "whose mobility is facilitated, and whose fixed?" "In addition," she continues, "I don't want to lose sight of Eve—the maiden at stake." Who is Eve? For Meiners, Eve is played as an icon, as "signifying a project of re-mythologization," as always " 'technologically' mediated." "Eve is," she writes, "as natural as a Ford." In "the doubled interests of tainting economic theory and economizing on the production of queer theory," Erica encourages Eve to come out as a Post-Fordist.

A Post-Fordist? Patience dear reader; Meiners makes this designation perfectly sensible. Remember that Erica wishes to question the elitism in queerness and queer theorizing. In particular, she wants to call attention to the whiteness of queer theory, quoting Evelyn Hammonds (1991), who observed that "the canonical terms and categories of the field: 'lesbian' 'gay' 'butch' 'femme' 'sexuality' and 'subjectivity' are . . . defined with white as the normative state of existence."

Recent work in queer theory embraces a notion of mobility in practices and pleasures and degrees of difference(s) in context(s). Queer discourses have moved away from Hammond's "canonical terms" of the field and an unself-conscious association with Eurocentric values. Recent queer discourses (she borrows the term "post-al" from Donald Morton) emphasize mobility in desire; queer is now "about perpetual desires in motion and body-morphing, about the identity or identification a body occupies." Now desire is characterized by movement: "becomings"; "intensifications"; "outside belongings"; "cruising machines"; "unfixing desire." Quoting Probyn and Crosz, she writes that the goal is "to queer oneself through movement," to "free desire from its location." For these "post-al" theorists, a "Deleuzian nomadism and fluidity are romanced." Certain travel metaphors (flight and migrancy, not deportation or homelessness, she points out) are common. Bodies and identities are presumed to be in a constant state of "becoming," and can be characterized, in Deleuzian fashion, as consuming desiring machines. She quips: "everybody who is anybody has a frequent flier plan." But her tone changes quickly and she asks again: "Who benefits from these discourses, who doesn't, and why?" In this post-al move to "becoming" and constant motion, gendered acts and identities risk ahistoricality and decontextualization. Without a context, she worries, the modifier of "queer" becomes too easily appropriated:

> How (and whether) to distinguish between every/any dick or harry who publicly positions as "heterosexual" and accrues privileges, yet considers their ("heterosexual") practices, for example child prostitution, S/M, or fetish gear, as "queer," and those bodies who publicly or not, do not identity as "heterosexual" and engage in same sex-desire and sex?

What can queer be when it is construed as excess, referring to recent work on piercing, tattooing, and addictions as forms of queer desire. Decontextualized, ahistoricized, what is queer? What, she asks, "is the queer enough difference that makes a difference 'queer.'" Returning to the "angst-ridden Eve," she asks, "is she now as-queer-as . . . or queer-than. . . ?" Or, she wonders, has queer become a self-applied adjective, handy when one wants to modify more "static" identities and identifications. If yes, then queer becomes a modifier available to anybody who chooses to self-identify their practice(s) as such.

Meiners calls for an analysis that "works to dis-place and de-naturalize the reified binaries of homo and hetero, and to expose the social, economic and political privileges embedded in these positionings." Additionally, she wants to explore relationships between constructed sexualities and other identity positionings, such as race. Without such analysis, she warns:

> the post-al queer theory move to focus on practices or pleasures or mobile "difference(s) in context(s)" as a marker of queerness introduces a slippery slope. The modifier "queer" can be rendered superficial. To appropriate Cindy Patton's term, "queer" can play as a "disidentification," or a type of "logofellatio."

Boys' play you say. Meiners refuses to binarize the discussion into a matter of performing a public identity or not. Clearly, invisibility is not a good thing. But, she says, we must do more than perform deviance; we must remain clear regarding "the costs of identity positionings." Meiners employs an economic and cultural geography to "flesh out" questions of mobility. Mobility is a metaphor, she points out, directly related to economic and identity privileges. "Who," she asks, "is permitted to drive, who has access to which forms of transportation, who is moved by 'choice' and who is not?" Meiners thinks of Fordism "because of the social contract or scaffolding relationships the theoretical term Fordism acknowledges between the production of the identities of workers and the production of consumers for goods." Post-Fordism poses questions (as do Said's and Spivak's critiques of post-colonialism) regarding the use of the marker *post.*

Who travels the post-al highway? "Forms of transportation," she observes, "whether material, epistemological or sexual, are produced and facilitated by Others." Although such "technological apparatuses" shape and influence the spheres in which they function, they do not exist independently from pre-existing social relations. Neither the mass production of Fords nor post-al queer theory, she cautions, produce more liberatory vehicles. Further, as in post-colonialism or post-modernism, post implies progression. But is it so? Often, post obscures or even erases those contextual, historical, economic, and political conditions and/or constituencies that produced and/or profited from the post. Queer implies post, implying that there has been a radical shift in sexualities, but, Meiners worries, "these possibilities are only afforded to a few. . . . I ask what is the cost of this often marked as progressive de-centralization?" Is it possible that the "fluid queer subject" posited by some queer theorists amounts to an ideal consuming subject for late capitalism? What larger ideological and economic shifts and interests does queer scholarship reflect and serve? "Is the post-al production of a consuming queer subject," she asks, "a form of scaffolding for late northern industrialized capitalist regimes?" She answers:

> most post-al queer theorizing does not, as Patton suggests "queery social theory," but romances mobility. The tenacious analogy I have constructed. . . . Eve is always, as natural as a Ford, is intended to highlight the necessity of persistent work evaluating . . . the goals and spaces in which discourses of post-al queer theory reside and are circulated.

Eve, take us there.

Susanne Luhmann shares an interest in "post-al" queer theory, although her sense of it differs. She begins her provocative essay by asking "how can one imagine a queer pedagogy?" Is such a pedagogy about queer students and teachers? Or is it more a matter of a queer curriculum? Queer pedagogy is more, she asserts, than these, more than the incorporation of queer content in extant curricula, more than devising teaching strategies designed to make queer content more palatable to students. A queer pedagogy must address:

> both pedagogy's curiosity in the social relations at stake in the process of learning, and on queer critiques of identity-based knowledges. Thus, I will

suggest that a queer pedagogy traverses identity demands central to other critical pedagogies and instead poses the question of how a "post-identity pedagogy" becomes thinkable.

Luhmann has grown somewhat skeptical of so-called "subversive" teaching practices. Perhaps the idea promised too much. There are limitations to what we can do (as Marla Morris will also note), and Luhmann suggests that queer pedagogy requires a self-reflexive examination of limitations. Take the matter of representation, for example. Lesbian and gay curricular content is fantasized by some as both a remedy for homophobia and a prerequisite for queer self-esteem. The idea is that homophobia is primarily a problem of representation, an effect of distorted or absent images. To correct such absences and distortions, mainstream lesbian and gay strategists demand "accurate" (that is, positive) representations of lesbian and gay life. This demand for equal cultural and political representation is, she judges, assimilationist in its politics and "modernist" (or "structuralist") in its construction of identity.

What if difference is a necessary condition for identity? Then homosexuality must experienced—she quotes Fuss—as an "indispensable interior exclusion"; only through the performance of this exclusion does heterosexuality become possible. A queer pedagogy, Luhmann argues, must labor to disrupt both the binary of heterosexual normalcy on the one hand and homosexual defiance on the other. Queer pedagogy works, once again in Fuss's words, "to bring the hetero/homo opposition to the point of collapse." Representational equity is not enough. "With the difficult suggestion that knowable subjects are merely another form of subjection to normalization," Luhmann writes, "queer shatters the hopes associated with representational inclusion of lesbians and gays into curricula as a viable strategy against homophobia or a strategy of subversion."

If not a representational matter, perhaps the queer is a matter of method? If so, can we teach in ways that do not reproduce those political and institutional forms we have criticized? "Can a queer pedagogy," Luhmann asks, "resist the desire for authority and stable knowledge; can it resist disseminating new knowledge and new forms of subjection?" This question, she argues, renders suspect the very basics of pedagogy as it questions its appeal to rational subjects who are cognitively capable of tolerance through learning accurate representations. Luhmann's question shifts the focus from the common concerns of teaching (what should be learned and how, what should be known, and how this can be taught) to "the question of how we come to know, or, how knowledge is produced in the interaction between teacher/text and student." Now the focus of pedagogy begins "to shift from transmission strategies to an inquiry into the conditions for understanding, or refusing, knowledge." What is at stake, she continues, is the *relation* of student to subject matter. The questions we ask change; now they become: How does the reader insert herself into the text? What kind of identifications are at stake in this process? What structures these identifications? How do identifications become possible, what prevents them, and ultimately, makes learning (im)possible.

Teaching then becomes more interested in the resistance to knowledge than in supplying missing information. "The desire for ignorance," Luhman explains, "is performative rather than cognitive." Rather than "dismissing the resistant student as ignorant, troublesome, or politically blinded," she advises, "we might begin to ask about the conditions and limits of knowledge, and of what one can bear to know. Where is the resistance to knowledge located?" "What is at stake in a queer pedagogy," Luhmann explains:

> is not the application of queer theory (as a new knowledge) onto pedagogy, nor the application of pedagogy (as a new method) for the dissemination queer theory/knowledge. . . . A queer pedagogy aims at the infinite proliferation of new identifications. A queer pedagogy suggests that, rather than finding the self in knowledge and representations, learning is about the process of risking the self.

The queer pedagogy Luhmann imagines, then, "would engage students in a conversation about how, for example when reading lesbian and gay texts, when listening to somebody speaking gay, textual positions are being taken up, or refused, by students." What happens to the self in such a conversation? Rather than assuming and affirming identities, can a queer pedagogy confront the complicated problem of how identifications are made and sometimes refused? "What is at stake," Luhmann concludes, "is the deeply social or dialogic situation of subject formation, the processes of how we make ourselves through and against others." After Leigh Gilmore (1994), I think of an "autobiographics" of alterity.

Rinaldo Walcott, too, is concerned about identification and the construction of the "other," but he looks to popular culture and Black canonical literature to think about "the dynamics of identity, community, and new desires." He wonders about "new forms of life" that require us to become engaged "in the question of the social." Walcott draws on textual examples that "refuse to stabilize boundaries of identification and endorse the demands for the proper body." He reads Zora Neale Hurston's *Moses Man of the Mountain* juxtaposed to rap music to question the concept of community, specifically Black community. I leave Walcott's intriguing reading of Hurston to the reader. His approach is evident, perhaps, in his discussion of rap, specifically N-Trance. This group performed a version of the Bee Gees "Stayin' Alive," a version that exhibited a hyper-masculinity. "What is interesting about performance and performativity in relation to

N-Trance's 'copy' is," Walcott explains, "that N-Trance used one of the songs or anthems of gay bars to reproduce authentic notions of hetero-masculinity."

"Staying alive" is, as Rinaldo reminds, a poignant priority for those of us living with or at-risk for HIV/AIDS, an "us" who, in his words, "cross-cuts and creates new figurations of communities." Old bipolar categories of "us" and "them" are called into question by such a view. He continues: "What the fluid traces of HIV/AIDS suggest is how interconnected we all are. Bodies then are not discreet entities but rather connect in space and time: they in effect reveal cross-cultural resonances."

Certain "cross-cultural resonances" constitute "sites" where "new kinds of conversations, dialogues and pedagogy" might be formulated. Calling on Douglas Crimp, Walcott discusses the idea of *intersectionality*, which he sees as an elaboration of "relational identities." It is in the recognition of the intersectionalities of identities that political identifications can occur. N-Trance's "Stayin' Alive" brings various social identities (race, gender, class) into collision. Two lines in particular—"Move to the side/Ev'rybody wants to stay alive"—reconfigure the meaning of sociality. Walcott is intrigued by the possibility of new publics and communities who might be capable of moving beyond familiar and facile notions of sameness.

Both rap and hip-hop culture may be examples of such communities. These Black communities have produced, he argues, new networks that have moved beyond earlier narrow parameters of these musical forms. He thinks of the Disposable Heroes of Hiphoprisy (DHH; 1992) whose album *Hypocrisy Is the Greatest Luxury* articulates the desire for more complicated and multipolar notions of community. DHH's "Language of Violence" narrates a story of violence: a group of boys violate another by calling him "faggot, sissy, punk, queen, queer." After school, they attack him. One of the offenders is convicted of the crime; he is sent to prison where he too encounters violence. In this song, race and sexuality are "intersectional," but those sites where the song is played also constitute intersectionality. Walcott explains:

> In queer spaces like dance clubs, rap can often get most people dancing because queer listeners can rewrite the lyrics of many rap songs. Queer men often eroticize hypermasculine rappers in a sexualized dance economy that undermines reading some rap songs as only heteronormative.

Pedagogy, then, must work to demonstrate how we are all bound up together, thereby moving beyond bipolar understandings of the social. This may be the most difficult task for pedagogy, to account for our interconnectedness outside the discourse of victims and victimizers. Pedagogies of the oppressed, Walcott worries, continue to reproduce a bipolar paradigm. "What is ultimately at stake," he concludes, is a shift in reading practices that might lead to an appreciation of complex, shifting identities ... a discussion which is not stuck in the fictive, stable categories we imagine, but never perform as identity. Our reading practices might aspire to continually subvert Us/Them positions and scenarios.

Nelson Rodriguez too is interested in Us/Them scenarios and the cultural politics of youth. He begins his intriguing essay by observing that as the gay community becomes more vocal and assertive in claiming its civil and human rights to equality, respect, and dignity, segments of the right—I think of the Southern Baptist Convention's 1997 boycott of Disney—must retaliate, must "defend" the family, must reiterate tired quasibiblical pseudoarguments to preserve their eroding foundations. He quotes Janet E. Haley (1993) to underline the instability of any sexual class and hence the impossibility of the neoconservatives' project. "The . . . class of heterosexuals," Haley writes, "is a default class, home to those who have not fallen out of it. It openly expels but covertly incorporates the homosexual other, an undertaking that renders it profoundly heterogeneous, unstable, and provisional."

Battles over sexuality and the family often occur, Rodriguez points out, at that site we call "youth," emphasizing that in our time, youth is a political site. As soon as this youth is understood, youth must be understood also as pedagogical. As we know by now, the pedagogical and the political are intertwined. The ways youth use their bodies, language, and culture to contest the mainstream adult world, Nelson points out, suggests that they are engaging in a pedagogical enterprise to educate us—the teachers, the parents, all of us older ones.

Rodriguez concentrates on queer youth, and in particular the pedagogical politics surrounding queer youth, which, he believes, can support the struggle for radical democracy, a civic state that takes seriously the issue of "difference" and challenges the violence of normativity. Having established that (queer) youth must be understood as political and pedagogical, Nelson now moves to make a second and related argument, namely that:

> the political and pedagogical practices and struggles of subcultural groups such as youth need to be linked to the practices and struggles of other (subcultural) groups, and that schools and colleges of education need to provide the critical/theoretical/pedagogical space for imagining how such coalitions might take place.

The field of education's obsession with the practical is complicated of course, but one of the consequences is that theoretical character of the practical goes unrecognized. In an attempt to challenge this pervasive problem, Nelson examines the case of Aaron Fricke. As many readers will recall, Fricke (a high-school senior in 1980) wanted to attend his high-school prom with a male date; he was refused permission by the principal who argued that his attendance with another male would place both Aaron and his classmates in danger. Fricke sued, and "the Rhode Island District Court determined that the school's claim that Fricke's attendance at the dance posed a threat to security was not sufficiently compelling to override Fricke's first amendment rights to free speech and association." What we see in this moment of youth resistance, Rodriguez explains, is the way such cultural political action can challenge both a particular school's authority and the legal governance of institutional pratices. Fricke's action rippled across a broader social surface as it forced the authority of the state of Rhode Island to confront and negotiate a "clash in ideologies." Rodriguez continues:

> Fricke's cultural work connects to even broader terrain. That is, his resistance contests what Judith Butler calls the heterosexual matrix, "that grid of cultural intelligibility through which bodies, genders, and desires are naturalized." To be sure, Fricke's attendance at "a paradigmatic heterosexual ritual like a prom [with another male] cannot but call into question our normative assumptions about dating, romance, and the nature of desire."

Fricke, then, is engaging in a form of pedagogy that performs identity politics. His case, and others, need to be taught in teacher education classes, so that educators—in schools and in colleges and universities—might help youth recognize, in Rodriguez's words, that:

> homophobic representations in culture engender undesirable consequences not only for gays and lesbians but for so-called "straights" too. [Perhaps] youth can then begin to consider the importance and necessity of constructing a politics that connects particular interests and struggles to a broader democratic project.

Who suffers from homophobia and heterosexism? Who should care? Not only gays and lesbians, Rodriguez answers.

In an insightful essay, Shirley Steinberg discusses queer visibility in the cinema. Although she concedes that queer visibillity has taught something to straight viewers, "I am concerned that this curriculum is a liberal attempt to cover up, sanitize and Disneyfy queerness. This cleansing, then, becomes a reinscription of homophobia and heterosexism."

Homosexuality has been implied, and occasionally explicit, in films since the beginning. In early films, flirtatious scenes could be interpreted as either "gay" or "straight," the ambiguity itself permitting visiblity. In the 1940s and 1950s, Hollywood was instructed to stop fooling around. In order to prevent "sleazy" and suggestive or compromising scenes, the Hays

Code censored producers' and directors' film work. For more than 20 years it was followed and "ugly sex situations" were avoided in the cinema. Slowly, however, the Code came to be disregarded in the 1960s, and by the 1970s, it had been forgotten.

Drag became funny and acceptable, provided, of course, the male characters dressed in dresses in order to seduce women. *Tootsie, Victor/Victoria, Yentl,* and *Mrs. Doubtfire* illustrate this phase. In the 1980s and 1990s, films with homosexual themes and/or characters were "sanitized" in order to make them "palatable" to (straight) moviegoing audiences. To illusrate the point, Steinberg reminds us that *Philadelphia* was a film that portrayed a gay man with AIDS—a gay man played by a straight man who was conspicuously asexual throughout the film. Heterosexual audiences were not uncomfortable, Steinberg points out, because the film focused on the prejudices surrounding the illness. But what gay men do in bed was acknowledged only by its absence. In contrast, *Torch Song Trilogy* is a film about gay men and in fact shows men in bed together. Becuase men kiss and express desire, the film never caught on with mainstream audiences. Steinberg characterizes *Philadelphia* as *liberal,* tolerable to the American (het)mainstream. It was considered for public awards; it was discussed in the news media. *Torch Song Trilogy* she terms *queer*: to the straight American public it was unacceptable; the movie was not discussed in the media. Liberal movies normalize the queer, she argues, legitimating homophobia, if in tacit ways.

After viewing *To Wong Fu, Thanks for Everything, Julie Newmar,* a gay man tells Steinberg that he was pleased that so many straight men in the movie audience appeared in no way "offended." Steinberg thinks that he should not conclude too much, "that he should *still* not walk down frat row at night without an escort. . . . These males were not legitimizing queerness," she argues, "they were merely enjoying Flip Wilson turned into Wesley Snipes in an updated romp through dragdom." For Steinberg, both *To Wong Fu . . .* and *Priscilla, Queen of the Desert* are liberal films that "reinscribe heterosexism and avoid the political." She elaborates:

> Sex is not topical in either film, that is, no one has it. In both films queers romp around in high heels looking for the "right" man—but, no one has sex. Indeed, when a character in *To Wong Fu* does fall in love, holding hands is as far as they get. As queer as the drag queens appear, they are depicted as sexless, libidoless and there is no mention of what exactly it is that queers *actually do* sexually.

Queer females, Steinberg argues, appear to fare better in Hollywood, but for no *good* reason. "What man," she asks, "[what] heterosexual man, is not turned on by the thought of more than one woman?" And so, women in Hollywood's "lesbianesque" films function as heterosexual turn-ons. The male audience is titillated to watch their private fantasies acted out on the screen while the women watch. Steinberg points to several films to illustrate her point, including *Fried Green Tomatoes, Basic Instinct, Bound,* and *Chasing Amy.* "Thematically," she tells us, "these films come from the same root: it is evident that the women have had relationships with males and *being a lesbian is not the point—having sex with women is.*"

Films with women having sex with women "invert" those themes characterizing male movies. In male–male movies, there can be depictions of gay "lifestyles" as long as there is no (or minimal) sex. In female–female movies we see the opposite: the camera concentrates on explicit sexual experience, but rarely do we see detailed portraits of these women as lesbians. Current films "romanticize" queerness, Steinberg argues, by presenting "queerness without sex—and exploit women fucking women who are not *really* lesbians." She concludes:

> To take one step *out,* then two steps back, as in *Philadelphia, The Crying Game, M Butterfly,* etc. is not sufficient. Film as gay counter-hegemonic cultural work must not apologize to homophobes for the practices of queerness. Indeed, homophobes should not tacitly dictate the operation of gay cinema. . . . [V]isibility is not enough. Responsible, unsanitized and self-conscious film making is.

Thank you, Shirley.

Perhaps there is something in the psychological structure of the male, specifically the European (het)male, that requires the (homosexual) "other" to be like the heterosexual "us." Such speculation takes us directly to questions of identity, questions that Dennis Sumara and Brent Davis explore in their important essay. Sumara and Davis are interested in identity, particularly sexual identity, which they construe as a social relation, not an essential division between "us" and "them." They quote Deborah Britzman (1995b): "[E]very sexual identity is an unstable, shifting, and volatile construct, a contradictory and unfinalized social relation." It is this understanding of sexuality as relational that underpins the work of queer theory. "As a form of cultural study," they write, "queer theory aims to take account of the polyvalent ways in which desire is culturally produced, experienced, and expressed." As curriculum theory, queer theory asks "that the form of curriculum and the relations of pedagogy be appropriated as spaces to interpret the minutiae of differences among persons, not merely among categories of persons." *Queer* is an umbrella term—a representation of gay, lesbian, bisexual, and transgendered persons, but also an idea that functions:

> as a collecting place for interpreting instances of curriculum/pedagogy that refuse what Haley (1993) has called the "heterosexual bribe." . . . Queer

theory asks not that pedagogy become sexed, but that it excavate and interpret that ways it already is sexed and, further that it begin to interpret the ways in which it is explicit heterosexed.

Understanding curriculum as comprised of sets of relations, and understanding both identity and sexuality as relations embedded in the production of knowledge, Sumara and Davis argue that curriculum forms are always tied to expressions of the sexuality/identity matrix. They share with others a certain reservation regarding a queer curriculum theorized in content terms: "While we do not contest the importance of the 'coming out' literature and the work it accomplishes, we worry that it continues to participate in the construction of the identity of the homo as necessary other to the hetero." They are quick to add that they appreciate that this coming out of the closet work functions to disclose what Sedgwick (1990) called the "open secret," namely that identities other than hetero exist, and "that these identities do not depend upon particular bodily acts and particular forms of social organization for their existence."

But there is another, different, curriculum question that follows the content question, one that begins in thinking about identity as relational. What if, they ask, sex and sexuality were not construed as discrete acts enacted by specific and separate identities, but rather as sets of social relations in the service of physical, emotional, and psychic pleasure? One might then think of identities and sexualities as formed and reformed through fantasized acts of relationality. What if, they continue, sex is not so much the act of sex—even the particular genitalia of the participants— that mattered, but rather "it was a particular set of structures and associations continued with a particular narrative structure that permitted eroticism." What then?

Well, for starters it would mean that both cultural studies and curriculum theory would construe the pedagogical as profoundly relational. Curriculum would be understood as a form within which to enact certain interventions, transformations of thinking, and other cultural practices. "Understood as such," they write, "curriculum theory is not subsumed within the larger category of cultural studies, but is a necessary valence to it." What makes curriculum queer is not so much that it deals specifically and explicitly with sex, but that, following the work of Britzman (1995b, 1996), "it attempts to perform this understanding of sex as a relation rather than as an object."

Dennis and Brent elaborate by offering their understandings of what constitutes a queering of curriculum and pedagogy. First, queer curriculum attempts to come to a profound understanding of those forms curriculum might take. Sexuality may be included not as a specific subject of study but as "a necessary valence of all knowing." Second, rather than focusing on gay, lesbian, bisexual, and transgendered identities, queer curriculum "wonders about the unruly heterosexual closet and seeks to render visible the always known but usually invisible desires and pleasures that circulate throughout it." Third, because a queer curriculum understands forms such as sexuality, identity, and cognition as relations rather than objects and, moreover, accepts these as intertwined, it creates situations where this complexity is made present for study. This means that sexuality would not be studied as a subset of, say, cognition; rather, knowing would be taught as sexualized. Sexuality *is* cognitive. Fourth, queer curriculum is interested more in appreciating differences among persons than in understanding differences among categories of persons. Fifth, a queer curriculum is especially interested in matters of desire, pleasure, and sexuality, most importantly, in how we might interrupt our understandings of these, including how they make themselves known. Finally, a queer curriculum creates forms where the heterosexual matrix is made visible, available for interpretation and critique.

In one sense, my piece works to make visible the "heterosexual matrix." A few things have happened since December 1981, when I wrote "Understanding Curriculum as Gender Text": AIDS for one, the explosion in lesbian and gay scholarship for another. At the time I was angry with the "macho Marxists" in our field, at their (apparently unconscious) insistence that "power" (i.e., the phallus) not gender (i.e., [heterosexual] women let alone queers), not race, construed especially as "class" (that same reactionary American working class that, in a final act of self-hatred and self-immolation, had just helped elect Reagan president the year before) was the primary category of curriculum theory. To whittle them down to size (as it were), I relied on Chodorow's (1978) study of mothering (which I modified). Although object relations theory has since been critiqued for its class- and race-blindness (see Bordo, 1993, or Cornell, 1992, for commentary), it seemed suitable to me at the time: after all, I was taking aim at middle-class White boys. Well, these boys are middle-aged now, and not so macho anymore. Their tired, self-serving pseudo-Marxism has long been eclipsed by feminist theory and racial theory, joined now by queer theory.

So why reprint the piece? Am I still angry? Maybe a little. Mostly I reprint the piece because machismo still works its way through a number of scholarly disciplines—including cultural studies and curriculum theory—and because it is machismo itself that remains an important problem we queers face. I am thinking specifically of "us" (male queers), as our ambivalence toward traditional masculinity continues to complicate our efforts to move past internalized, self-hating, and mystifying conceptions of who we—and they—might be. I reprint the piece because it names the body, specifically parts of the body, and links them to political and autobiographical ideas. The "phallus"—no matter how densely and brilliantly Lacan insists (and Zizek defends)—is still a dick, a private part yes, but a public weapon too.

Ask the victims of rapists and stalkers, including those college girls who continue to visit fraternity houses on date(s) (rapes; see, for instance, Schwartz & DeKeseredy, 1997). Ask female soldiers, ask the military faggots, who get it every day, unless they're outed (of the military that is). The phallus is still a dick; the anus is still an asshole. But both are also symoblic currency in a psychocultural exchange of patriarchy, misogyny, heterosexism, all encoded on and in the body. Body matters: the male body comes from the female body (repudiated then desired/not desired) and from the male body (the father in whose sperm sack "I" lived before reaching the womb, before the egg and "I" merged), and in the settlement of (male) identity an "other" is split-off. Queer theory as I perform it, as I see it anticipated in my 18-year-old paper, is, in part, about the self-splitting other-producing phenomenon of masculinity production in (White/het) America. To be a White middle-class male and a rebel in America means becoming an "other," and becoming queer was the last move (after the defeat of 1968 and the shift from political to cultural revolution) this White boy could think to make. If the world were queer, I suppose I would be straight. It isn't; I'm not.

"What would we make," Suzanne de Castell and Mary K. Bryson ask in their succinct and provocative piece, "of a school-based research study in which all of our informants were heterosexual?" They answer:

> This should be an easy question to answer, given that practically all educational research finds exactly this. Now, speaking hypothetically for a moment, what of a study in which all of the informants were lesbians? What might we say? That this must be a very unique situation? That the researchers must be being led astray by her own desires? That she must be being duped, like Margaret Mead in Samoa? Or. . . . what indeed *would* we say in such a case?

The absence and/or invisibility of lesbian students, teachers, administrators, and, indeed, researchers, in educational research accounts is profoundly troubling. "But," de Castell and Bryson wryly note, "it has seemed rather impolite to mention this and, when we have dared nonetheless to raise this question of other peoples' research, we have made all too clearly aware of its impropriety."

It is essential to ask this question; our absence is not insignificant. Probably it matters very much as to what is discovered who is doing the research, and from what identity position. It matters, they point out, that only heterosexual or "faux-heterosexual" people are usually welcome to do school-based educational research? They assert:

> [I]t surely matters if these same heterosexual people are either unable or unwilling to see or to report the presence of gay and lesbian subjects in their research population. . . . Must we then accept and sanction incomplete

and deceptive research because the homophobic environment of school sites and workplaces puts certain knowledges and certain identities out of sight and out of mind?

What can be done? Suzanne and Mary answer with what they term "notes toward a queer researcher's manifesto," asking afterward: "Alright then, can you sign on? What will it mean for the future of your research if you do? What does it mean for the condition of your research if you cannot?" A (extraordinarily important) point well taken.

Kenn Gardner Honeychurch (whose artwork appears on the cover of this book) has also been thinking about research. Sexually neutral research is, presumably, methodologically optimal. Honeychurch declines to do the optimal. Perhaps a bit like Jane Gallop, he eroticizes his professional activity. After all, the neutered researcher is nothing more than an impersonation. To illustrate eroticized research, he describes his interview with Gayle Ryon, as part of a larger research project concerning adult gay male artists. You'll get the picture:

> Prior to beginning the first body-to-body interview, I edged towards the still sticky surface of the wet-into-wet blended gradations of the various lights of painted flesh. The first canvas offered an unfinished nude portrayal of the artist who, in oils, as well as in the regimes of his life, courts the viewer, constructing and presenting himself as an object of sexual desire. . . . On the floor were tempting, color nude photographs, on which the painting was based.

Honeychurch thinks of Nietzsche, who suggested that "aesthetic experience had more in common with sexual ecstasy . . . than it did with the quiet individualistic contemplation of a work of art in a spirit of disinterested, rational inquiry." Glancing over at Gayle, Honeychurch is amazed "how much I had learned about his body in a very short time."

He now proceeds with the interview process:

> After seating ourselves at a long, hand-constructed table, the first formal, recorded interview began. With fluent lips and a brave tongue, Gayle provided interview data which was substantial and provocative. Perhaps predictably however, despite the seductive constituents, the conversation concluded without any mention of the body and sexuality outside of abstract terms of inquiry. Clad in the demand for the body's denunciation, I spoke not a word about it and in that omission, there was created a paradox: an insistence on considering and affirming the homosexual body and desire as topic . . . but denying them in the flesh.

How did Honeychurch become so clothed, "clad in the demand for the body's denunciation?" Could it be . . . the university? He observes that "any text of the Academy which expresses sexuality through erotic words and phrases may be deemed tense and unacceptable." He acknowledges (smiling surely) this not a simple matter of loosening restraints: "[I]f considering, or cruising, the body as an sexual site of agency, and, allowing for at least a peek at the possibilities of desire in social research, are deemed permissible, any ensuing discussion is still not without its kinks." One such kink is that fundamental sexual repression institutionalized in schools: "It is, after all, at the critical places of pedagogy where bodies of the learner, the teacher, and knowledge come together." It is clear that "the sensual, sometimes hot, pleasures of the body may not easily, or always, be extricated from the cool demands of inquiry."

Nor should it, perhaps. "How might," Honeychurch asks, "a recognition of the body contribute to understanding?" He lists three ways:

> 1) [E]ros, as a source of human motivation, may not only influence the researcher's ideas for research, but, as well, may invigorate and fuel the entire body-to-body inquiry process; 2) as motivating life-force, the possibility of strong erotic feelings may influence rapport, and therefore, candor; and 3) as emotion is rooted in the visceral, strong emotions which include sexual desire, may also, perhaps most importantly, influence perception.

Social research has to do with the experience of bodies, Honeychurch reminds. By emphasizing sex and the body, he argues for "a more conscious inclusion of the corporeal, for a recognition of a fuller range of the body's sensual capacities, and, as well, for a recognition of how some inquires are impacted by the presence of specific desires." Sensing and sexual bodies, then, become central not marginal, both to theory as well as to the day-to-day labors of social research. Sexual bodies become allies in, not aliens to, understanding. Such acknowledgment of sexuality and the body might well, he writes, "fall outside of the pervasive and powerful shadow of an exclusive masculinist and heterocentric perspective." The significance of the body, Honeychurch concludes, can perhaps best appreciated by imagining a world in which sensuality plays no part. The overwhelming disappointment that accompanies such a conjecture speaks "to the irrepressible itch of the body, of the connections of pleasure, desire and knowledge which this project has only begun to scratch."

Marla Morris wants to scratch the curriculum . . . well, "unrest" it, to use her evocative verb. Queer it. Starting with Gertrude Stein, Marla asks what would it mean to queer the curriculum? Were she a curriculum theorist, Stein might insist that the curriculum become strange—one way to describe the word queer is as strangeness. But to define queer as an attitude stretches the term too far, risks rendering it meaningless (as Meiners too has worried). If defined as concerning only the problematics of gender, queer risks becoming too narrow. Subsuming differences within it, the concept of queer risks obliterating the situatedness of individuals. So, Morris is left questioning the very category itself, wondering if the notion of queer simply instantiates yet another binary: queer/not queer?

In the echo of these important questions, Morris elaborates her own theory of the queer, a provocative one based in aesthetics. She argues that a queer aesthetic or queer sensibility extends the current discussion on queerness by side-stepping identity politics. She advances a three-part definition of queerness, each part of which includes an aesthetic dimension. First, queerness understood as a subject-position digresses from normalized, rigid identities that adhere to the sex = gender paradigm. It surpasses the liberal humanist project that pretends that straights/lesbians and gays/transgendered people are all somehow alike. Second, queerness as a politics challenges the status quo, rejecting assimilation. The politics of queer is, she suggests, "digressive," requiring examination of those cultural codes and discursive strategies located in the dominant culture. Unlike resistance, a digressive politics is not utopian. Like Luhmann, Morris says we must entertain a certain cynicism about what, realistically, is possible. To digress from dominant cultural codes is to move away from mainstream discourses. She writes: "Becoming queer is just that: a constant becoming, a constant transformation. . . . A queer identity is a chameleon-like refusal to be caged into any prescribed category or role." Third, queerness as an aesthetic or sensibility reads and interprets texts (art, music, literature) as potentially politically radical. As illustrative of a queer aesthetic she discusses—intriguingly—Mark Rothko, Philip Glass, and François Rabelais whose works, across gender and time, provoke queer readings. Morris posits the idea of a queer curriculum worker, one who might trouble curriculum, trouble the very relationships of the day to day lived experience of school life. A queer project, she concludes, unrests curriculum. That it would.

Mary Aswell Doll wants to queer our gaze. To do so, she writes about the pun, "the lowest form of humor." Why is it, she asks, that when someone puns, people groan, a sound, she notes, that mixes moan with growl, pleasure with pain. The pun, she asserts, ought to be remembered as a kind of *opus contra naturam*, a work against nature, a move into lower forms. That appeals to Doll, who has pledged herself—heroically I would say—to work against the dulling institutionalized tendency toward "niceness." To do so, she "must teach the non normal, be the non normal." How does one queer the gaze? Doll gives us four ways, each, like the pun, an *opus contra naturam*. First is the way of shock; second is the joke; third is myth; and the fourth is the way of the perverse. Let's take them one at a time. Shock, she explains, is nonphallic, yet confrontational. She discusses Frida Kahlo's painting as an instance of shock. Less confrontational is the second way, that of the joke. Here she cites the playwright Tom Stoppard, who once described himself as a "bounced Czech." Stoppard's plays, Doll explains, unsettle an audience's expectations of what it is to be an audience, what it means to take on the spectator role. It is, she writes, "insouciant art, wrong representations which function to queer the gaze."

A third way to queer the gaze is myth. Myths are narratives on a different plane, not "out" but "down." In myth, forms that appear human are also divine, possibly animal or vegetable, even mineral. Doll recalls the myth of Persephone as illustration. The motifs of the Persephone myth—the virgin, rape, Hades, natural change—resonate with queer theory; they queer normalized perception. The fourth way, that of the perverse, means "to follow a left (non right) path, a way not of the will." Here she discusses the work of Beckett—on whose work she has written before (Doll, 1988). How do these four ways function to queer the gaze? Doll explains: "To be wretched . . . away from ourselves, finally, is to leave our ego claims behind. It is to open to a far-flung imagination, an exotic otherness, a vaster vision that expresses a freedom from limits. This move contra-naturam," she concludes, "might be accomplished in these four ways, ways which both allow us to confront the homophobe while we chart a path away from the straight and narrow." Indeed.

Away from the straight and narrow is exactly where Alice Pitt is headed. "Lesbians are not women," she begins provocatively, quoting Monique Wittig's "The Straight Mind." This declaration is amplified by Wittig in a footnote, where she adds: "No more is any woman who is not in a relation of personal dependency with a man." What is "woman" and what is her relation to "lesbian"? These questions are audible in Women's Studies classrooms, where commonsense notions of woman are challenged regularly. In the classroom, Pitt reports, "the figure of the lesbian continues to be a disturbing, perhaps even uncanny presence." This project points to the pedagogical problem that the labor of learning often occurs in the unconscious. There the sense of self is anchored as cohesive and coherent. Education involves the labor of identification, she explains, and its processes are implicated in relations of domination and subordination. So conceived, "theorizing curriculum and pedagogy might benefit from understanding learning as a psychic event that involves the realms of both conscious and unconscious operations." What might such understanding entail? To explore this question, Pitt suggests studying "certain disturbances in one woman's imagined relation to femininity," a White woman in her late 30s named Lynne Hunt who volunteered for the project.

Wittig's conclusion ("lesbians are not women") works against the grain of mainstream North American feminist education. Lesbians are regarded as being within, not apart from, the category of women. Within this mainstream practice, lesbians are perceived as sharing gender identity with heterosexual women, and are oppressed both as women and as lesbians.

But for Lynne, the woman Pitt studied, the figure of the "lesbian exceeds the bounds of what she will identify as a women's issue. . . . [L]esbians are oppressed because they are lesbians, not because they are women."

Pitt excerpts Lynne's account of her participation in an introductory Women's Studies course in order to examine the relationship between Lynne's self-understandings as a woman and those subject positions— woman, feminist, lesbian—articulated by the course curriculum. "I focus," Pitt explains, "on the ways in which this relationship can be seen as relying on, even if it is bothered by, the place within the course of the figure of the lesbian." It is this student's refusal to recognize herself in relation to the figure of lesbian, her generalized resistance to Pitt's pedagogical efforts, that provides Pitt with the opportunity to study the labor of theorizing identity that Lynne—and no doubt many other students—undertake.

What does it mean to interpret the work of students' resistance as part of the work of identification? What are the "symptoms" of educational engagement? By asking such questions, Pitt is conceiving of pedagogy as creating conditions that invite students to examine the structure of their responses to the curriculum. Wittig's "The Straight Mind" is pedagogically interesting in this regard, not because it "represents lesbians" or problematizes heterosexuality, but because "it allows us to think about representations of gender and sexual identities as sites of identification where our fantasmatic ideals might be called into question, assessed, and perhaps even reconfigured." This is extraorindarily important work, in which Deborah Britzman has more than a passing interest.

Britzman has been wondering, among other things, about pedagogy's capacity to address the ego. She has grown skeptical of "pedagogy's current preoccupation with making the proper curriculum that can somehow prop up the coherence of knowledge and its subjects." The author of the ground-breaking "Is There a Queer Pedagogy?" (1995a), Britzman here focuses on AIDS education, noting that as "we attempt to offer less damaging information and ready ourselves to rethink current representations of the virus . . . we also know those appeals to a rational, cohesive, and unitary subject in the name of toleration, role models, and affirmation of and reliance on identity return the damage." What does she mean? She explains by challenging educators' preoccupation with the ego. What is the ego, she asks, that it should be "the destination of a pedagogical address?" After Freud, she suggests that the ego is first of all a bodily ego, a "frontier creature." Its work is that of perception, hallucination, reality-testing. The ego attempts to resolve that which cannot be resolved, namely the problem (i.e., the difference) between psychic dynamics and social demands. It is in this difference, Britzman writes, that "we have the most intimate expression of the failure of knowledge." Due to ego's interest in resolution, in synthesis, when confronted with the impossibility of escape from itself when things (inevitably) do not work out, the ego employs its "special methods," those famous defense mechanisms. When put in operation, the defenses allow the ego to live its irresolvable dilemmas. This concise and compelling account of the ego's coming to knowledge is complicated by Freud's portrayal of the ego as tragic. Britzman explains:

> For the ego's defense mechanisms are formed at a time when the ego is just emerging, too young really, to understand that in its lonely attempts to defend itself, to differentiate itself from its own anxieties, it will set in motion the very dilemmas it desires to flee. . . . Freud suggests that the very work of the ego causes it to fall ill.

The tragedy does end there. Freud theorized that the forces at work within the ego also compel the ego to change the world, rather than merely adapting to it. Does the "longing for total revolution" (Yack, 1986) originate in the birth of the modern subject?

Where does this leave us in our effort to understand our dilemma as students and teachers? We must acknowledge, Britzman writes, that "knowledge will always be fragile, subject to reversal, displacement, substitution and condensation. For the ego is a precipitate of its own libidinal history, its capacity to touch and be touched." It is within such dynamics that student "learn" and teachers "teach."

Freud suggests another potential—which Britzman characterizes as queer—that will interest those who think about pedagogy: "Where id was, there ego shall be." "Suppose," she asks, "that pedagogy could attend to the time of delay. . . . If pedagogy can reside in the fallout lines of these sentences—promising nothing, not expecting so much—it might begin again with another sentence of delay."

What if our professionalized obsession with smooth relations (what Doll calls "niceness") is in fact a defense against our incapacity to acknowledge the fragility and complexity of our mission? To risk controversy would mean speaking to this phenomenon of symptom-formation, our investment in ignorance. We educators obtain some (perverse?) satisfaction in our victimization. Freud termed this "resistance" or "the gain from illness," that clinging to illness in the name of innocence. Britzman cites Christopher Bollas who speaks of "the violence of innocence," characterizing "innocence" as a refusal of relationality. Innocence, Bollas says, is a form of denial, but "one in which we observe not the subject's denial of external perception, but the subject's denial of the other's perception." Britzman adds: "We might venture to speculate that two relations are being denied: the self's otherness and the other's otherness." Exactly.

The tendency to identify with others is a symptom of the ego's capacity to hallucinate. Citing Alice Balint, Britzman asserts that identificatory thought is an expression of resistance, not love.

Because resistance is carried within so many interminable disguises and
essentially recreates the logic of dream-work through condensation, distortion, reversal of content and so on, even resistance, itself a symptom formation, requires interpretation as opposed to the centering of the educator's
moral judgment.

Resistance is one of the most difficult concepts in psychoanalysis. Why?
Because it implicates thinking itself as one of its primary strategies. Is
"reason" in this sense a reactionary instrument of obfuscation and denial?
Perhaps the pedagogical problem cannot be solved by a "better idea"
devised by bureaucrats of the mind who foolishly try to heal psychical
wounds programmatically. Is this why Lyotard (1991) says that thinking is
a form of suffering?

We are left with the problem of the ameliorative orientation of the
educator, a mode-of-relation to oneself and to one's students that is exceedingly innocent. Hidden in its innocence is aggression. Britzman writes:
"Because the desire to make reparation begins with a working through of
aggression, pedagogy may need to attend to the question of the ego's
capacity to repress." Repression, she writes (quoting Anna Freud), is one
of the ego's most special methods of defense, a mechanism in the service
of the "struggle against painful or unendurable ideas or affects." The educator is inconsolable. Not only can he or she not be in mastery of himself
or herself, but he or she employs—in ways that often escape notice—his
and her own rather unpedagogical anxieties and defenses.

To the educational question of AIDS is where Britzman is taking us, to
what she terms "the ego's tragic defense against being touched by AIDS."
Quoting Freud:

> If we ask ourselves why the avoidance of touching, contact, or contagion
> should play such a large part in this neurosis and should become the sub-
> ject-matter of complicated systems, the answer is that touching and physical
> contact are the immediate aim of the aggressive as well as the loving object-
> cathexes. Eros desires contact.

In this touching sense, it is clear that AIDS education makes especially
threatening demands on the ego. These are demands that ask the ego to
relinquish its defenses, to be touched precisely by that which endangers
it. AIDS education obligates teachers and students to change their conceptual and affective structure, "attempt," Deborah writes, "to acknowledge
a thought in excess of itself." AIDS education—and a queer pedagogy—find
themselves immersed in questions of disavowal, withdrawal, wracked by
the ambivalence of touching and being touched, but pressed onward by
the desire to be touched. These intimate dynamics are enacted socially
and epistemologically.

Britzman concludes her important and provocative essay by sketching "three moves in relation to a pedagogy of AIDS that attempts the work of reparation." "[T]his belated work," she says soberly, "begins with the recognition that something can be destroyed, that education can inflict harm." That acknowledged, Britzman believes that such a pedagogy, which attempts to address the question of AIDS, is possible. How? Its first move must be to teach what she terms "ethnographic stories of AIDS," stories that notice "the contradictory details of syndrome, of the HIV virus, of the woeful disregard of the event, of ACT-UP, of the language of AIDS." These ethnographic narratives are also the stories of discourses, "the constitution of bodies of knowledge and knowledge of bodies." Second, the history of AIDS needs be situated in a broader study of illness, including the study of how societies have historically distinguished "the healthy from the ill, the guilty from the innocent, the general public from the risk group." She continues:

> [T]he ethnographic must be returned, disrupted with a second move, a reflective narrative addressed to the ego's anxieties and defenses and the strange time of delay. The significance at stake has to do with the work of perception, hallucination, and reality testing. The ego will be warned that it is being interfered with, that it should try to notice when it stops noticing, that it should confront its fears before its fears diminish its capacity to respond.

Finally, there is a third movement. Britzman is referring here to what she terms "the uncanny, where the force of the return of the repressed can bother the ego's work of consolation." In this third move, the taboo against touching is refused, the taboo against becoming touched and touching AIDS: "The ego shall become as generous as the id." Such a pedagogy supports "a community of egos" to move toward "a community of daydreams." Such a (queer?) pedagogy crafts a certain "in-betweeness, a potential space, an impossible geography, a question of freedom." Now, Britzman concludes, the question is no longer "why speak of the unspeakable" but becomes instead: "what is reparation in this learning?"

One form of reparation is remembrance, and how we remember, Roger Platizky reminds, is as important as what we remember. In fact, in response to AIDS, "remembering [does] become a central act." Roger helps us remember by reviewing, sometimes cryptically, often lyrically, "before" and "after" AIDS in nearly three decades of gay fiction. What's next? There is not yet an "after" stage of AIDS. Of course, there is still no cure, despite the promise of the new protease inhibitors and combination therapies. Maybe HIV will become a chronic instead of an always fatal disease. He sees hope in the World AIDS conferences, as well as other global, national, and grassroots efforts. But, he laments, it will take years before the expensive treatments are widely available.

Given this situation, Platizky is not surprised to see signs of what he terms a "guarded optimism" in contemporary works about AIDS. In plays like *Jeffrey* and *Angels in America*, he sees evidence of humor and spirituality. AIDS is less foregrounded in these works, more situated in a broader view of life and death. Gallows humor and spirituality have been present from the onset of the disease (he thinks of *And the Band Played On* and *Longtime Companion*), but the humor in more recent work might function as "countermythologies," ways (quoting Linda and Michael Hutcheon) to "wrest from the dominant culture the wholly negative if not annihilative representation of HIV infection and AIDS to instruct in its stead a discourse of empowerment, meaning, and possibility."

Platizky finds in Peter Cashorali's *Fairy Tales: Traditional Stories Retold for Gay Men* an instance of "countermythology." Rumpelstiltskin's new riddle is addressed to a gay man rather than a maiden: "Why are you HIV positive?" The reply: "It's just something that was there—a terrible one, but just a virus." Roger locates other tales of healing in the spiritual and secular testimony of long-term survivors, AIDS activists, and in tales of celebrities, including Michael Callen, Mary Fisher, Greg Louganis, and Magic Johnson. "While future works about AIDS will continue to witness, warn, and commemorate those who have already been impacted by this disease," Roger suggests:

> the shapes those works take, the voices invoked, and the details emphasized are likely to be richly variable. Among the many different groups now affected worldwide by this disease—people of different races, genders, ages, classes, religions, and ideologies—the narrative responses to AIDS in future years will be as mutable as the virus—and the treatments used to combat it—may become.

Platizky concludes by asking: who would not agree with Willy of *Longtime Companion* who, when remembering all of it, affirms, "I just want to be there if they ever find a cure?" Who would not agree with Holleran when he writes in *Ground Zero*, "We want there to be a whistle, or siren, that signals 'All Clear' " (p. 48). Indeed, may we all be there. Following this essay are four of Roger's poems.

"For a very long time," William Haver begins his remarkable essay, "we—teachers and those who think about teaching—have come perilously close to a consensus." What is this consensus, to which we've come "perilously" close? "Almost unanimously," he explains,

> we have very nearly agreed that the pedagogical enterprise is about the production of subjects. True, we disagree ... about the nature of that subjectivity. ... [but] we incessantly confirm our agreement ... that pedagogy

is the work of Bildung, a coming to subjectivity as jubilant and relieved self-recognition. Born to stupidity, our students needs us, we are almost agreed.

Such near consensus, he asserts, is "stultifying if not fatal for any thought of the queer."

At least since Kant, Haver asserts, pedagogy, like philosophy, has aspired to explain the world, to make sense, and to transmit the sense that it makes. And in that transmission pedagogy has labored "to bring the stupid to subjectivity, however construed." Our hope has been the production of a subject who might, in Haver's phrasing, "master that of which it thinks . . . [A] subjectivity rescued from stupidity would be that enlightened mastery of Enlightenment itself, divorced from its object, almost." It is clear now that this near consensus cannot be sustained in the face of what he terms "the existential insistence of the social, of which queer studies, queer politics, queer thought, and our queer lives are multiple articulations." It is this idea—"the existential insistence of the social"—Haver's essay elaborates, an idea that comes to us first "as that infinite loss we call the AIDS pandemic." The "existential insistence of the social" must be understood first as "that untranscendable interruption that is the death of friends, lovers, and strangers." The existential insistence of the social means, in Haver's powerful phrase, "utter abjection, absolute extremity." There is another "extremity," that of pleasure. The social exists, then, in "the affirmation of the impossibility of dissociating pleasure from abjection." Nowhere is this complex and wrenching fact more apparent than in the discourses on safer-sex education.

The existential insistence of the social makes itself felt as an irrecusable encounter with extremity, and by extremity Haver emphasizes the extremity of suffering and pleasure. Not coincidentally, he adds, this insistence becomes articulated as "an infinite proliferation of difference, of identities and identifications, as a certain impossibility of containment." This proliferation exceeds the capacity of any polity to adjudicate difference. Traditional Western (that is, we might add, patriarchal) political theory has assumed that subjects are autonomous and finite. The proliferation of subjectivities that characterizes the social sphere now makes it impossible to say what (least of all who) a political subject is.

Queer thought, queer politics, queer pedagogy exist in a double relation to the social. First, queer exists in relation to the existential exigencies of the AIDS pandemic. Second, queer exists in relation to the unending proliferations of the social for which thought is its supplement. Queer exists, then, in a double relation to extremity. At stake in both relations is the erotic. There is an erotic relation to the extremity of pleasure, of course, but as well (here he sounds more like Foucault than Derrida) an erotic relation to the extremity of abjection, to death.

Queer theory is queer, Haver explains, "to the extent that it sustains an erotic relation/non-relation to the extremity that interrupts it." That is to say, "queer theory is queer precisely in its incompletion." Like Britzman and Sumara and Davis, the object of desire seems less crucial than the nature of the relation. After Samuel Delany Haver asks, what if queer theory is "not so much about feeling good about oneself as about feeling good?" [Here one hears an echo of Guy Hocquenghem.] Haver discusses these questions by telling us about Delaney's novel *The Mad Man*, which he describes as "at once a Bildungsroman of a coming-to-philosophical-subjectivity (a pedagogy, therefore) and the unworking of that subjectivity." The novel, he continues, "is an erotic relation of non-relation to heteroclite, queer, sociality in extremis that interrupts the philosophic–pedagogical reunion of thought with itself in the concept." I will leave the telling to Haver—he does so most effectively—and move to his conclusion.

He asks us to remember that "the social" is heteroclite, an "irregular declension or conjugation of our being-in-common." Kierkegaard walking in the shadows, he reminds us that "there is nothing one can say of the social altogether, except that it belongs to that which it is impossible to characterize in general." Consequently, no one particular description or articulation of the social can function as a synecdoche for the whole. Sociality is, he insists (denying Sartre), "the very non-accomplishment of the totality, the very impossibility of totalization." But this does not leave us silent. What is at stake, he says:

> is an erotic relation of non-relation, that extreme relation that is sovereignty, to destitution (homelessness), to an economy of pleasures and love rather than a psychic economy of desire and possession, and thus an erotic relation of contamination to all that philosophy must refuse in order to become what it is resumptively is.

It is unsurprising, Haver continues, that no history has been written of the Lumproletariat. Pasolini insisted that only among the most destitute could humanity be seen; the bourgeoisie were victims of anthropological genocide, an ontological consequence of consumer capitalism. Contrary to the Party and to mainstream Marxism, Fanon insisted that the lumpen-proletariat had revolutionary potential in colonized Africa. What interests Haver is how this growing population in the United States is increasingly defined in terms of exteriority, in terms of their non-relation to the property, including genealogical property. In this respect "homelessness" draws the boundary around the social:

> The term *homelessness* here points toward all that which most nearly ap-proaches absolute abjection in any society such as "ours" entirely organized according to a logic of production. . . . [H]omelessness designates pure lux-

ury (all time is "free," time is not transmuted into labor value), but also the suffering and destitution of pure poverty. . . . Homelessness designates the outside not only of philosophical culture, but of the cultural altogether; the economies, etiquettes, and protocols of the homeless, no less rigorous than those which obey the logic of production, are nevertheless entirely other than the latter.

A queer economy, that is to say, an economy of pleasures, is bankrupt in the eyes of those who conflate the logic of production with what the world. A queer economy is, he writes, "the surplus, supplement, or excess of the subjectivity that is presumptively the telos, the object, of their desire." Erotic sociality is less a relation between and among bodies as it is the fact of existential embodiment itself, what Cindy Patton terms the "ob-scene." The body is less an object in fantasy one can desire or loathe, but the very location of sociality, as Honeychurch and Walcott also suggest. The body is not a "thing" but an "event." This is, Haver says, (with the loud echo of Butler) the body that matters. In other words:

> [T]he "body" is the fact of a primordial contamination, a transgression more original than the law (logos) that is transgressed. It is not a matter of an undifferentiated primal fusion of self and other, but of the primordial alterities of the self. . . . And, of course, it is this contamination that what counts as philosophy must disavow in order to be "itself."

The erotic is, then, a contamination of the categories of "self" and "other." It is the queer that interrupts thought's aspiration for reunion with itself. It is the queer that denies the possibility of a secure separation. The queer constitutes subject as "essential incompletion." Erotic contamination is, then, "the permanent interruption of the pedagogical project of coming to philosophical culture." "It is," he concludes, "to this relation of non-relation to extremity, to this interruption, that we must bring those whom we call our students."

Janet L. Miller begins by remembering a session at the 1991 Bergamo Conference. The organizers invited participants to explore, autobiographically, those tensions and contradictions they experienced as women and men working in the academy. Particpants were ecouraged to describe any experience that exceeded those institutional practices that contained and regulated their academic labor. Miller tells us:

> I listened for a long while, and then suddenly decided to share my rough draft, although this was not something that I usually felt comfortable doing in a large group. I called my piece "Yellow Paper" and in it described the writing, more than twenty years ago, of my dissertation in long-hand on the same kind of legal yellow writing paper that I had grabbed for this particular

writing event. My theme in this free verse was the distancing of my self from my own work through the mandated use of others' words to support my dissertation thesis. And in the last part of "Yellow Paper," I spoke of not wanting to avoid or go back on my own words now and of my desires to share those words with the woman I love.

What struck Janet about this event was the way she had employed autobiography, a genre she had been studying and using (may I point out, with insight and beauty) for 20 years. She writes: "Without any preconceived intentions, I had queered an 'educational' use of autobiography in this session by spontaneously declaring my new and, until then, fairly private relationship with a woman to a room full of colleagues, friends, and strangers."

Miller's autobiographical statement was no "modernist tale about how to claim an authentic lesbian identity" (Martindale, 1997, p. 29), a narrative form she rejected in favor of exploring autobiography in ways that exemplified Judith Butler's notion of "permanently unclear" identity categories. Miller's interest in autobiography concerns its potential to defamiliarize or queer static versions of academic, woman, teacher, researcher, lesbian selves. She employed the genre "in ways that shifted autobiography in education from its modernist emphasis on producing predictable, stable, and normative identities and curricula to a consideration of 'selves' and curricula as sites of 'permanent openness and resignifiability.' "

When autobiography is understood as a queer curriculum practice, it can support a certain dis-identification with oneself and others, producing difference from what was once familiar or the same. Problematizing what it means to "be" a teacher or student or researcher or woman cannot occur by "telling my story" if that story repeats or reinscribes already normalized identity categories. Further, strategically producing a difference cannot occur if difference is only construed as "binary and oppositional rather than nuanced, plural, and proximate" (Greene, 1996, p. 326). Addressing such a "self" as a "site of permanent openness and resignifiability" queers autobiography, as it recasts the ways in which "we might investigate our multiple, intersecting, unpredictable, and unassimilatable identities." "Autobiography as a queer curriculum practice," Miller continues, "suggests a focus on a range of sexualities as well as racialized and classed identities that exceed singular and essential constructions of 'student' and 'teacher.' "

An educator who understands autobiography as a queer curriculum practice realizes that such practice is not a simple matter of looking into the mirror of self-reflection and there seeing her already familiar, identifiable self. Instead, Janet explains,

she finds herself not mirrored—but in difference. In difference, she cannot simply identify with herself *or* with those she teaches. In the space she explores between self and other, nothing looks familiar, everything looks a little unnatural. To queer the use of autobiography as a curriculum practice is to produce a story of self and other that can't be identified with. It is to recognize that there are times and places in constructing versions of teaching, research, and curriculum when making a difference requires making one's autobiography unnatural.

Janet Miller reconceives autobiographical practice as a performance of queer theory, showing us how we might recognize what we have constructed as "other," as a split-off, imaginary product of our own egos. In so doing she extends our understanding of both the autobiographical and the queer, of self and other. In a curriculum of individuals not categories, such a queer autobiographical practice will be indispensable.

CONCLUSION

The boys in New York may be headed to the suburbs (i.e., assimilationism) but queer theorists in education, it seems, plan to stay in the city. True, we drink lots of coffee and we have an interest in Rome, although it is quite specific. Our tools are not as provocatively performative as were those employed by ACT UP; they are, given the highly conservative character of the field of education, probably provocative enough. Those tools are discursive; they are pedagogical. Gazes will be queered, curricula unrested, pedagogies addressed not just to the ego but to the id as well. In so doing we might glimpse what teaching positions we occupy, including our investments in our own suffering and failure. Maybe we will change positions.

There is now a modernist moment of mobilization, a clarity of insight if not a consensus of agenda that is queer theory in education. There is as well as a post-modern appreciation for decentered, eroticized, relational selves, bodies of knowledge (and knowledge of bodies), which work to undo binary oppositions that lead to alterity identities. The subsumption of difference into (male) indifference associated with the ancient Greeks ends here. Woman is no longer erased but transgendered into self-affirmative, homoeroticized, politically engaged subject positions. This is not boys' play. Hey, Eve . . . you driving machine . . . take us there.

What is the queer? Queer is non-canonical, a term of perhaps momentary coalition. Are queers revolutionaries against the patriarchal heteosexist social order? Or just plain folks? There is something of a separatist moment among some of us; many reject assimilationism despite continuing hopes for broader alliances and coalitions. Yet, probably not one of us can feel the revolutionary optimism of Herbert Marcuse. We work toward a future that is not visible, not even a lavender glimmer on the horizon. Despite the explosion in scholarship and an apparent clearing in the public space, we remain, fundamentally, in a defensive position. We work overtime to teach tolerance, to teach the truth, to try to find ways to decenter, destabilize, and deconstruct (forgive me) the heterosexist normalizations that so essentialize many of the students we teach. Homosexuality is erased by "hommo-sexuality," by the self-reproduction of (het)male gender that universalizes his experience and obliterates singularity, difference, individuality. Perhaps for now it is enough to assert difference, to theorize queer curriculum and pedagogy, and to watch the horizon.

ACKNOWLEDGMENTS

I thank Naomi Silverman, my most remarkable editor at LEA, for her sound editorial advice, good humor, and for sending me Mendelsohn's *New York Times Magazine* article (which I had missed). Special thanks as well to William Tierney and Deborah Britzman, who suggested names of possible contributors, and to Kenn Gardner Honeychurch, who generously donated his work for the cover of this book.

REFERENCES

Berlant, L., & Freeman, E. (1993). Queer nationality. In M. Warner (Ed.), *Fear of a queer planet: Queer politics and social theory* (pp. 193–229). Minneapolis: University of Minnesota Press.

Block, A. A. (1997). *I'm only bleeding: Education as the practice of violence against children.* New York: Peter Lang.

Bordo, S. (1993). *Unbearable weight: Feminism, western culture, and the body.* Berkeley & Los Angeles: University of California Press.

Boykin, K. (1996). *One more river to cross: Black and gay in America.* New York: Anchor Books.

Bredbeck, G. W. (1995). Analyzing the classroom: On the impossibility of a queer pedagogy. In G. E. Haggerty & B. Zimmerman (Eds.), *Professions of desire: Lesbian and gay studies in literature* (pp. 169–180). New York: Modern Language Association of America.

Britzman, D. (1995a). Is there a queer pedagogy: Or, stop reading straight. *Educational Theory, 45*(2), 151–165.

Britzman, D. (1995b). What is this thing called love? *Taboo, 1*(1), 65–93.

Britzman, D. (1996). On becoming a "little sex researcher": Some comments on a polymorphously perverse curriculum. *Journal of Curriculum Theorizing, 12*(2), 4–11.

Bryson, M., & de Castell, S. (1993a). Engendering equity: On some paradoxical consequences of institutionalized programs of emancipation. *Educational Theory, 43*(3), 341–355.

Bryson, M., & de Castell, S. (1993b). Queer pedagogy: Praxis makes imperfect. *Canadian Journal of Education, 18*(3), 285–305.

Castle, T. (1993). *The apparitional lesbian: Female homosexuality and modern culture.* New York: Columbia University Press.

Cornell, D. (1992). What takes place in the dark. *Differences, 4*(2), 45–71.

Crimp, D. (1993). Right on, girlfriend. In M. Warner (Ed.), *Fear of a queer planet: Queer politics and social theory* (pp. 300–320). Minneapolis: University of Minnesota Press.

de Castell, S., & Bryson, M. (in press). Don't ask, don't tell: "S'niffing out queers" in education. In W. F. Pinar (Ed.), *Curriculum: New identities in/for the field.* New York: Garland.

Dellamora, R. (1995). Queer apocalypse: Framing William Burroughs. In R. Dellamora (Ed.), *Postmodern apocalypse: Theory and cultural practice at the end* (pp. 136–167). Philadelphia: University of Pennsylvania Press.

Doll, M. A. (1988). *Beckett and myth: An archetypal approach.* Syracuse, NY: Syracuse University Press.

Ellsworth, E. (1986). Elicit pleasures: Feminist spectators and *Personal Best. Wide Angle, 8*(2), 45–58.

Ellsworth, E. (1987a). Educational films against critical pedagogy. *Journal of Education, 169*(3), 32–47.

Ellsworth, E. (1987b). Media interpretation is a social and political act. *Journal of Visual Literacy, 8*(2), 27–38.

Ellsworth, E. (1989). Why doesn't this feel empowering? Working through the repressive myths of critical pedagogy. *Harvard Educational Review, 59*(3), 297–324.

Ellsworth, E. (1992, February). Teaching to support unassimilated difference. *Radical Teacher.*

Ellsworth, E. (1994). Representation, self-representation, and the meanings of difference: Questions for educators. In R. Martusewicz & W. Reynolds (Eds.), *Inside out: Contemporary critical perspectives in education* (pp. 99–108). New York: St. Martin's Press.

Ellsworth, E., & Miller, J. L. (1992, October). *Working difference in education.* Paper presented to the Bergamo Conference on Curriculum Theory and Classroom Practice, Dayton, OH.

Fichte, H. (1996). *The gay critic* (K. Gavin, Trans.). Ann Arbor: University of Michigan Press.

Fuss, D. (1993). Freud's fallen women: Identification, desire, and "a case of homosexuality in a woman." In M. Warner (Ed.), *Fear of a queer planet: Queer politics and social theory* (pp. 42–68). Minneapolis: University of Minnesota Press.

Gallop, J. (1988). *Thinking through the body.* New York: Columbia University Press.

Gilmore, L. (1994). *Autobiographics: A feminist theory of women's self-representation.* Ithaca, NY: Cornell University Press.

Greene, F. L. (1996). Introducing queer theory into the undergraduate classroom: Abstractions and practical applications. *English Education, 28,* 325–339.

Greene, N. (1990). *Pier Paolo Pasolini: Cinema as heresy.* Princeton, NJ: Princeton University Press.

Grumet, M. R. (1988). *Bitter milk: Women and teaching.* Amherst: University of Masschuetts Press.

Haggerty, G. E., & Zimmerman, B. (1995). Introduction. In G. E. Haggerty & B. Zimmerman (Eds.), *Professions of desire: Lesbian and gay studies in literature* (pp. 1–7). New York: Modern Language Association of America.

Haley, J. (1993). The construction of heterosexuality. In M. Warner (Ed.), *Fear of a queer planet: Queer politics and social theory* (pp. 82–102). Minneapolis: University of Minnesota Press.

Halperin, D. M. (1990). Why is Diotima a woman? In *One hundred years of homosexuality and other essays on Greek love* (pp. 113–152). New York: Routledge.

Hammonds, E. (1991). Black (w)holes and the geometry of black female sexuality. *Differences, 3*(2).

Lyotard, J.-F. (1991). *The inhuman: Reflections on time* (G. Benning & R. Bowlby, Trans.). Stanford, CA: Stanford University Press.

Marcuse, H. (1966). *One-dimensional man: Studies in the sociology of advanced industrial society.* Boston: Beacon Press.

Marcuse, H. (1971). *Eros and civilization.* Boston: Beacon Press.

Mendelsohn, D. (1996, September 30). We're here! We're queer! Let's get coffee! *New York Times Magazine,* pp. 26–31.

Murray, S. O. (1996). *American gay.* Chicago: University of Chicago Press.

O'Brien, M. (1981). *The politics of reproduction.* Boston: Routledge & Kegan Paul.

Patton, C. (1993). Tremble, hetero swine! In M. Warner (Ed.), *Fear of a queer planet: Queer politics and social theory* (pp. 143–177). Minneapolis: University of Minnesota Press.

Pinar, W. F. (Ed.). (1997). *Curriculum: New Identities in/for the field.* New York: Garland.

Pinar, W. F., & Grumet, M. R. (1988). Socratic *caesura* and the theory–practice relationship. In W. Pinar (Ed.), *Contemporary curriculum discourses* (pp. 92–100). Scottsdale, AZ: Gorsuch Scarisbrick.

Pinar, W. F., & Reynolds, W. M. (1992). Appendix, section two: Genealogical notes on post-structuralism in curriculum studies. In W. F. Pinar & W. M. Reynolds (Eds.), *Understanding curriculum as phenomenological and deconstructed text* (pp. 244–259). New York: Teachers College Press.

Pinar, W. F., Reynolds, W. M., Slattery, P., & Taubman, P. (1995). *Understanding currciulum.* New York: Peter Lang.

Reiniger, M. (1982). *Autobiographical search for gyn/ecology: Traces of misogyny in women's schooling.* Unpublished doctoral dissertation, University of Rochester, Graduate School of Education and Human Development, Rochester, NY.

Reiniger, M. (1989). Autobiographical search for gyn/ecology: Traces of misogyny in women's schooling. *JCT, 8*(3), 7–88.

Rorty, R. (1991a). *Philosophical papers. Vol. 1: Objectivity, relativism, and truth.* Cambridge, England: Cambridge University Press.

Rorty, R. (1991b). *Essays on Heidegger and others. Philosophical papers. Vol. 2.* Cambridge, England: Cambridge University Press.

Schwartz, M. D., & DeKeseredy, W. S. (Eds.). (1997). *Sexual assault on the college campus.* Thousand Oaks, CA: Sage.

Sears, J. (1983, Spring). Sexuality: Taking off the masks. *Changing Schools, 11,* 12–13.

Sears, J. (1987a). Peering into the well of loneliness: The responsibility of educators to gay and lesbian youth. In A. Molnar (Ed.), *Social issues and education* (pp. 79–100). Alexandria, VA: ASCD.

Sears, J. (1987b, October). *Developing a sense of difference among gay and lesbian children in the deep South: The difference between being queer and being different.* Paper presented at the 1987 Bergamo Conference, Dayton, OH.

Sears, J. (1988). Growing up gay: Is anyone there to listen? *American School Counselors Newsletter, 26,* 8–9.

Sears, J. (1989a). Playing out our feelings: The use of reader's theater in anti-oppression work. *Empathy, 2,* 33–37.

Sears, J. (1989b). The impact of gender and race on growing up lesbian and gay in the South. *NWSA Journal, 1*(3), 421–456.

Sears, J. (1990a). *Growing up gay in the south.* New York: Haworth Press.

Sears, J. (1990b, April). *On conducting homosexual research.* Paper presented at the annual meeting of the American Education Research Association, Boston, MA.

Sears, J. (Ed.). (1992). *Sexuality and the curriculum.* New York: Teachers College Press.

Sedgwick, E. K. (1990). *Epistemology of the closet.* Berkeley: University of California Press.

Seidman, S. (1993). Identity and politics in a "postmodern" gay culture: Some historical and conceptual notes. In M. Warner (Ed.), *Fear of a queer planet: Queer politics and social theory* (pp. 105–142). Minneapolis: University of Minnesota Press.

Silin, J. (1992). School-based HIV/AIDS education: Is there safety in safer sex? In J. Sears (Ed.), *Sexuality and the curriculum* (pp. 267–283). New York: Teachers College Press.

Silin, J. (1995). *Sex, death and the education of children: Our passion for ignorance in the age of AIDS.* New York: Teachers College Press.

Taubman, P. M. (1979). *Gender and curriculum: Discourse and the politics of sexuality.* Unpublished doctoral dissertation, University of Rochester, Graduate School of Education and Human Development, Rochester, NY.

Tierney, W. G. (1997). *Academic outlaws: Queer theory and cultural studies in the academy.* Thousand Oaks, CA: Sage.

Waller, W. (1932). *The sociology of teaching.* New York: Wiley.

Warner, M. (Ed.). (1993). *Fear of a queer planet: Queer politics and social theory.* Minneapolis: University of Minnesota Press.

Watney, S. (1996). Queer Andy. In J. Doyle, J. Flatley, & J. E. Munoz (Eds.), *Pop out: Queer Warhol* (pp. 20–30). Durham, NC: Duke University Press.

Williams, P. (1991). *The alchemy of race and rights.* Cambridge, MA: Harvard University Press.

Yack, B. (1986). *The longing for total revolution: Philosophic sources of social discontent from Rousseau to Marx and Nietzsche.* Princeton, NJ: Princeton University Press.

Chapter 1

Constructing Knowledge: Educational Research and Gay and Lesbian Studies

William G. Tierney
Patrick Dilley
University of Southern California

Arguably, during the last decade, few issues have become more contentious in schools, colleges, and universities than lesbian, gay, and bisexual topics. New York City's rainbow curriculum, for example, was truncated, and its school chancellor fired in large part due to the controversy over teaching lesbian and gay topics ("Teaching About Gay Life," 1992). Salt Lake City's school system decided to ban all after-school activities when faced with the possibility of having to allow a lesbian and gay youth group to meet in a school (Brooke, 1996). Auburn University in Alabama ended up in the state supreme court when the student senate decided to de-fund a gay campus group ("Alabama Denies Aid," 1992). Campus surveys at multiple universities (e.g., University of California at Los Angeles; Shepard, 1990) rated campus intolerance of homosexuality as more serious than racial or gender intolerance.

Such problems are relatively recent; a generation ago, much less a half century ago, schools, colleges, and universities never had visible and vocal complaints about lesbian and gay issues on the magnitude that occurs today. Indeed, if homosexuality were ever discussed, it was usually only as an aberration, an issue to be expunged from education. More often than not, however, homosexuality and homosexuals were never considered.

How researchers have studied homosexuality, and who studies topics related to lesbian and gay issues, also has changed dramatically. Although research on homosexuality was not prolific a generation ago, it existed. However, whereas researchers once came primarily from psychology or sociology, today lesbian and gay studies—or "queer studies"—has mush-roomed into multiple disciplines and areas of inquiry. What was once a topic that fell under the rubric of "deviancy" has branched out into numerous intellectual arenas.

In this chapter we trace the history of inquiry into lesbian and gay issues primarily in the United States.[1] We point out the discourses that have surrounded the topic and focus exclusively on how these discourses have derived from, and impacted, educators and educational institutions. We do not consider, for example, studies about life-span development of lesbian and gay people, or issues pertaining to the personal counseling of lesbian and gay youth. Frankly, the research literature on lesbian, gay, and bisexual issues has become too vast; our purpose here is to offer conceptual clarity to one domain of inquiry and to consider how primarily North American educational researchers have reconfigured their own stances and an area of inquiry throughout the century. We suggest that the implications of such findings are quite significant for how one thinks about knowledge production. We conclude by pointing out gaps in the literature and considering arenas that await further inquiry.

HOMOSEXUALITY AND DEVIANCY

Until the mid-1970s, the literature about homosexuality and its relationship to education was framed in one of two ways: either by absence, or by defining the topic as deviant. The professional guardian of academic freedom, the American Association of University Professors (AAUP), lists no instances where a scholar who tried to study homosexuality had his or her academic freedom abridged. One might assume that a controversial topic such as homosexuality would have engendered tests of academic freedom in much the same way that other similarly contested topics did at the turn of the century. However, we have found very little research that pertains to education and homosexuality. Simply stated, few scholars studied the topic unless they were psychologists or sociologists interested in deviancy (Tierney, 1993).

The research that existed always used the framework of deviance as the way to define the topic. Willard Waller's classic, *The Sociology of Teaching* (1932), for example, pointed out the danger of allowing homosexuals to teach. As homosexuality was considered a disease infecting homosexuals, Waller suggested that homosexual teachers would be able to contaminate students and spread the illness.

---

[1]A caveat is in order. Although we make reference to literature that has been published in Europe and elsewhere, our focus is primarily on United States educational institutions.

"Nothing seems more certain than that homosexuality is contagious" wrote Waller (1932, p. 147). The import of such a finding, of course, was that a noted scholar brought to light the problems schools encountered with homosexuals. Homosexual teachers also were believed prone to falling in love with their charges. "The homosexual teacher develops an indelicate soppiness in his relations with his favorites," suggested Waller, "and makes minor tragedies of little incidents when the recipient of his attentions shows himself indifferent" (p. 148). Obviously, no school principal would desire someone who either infected children with a disease or fawned after them. Accordingly, Waller encouraged principals and superintendents not to hire homosexuals; and the way one identified a homosexual was by personality traits such as "carriage, mannerisms, voice, speech, etc." (p. 148); if discovered, they should be fired.

Waller's work is helpful for a variety of reasons: it lends insight into how we once defined homosexuality and educational practice. Waller's text was considered a landmark study in the United States that employed sociological methods to investigate education. And yet, he had no empirical evidence on which to base his findings that homosexuality was a disease or contagious. He based his certitude about homosexuality's contagion, then, on opinion and belief, rather than on fact and evidence.

Waller also had no comparative data about whether homosexuals developed more or less "soppiness" toward students than heterosexual teachers. Indeed, he provided no statistical or qualitative data about the percentage of homosexual teachers who developed crushes on students. We also do not know how he derived his finding that homosexuals acted in one particular manner, or utilized one specific speech pattern. Curiously, in a profession with a significant percentage of females, Waller also overlooked lesbians and concentrated strictly on male homosexuals.

Of course, one might easily deride the comments Waller made as ancient history, albeit only 60 years ago. Nonetheless, Waller's book remains a classic that continues to garner respect as a study that will be considered a landmark of the 20th century; indeed, Webb (1981) suggested the book as "a classic study . . . remarkably fresh" (p. 239). Waller's comments on homosexuality are certainly in keeping with general discussions about lesbians and gay males that were made at the time; however, his work did not reflect any research in a manner that we would accept today. Nevertheless, such work has had vast influence in providing direction for studies about homosexuality and schooling.

Even in the 1970s, research about homosexuality and its influence on education still primarily worked from a psychoanalytic framework of deviance. Fromhart (1971), for example, wrote that "Homosexuality represents only one of the possible variations of sexual identity confusion seen by therapists and counselors who treat college students" (p. 247). DeFries

(1976) wrote that lesbian students also had ambiguous identities. Bauer and Stein (1973) similarly suggested that homosexual students had confused identities. Echoing Waller, they noted: "The [homosexual] male student may also possess qualities that he or others characterize as effeminate, such as a lack of athletics, graceful and fragile carriage, and particularly, an inability to be directly assertive" (p. 835).

NORMALCY AND ASSIMILATION

The 1970s also saw a rise in a second, more intensive and prolonged, burst of research that looked at lesbian and gay people not as deviants, but as "normal" or quasi-normal. This line of research primarily began after the Stonewall Riots in a New York City bar in 1969, and after the American Psychological Association (APA) removed homosexuality as a form of mental disorder in 1973. As historian John D'Emillio (1992) observed, Stonewall was the spark that ignited a powder keg of gay anger and resistance.

> By 1973, just four years later, almost a thousand lesbian and gay organizations had been created. . . . These organizations come in all sizes and shapes: national, state, and local; political, religious, cultural, service, recreational, and commercial; organizations based on gender, ethnic, and racial identity; and organizations based on occupational and professional affiliation. (p. 164)

To be sure, no single event demarcates one line of research from another, but one of the points we suggest in the next section is that research streams have the potential to mirror and/or advance actions in the general society. In this light, a riot by gay men and lesbians in a bar in Greenwich Village signaled that those who had been defined as deviant and faceless were no longer going to submit to harassment such as the police action in the bar. The action by an association of the size and prestige of APA symbolized how the principle academic arena where homosexuality had been studied and defined also admitted past mistakes and pointed toward alternative ways to think about and define a particular area of inquiry.

The results were quite significant for the research community. The clinical term *homosexual* gave way to the terms *gay* and *lesbian*. Although, as we will show, a third line of work has developed in the last decade and a small fragment of research still clings to the original thesis of homosexuals as a mentally ill group, the vast majority of research about gay and lesbian people in education falls into the categories of normalcy and assimilation, what historian Lisa Duggan (1992) might call research that appeals to the liberalism of educators. Instead of deranged, psychologically stunted "cases," gays and lesbians were (and are) studied and presented as a minority (presumed by oppressive public misunderstanding and hatred) and like heterosexuals except for "sexual preference," and in need of "the 'liberal' rights of privacy and formal equality" (Duggan, 1992, p. 13).

At the same time, educational research moved out of the strictly psychological and sociological domains and into multiple arenas. Researchers were no longer only positivist scientists but also individuals who mirrored the broad fabric of theoretical work that had come to enrich the field of educational theory. And finally, researchers were not only disengaged scientists—presumably heterosexuals—studying lesbian and gay people; frequently, we discover the "natives"—lesbian and gay researchers—studying issues pertaining to their group, giving an insider's voice and perspective. Louie Crew's *The Gay Academic* (1978) is a good example.

Four primary categories of research may be found that use the idea of normalcy in the study of gay and lesbian topics and how they interface with educational issues and systems: (a) issues of visibility; (b) studies of the climate of the organization; (c) studies that suggest ways to improve educational organizations for lesbian and gay people; and (d) studies about gay and lesbian studies.

Visibility

A popular phrase often used for individuals who are open about their gay or lesbian sexual identity is that they have "come out of the closet." We use the term *visibility* to denote the inclusion of, and the presentation of, individuals, groups, and topics of gay, lesbian, or bisexual interest as a part of society and a part of our educational systems. Cullinan (1973) was one of the first researchers in higher education to reflect this paradigm shift of research—and of gay self-identity. He interviewed 10 gay men from Wayne State University's student organization, summarizing that, "[w]hile society often labels him as sick, perverted and having a criminal mind, the homosexual sees himself as a moral and ethical being," representing "the 'new' homosexual on campus whose identity is emerging from the midst of a sea of prejudice" (pp. 346–347). Harbeck's (1992) book, *Coming Out of the Classroom Closet,* is an example of a research emphasis that gives visibility to lesbian and gay issues within education. That edited text, although vastly different from Waller's epic, is emblematic of research that seeks to prove the normalcy of lesbian and gay people. The work is multidimensional; topics cover areas such as legal issues, historical work, curricular change, psychological health, and school-based projects. Much of the work seeks to prove that lesbian and gay educators and students always have existed, to expose the costs of invisibility, and to suggest how to correct the wrongs against gays and lesbians. The work combines empirical and exhortative approaches, and frequently adopts an emancipatory voice. Additionally, Ringer (1994) reported on a survey of the effects of faculty coming out in the classroom, and Opffer (1994) used interviews to note the experiences of college instructors who had become visible to their classes.

The principle goal of visibility research is not unlike research that involves other oppressed, or multicultural, groups. Weis and Fine (1993), for example, edited *Beyond Silenced Voices*, and McLaughlin and Tierney (1993) edited *Naming Silenced Lives*. Both texts involve qualitative research practices that seek to understand "silencing in public schools" (Weis & Fine, 1993, p. 1). Among groups who are included as silenced and deserving voice are lesbian and gay educators and students. In the Weis and Fine text, Friend (1993) wrote, "serious discussion of how inequalities in terms of sexual orientation are reproduced and sanctioned by schooling has been absent in the social analyses of diversity, equity and power in education" (p. 210). His work involved an analysis of what he defined as the ideology of silencing: heterosexism and homophobia. *Naming Silenced Lives* includes a chapter that is a life history of a gay person of color (Tierney, 1994). What we discover, then, is not only the visibility of lesbian and gay educators, but also the claimed relationships with other marginalized groups in education. Rather than focusing on fractured identities in need of repair or as the problem, the focus of work shifted to the larger society's homophobia and heterosexism as the problem.

Similarly, Khayatt's (1992) book utilizes feminist concepts of patriarchy to understand the standpoint of lesbian teachers. Khayatt interviewed 19 lesbian teachers in order to ground the experiences of such women in the social organization of the school. In effect, Khayatt's work struggles to contradict mainstream assumptions about female teachers, and to give voice to a group that had previously been invisible. Rensenbrink (1996) published the life history of a lesbian elementary school teacher, including her primarily positive experiences, and the consequential effects on her school and her students, of coming out both to a fifth-grade class and to fellow teachers. Bensimon (1992) presented an academic-life study of one lesbian faculty member where she utilized a "feminist-lesbian standpoint from which to view the effects of the public/private logic has on her as a professor" (p. 100).

Family members, as an integral part of the educational process, offer more opportunities for visibility and voice in education. Casper, Schultz, and Wickens (1992) analyzed data from a longitudinal interpersonal study of the relationships between gay and lesbian parents and school administrators and teachers; they urged "breaking the silences" by "opening a dialogue" to replace "an active but 'silenced' dialogue under the surface of parent–teacher discourses" (1992, p. 109). Sears' (1993/1994) extensive literature review categorizes current research on the impact of schools and teachers on families with gay, lesbian, or bisexual members, emphasizing the importance of issues of disclosure.

Other research has delineated the social atmosphere for gay, lesbian, and bisexual students, whether visible, invisible, or coming into focus. D'Augelli (1989a, 1989b, 1989c, 1991a), for example, employed survey research to understand the problems and challenges that confront lesbian and gay college students, and Griffin (1992) involved herself in a partici-patory research project in order "to understand the experiences of lesbian and gay educators and to empower the participants through collective reflection and action" (p. 167). Sears (1993b) presented a similar, critically reflective analysis of sexual diversity of faculty and students, targeted toward educational administrators; Sears based that analysis on his qualitative in-vestigations of the lives of gays and lesbians who were in school (1992, 1993a).

Analyzing a 2-year-long ethnographic study of gay male students, Rhoads (1994, 1995) outlined how gay men struggle to come out of the closet on campus and the consequences of such visibility. MacKay (1993) collected the personal narratives of the college experiences of Vassar lesbians (and gays) from 1930 to 1990. O'Conor (1995) utilized a form of ethnographic fiction, arranging actual comments from gay and lesbian high-school stu-dents as a composite narrative. Chandler (1995) and Due (1995) both depicted U.S. gay and lesbian high-school and college students they inter-viewed, portraying the effects of "growing up hidden," of the consequences of "coming of age not only invisible but embattled in that invisibility" (Due, 1995, p. xxvi), "continuing to make their own circles of support, their own safe havens, their own cultural niche" (Chandler, 1995, p. 339). Khayatt (1992, 1993, 1994) interviewed lesbian secondary-school students in Can-ada, portraying lives lived in, and identities formed in, silence. Although the students Due, Chandler, and Khayatt bring to life in their studies by no means feel fully connected as a community (as gay people or gay students), the effects of increased visibility are evident in the changes in the experiences and identities of MacKay's Vassar alumna and the gay students of the 1990s.

Organizational Climate

A great deal of research focused on the climate at colleges and universities for lesbian and gay people. Reynolds (1989), for example, pointed out that gay men rated the climate at the University of Virginia lower than straight men with regard to emotional support, intellectualism, change, and innovation. Many other campuses—Rutgers, Pennsylvania State Uni-versity, University of California–Santa Cruz, University of Oregon, University of Kansas, among others—also undertook analyses of the climate for lesbian and gay students, faculty, and staff (Gay, Lesbian and Bisexual Concerns Study Committee, 1993; Herek, 1986; Nelson & Baker, 1990; Nieberding, 1989; Shepard, 1990; Task Force on Lesbian and Gay Concerns, 1990; Tierney, 1992; Yeshel, 1985). In virtually every study, analogous findings were reported: Lesbian and gay students were significantly more likely to face physical and verbal harassment than their heterosexual counterparts. In multiple studies (e.g., D'Augelli 1989a, 1989b; D'Augelli & Rose, 1990; D'Emillio, 1990; Norris, 1992), authors investigated various facets of campus life—dormitories, out-of-class experiences, classrooms—and reported survey research documenting the problems gay and lesbian students encountered during their academic careers.

The emphasis on exploring, examining, and explaining the quality of gay life on campus extends beyond students. Grayson (1987) presented an overview of homosexual issues in education for students and professionals. Crew and Keener (1981) reported on the results of a study of the National Council of Teachers of English, documenting the frustration of and discrimination against lesbians, bisexuals, and gays in their profession.

The focus, framework, and findings of these studies were remarkably similar. The studies were usually single-campus investigations that utilized survey research coupled with interviews (e.g., Nelson & Baker, 1990; Reynolds, 1989; Shepard, 1990; Tierney, 1992). Invariably, the results were that the site under study was hostile to lesbian and gay populations. In contrast to previous investigations that looked at homosexuality as a pathology, these studies argued that the results of such assumptions were that the population suffered mental stress and harassment in the organization. One link to the past was that most of the work done here came from a social-psychological perspective, albeit from a dramatically different vantage point.

Strategies for Improvement

A good deal of research that was often linked to studies about campus climate pertained to ways to improve the plight of lesbian and gay people in schools, colleges, and universities. Grayson (1987), for example, outlined issues of equity in educational organizations for lesbian and gay people. She focused on policy issues that were beyond the institutional level, psychological and counseling support services for youth in the institution and community, and specific strategies that might be attempted in educational organizations. Similarly, Sears (1987) pointed out the role of school educators in improving the lives of lesbian and gay youth, and proposed that "schools must also enhance [all] students' understanding of the sexual diversity within each person" (1991, p. 54). Tierney and Rhoads (1993) discussed how to better the lives of college faculty.

Addressing the needs of gay, lesbian, and bisexual students often involves strategies of supported visibility. The efforts and effects of implementing a high-school outreach program for gay youth have been chronicled by Uribe (1995; Uribe & Harbeck, 1992). Croteau and Kusek (1992) presented their quantitative findings on the effectiveness of gay and lesbian speakers' panels in college, along with guides for implementation; Geasler, Croteau, Heineman, and Edlund (1995) addressed qualitative data of the effectiveness of such programming. Other researchers have also studied the effects of speakers' panels consisting of gays and lesbians on student attitudes toward homosexuality and AIDS (Chng & Moore, 1991; Green, Dixon, & Gold-Neil, 1993). Geller (1991) outlined steps for making gay and lesbian topics more visible and addressed among college student populations, whereas Good (1993) suggested coordinating campus activities programming for gay students to stages in gay identity development theory. Schreier (1995) argued for a new paradigm for campus programming about gay, lesbian, and bisexual issues, away from tolerance of gays and toward a nurturing environment for gays.

Much of this work parallels policy-oriented research in other arenas. Rather than psychological or sociological, such research derives primarily from the organizational change and public administration literatures that focus on practice. The work utilizes theoretical vantage points that assume change by individuals or groups is possible and desirable. Problems are identified and solutions are proposed. Again, problems do not lie with the victims of harassment, but with the perpetrators, or more likely, the amorphous climate that allows, or countenances, victimization. As with most public policy research, causal solutions are neither proposed nor assumed possible; instead, the authors delineate the problems and pose steps to resolve them.

Studies on Gay and Lesbian Studies

The newest and most prolific line of research from the vantage point of normalcy is epistemological in nature; it uses as its referent point the curriculum in general, and departmental configurations in particular. Researchers in this line of investigation have formed the most dramatic break from previous investigations. Their work is not psychological and it is not empirically based. Many of the researchers come out of literary, linguistic, philosophical, or anthropological arenas.

Richard Mohr (1989) has focused on the moral and epistemological imperatives to create gay studies departments. Crew's (1978) edited text utilized different disciplinary frameworks to analyze texts and issues. D'Emillio (1992) posited the question of gay studies in a traditional curricular manner:

The building blocks of gay studies, as of any program or discipline, are individual courses, and course development is a first priority. But beyond that, a whole host of implementation issues will arise: should we strive to establish an interdisciplinary "program," or a separate "department"? Do we want a minor or a major? Are we talking about undergraduate education, or graduate training as well? Should a gay studies program have hiring authority, or will faculty be jointly appointed, with a department as a home base? (p. 170)

D'Emillio answers his rhetorical questions in the following manner:

The answers to these questions will be rooted in the distinctive histories of particular institutions: How have other programs, such as women's studies or Chicano studies, been developed on a campus? . . . Another important strategic issue involves the choice between mainstreaming and ghettoization. I suppose the very way I've phrased the problem displays my prejudice: mainstreaming of gay and lesbian issues is my goal. I would like to see the time come when so much research has been done, and our ways of thinking so thoroughly revised, that the gay and lesbian experience, the varieties of same-sex intimacy, and the role of sexuality in social life are all fully integrated into the curriculum. (p. 171)

Several studies have looked at how curricula might be used to alter understandings of lesbian and gay identity (Britzman, 1995; Cady, 1992; D'Augelli, 1991b, 1992; Duggan, 1995; Garber, 1994; Leap, 1996; Lipkin, 1993/1994; McCord & Herzog, 1991). On the one hand we have work that has looked at arts, books, films, and teaching strategies that might be employed in high-school or junior-high classrooms (Athanases, 1996; Besner & Spungin, 1995; Boutilier, 1992; Brogen, 1993/1994; Epstein & Johnson, 1994; Harris, 1990; Lampela, 1996; Linne, 1996; Patrick & Sanders, 1994; Pollak, 1994), and on the other hand, we have calls for curricular integration at the university level (Abel, 1994; Berg, Kowalski, Le Guin, Weinauer, & Wolfe, 1994; Blinick, 1994; Faderman, 1995; Fonow & Marty, 1992; Gaard, 1992; Grossman, 1993; Jackson, 1995; Keating, 1994).

The few institutions that have created a cohesive lesbian and gay studies academic department are models for this type of research. Collins (1992) outlined the creation of the first gay and lesbian studies department in the United States, at City College of San Francisco Community College, and Klinger (1994) reflected on the difficulty of beginning a similar program at the University of California at Berkeley. Roman (1995) discussed combining theory and practice in a seminar on gay and lesbian issues. Minton's (1992) edited text focused on gay and lesbian studies and curricula, and a case study of such a curriculum (including teaching theory and strategies) was presented by Grossman (1993). Non-U.S. models are also represented in the literature (Gammon, 1992; Hekma & van der Meer, 1992).

We derive several points from these works. As might be expected from social scientists in general, and linguists in particular, a concern for language becomes important. The use of *homosexuality* is dropped because of its clinical connotations, and *gay and lesbian* is called into question as the idea of bisexuality gains currency. Alliances with, and modeling from, other groups perceived as distinct from the norm take place; a certain solidarity (born from liberalism) bolsters inclusion of gay issues in the curriculum (Pope, 1995). Thus, as curricular controversies erupted over representative practices in school and college curricula for Blacks and women, so similar arguments take place with regard to lesbians and gays. And the concurrent message, that gays are just like most everyone else (well, at least like the non-majority), means they can fit into society just like Blacks and women could. Textual practices and structural arrangements come in for questioning and criticism as theoreticians and philosophers argue for less marginalization of lesbian and gay life.

The overriding concern of each of these vantage points has been with the idea of normalcy. Rather than consider how to deal with social deviants, the research here has argued that the problem exists not with the group under study—lesbian and gay students, faculty, and staff—but with the organizational constraints and constructs developed over time. Solutions pertained to incorporation as a way to end victimization. In effect, the underlying assumption was that if society could just get over its homophobia and heterosexism, then lesbian and gay people's second-class status would end. Gay and lesbian people were no different from straight people, and only wanted what everyone else wanted. Equal rights in educational organizations, and incorporation and representation in curricular and organizational structures was fair and just. Perhaps not surprisingly, the next moment in research has been an extension of, and in opposition to, this line of reasoning.

QUEER THEORY

The conceptual linkages that we have seen between the first two areas of investigation are virtually nonexistent with queer theory. The research does not come out of psychology, it is not survey-based, and rather than deal with how to contain deviance or treat everyone similarly, queer theory seeks to disrupt and to assert voice and power. Indeed, even the evocation of the term *queer* is decidedly defiant; as opposed to the clinician's use of medical terminology (homosexual) or the assimilationist's deployment of less explicitly confrontational terms (gay, bisexual, and lesbian), the theorist from this perspective seeks to bring even language itself into question. As opposed to a previous era when queer was used as a derogatory term for the homosexual, theorists of this persuasion claim the term as a linguistic badge of pride. As Case (1991) nicely summarized, "the queer, unlike the rather polite categories of gay and lesbian, revels in the discourse of the loathsome, the outcast, the idiomatically-proscribed position of same-sex desire. Unlike petitions for civil rights, queer rebels constitute a kind of activism that attacks the dominant notion of the natural" (p. 3).

To understand queer theory, we must first realize that it stems from a social reform movement. Queer activism seeks to break down traditional ideas of normal and deviant, by showing the queer in what is thought of as normal, and the normal in the queer. As Slagle (1995) noted, "By shaking up modernistic conceptions of classification, queers create a climate around which collective action and change can occur" (p. 93). Berlant and Freeman (1992) assessed this activism through the motives and actions of the American group Queer Nation (QN):

> QN redeploys these tactics in a kind of guerrilla warfare that names all concrete and abstract spaces of social communication as places where "the people" live and thus as natural sites ripe for both transgression and legitimate visibility. Its tactics are to cross borders, to occupy spaces, and to mime the privilege of normality. (p. 152)

Queer theory transforms those actions into an analytical operation, by utilizing similar tactics to conceptualize new ways of knowing and understanding what it means to be "normal" and/or "other." Chauncey (1994) utilized the spirit of queer theory to map "the spatial and social organizations of [the gay] world in a culture that often sought to suppress it" (p. 24), and to display "the shifting boundaries drawn between queers and normal men, as well as among queers themselves" (p. 24). Bryson and de Castell (1993) created a queer pedagogy to try to discover, "What difference does it make—being 'queer' in the classroom? What would that mean, anyway—*being* queer? How does it matter—with whom, or how, we re/construct sexual and affectional relations?" (p. 287). Queer theory, then, is about questioning what (and why) we know and do not know about things both normal and queer.

Obviously, queer theorists conceptualize the questions of inquiry and research differently than do assimilationists. Duggan (1995) succinctly delineated the distinction between the two approaches to history:

> Queer theory, located within or in proximity to critical theory and cultural studies, has grown steadily in publication, sophistication, and academic prestige. Queer theorists are engaged in at least three areas of critique: (a) the critique of humanist narratives that posit the progress of the self and of history, and thus tell the story of the heroic progress of gay liberationists

against forces of repression; (b) the critique of empiricist methods that claim directly to represent the transparent "reality" of "experience," and claim to relate, simply and objectively, what happened, when, and why; and (c) the critique of identity categories presented as stable, unitary, or "authentic." (p. 181)

As Duggan stated, queer theory is a contemporary idea related more to critical theory and cultural studies than to positivist or modernist theories.

To be sure, some linkages exist between queer theorists and theorists who strive for normalcy. Both viewpoints claim relationships between society and their theoretical arguments. Neither group is strictly theoretical, occasionally offering suggestions to better life experiences of queer people. Assimilationists and queer theorists both reject the clinician's focus on fixing ostensibly damaged individual identities. An end to discrimination and harassment is seen as a valid goal, although the means proponents of both groups would take to achieve social justice are dramatically different.

Educational organizations are particularly germane areas to highlight the differences between assimilationists and queer theorists. Whereas those who desire gay studies departments fall in line with traditional disciplinary configurations, queer theorists argue for alternative conceptualizations of knowledge, and in turn, organizational structures (Tierney, 1997). The implications of both views are distinct. If we are to professionalize a new area of inquiry in a manner consistent with previous areas, then we develop journals, conferences, and academic lines of appointment that seek to move power and authority within a disciplinary structure. Such activity is consistent with what we have seen by the creation of American Studies departments at the turn of the century, and more recently, departmental areas such as biochemistry and Women's Studies.

In contrast, queer theorists seek to disrupt "normalizing" discourses. Haver (in press) noted:

What if, that is to say, queer research were to be something more essentially disturbing than the stories we tell ourselves of our oppressions in order precisely to confirm, yet once more, our abjection, our victimized subjectivity, our wounded identity? What if, therefore, queer research were actively to refuse epistemological respectability, to refuse to constitute that wounded identity as an epistemological object such as would define, institute and thus institutionalize a disciplinary field? (pp. 1–2)

Haver's argument, however dense, assumes that a social field of knowledge ought not be contained or controlled; instead, a line of thought ought to be, as he notes, "an interruption rather than a reproduction" (p. 2). Queer theorists, then, do not look at the homosexual/gay body and wonder how one deals with the deviance of the individual or repression by the organization, but instead they see their work as a movement for cultural change of the notions of *normal* and *deviate*. Representation and its meanings (who says who is normal and who is deviant) become central to the struggle. Gay identity, then, is not simply a discussion about rights, but also about how identity and power intersect, how institutions control and legitimate certain discourses (Tierney, 1993).

This shift in focus occurred in a generation of gay activists and scholars who grew up during or after Stonewall and the resultant changes in societal views of homosexuality. As Lucas (1994) noted, discussing the British queer movement's main organization, "OutRage! have tapped in to a young and confident gay generation who are able to live openly gay lives, and who are willing to risk arrest where necessary in order to achieve their civil rights" (p. 160).

Most queer theorists acknowledge that those who sought assimilation with the mainstream, by continuing to address and discuss gay people, have made queer theory possible. Again, societal activists and academic scholars have interacted symbiotically with one another so that queer theory has become a central area for scholarship and research. Activists involved in groups such as Queer Nation, and queer theorists from multiple disciplines might occasionally talk past one another, but what unites them is an overriding concern for understanding norms and ideologies and coming to terms with how individuals and groups are marginalized, and how they might gain voice. Further, "the mainstreaming of lesbian and gay intellectual culture," noted Seidman (1995), "means that the university has become a chief site for the production of lesbian and gay discourses" (p. 122). Thus, gay and lesbian historians, for example, have in part made possible the alternative configurations called for here (Duggan, 1995). Of consequence, how gay/queer culture gets defined on campus has broad implications for society in general, and schools in particular.

Additionally, who the author/researcher is has come into question. Whereas at the start of the century the assumption was that neutral scientists studied homosexuals in much the same way that the colonial anthropologist studied the native, in queer theory such a vantage point has been destroyed. Further, from an assimilationist perspective, the sexual orientation of the researcher was not, in general, a question. Rather, the theoretical vantage point of the researcher was what mattered. That is, whether one was gay or straight mattered little as long as the perspective of deviance was dropped. Queer theory, however, raises questions about the nature of the author. Is it possible for a straight author to write a queer text? Such a question has no answer, or rather, it has multiple responses insofar as it brings into question issues of identity and narrative construction.

Britzman (1995), for example, considered if a "queer pedagogy" exists, and by implication, she pointed out how a heterosexual, or "straight," reading permeates teaching and curricula in schools, colleges, and universities. Straight reading continues to produce binary distinctions of self–other and normal–deviate. From Britzman's perspective, a queer pedagogy would examine the social constructions that create, and result from, such designations. *Queer*, then, would denote not who gay people "are" but how non-straight people understand and respond to society. Again, she was not simply claiming "visibility"—as if adding a gay author to the curriculum were sufficient, or a lesbian announcing her sexual orientation to her class was satisfactory. Instead, Britzman (1995) suggested that "queer theory offers methods of critiques to mark the repetitions of normalcy as a structure and as a pedagogy" (p. 154). Thus, the idea of normalization becomes the subject of investigation as a problem of culture and thought. Queer theorists suggest, then, that a cultural politics surrounds how knowledge gets defined, studied, and enacted.

Honeychurch (1996) examined the multifaceted dimensions of the term *queer* in comparison to more limiting terms.

> The familiar term "gay/lesbian sensibilities" does not adequately account for either the multiplicity of differences (race, class, ethnicity, etc.) Within those identities, or the anticipation of common grounds between them. It is perhaps in the more expansive term "queer" that most possibilities emerge for the denominating and declaring of differences and positions arising from the gamut of sexual diversities. (p. 341)

These overlapping, perhaps competing aspects of the term *queer*, foster a questioning of not just a single position or epistemology, but of all positions of knowledge: "Approaching social knowledge from a queered position is a postmodern rejection of epistemological certainty" (Honeychurch, 1996, p. 344).

In a reversal of traditional ways of understanding others (in contrast to the norm), queer theory attempts to understand the norm in contrast to others. Rofes (1993/1994) challenged notions of normalcy of school socialization, of "bullies" and "sissies." He made clear that the social construction of identity (what others think about us) is based on power and appearances rather than innate qualities:

> Throughout my primary and secondary school years, the words hurled at non-traditional boys were "sissy," "pansy," and "nancy-boy." Today the words are "gay," "faggot," and "queer." In fact, many students, when challenged by teachers on using the word "gay" as an epithet, insist that it has nothing to do with homosexuality. Instead, they are using the word to brand an individual as odd, non-traditional, or "girlish." The links to youthful misogyny are evident. Whether or not sissy boys grow up to be adult gay men, no attempt to prevent violence in our schools will succeed without addressing the attacks on sissies. (Rofes, 1993/1994, p. 38)

We quote this passage to highlight the interaction of language and action, self- and social identity, power and difference, experience and what is taken for knowledge, and the function of institutions to ensure equity beyond tolerance or representation. These issues (no matter the discourse level of the discussion) are key to queer theory.

Queer theory, then, rejects the view of homosexuality as a property of an individual or group (Seidman, 1995). Echoing Michel Foucault, queer theorists seek to develop a theoretical and political project that challenges a social regime that perpetuates the production of subjects and social worlds organized and regulated by the heterosexual–homosexual binary. Thus, to understand sexual orientation, queer theorists situate their work in present social contexts and analyze how sexual identity has been institutionalized. Such a focus is precisely why the author function comes in for investigation and debate.

Bryson and de Castell (1993) utilized a "queer pedagogy" in a college course on lesbian identity to construct nontraditional exercises to examine identity, gender, and issues of privilege and power. Lesbians from the community (an echo of the early gay and lesbian scholarship by activists) instructed the students in ways to utilize technology and art as ways of providing their own texts about their lives, thus providing and representing their own sense of identity. Bryson and de Castell's experience with nine non-heterosexual women—and one heterosexual woman, who appeared to resist the challenge to question her identity—highlights the difficulty of how to construct a pedagogy that will provide stimuli for all people to position their identities in relation to the norm. We need to come to terms, then, with how sexual identity gets defined and how such definitions vary or are in congruence with previous definitions so that we do not merely accept a transparent queer identity. As Sarah Chinn (1994) pointed out, the particular situations of individual schools and colleges affect (and effect) sexual identity and related scholarship:

> The stakes of queer affiliation cannot be separated from those of institutional affiliation—how much room the institution allows to explore and teach lesbian and gay material, for example; whether there are more than a handful of out students in the entire college or university...; how the resistance and homophobia of students and peers can make us bitter, resentful, and hateful and can blind us to the liberatory power that queer theory can embody. (p. 249)

If we decenter the norms that exist in culture in this manner then the idea of knowledge in the academy becomes much more a question of understanding not the objective nature of a study, but instead, the epistemological relationship of the study to larger social issues. We investigate how lesbian and gay people are situated in the academy and in schools in their present contexts and how these contexts have evolved (Chesler & Zuniga, 1991; Leck, 1995). We look at the study of homosexuality and try to come to terms with how it was investigated, what ideological norms existed, and how they might change (Eyre, 1993; Honeychurch, 1996; McLaren, 1993/1994). Thus, by decentering norms we move away from a politics of identity that situates analyses within individuals and we struggle to move toward an understanding of institutional and cultural practices that frame sexual orientation in a particular manner.

CONCLUSION

We have suggested here that three distinct, but overlapping, domains of research have existed with regard to lesbian and gay research in education. Well into the second half of this century, scholars interested in the study of deviance investigated homosexuality as a disease to be contained. Up until the 1970s any serious academic scholar who had argued that homosexuality should be considered normal would have been thought intellectually and morally irresponsible. To suggest that an academic department needed to be started, or that schoolchildren should learn of lesbian and gay issues, would have been unthinkable. From the 1970s to the present we have seen a great deal of work that seeks to shed light on the problems that lesbian and gay individuals face and to offer solutions to those problems. One primary area of research has concentrated on how to improve the site—educational institutions—for lesbian and gay people, and on the idea—education—as a way to increase understanding in the society at large.

In contrast, queer theorists argue that proponents of normalcy and deviance have accepted a sexual binarism—heterosexual–homosexual—that privileges some and silences others. Rather than concentrate exclusively on what they claim to be surface-level issues—faculty appointments, an inclusive curriculum, a gay-friendly environment—queer theorists argue that structures need to be disrupted. If one assumes that the structures of knowledge in part have defined normalized relations that have excluded homosexuals, then one needs to break those structures rather than merely reinvent them. To quote Audre Lorde (1984), "The master's tools will never dismantle the master's house" (p. 112).

The competing discourses that have existed surrounding this topic throughout the century in many respects mirror and extend intellectual arguments in multiple other arenas. The interplay of societal understanding and academic argument, for example, has occurred in numerous areas. Assimilationists assume that the oppression of lesbians and gays is akin to the norm's oppression of other groups (e.g., African Americans, Native Americans). The queer theorists' argument that sexual identity is more than genetic or social predisposition has also been suggested with regard to race and gender. One point for future work is to investigate how these problems intersect and diverge so that, for example, we do not essentialize oppression or assume that the process or experience of assimilation for one group is the same for another. More work also awaits us as we struggle to come to terms with what it means to be different (both specifically and collectively) in a postmodern world, and how educational organizations might foment and advance an understanding of difference.

REFERENCES

Abel, S. (1994). Gay and lesbian studies and the theatre curriculum. *Theatre Topics, 4*(1), 31–44.

Alabama denies aid to gay student groups. (1992, May 16). *New York Times*, L9.

Anthanases, S. Z. (1996, Summer). A gay-themed lesson in an ethnic literature curriculum: Tenth graders' responses to "Dear Anita." *Harvard Educational Review, 66*(2), 231–256.

Bauer, R., & Stein, J. (1973). Sex counseling on campus: Short-term treatment techniques. *American Journal of Orthopsychiatry, 43*(5), 824–839.

Bensimon, E. M. (1992). Lesbian existence and the challenge to normative constructions of the academy. *Journal of Education, 174*(3), 98–113.

Berg, A., Kowaleski, J., Le Guin, C., Weinauer, E., & Wolfe, E. A. (1994). Breaking the silence: Sexual preference in the composition classroom. In L. Garber (Ed.), *Tilting the tower: Lesbians teaching queer subjects* (pp. 108–116). New York: Routledge.

Berlant, L., & Freeman, E. (1992). Queer nationality. *Boundary 2, 19*(1), 149–180.

Besner, H. F., & Spungin, C. I. (1995). *Gay and lesbian students: Understanding their needs.* Washington, DC: Taylor & Francis.

Blinick, B. (1994). Out in the curriculum, out in the classroom: Teaching history and organizing for change. In L. Garber (Ed.), *Tilting the tower: Lesbians teaching queer subjects* (pp. 142–149). New York: Routledge.

Boutilier, N. (1992). Reading, writing, and *Rubyfruit Jungle*: High school students respond to gay and lesbian literature. *Out/Look, 4*(3), 71–76.

Britzman, D. P. (1995). Is there a queer pedagogy? Or, stop reading straight. *Educational Theory, 45*(2), 151–165.

Brogan, J. (1993/1994). Gay teens in literature. *High School Journal, 77*(1 & 2), 50–57.

Brooke, J. (1996). To be young, gay, and in the schools of intolerant Utah. *New York Times, CXLV*(50,351), A1, B8.

Bryson, M., & de Castell, S. (1993). Queer pedagogy: Praxis makes im/perfect. *Canadian Journal of Education, 18*(3), 285–305.

Cady, J. (1992). Teaching homosexual literature as a "subversive" act. In H. L. Minton (Ed.), *Gay and lesbian studies* (pp. 89–107). Binghamton, NY: Harrington Park Press.

Case, S. (1991). Tracking the vampire. *Differences: A Journal of Feminist Cultural Studies, 3*(2), 2–20.

Casper, V., Schultz, S., & Wickens, E. (1992). Breaking the silences: Lesbian and gay parents and the schools. *Teachers College Record, 94*(1), 109–137.

Chandler, K. (1995). *Passages of pride: Lesbian and gay youth come of age.* New York: Times Books.

Chauncey, G. (1994). *Gay New York: Gender, urban culture, and the making of the gay world 1890–1940.* New York: Basic Books.

Chesler, M. A., & Zuniga, X. (1991). Dealing with prejudice and conflict in the classroom: The pink triangle exercise. *Teaching Sociology, 19*, 173–181.

Chinn, S. (1994). Queering the profession, or just professionalizing queers? In L. Garber (Ed.), *Tilting the tower: Lesbians teaching queer subjects* (pp. 243–250). New York: Routledge.

Chng, C. L., & Moore, A. (1991). Can attitudes of college students towards AIDS and homosexuality be changed in six-weeks?: The effects of a gay panel. *Health Values, 15*(2), 41–49.

Collins, J. (1992). Matters of fact: Establishing a gay and lesbian studies department. In H. L. Minton (Ed.), *Gay and lesbian studies* (pp. 125–136). Binghamton, NY: Harrington Park Press.

Crew, L. (Ed.). (1978). *The gay academic*. Palm Springs, CA: ETC Publications.

Crew, L., & Keener, K. (1981). Homophobia in the academy: A report of the Committee on Gay/Lesbian Concerns. *College English, 43*(7), 682–689.

Croteau, J. M., & Kusek, M. T. (1992). Gay and lesbian speaker panels: Implementation and research. *Journal of Counseling & Development, 70*, 396–401.

Cullinan, R. G. (1973). A "gay" identity emerges on campus amidst a sea of prejudice. *NASPA Journal, 10*(4), 344–347.

D'Augelli, A. R. (1989a). Homophobia in a university community: Views of prospective resident assistants. *Journal of College Student Development, 30*, 546–552.

D'Augelli, A. R. (1989b). Lesbian and gay men on campus: Visibility, empowerment, and educational leadership. *Peabody Journal of Education, 66*(3), 124–142.

D'Augelli, A. R. (1989c). Lesbians' and gay men's experiences of discrimination and harassment in a university community. *American Journal of Community Psychology, 17*(3), 317–321.

D'Augelli, A. R. (1991a). Gay men in college: Identity process and adaptations. *Journal of College Student Development, 32*, 140–146.

D'Augelli, A. R. (1991b). Teaching lesbian and gay development: A pedagogy of the oppressed. In W. Tierney (Ed.), *Culture and ideology in higher education: Advancing a critical agenda* (pp. 213–233). New York: Praeger.

D'Augelli, A. R. (1992). Teaching lesbian/gay development: From oppression to exceptionality. In K. M. Harbeck (Ed.), *Coming out of the classroom closet: Gay and lesbian students, teachers and curricula* (pp. 213–227). Binghamton, NY: Harrington Park Press.

D'Augelli, A. R., & Rose, M. L. (1990). Homophobia in a university community: Attitudes and experiences of heterosexual freshmen. *Journal of College Student Development, 31*, 484–491.

DeFries, Z. (1976). Pseudohomosexuality in feminist students. *American Journal of Psychiatry, 133*(4), 400–404.

D'Emillio, J. (1990). The campus environment for gay and lesbian life. *Academe, 76*(1), 16–19.

D'Emillio, J. (1992). *Making trouble: Essays on gay history, politics, and the university*. New York: Routledge.

Due, L. (1995). *Joining the tribe: Growing up gay & lesbian in the '90s*. New York: Anchor Books.

Duggan, L. (1992). Making it perfectly queer. *Socialist Review, 22*(1), 11–31.

Duggan, L. (1995). The discipline problem: Queer theory meets lesbian and gay history. *GLQ, 2*, 179–191.

Epstein, D., & Johnson, R. (1994). On the straight and the narrow: The heterosexual presumption, homophobias and schools. In D. Epstein (Ed.), *Challenging lesbian and gay inequities in education* (pp. 197–230). Buckingham, England: Open University Press.

Eyre, L. (1993). Compulsory heterosexuality in a university classroom. *Canadian Journal of Education, 18*(3), 273–284.

Faderman, L. (1995). What is lesbian literature? Forming a historical canon. In G. E. Haggery & B. Zimmerman (Eds.), *Professions of desire: Lesbian and gay studies in literature* (pp. 49–59). New York: Modern Language Association of America.

Fonow, M. M., & Marty, D. (1992). Teaching college students about sexual identity from feminist perspectives. In J. T. Sears (Ed.), *Sexuality and the curriculum: The politics and practices of sexuality education* (pp. 157–170). New York: Teachers College Press.

Friend, R. A. (1993). Choices, not closets: Heterosexism and homophobia in schools. In L. Weis & M. Fine (Eds.), *Beyond silenced voices: Class, race, and gender in United States schools* (pp. 209–235). Albany: State University of New York Press.

Fromhart, M. V. (1971). Characteristics of male homosexual college students. *Journal of the American College Health Association, 49*(4), 247–252.

Gaard, G. (1992). Opening up the canon: The importance of teaching lesbian and gay literatures. *Feminist Teacher, 6*(2), 30–33.

Gammon, C. (1992). Lesbian studies emerging in Canada. In H. L. Minton (Ed.), *Gay and lesbian studies* (pp. 137–160). Binghamton, NY: Harrington Park Press.

Garber, L. (Ed.). (1994). *Tilting the tower: Lesbians teaching queer subjects.* New York: Routledge.

Gay, Lesbian and Bisexual Concerns Study Committee. (1993). *The final report to the executive vice chancellor from the gay, lesbian and bisexual concerns study committee.* Lawrence: The University of Kansas Press.

Geasler, M. J., Croteau, J. M., Heineman, C. J., & Edlund, C. J. (1995). A qualitative study of students' expression of change after attending panel presentations by lesbian, gay, and bisexual speakers. *Journal of College Student Development, 36*(5), 483–492.

Geller, W. W. (1991). Lesbian and gay topics: Awakening a campus. *Journal of College Student Development, 32,* 91–92.

Good, R. T., III. (1993). Programming to meet the needs of the lesbigay community. *Campus Activities Programming, 26*(2), 40–44.

Grayson, D. A. (1987). Emerging equity issues related to homosexuality in education. *Peabody Journal of Education, 64*(4), 132–145.

Green, S., Dixon, P., & Gold-Neil, V. (1993). The effects of a gay/lesbian panel discussion on college student attitudes toward gay men, lesbians, and persons with AIDS (PWAs). *Journal of Sex Education and Therapy, 19*(1), 47–63.

Griffin, P. (1992). From hiding out to coming out: Empowering lesbian and gay educators. In K. M. Harbeck (Ed.), *Coming out of the classroom closet: Gay and lesbian students, teachers and curricula* (pp. 167–196). Binghamton, NY: Haworth Press.

Grossman, A. H. (1993). Ten percent of those we teach and they serve: A case study of incorporating gay and lesbian studies into the curriculum. *Schole, 8,* 51–60.

Harbeck, K. M. (Ed.). (1992). *Coming out of the classroom closet: Gay and lesbian students, teachers and curricula.* Binghamton, NY: Haworth Press.

Harris, S. (1990). *Lesbian and gay issues in the English classroom: The importance of being honest.* Buckingham, England: Open University Press.

Haver, W. (in press). Queer research. *East Asian Studies.*

Hekma, G., & van der Meer, T. (1992). Gay and lesbian studies in the Netherlands. In H. L. Minton (Ed.), *Gay and lesbian studies* (pp. 125–136). Binghamton, NY: Harrington Park Press.

Herek, G. M. (1986). Heterosexuals' attitudes toward lesbians and gay men: Correlates and differences. *Journal of Sex Research, 25*(4), 451–477.

Honeychurch, K. G. (1996, Summer). Researching dissident subjectivities: Queering the grounds of theory and practice. *Harvard Educational Review, 66*(2), 339–355.

Jackson, E., Jr. (1995). Explicit instruction: Teaching gay male sexuality in literature class. In G. E. Haggery & B. Zimmerman (Eds.), *Professions of desire: Lesbian and gay studies in literature* (pp. 136–155). New York: Modern Language Association of America.

Keating, A. (1994). Heterosexual teacher, lesbian/gay/bisexual text: Teaching the sexual other(s). In L. Garber (Ed.), *Tilting the tower: Lesbians teaching queer subjects* (pp. 196–207). New York: Routledge.

Khayatt, M. D. (1992). *Lesbian teachers: An invisible presence.* Albany: State University of New York Press.

Khayatt, M. D. (1993). Proper schooling for teenage lesbians in Canada. In A. Hendriks, R. Tielman, & E. van der Veen (Eds.), *The third pink book: A global view of lesbian and gay liberation and oppression* (pp. 123–139). Buffalo, NY: Prometheus Books.

Khayatt, M. D. (1994). Surviving school as a lesbian student. *Gender and Education, 6*(1), 47–61.

Klinger, A. (1994). Moving the pink agenda into the ivory tower: The "Berkeley Guide" to institutionalizing lesbian, gay, and bisexual studies. In L. Garber (Ed.), *Tilting the tower: Lesbians teaching queer subjects* (pp. 186–197). New York: Routledge.

Lampela, L. (1996, Fall). Gay and lesbian artists: Toward curricular inclusiveness. *Taboo: The Journal of Culture and Education, II,* 49–63.

Leap, W. L. (1996). *Word's out: Gay men's English.* Minneapolis: University of Minnesota Press.

Leck, G. M. (1995). The politics of adolescent sexual identity and queer responses. In G. Unks (Ed.), *The gay teen: Educational practice and theory for lesbian, gay, and bisexual adolescents* (pp. 189–200). New York: Routledge.

Linne, R. (1996, Fall). Coming of age and coming out: Representations of gays and lesbians in young adult literature. *Taboo: The Journal of Culture and Education, II,* 71–86.

Lipkin, A. (1993/1994). The case for a gay and lesbian curriculum. *High School Journal, 77*(1 & 2), 95–107.

Lorde, A. (1984). *Sister outsider.* Freedom, CA: The Crossing Press.

MacKay, A. (1993). *Wolf girls at Vassar: Lesbian and gay experiences 1930–1990* (rev. ed.). New York: St. Martin's Press.

McCord, D. M., & Herzog, H. A. (1991). What undergraduates want to know about homosexuality. *Teaching of Psychology, 18*(4), 243–244.

McLaren, P. (1993/1994). Moral panic, schooling, and gay identity: Critical pedagogy and the politics of resistance. *High School Journal, 77*(1 & 2), 157–168.

McLaughlin, D., & Tierney, W. G. (Eds.). (1993). *Naming silenced lives: Personal narratives and the process of educational change.* New York: Routledge.

Minton, H. L. (Ed.). (1992). *Gay and lesbian studies.* Binghamton, NY: Harrington Park Press.

Mohr, R. D. (1989). Gay studies as moral vision. *Educational Theory, 39*(2), 121–132.

Nelson, R., & Baker, H. (1990). *The educational climate for gay, lesbian, and bisexual students at the University of California, Santa Cruz.* Santa Cruz: Student Services, University of California, Santa Cruz.

Nieberding, R. A. (1989). *In every classroom: The report of the president's select committee for lesbian and gay concerns.* New Brunswick, NJ: Office of Student Life Policy and Services, Rutgers—The State University of New Jersey.

Norris, W. P. (1992). Liberal attitudes and homophobic acts: The paradoxes of homosexual experience in a liberal institution. In K. M. Harbeck (Ed.), *Coming out of the classroom closet: Gay and lesbian students, teachers and curricula* (pp. 81–120). Binghamton, NY: Haworth Press.

O'Conor, A. (1995). Who gets called queer in school? Lesbian, gay, and bisexual teenagers, homophobia and high school. In G. Unks (Ed.), *The gay teen: Educational practice and theory for lesbian, gay, and bisexual adolescents* (pp. 95–101). New York: Routledge.

Opffer, E. (1994). Coming out to students: Notes from the college classroom. In R. J. Ringer (Ed.), *Queer words, queer images: Communication and the construction of homosexuality* (pp. 296–321). New York: New York University Press.

Patrick, P., & Sanders, S. A. L. (1994). Lesbian and gay issues in the curriculum. In D. Epstein (Ed.), *Challenging lesbian and gay inequities in education* (pp. 118–130). Buckingham, England: Open University Press.

Pollak, J. (1994). Lesbian/gay role models in the classroom: Where are they when you need them? In L. Garber (Ed.), *Tilting the tower: Lesbians teaching queer subjects* (pp. 131–134). New York: Routledge.

Pope, M. (1995). The "salad bowl" is big enough for us all: An argument for the inclusion of lesbians and gay men in any definition of multiculturalism. *Journal of Counseling & Development, 73*, 301–304.

Rensenbrink, C. W. (1996, Summer). What difference does it make? The story of a lesbian teacher. *Harvard Educational Review, 66*(2), 257–270.

Reynolds, A. J. (1989). Social environmental conceptions of male homosexual behavior: A university climate analysis. *Journal of College Student Development, 30*, 62–69.

Rhoads, R. A. (1994). *Coming out in college: The struggle for a queer identity.* Westport, CT: Bergin & Garvey.

Rhoads, R. A. (1995). Learning from the coming-out experiences of college males. *Journal of College Student Development, 36*(1), 67–74.

Ringer, R. J. (1994). Coming out in the classroom: Faculty disclosures of sexuality. In R. J. Ringer (Ed.), *Queer words, queer images: Communication and the construction of homosexuality* (pp. 322–331). New York: New York University Press.

Rofes, E. E. (1993/1994). Making our schools safe for sissies. *High School Journal, 77*(1 & 2), 37–40.

Roman, D. (1995). Teaching differences: Theory and practice in a lesbian and gay studies seminar. In G. E. Haggerty & B. Zimmerman (Eds.), *Professions of desire: Lesbian and gay studies in literature* (pp. 113–123). New York: Modern Language Association of America.

Schreier, B. A. (1995). Moving beyond tolerance: A new paradigm for programming about homophobia/biphobia and heterosexism. *Journal of College Student Development, 36*(1), 19–26.

Sears, J. T. (1987). Peering into the well of loneliness: The responsibility of educators to gay and lesbian youth. In A. Molnar (Ed.), *Social issues and education: Challenge and responsibility* (pp. 79–100). Alexandria, VA: Association for Supervision and Curriculum Development.

Sears, J. T. (1991). Helping students understand and accept sexual diversity. *Educational Leadership, 49*(1), 54–56.

Sears, J. T. (1992). Researching the other/searching for self: Qualitative research on [homo]sexuality in education. *Theory Into Practice, 31*(2), 147–156.

Sears, J. T. (1993a). Alston and Everetaa: Too risky for School? In R. Donmoyer & R. Kos (Eds.), *At-risk students: Portraits, policies, programs, and practices* (pp. 153–172). Albany: State University of New York Press.

Sears, J. T. (1993b). Responding to the sexual diversity of faculty and students: Sexual praxis and the critically reflective administrator. In C. A. Capper (Ed.), *Educational administration in a pluralistic society* (pp. 110–172). Albany: State University of New York Press.

Sears, J. T. (1993/1994). Challenges for educators: Lesbian, gay, and bisexual families. *High School Journal, 77*(1 & 2), 138–156.

Seidman, S. (1995). Deconstructing queer theory or the under-theorization of the social and the ethical. In L. Nicholson & S. Seidman (Eds.), *Social postmodernism: Beyond identity politics* (pp. 116–141). New York: Cambridge University Press.

Shepard, C. F. (1990). *Report on the quality of campus life for lesbian, gay, and bisexual students.* Los Angeles: Student Affairs Information and Research Office, University of California - Los Angeles.

Slagle, R. A. (1995). In defense of Queer Nation: From *identity politics* to a *politics of difference. Western Journal of Communication, 59*, 85–102.

Task Force on Lesbian and Gay Concerns, University of Oregon. (1990). *Creating safety, valuing diversity: Lesbians and gay men in the university: A report to the president of the University of Oregon.* Eugene: The University of Oregon Press.

Teaching about gay life is pressed by chancellor. (1992, November 17). *The New York Times,* B3.

Tierney, W. G. (1992). *Enhancing diversity: Toward a better campus climate: A report of the Committee on Lesbian and Gay Concerns.* College Station, PA: Pennsylvania State University.

Tierney, W. G. (1993). Academic freedom and the parameters of knowledge. *Harvard Educational Review, 63*(2), 143–160.

Tierney, W. G. (1994). Self and identity in a post-modern world: A life story. In D. McLaughlin & W. G. Tierney (Eds.), *Naming silenced lives: Personal narratives and the process of educational change* (pp. 119–134). New York: Routledge.

Tierney, W. G. (1997). *Queer Outlaws: Queer theory and cultural studies in the academy.* Beverly Hills, CA: Sage.

Tierney, W. G., & Rhoads, R. A. (1993). Enhancing academic communities for lesbian, gay, and bisexual faculty. In J. Gainen & R. Boice (Eds.), *Building a diverse faculty* (pp. 43–50). San Francisco: Jossey Bass.

Uribe, V. (1995). Project 10: A school-based outreach to gay and lesbian youth. In G. Unks (Ed.), *The gay teen: Educational practice and theory for lesbian, gay, and bisexual adolescents* (pp. 203–210). New York: Routledge.

Uribe, V., & Harbeck, K. M. (1992). Addressing the needs of lesbian, gay, and bisexual youth: The origins of PROJECT 10 and school-based intervention. In K. M. Harbeck (Ed.), *Coming out of the classroom closet: Gay and lesbian students, teachers and curricula* (pp. 9–28). Binghamton, NY: Haworth Press.

Waller, W. (1932). *The sociology of teaching.* New York: Wiley.

Webb, R. B. (1981). *Schooling and society.* New York: Macmillan.

Weiss, L., & Fine, M. (Eds.). (1993). *Beyond silenced voices: Class, race, and gender in United States schools.* Albany: State University of New York Press.

Yeskel, F. (1985). *The consequences of being gay: A report on the quality of life for lesbian, gay and bisexual students at the University of Massachusetts at Amherst.* Amherst, MA: Office of the Vice Chancellor for Student Affairs, University of Massachusetts at Amherst.

Chapter 2

A Generational and Theoretical Analysis of Culture and Male (Homo)Sexuality

James T. Sears
Independent Scholar

As the homophile movement emerged following World War II against the foreground of virulent homophobia within the medical establishment, law enforcement, the media, and the political arena, homosexual leaders distanced themselves from gay youth or those advocating reform of age-of-consent laws. As the movement enlarged numerically, broadened politically, and evolved theoretically during succeeding generations, it continued to meet resistance among political and religious groups often employing the "homosexual as sodomizer of youth" theme. Always marginalized, those who defend intergenerational relationships have long been at the end of the gay pride parade and sometimes ejected from it. Interestingly, both mainstream movement leaders and their opponents have found common ground in denouncing the "perversity of pederasty."[1]

Here, I outline the evolution of postwar gay politics along the axes of assimilationism/separatism from the homophile era, to the era of liberation, to the current identity era. Distinguishing each by a central conflict, I discuss how the generations approached the subject of adult–adolescent homoerotic relationships.[2] Arguing that these postwar ideological divisions reflect different concepts about culture and sexuality, the second section of this chapter elaborates on (homo)sexual discourses formed from these

---

[1]Pederasty, commonly found across cultures and historical epochs, is defined here as an intimate adult–adolescent relationship that includes a sexual element.

[2]For a discussion of the generations concept, see Sears, 1997, p. 10.

intersecting conceptions. A nine-cell framework situates the conflicts of postwar gay intellectual history, suggesting alternative frames for rethinking sexualities.

POSTWAR SOCIAL AND INTELLECTUAL GAY MOVEMENTS: AXES OF ASSIMILATIONISM AND SEPARATISM

From the emergence of the homophile movement during the era of McCarthyism to its visible radicalization as gay liberation following the summer riots in Greenwich Village, to identity politics of the 1980s and 1990s, the lesbian and gay movement has embraced differing intellectual foundations that have pivoted on distinct cultural assimilationist/separatist axes evident in the major wars of each era.[3]

Homophile Movement: The Sickness Wars

In the spring of 1953 leftists—most notably Harry Hay, who was a founding member of the Mattachine Society forming secret communist cell-like groups and championing the homosexual as a "special people"—were ousted by the cultural assimilationists. One of those renegade conservatives, San Franciscan Hal Call, described the radical founders as "sort of pie in the sky, erudite, and artistically inclined. . . . We saw Mattachine as a here-and-now, practical. . . . We knew that if we were going to get along in society, we were going to have to stay in step with the existing and predominant mores and customs" (Marcus, 1992, pp. 62–63). The engineer behind the palace coup, Ken Burns (1956), later underscored the new Mattachine position on the sickness issue:

> Psychiatry especially has made great strides forward in its analysis and comprehension of homosexuality. . . . Yet it is the homosexual himself who cries out for help in controlling this continuous cycle by constructive means. Castigating homosexuals now living is sheer stupidity. The solution of the problem of persons yet to be born who will become homosexual—who are maybe even destined to be homosexual—lies in preventive means. (p. 287)

---

[3]Excellent historical resources include Blasius and Phelan, 1997; Marcus, 1992; Miller, 1995. For helpful analyses of various ideological camps within the lesbian and gay communities during these eras, see Escoffier, 1992. There are also outstanding histories and anthologies of the homophile era (e.g., D'Emillio, 1983) and the liberation era (e.g., Martindale, 1997; Teal, 1971). For illustrative works of the identity era, see de Lauretis, 1991; Fuss, 1991; Morton, 1993, 1996; Phelan, 1994; Sedgwick, 1990. Each of these eras as well as the two preceding ones are chronicled in my multivolume project on Southern gay history, beginning with the homophile era (Sears, 1997).

Although the homophile movement was largely male-led and certainly male-controlled, women such as Del Martin, Phyllis Lyon, Barbara Gittings, and Barbara Grier emerged to develop parallel organizations and magazines—most notably Daughters of Bilitis and *The Ladder*. Founded in 1955, the organization's name honored the fictional heroine of Louys' *Songs of Bilitis* who, as Sappho's contemporary, lived as a lesbian; the magazine's title, *The Ladder*, conveyed the means by which the lesbian could ascend from her well of loneliness.

Although conscious of the special problems facing women within the Ozzie and Harriet life expectations of the 1950s and early 1960s, most of these women viewed themselves as homosexuals—lesbian or the "L word" was viewed as derogatory by women who loved women. Collaboration—be it going on "fake dates" or sharing a picket line—between gay women and men struggling to develop a broader-based homophile movement was the norm.

During this era, the movement's intellectual foundation was supported by the work of Donald Webster Cory's *The Homosexual in America*, the pioneering research studies of Alfred Kinsey (1948, 1953) and Evelyn Hooker (1956). The pseudonymous Cory (Edward Sagarin), echoing the earlier generations of Walt Whitman and Edward Carpenter, asserted that being homosexual—far from a handicap—was, in fact, a great democratic strength that bonded persons across social class lines. The research of Kinsey and his colleagues at Indiana University established the prevalence of homosexual behavior at a rate unimagined by most persons—gay or straight—during the 1950s. Finally, Hooker's pioneering work, funded by a grant from the National Institute of Mental Health, consisted of psychiatric profiles of a non-clinical sample of homosexual men, which found them to be as psychologically adjusted as their heterosexual counterparts.

Relying on outside experts to defend the normalcy of homosexuality, movement activists struggled during a time when conventional gender roles was the norm, heterodoxy was at its zenith, and police harassment and political intimidation of lesbians and gay men were common (Sears, 1997). During this era, newspaper accounts—when homosexuality was addressed at all—was generally under headlines such as: "$200,000 Outlay Urged for Center to Treat Deviates"; "Police to Harass Pervert Hangouts"; "Stiff Laws Urged on Perversion"; "Homosexual Cure Unlikely"; "16, He Gets 15 Years as Sex Deviate."

The homosexual male (women were seldom mentioned) was often portrayed as a nighttime marauder of public parks or molester of boys. Even in those circumstances where willing adolescents engaged in homosexual relations for money or enjoyment, the boy was cast as an unwilling or naïve innocent. The Boise scandal involving adults and young men (Gerassi, 1966) or the hitchhiking scam off Miami's Biscayne Boulevard during the

1950s resulted in long prison sentences for homosexual adults coupled with light sentences for teen hustlers who robbed, assaulted, and sometimes murdered their less sophisticated clients (Sears, 1997).

The tenor of these times was well-reflected when a Senate subcommittee paid a winter visit to Miami in 1954. Targeting juvenile delinquency, Tennessee Senator Estes Kefauver, his eyes fixed on the presidency, was a member of this "fact-finding" group. Armed with documents collected by Daniel Sullivan, who led the Senate's underworld crime hearings in Miami 4 years earlier, much of the testimony focused on the "recruitment by adult perverts" of teenagers into "homosexual practices." Assistant Counsel James Bobo pursued the homosexual-as-menace theme, asking the acting director of the police juvenile division, Sergeant Earl Owens: "What is the usual type of employment that these 16-year-olds can get?"

"Well, dishwashing. . . ."

"Has any investigation been made into who they might be living with?"

"We have found that some of these homosexuals that you speak of try to prey on this type. . . ."[4]

Daniel Sullivan, the chief investigator of the Florida State Racing Commission, then testified that the tendency of these homosexuals

> is for those people to move to the innocent, the uninitiated, the people who are sexually inexperienced and naturally they move to the young. . . . They tend to recruit new members into their group . . . [with] that person . . . lost for life to common normal standards of morality.[5]

Given the equation, male homosexual = child molester, homophile movement leaders and their organizations were reluctant to assist gay men under the age of 21, and ignored or joined in the chorus of condemnation against homosexual adults victimized because of intimate consensual relationships with teens.

Meanwhile, within the movement, the ideological debate swirled around the role of the homosexual in society and the "sickness issue." By the 1960s, more radical homophile activists, like Washington, DC leaders Frank Kameny and Jack Nichols, were arguing vociferously that not only was homosexuality *not* a psychological deformity but that lesbians and gay men—not psychiatrists and physicians—could best speak on behalf of the homophile movement. Kameny, a scientist and self-described skeptic and iconoclast, for example, penned in 1965:

> Our approach to the question of homosexuality as sickness . . . is one of the most important issues—probably THE most important single issue—facing

---

[4]*Hearing Before the Subcommittee*, 1956, p. 9

[5]*Ibid*, pp. 56–59

our movement today. . . . There are some who say that WE will not be accepted as authorities, regardless of what we say, or how we say it, or what evidence we present, and that therefore we must take no positions on these matters but must wait for the accepted authorities to come around to our position—if they do. This makes of us a mere passive battlefield across which conflicting "authorities" fight their intellectual battles. . . . We argue for our RIGHT to be homosexuals, to remain homosexuals, and to live as homosexuals. In my view and by my moral standards, such an argument is immoral if we are not prepared, at the same time, to take a positive position that homosexuality is not pathological. If homosexuality indeed IS a sickness, then we have no right to remain homosexuals; we have the moral obligation to seek cure. (pp. 335–337)

Not surprisingly, this position met with strong opposition from assimilationist leaders. As later recalled by Jack Nichols: "Bill Beardemphl of the Society for Individual Rights denounced aspects of our East Coast militancy. On the floor Kameny and Beardemphl traded—in bombastic tones—the disagreements." The delegates gave near-unanimous approval (44–1) for a resolution demanding an end to discrimination in the workplace and the military as well as the cessation of police harassment and Gestapo-like "purges." From Nichols' vantage point, however, it lacked substance resulting "in a mediocre statement that meant nothing. The Conference statement on pathology was hopelessly watered-down."[6]

Though the split between the assimilationists and separatists on the sickness issue was profound, both camps were only represented by a few dozen activists, and subscribers to their magazines, at best, accounted for several thousand persons (Streitmatter, 1995). Within the homophile movement, the sickness issue was not resolved; male–female relations within the emerging movement, the legalization of same-sex marriage, pornography age of consent laws, or linkages among various anti-oppression movements were non-issues. It would take rebellious hustlers, drag queens, and politicized hippies at a seedy Greenwich Village bar and the radicalism of the student antiwar and feminist movements to shift the ideological terrain as the winds of social change buoyed a fledgling movement.

Liberation Movement: The Gender Wars

As the 1960s ended, Gay Liberation coupled with the radical politics of the student resistance movement, brought an analyses of power and ideology to homosexual relations. In "Refugees from Amerika: A Gay Manifesto," Carl Wittam (1972), an SDS founding member, linked gay liberation to issues of equality and the hierarchy of oppression:

---

[6]Interview with Jack Nichols by James T. Sears, January 1995, Cocoa Beach, Florida. Located in Sears Papers at the Special Collections Library of Duke University, Durham, NC.

We are children of straight society. We still think straight; this is part of our oppression. One of the worst of straight concepts is inequality. Straight (also white, English, male capitalist) thinking views things in terms of order and comparisons. . . . This idea gets extended to male/female, on top/on bottom, spouse/not spouse, heterosexual/homosexual, boss/worker, white/black, and rich/poor. Our social institutions cause and reflect this verbal hierarchy. This is Amerika. . . . It is important to catalogue and understand the different facets of our oppression. There is no future in arguing about degrees of oppression. A lot of "movement" types come on with a line of shit about homosexuals not being oppressed as much as black or Vietnamese or workers or women . . . We don't happen to fit into their ideas of class or caste. Bull! (pp. 333, 335)

On the crest of the second wave of feminism—sparked by *The Feminine Mystique* and *Sexual Politics*—a tidal wave of feminism redefined relationships between men and women and among women. By the early 1970s, gay liberationists separated as gender defined the homosexual landscape much as the sickness issue had done in the previous era. Lesbian separatists writing for *The Furies, Feminary, Off Our Backs, Amazon Quarterly,* and *Sinister Wisdom*—many of whom were Southerners rebelling against gender codes of the Old South—championed lesbianism as a new feminist generation emerged. Walking out of NOW's New York chapter—whose members she denounced as "sexist, reformist clubwomen" (as she had earlier left NYU's homophile student group, which she found "male-dominated and irrelevant to women")—Rita Mae Brown organized the "first meeting of radical young lesbians without gay men" forming the first all-lesbian consciousness-raising group. From these efforts emerged the lesbian-feminist-separatist newspaper, *The Furies,* and the ground-breaking, collectively-written essay "The Woman-Identified Woman" that proclaimed:

Only women can given each other a new sense of self. That identity we have to develop with reference to ourselves, and not in relation to men. This consciousness is the revolutionary force from which all else will follow, for ours is an organic revolution. For this we must be available and supportive to one another, give our commitment and our love, give the emotional support necessary to sustain this movement. Our energies must flow toward our sisters, not backwards toward our oppressors. (Radicalesbians, 1972, p. 176)

While radicals separated in the gender wars, male and female homosexual assimilationists worked within sacred and profane traditions to establish religious organizations and political lobbying groups. From scriptural condemnation and organized religious bigotry, gay affirmation was linked to Baptist-based theology as a former southern Pentecostal minister, Troy Perry, established the Metropolitan Community Church, performing the first gay marriage in the United States. Meanwhile, other religious assimilationists worked within established denominations such as the Episcopalism and Catholicism to form support groups like Integrity and Dignity.

Within the political realm there was an emergence of gay organizations, most notably the National Gay Task Force (NGTF) and the Lambda Legal Defense and Education Fund. Founded in 1973, NGTF lobbied public officials and lent support to lesbians and gay men and their supporters seeking political office. The selection of Elaine Noble, the first openly gay person elected to public office (the Massachusetts House of Representatives), and Harvey Milk's election 3 years later in 1977 as a member of the San Francisco Board of Supervisors, signaled the dawn of gay visibility in mainstream politics.

Meanwhile, sexual radicals argued in favor of elimination of age-of-consent laws. For example, a group of young Turks, led by Stephen Donaldson, offered such a motion at the 1969 meeting of the North American Conference of Homophile Organizations (an umbrella group of loosely affiliated organizations)—which was unceremoniously defeated. By the early 1970s, groups such as Youth Liberation of Ann Arbor published newsletters and booklets defending the right of young adults to render decisions about their body. Again, though, such efforts paled in the face of mainstream gay agendas and the rapid devolution of the left.

As enlarging gay and lesbian communities led by social, religious, political, and economic assimilationists rallied against Anita Bryant in Florida and John Briggs in California, the voice and influence of the separatists—male or female—waned. For both war horses of the homophile movement, like Barbara Gittings, and a new generation of assimilationists, such as Harvey Milk, the unraveling of the left was welcomed. And, in academia the one-issue Gay Activist Alliance towered over the multiple-oppression oriented Gay Liberation Front. It would not be until the next generation that the radicals—now incarnated as queer theorists—would triumph over their moderate academic predecessors.

Identity Movement: The Sex Wars

By the early 1980s, the sex wars pitted lesbian-feminists and pro-feminist men such as Marilyn Frye and John Stoltenberg against sex radicals like Pat Califia and John Preston on issues of pornography, sadomasochism, pederasty, and public sex. As the mid-1980s witnessed the emergence of AIDS, however, there was some realignment among lesbians and gay men on issues of health and politics evidenced in the emergence of ACT–UP and Queer Nation, whose street politics differed from mainstream organizations such as the Human Rights Campaign Fund. Finally, during this era lesbians and gay men of color challenged the long hegemony of White middle-class political and intellectual leadership of the gay liberationists while openly questioning the primacy of race over sexuality among their heterosexual colleagues (e.g., Hemphill, 1991; Moraga & Anzaldúa, 1981; Smith, 1983).

The sex wars, though, dominated movement discourse. For example, in the now classic essay, "Lesbian Feminism and the Gay Rights Movement: Another View of Male Supremacy, Another Separatism," philosophy professor Marilyn Frye (1997) wrote:

> A look at some of the principles and values of male-supremacist society [e.g., worship of the penis, male homoeroticism, contempt for women] and culture suggests immediately that the male gay rights movement and gay male culture, as they can be known in their public manifestations, are in many central points considerably more congruent than discrepant with this phallocracy, which in turn is so hostile to women and to the woman-loving to which lesbians are committed. The phallocratic orthodoxy about the male body's pleasure seems to be that strenuous muscular exertion and the orgasm associated with fucking are its highest and greatest forms. This doctrine suits the purposes of a society which requires both intensive fucking and a population of males who imagine themselves as warriors. (pp. 500, 508)

In contrast, that same year John Preston (1997), one time *Advocate* editor and writer of erotica, countered that the gay man

> does not discuss the power issues of sadomasochism in workshops; he experiences it as an often positive force which can break through his inhibitions. He is not a pedophile in the classic sense of the word, but he is certainly attracted to situations in which an age discrepancy heightens erotic appeal between men whom he sees as peers. He very probably does seek emotional attachments and worries great about his and other men's abilities to construct meaningful relations, but sex for him is play.... It is very clear that the maleness of gay men presents an image that many feminists find impulsive. It also should be very clear to gay men that we cannot afford to give up the victory which is the celebration of that maleness. (p. 512)

Meanwhile, the assimilationists of this era—epitomized by business guilds, Metropolitan Community Church congregations, Log Cabin Republicans, and Human Rights Campaign Fund supporters—sought equality within existing institutional structures. Their goal (like those of their homophile forbears) was to integrate lesbians and gay men into the economic, religious, and political fabric of society where one's sexual orientation, now portrayed as a genetic fact of life, would eventually diminish in importance. Gay marriage and military service were their causes célèbres; proponents of abandoning age-of-consent laws, now organized as the North American Man–Boy Love Association, were branded sexual outlaws in a once hostile heterosexual frontier only recently tamed by the assimilationists.

The radical intellectual critique of mainstream homosexual activism and cultural separatism moved from Marxist and lesbian feminist analyses to queer theory, with its reliance on deconstructionism and post-modernism. Through discourse analysis, queer theorists often drew on the work of Jacques Derrida, Jacques Lacan, and Michel Foucault. Though some of its proponents were well-represented in activist groups such as ACT-UP and Queer Nation, their domain of influence resided largely within academe, which prized such abstract and distant discourse.

COMPETING UNDERSTANDINGS OF CULTURE AND SEXUALITY

These postwar divisions between and among cultural assimilationists and separatists pivoted on competing understandings of culture and sexuality. The concept of culture, be it the dominant heterosexual one into which many assimilationists sought access and respect such as the Daughters of Bilitis and the Gay Activists Alliance or the emerging countercultural ones that ranged from lesbian separatists to the California Castro clones, was central.

Similarly, discrepant views about (homo)sexuality—as universal and trans-historical, as constructed and pliable, or as an instrument for transcendence—were foundational firewalls between groups struggling within an era. Gay liberationists, for example, developed their ideological frame on the basis of a constructivist view of sexuality and a materialist view of culture. Homosexual assimilationists—be they religious or political—tended to view sexuality from the lens of essentialism while centering culture in texts—be they sacred (e.g., Bible, Torah) or profane (Constitution, legislative statutes).

Thinking About Culture

There are three distinctive anthropological vantage points to thinking about culture.[7] Traditionally, anthropologists have believed that "culture

---

[7]Culture, of course, has a multitude of meanings and interpretive approaches to its study (Kroeber & Kluckhohn, 1952). From the debate on the relationship between culture and society, Eagleton (1968), for example, cites three main uses of the term: particular artistic or intellectual works commonly associated with high culture; the more generalized but abstract, "shifting, intangible complex of its lived manners, habits, morals, values" (p. 3); and a way of life commonly associated with "the totality of interacting artistic, economic, social, political, ideological elements which composes its total lived experience" (p. 4). From the concern about the adequacy and accuracy of anthropological inquiry and rooted in the ancient debates between enlightenment and romanticism, realism and idealism are contemporary ethnographic arguments such as the universals and the particularities of cultures and the emic and the etic perspectives on culture (Brown, 1991; Shweder & Levine, 1984). Also see Alexander & Seidman, 1990; Austin-Broos, 1987; Barrett, 1984; Brown, 1991; Cliford & Marcus, 1986; Kaplan & Manners, 1972; Marcus & Fischer, 1986; Rohner, 1984; Shweder & Levine, 1984.

consists of *patterns . . . of and for behavior*" (Kroeber & Kluckholn, 1952, p. 181, italics added). Thus, they have studied cultures and those who inhabit them by entering into their societies, recording their native customs and actions, examining their artifacts, describing these behaviors and deciphering the patterns—usually in reference to "civilized" cultures (e.g., Frazer, 1890; Morgan, 1877; Redfield, 1953; Tylor, 1871). Through extensive fieldwork they observed, cataloged, and described a culture with respect to its economic, political, and social organization, and its members' patterns of behavior regarding kinship and marriage, religious practices, and the arts (e.g., Radcliffe-Brown, 1952; Wissler, 1923).

For most of this century, however, the dominant anthropological image of culture has been that of a coherent system of shared symbols and meanings that cluster people into one interconnected, conceptual web. This ideational, constructivist view of culture—grounded in the early anthropological work of Franz Boas (1938), Ruth Benedict (1934), and Lucien Lévy-Bruhl (1936) along with the philosophical writings of Wilhelm Dilthey (1976) and Ludwig Wittgenstein (1966)—is well represented in the distinctively unique works of cultural anthropologists (e.g., Douglas, 1973; Geertz, 1973, 1983; Goodenough, 1981). Here, culture is viewed from the inside out; to understand a cultural system anthropologists must understand the intersubjective meanings and symbols constructed by those who reside within that culture.

Some social theorists, though, have found problematic the view that culture is ordered with meanings and symbols available for ready translation by knowledgeable scholars who access "local knowledge" (e.g., Holly, 1989; Parkin, 1982). Conceptualizing culture as language and text, post-structural anthropology (e.g., Crapanzano, 1980; Rabinow, 1977; Tyler, 1987) considers the reading of cultural texts and the production of ethnographic texts to be problematic. Stephen Tyler (1986a, 1986b, 1987), for example, advocates an "ethnography of evocation," which rejects modernist attempts to present or represent the Other unproblematically in cultural texts.[8] The result is the construction of dialogic texts that "make available through absence what can be conceived but not represented" (Tyler, 1986a, p. 123). This contemporary convergence between anthropology and postmodernism is well articulated by Peter McLaren (1991):

A radical reconceptualization of culture as a field of discourse or text has helped to make our common understanding of culture quite uncommon. . . .

---

[8]For an insightful feminist critique of postmodernist anthropology and their uncritical use of the Other vis-à-vis women, see Mascia-Lees, Sharpe, & Cohen (1989). They conclude, "Those anthropologists sensitive to power relations in the ethnographic enterprise who wish to discover ways of confronting them ethically would do better to turn to feminist theory and practice them in postmodernism" (pp. 32–33).

Postmodern social theory has given us a differentiated view of culture as distinct from the unitary one. . . . Culture has come to be understood as more distinctly multiplex and political than its usual conception as the proliferation of historically produced artifacts forged within a neutral arena of social relations. (pp. 235, 237)

Thinking About Sexuality

There are also competing understandings about sexuality: essentialist, constructivist, transformationist. The most common view of sexuality is from the perspective of essentialism: sexuality as a universal human *trait* reflecting a body–mind dualism. In Western societies, our understanding of sexuality and its associated artifacts and behaviors has been seen through one of three essentialist discourses: techno-behavioral, Freudian, and Judeo-Christian. While each of these is distinct, all fall within a modernist framework.[9] In Western societies, modernism is manifested in an essentialist understanding about sexuality as a universal and transhistorical trait and, within the field of cultural anthropology, a frozen depiction of the Other in cultural accounts.

More recently, feminist theorists, neo-Marxist analysts, and post-structural scholars have embraced constructivism: sexuality as a socially constructed *concept*. The constructivist perspective emphasizes the plasticity of human sexuality, asserting the power of society's beliefs, artifacts, and values to mold it. Embodied in cultural myths, social relations, or language, sexuality is foremost a mental concept, not a biological phenomenon.[10]

Finally, from the transformationist perspective (as of yet not widely appropriated by gay/lesbian scholars or activists), sexuality qua sexuality is an *instrument* for individual or social evolution in which mind–body dualisms collapse. Rather than conceptualizing sexuality as a fixed essence of humankind or as constructed materially, symbolically, or linguistically others view sexuality as a profound transformational force. Focusing on culture as behavior, symbol, or text, sexuality is the principal instrument in the work of sociobiology, Jungian analyses, and erotica.

The competing understandings of culture and sexuality, therefore, intersect into nine (homo)sexual discourses (see Fig. 2.1). This framework helps to situate intellectually the sickness, gender, and sex conflicts of postwar gay intellectual history; here, though, I principally use this model to suggest alternative frames for rethinking the "perversity of pederasty."

---

[9]See, for example, Ardener, 1985; Burniston, Mort, & Weedon, 1978; Clifford & Marcus, 1986; Manganaro, 1990; Marcus & Fischer, 1986; Tong, 1989.

[10]See Alcoff, 1988; Ardener, 1985; Fromm, 1961; Manganaro, 1990; Marcus & Fischer, 1986; Tong, 1989; Walby, 1990.

Sexuality as / Culture as	BEHAVIORS & ARTIFACTS	SYMBOLS & MEANINGS	LANGUAGE & TEXT
ESSENTIALIST	SEX AS PLEASURE/DANGER Techno-Behaviorist	SEX AS LIBIDINAL ENERGY Freudian	SEX AS SIN/SACRAMENT Judeo-Christian
CONSTRUCTIVIST	SEX AS CONTROL & POWER Marxist	SEX AS CULTURALLY RELATIVE Culturalist	SEX AS DISCOURSE Post-Structuralist
TRANSFORMATIONIST	SEX AS CULTURAL SELECTION/ GENETIC PREDISPOSITION Evolutionist	SEX AS TRANSCENDENT Mythologist	SEX AS EROTIC IMAGINATION Liberationist

FIG. 2.1.   Sexuality and culture grid.

(HOMO)SEXUAL DISCOURSES: RETHINKING PORNOGRAPHY AND PEDERASTY

Sex as Pleasure/Danger

From the technobehavioral perspective, sexuality provides the sexual free-dom experienced by many gay men during the 1970s and early 1980s. Within the behavioral tradition are sexual liberationists such as Pat Califia and Susie Bright who view sexual behavior as pleasurable, and rationalists represented by some AIDS organizations whose message, delivery, and evaluation reflect a technobehavioral worldview as well as antipornography feminists like Catherine MacKinnon and Andrea Dworkin for whom sexu-ally explicit words and images and sexual behaviors are linked. Whereas the sexual rationalists and the sexual liberationists engaged in prolonged battles with respect to picketing adult bookstores, developing restrictive zoning laws, enacting harsher age-consent laws, and closing the bathhouses, both the liberationists and the rationalists viewed gender and sexual behavior in essentialist terms.

In 1983, for example, success found two University of Minnesota professors earning approval from the Minneapolis City Council for their proposed antipornography ordinance. The law declared pornography as "a practice of sex discrimination" authorizing lawsuits for offenses that included trafficking of or coercion into pornography and assault or physical attack due to pornography. Although pornography was defined as "graphic sexually explicit subordination of women through pictures and/or words," it also stipulated that "the use of men, children, or transsexuals in the place of women . . . is pornography for purposes of this law" (Strossen, 1995, pp. 75, 106). This morphing of victims was defended by Dworkin (1979, p. 23): "Fucking requires that the male act on one who has less power. . . . [T]he one who is fucked is stigmatized as feminine during the act even when not anatomically female."[11]

Another example of the pleasure/danger construct is the debate about intergenerational intimacy. The traditional view of "child sexual abuse" assumes that youth are nonsexual and non-pleasure-seeking, or at least incapable of making informed sexual decisions, and the adult is the corrupting influence. In contrast, liberationists, such as members of the Rene Guoyn Society, view young people as sexual beings whose happy sexual childhood behavior leads to a creative and guilt-free adulthood. Despite holding such disparate positions, both share an essentialistic and behavioristic view of sexuality.

Sex as Libidinal Energy

The psychoanalytic perspective, appropriating Freud's concept of mechanics to the human body, views sex as libidinal energy. Classic Freudianism is rooted in the epistemology and ontology of the late 19th century and constructed within the cultural context of the Victorian age.

But, it is the realm of sexual symbolism and unconscious meanings that is at the heart of this discourse. The propositions that neurosis resulted from factors arising from sexual life—especially in childhood—that sexuality is converted into anxiety, and that adult sexual development rests on sexual childhood fantasies—particularly about one's mother and father—have been incorporated in a significant way into our secular understanding of sexuality.

---

[11]For further discussion of this debate along feminist lines, see, for example, Gubar, 1987; Toolin, 1983.

Adult sexuality evolves from polymorphous, infantile sexual forms. One of these infantile sexual forms, according to Freud (1963), is homosexuality. Throughout the homophile movement, a principal concern was how to deal with the psychiatric establishment, in general, and the work of men such as Irving Bieber (1962) and Charles Socarides (1968), in particular. It was here that the fissure between conservatives like Hal Call and radicals such as Frank Kameny occurred.

A generation later, while some psychiatrists, most notably Socarides, continued to advocate along these lines, feminist scholars incorporated a neo-Freudian understanding into homosexuality. De-emphasizing Freud's misogyny, Nancy Chodorow (1978) and Juliette Mitchell (1975), for example, focused on the importance of early childhood experiences using object relations theory and built on Freud's concept of the unconscious to explore gender relations.

Psychoanalytic thought has implications for children's sexuality and lends insight into intergenerational relationships. As articulated in Freud's classic 1907 essay, "The Sexual Enlightenment of Children":

> Puberty merely brings about attainment of the stage at which the genitals acquire supremacy among all the zones and sources of pleasure, and in this way presses eroticism into the service of reproduction . . . the child is long before puberty a being capable of mature love, lacking only the ability for reproduction. (Freud, 1963, p. 19)

The curricular implications for the more traditional Freudian perspective is perhaps best seen in the writings of Scottish educator A.S. Neill (1926, 1953). Steeped in the assumptions of Freud and a close friend of Wilhelm Reich, Neill wrote about the founding of Summerhill: "Freud showed that every neurosis is founded on sex repression. I said: 'I'll have a school in which there will be no sex repression'" (Croall, 1983, p. 153). Neill (1960) forcefully laid out his position on childhood sexuality:

> The sex taboo is the root evil in the suppression of children. . . . What then can we do to prevent sex suppression in children? Well, for one thing, from the earliest moment the child must be completely free to touch any and every part of his body. . . . When the children have no moralistic training in sex, they reach a healthy adolescence—not an adolescence of promiscuity. . . . Every older pupil at Summerhill knows from my conversation and my books that I approve of a full sex life for all who wish one, whatever their age. . . . The factual truth about sex is, of course, important, but what's more important is the emotional content. . . . If the child's natural curiosity has been satisfied all the way by open and unemotional answers to all his questions, sex will not stand out as something that has to be specially taught. (pp. 206–209)

It is within this realm of the sexualized nature of children and concept of polymorphous sexuality that some have rethought our understandings of pederasty and pedophilia (e.g., Brongersma, 1986; Sandfort, 1987; Sandfort, Brongersma, & van Naerssen, 1991). For example, Edward Brongersma writes: "a boy is mature for lust, for hedonistic sex, from his birth on; sex as an expression of love becomes a possibility from about five years of age; puberty is the best time for the 'oceanic,' the mystic experience and for using sex to unite one with nature" (p. 40).

Sex as Sin/Sacrament

As activists found themselves locked in fierce debate with the psychiatric community during the homophile era, the archnemesis for liberation activists were Christian conservatives who, following the formation of the Falwell's Religious Roundtable during the mid-1970s, challenged the increasingly public and powerful gay rights movement. Unlike the secular rhetoric of the technobehaviorists, the biblical interpretation of sexuality is not rooted in a concern for the physical danger posed by sexual behavior but in the spiritual corruption by the flesh.

In Paul's writings, sins against the human body—temples of the Holy Spirit—consisted of four types:

> on an ascending curve of sinfulness. The first group consists of those who prostitute themselves, *fornicarii*. The second group is that of adulterers, that is those who seduce another's wife, and women who allow themselves to be seduced. . . . The third group is that of the *molles* (*malakoi*) . . . *Mollities* is an ambiguous sort of word, not necessarily sexual by implication . . . acting just for pleasure. . . . After the *fornicarii*, the *adulteri*, and the *molles*, St. Paul adds the *maculorum concubitories*, the men who go to bed together. . . . Henceforth we have a code of sexual morals: sins against the body arising from the use or abuse of sexual organs—lust, in fact. (Aries, 1985, pp. 38–39)

Lesbian and gay scholars during the liberationist era re-appropriated Christian teachings through a rereading of scriptural and ancient texts (e.g., Boswell, 1980, 1994; Lance, 1989; McNeil, 1976; Scroggs, 1983). John Boswell's seminal works, for example, recovered evidence of a more tolerant early-Christian era with respect to homosexual behavior and same-sex unions. He shared, however, a universalistic and essentialist conception of sexuality. Other scholars, most notably Robin Scroggs, challenged the fundamentalist reading of these scriptural texts, linking it to youthful male prostitutes and their benefactors rather than to adult male homosexuality. Scroggs argues that in the case of Paul the frequently translated references against homosexuality were, in fact, not directed at pederastic relationships between lover and beloved in the gymnasium or symposium. They were targeted at "effeminate call boys" and their active partners who maintained them as "mistresses"—mere objects of desire (Scroggs, 1983, pp. 106–108). Though ignored by intergenerational advocates, the Bible thus provides a textual defense for non-exploitive adult–adolescent sexual relationships.

Sex as Control and Power

Classical Marxism, with its emphasis on historical materialism, asserts that social existence determines an individual's consciousness; thus as the economic conditions of production are transformed, so, too, are individuals' social consciousness. In capitalist societies (those emerging out of feudalism's inherent contradiction between the productive forces and the existing social organization), the production and reproduction of individuals' behaviors are guided by the requirements of their material situations; how individuals express themselves depends on what they produce and how they produce it.

It is upon this economic structure that the social and political superstructure is built. This superstructure encompasses institutions such as the church, school, family, and government. These, in turn, generate values, ideas, habits of life, and laws that correspond to and legitimate an economic structure that is inequitable and alien. Hence, those of privilege (those with surplus economic or cultural capital) maintain their position through economic power and ideological control.

Viewing sexuality as a human invention, Jeffrey Weeks (1982, 1985), among others, has argued that categorizing human beings according to their role in the biological process is central in the reproduction of the social order. Employing a materialist analysis of sexual regulation, he writes:

> Power no longer appears as a homogeneous force which can be straight-forwardly expressed or captured. Power, like the politics around it, can be seen as mobile, heterogeneous, insistent and malleable, giving rise to various forms of domination, of which the sexual is one. . . . The sexual only exists in and through the modes of its organisation and representation . . . it only has relevant meaning via cultural forms. (Weeks, 1985, pp. 9–10)

From this perspective, during recent decades of capitalist transition from production to consumption, sexuality was transformed into a commodity. "Sex had for long been something you were. By the 1950s it was also something you could buy" (Weeks, 1985, p. 23). Increasing public ambivalence to, if not acceptance of, pornography, pre-marital sex, and prostitution was coupled with the use of sexual imagery in mainstream marketing. This change resulted, in part, from the technological separation of sexual intercourse from pregnancy, from the search and expansion of capitalist markets, and from the "millions of people escaping from social privation and sexual puritanism" (Weeks, 1985, p. 258).

It is within this conception of sexuality and culture that serious concerns regarding intergenerational sex have been raised. The commodification of the sexual subject, the reduction of the relationship to an economic exchange, and the inherent inequality in power between the older and younger lover coupled with society's fetish on youth and innocence are common concerns (e.g., Spiecker & Steutel, 1997). And, it is within this domain that most discourse in defense of intergenerational relationships has occurred:

> We would challenge critics to identify just one example of any kind of relationship which involved two or more persons that isn't characterized by a structured or a *de facto* imbalance of power. . . . The anti-pedo advocates don't really object to the fact of inequality in an adult–minor relationship. Relationships they hold dear are full of inequalities: husband–wife, parent–child, government–citizen. What these critics dislike about their perceived idea of inequality in man–boy affairs is that they think it exactly duplicated the coercive and socially-imposed inequality in existing heterosexual and intra-family relationships. (NAMBLA, 1997, p. 565)

Support for this position is found in the studies of Dutch scholars, notably Theo Sandfort and Edward Brongersma. In Sandfort's (1987) study of 25 male minors engaged in sexual relationships with adult men, he found the youths were not recruited into the relationships. In fact, most youth initiated the contact, often exercising considerable power in the relationship. And, as Brongersma (1991) observes: "It is inherent in intimate human relations that both partners can exercise a profound influence upon each other. . . . [But] in any relationship between human beings he who needs the relationship most has the least power and the greatest dependence upon the other" (pp. 147, 166). The more dependent partner may just as easily be the adult as the adolescent. Interestingly, Brongersma asserts that the greatest potential of abuse from the adult is not sexual but lies in the adult partner being too permissive.

Sex as Culturally Relative

The vast array of gendered and sexual relationships is well expressed by cultural anthropologist Clyde Kluckhohn (1954), who defines culture as "distinctive ways of life" learned by individuals within that society: "Puberty is a biological fact. But one culture ignores it, another prescribes informal instructions about sex but no ceremony, a third has impressive rites for girls only, a fourth for boys and girls. . . . Each culture dissects nature according to its own system of categories" (p. 26).

Some detailed studies occasionally relied on by those defending pederastic relationships have been penned by anthropologists and historians (e.g., Beveridge, 1922; Englinton, 1964; Herdt, 1981; Licht, 1932; Mathers, 1972; Percy, 1990). The relationships between the older lover (*erastes*) and beloved young man (*eromenos*) typified in ancient Greece; the young protégé page of the warrior Samurai class in 12th-century Japan; the puberty rite of fellatio among the Sambia; and the rich Afghan legacy of pederasty are such examples.

Although such scholarship supports the fluidity of human sexual behavior, the meanings constructed about such intergenerational relationships may not be as clear. The reliance on cross-cultural or historical case studies to support intergenerational sexual relationships has limited utility. Observing that "New Guinea is not Amsterdam or Greenwich Village," Carole Vance (1982, p. 22) acknowledged that such studies encourage openness rather than premature closure in our thinking about the historical and cultural meaning of diverse sexual acts and identities. A similar point is made by two cultural anthropologists:

> The culturalist approach, first, stresses that no particular gender symbol can be well understood without an appreciation of its place in a larger system of symbols and meanings. In other words, it is not only that we must understand what "male," "female," "sex," and "reproduction," mean in any given culture, but that those meanings are best understood in terms of a larger context of interrelated meanings. (Ortner & Whitehead, 1981, p. 2)

Understanding how various cultural groups make sense of homosexuality and how we construct and reconstruct our subjectivities lies at the heart of sexual constructivism. However, for those seeking to move beyond the perversity of pederasty, an interactionist perspective focusing on meaning and process may be more helpful.

Symbolic interactionists are concerned with individuals' emerging sexual meanings and the process of negotiating one's sexual identities in interpersonal encounters. From this perspective, sexuality begins at the moment of an individual's first understanding of sex and continues over a lifetime of sexual meaning making.

In the interactionist-based sociological scholarship of John Gagnon and William Simon (1969), the meaning and symbology associated with sexuality has no deep meaning aside from those indirectly learned from peers or adults; one's adult sexuality is not the result of developmental stages that have unfolded since infancy. They write:

> The individual can learn sexual behavior as he or she learns other behavior—through scripts that in this case give the self, other persons, and situations erotic abilities or content. . . . People in different cultures construct their scripts differently; and in our society, different segments of the population act out different psychosexual dramas. (p. 10)

Thus, as the child grows older, the meaning associated with sexuality is directly learned through personal experiences; from these personal experiences children turned adults reinterpret their childhood experiences, re-evaluating the adequacy of the earlier sexual scripts (e.g., the script of secrecy) provided to them by peers and adults. Not surprisingly, sexual meanings constructed between perhaps well-meaning adults and pleasure-seeking adolescents about sexual relationships are often discrepant: "Both are looking at the same forms of behavior from very different experience levels, and both use the symbols and meanings that are perceived as appropriate to their respective level" (Petras, 1978, p. 144).

Anecdotal writing by a lesbian, Masha, and a gay man, Bill, both of whom engaged in consensual sexual relationships with adults during their adolescence, provide evidence for the rejection of a singular and static reading of intergenerational sexual experiences. Bill Andriette (1994) remembers:

> I started having gay sex with men as a 14-year-old boy. By and large my relationships were positive. They were the field on which I learned to negotiate the sexual terrain. . . . In these sexual encounters I found pleasures I hadn't anticipated based on what I knew from fantasizing or childhood sex play; the physical warmth and tenderness of love making, being the object of another person's arousal, the excitement of breaking the rules. But at the same time I often felt ambivalent and slightly troubled: by my lack of confidence in avoiding or initiating sexual situations, by my uncertainty about the criteria I should use in deciding whether or not to have sex with someone, by the fact that these relationships were completely separate from the other sets of relationships that constituted my fairly ordinary, suburban New York adolescent life. . . . It is not that sex is so extraordinarily troublesome and foreign that even young children cannot assimilate it to their understanding. I had no trouble knowing the kinds of sexual situations I liked—even when six years old; when life did not provide, I created them nightly in my fantasies. Rather, it is our society's bigoted intolerance that deliberately and at great cost makes intergenerational sex troublesome, and not the *nature* of children or adolescents and the *nature* of sex. (pp. 207–208)

In contrast, Masha Gessen (1994) writes:

> Each touch was the first, filling my body with the fear and thrill of the unknown. It wasn't really the first time I had been touched sexually, but for the first time I had willed it to happen. I felt powerful, for the first time in my twelve years. I explored my sexual power over the next few years. It became a game: At fourteen, I would walk into a discotheque with a (17-year-old) friend, and within the first five minutes point to the man I would bed that night. . . . I felt all-powerful. I could get anything, do anything, go anywhere—for sex. Since the sex was mine, my life was mine—and my life suddenly included that things I needed and/or wanted: affection . . . a place safer than my parents' home . . . alcohol and drugs . . . I had freedom as

long as I had sex. . . . But for the longest time when you asked if I thought children could consent to sex, I would say that at twelve I had been no child, I had not just consented but instigated quite competently. And when you asked if I thought the men I'd slept with should have said no, I would tell you to stop being patronizing. . . . But at nineteen, I still didn't know how to feel like you loved me if we didn't have sex. (pp. 213–215)

One of the few scholars to apply interactionist theory within this constructivist paradigm to rethink sexualities is Ken Plummer (1991):

[T]o show that boys can have erections and that girls can have orgasms at very early ages, that they can engage in masturbatory, homosexual and heterosexual play, and that they can develop a curiosity about birth and production is NOT to show that they are necessarily sexual. Sexuality certainly has its physiological and behavioural base: but amongst humans it has an essentially symbolic, socially constructed meaning. Nothing automatically translates itself for the child into sexual meaning—this, like everything else, has to be learned and is culture specific. . . . In discussing paedophilia, child sexual abuse, or the age of consent, the issue of "age" is clearly omnipresent. . . . The most common approach to age in social science suggests that it may best be viewed as a series of developmental stages or crises. . . . "Ages of consent," and "views of cross-generational sexuality" all harbour models of this development sequence. . . . [But] "childhood" itself is not a biological given but an historically produced social object; so is youth, and so on. . . . Within this approach there is no assumption of a linear sexual development. . . . And here lies a dilemma. It is precisely because of this "developmental" imagery being so pervasive that many children and adults collectively construct the sexual worlds of childhood around such a theme. Cross-generational sexuality may serve to reinforce such assumptions—the child is a child, the adult is an adult. But it also harbours the potential to suggest that the child is an adult and the adult is a child; that such categories are neither fixed nor universal. (pp. 237, 243–245)

Sex as Discourse

Our gendered and sexual identities are elaborate constructions based on discourse and cultural practice. Foucault's use of history, Lacan's use of psychoanalysis, and Derrida's use of grammar all challenge the belief of an *a priori* self. By examining sexuality in relation to society rather than in relation to other individuals, Michel Foucault (1978, 1980, 1988), for example, views sexuality as an inherently meaningless concept that only assumes meaning within an historical context such as the scientism of the 19th century. Jacques Lacan (1977) argued that through language a child internalizes and unconsciously accepts a symbolic order in a stage-like process of submission culminating in submission to the "Law of the Father."

Jacques Derrida (1987) asserted that our language (which constructs the symbolic order) is characterized by its logocentrism (primacy of speech), phallocentrism (instrumentalism), and dualism (embrace of binary oppositions). Common to all is the belief that through discourse we create sexual meanings.

Returning to the sex wars of the Identity Era, antipornography advocates such as Andrea Dworkin and Catherine MacKinnon, like their Christian conservative allies, assume an essentialistic reading of the sexual text and a behavioristic view of human action. From their perspective, erotica glorifies humiliation and degradation of women and encourages discrimination, abuse, and violence against them. However, as Nadine Strossen (1995) has pointed out:

> the insistence that all pornography conveys misogynistic messages to all viewers—or at least to all male viewers—ignores the complex, variegated nature of sexually explicit expression and the subjective, nuanced nature of any viewer's interpretation of such expression. . . . The reductionist approach of the procensorship feminists denies the existence of ambiguity, subtlety, and irony in the interactions between all individuals and a text or image. It overlooks the boundary between fantasy, imagination, and ideas, on one hand, and behavior, on the other. (pp. 142, 146)

Similarly, the insistence by most profeminists and Christian conservatives that pornography—particularly involving adolescents—is *ipso facto* exploitive and results in "child abuse" presumes a singular textual reading linked with a mistaken conflation of behaviors and fantasies, choice and coercion. It is, however, through the medicalizing of "child abuse," the constructing of "adolescence," and the politicizing of sexual imagery as "pornography" that we are socialized into the symbolic order.

Sex as Cultural Selection/Genetic Predisposition

Sociobiologists have viewed sexuality primarily in terms of genetic recombination through which a gradual transformation of the human species and culture occurs. Although their attempt to render a bioevolutionary analysis to social behavior has been criticized, their focus on sexual behavior as the instrument for multiple recombinations of genetic options and cultural evolution as shaped by "evolved genetically transmitted predispositions . . . [that] often result in highly adaptive behavior" (Richerson & Boyd, 1989, p. 195) allows for a rethinking of sexual behaviors. Evolutionary cultural theorists thus explain social behavior, including homosexuality and pornography, in terms of selection, adaptation, fitness, and reproductive altruism (Shepherd & Reisman, 1985; Trivers, 1974; Weinrich, 1986).

Sociobiologists (e.g., Findlay & Lumsden, 1988; Lumsden, 1989; Lumsden & Wilson, 1981, 1985), assuming the existence of "deep structures" that innately constrain cognition, "dig deeper and ask what role biological factors play in specifying the particulars of thought and in the differences observed among individuals and among societies with respect to social behavior" (Lumsden, 1989, p. 12). They argue that cultural behavior is linked to the genome: that is, within human cultures, a genetic predisposition exists for certain behaviors ranging from altruism to homosexuality. This reciprocal relationship between culture and biology is called gene-culture transmission: the process "in which evolved constraints help to organize mental development in the transmission of culture" (Lumsden, 1989, p. 12).

These evolved constraints, or *epigenetic rules*, "make culture learnable. Without them, there is no possibility of cultural inheritance, and therefore of dual inheritance and gene-culture coevolution" (Lumsden, 1989, p. 15). The adaptation of these rules is expected to enhance the reproduction and survival of the organism. And, it is the existence of these rules that affects the likelihood of a person using one or another *culturgen* ("transmissable behaviors, mentifacts, and artifacts" directly encoded in long-term memory as "node-link structures"; Lumsden & Wilson, 1981, p. 7).

There are a number of concepts critical for thinking through cultural transmission and the relationships between culture and genes. Two of these are *meme* and *meme product*. A meme is the fundamental element of culture existing as an informational unit in the brain (Dawkins, 1976, 1982). Further, as articulated by Ball (1984), memes can be divided into four categories reflecting the adaptive benefit for either the individual or the culture: those that are *symbiotic* promote behaviors that are adaptive for the individual and the culture; those that are *difficult* encourage behaviors that are maladaptive for the individual but adaptive for the culture; those that are *parasitic* promote behaviors that are individually adaptive but maladaptive culturally; and those that are *bad* encourage behaviors that are maladaptive for both the individual and the culture. A meme product is the external effect evidenced from the meme (i.e., behaviors and artifacts).

Although defenders of pederasty may find those who condemn such behavior "maladaptive," an equally strong case could be made that its recurrence across time and culture evidences a predisposition for such behaviors that, though viewed within our culture as "bad," may, in fact, be "symbiotic," particularly in a culture in which support for youth sometimes extends only as far as age-of-consent laws. From this perspective, one can revisit anthropological studies cited earlier (e.g., Herdt, 1981) to consider why cultures—ranging from ancient Greece and medieval Japan to contemporary New Guinea—normalize pederasty, and to reconsider the cultural and personal cost for this taboo in EuroAmerican culture.

Sex as Transcendent

Sexual understandings are transmitted through dreams, myths, and rites, which are themselves manifestations of archetypal images:

> The way the body has been envisioned and evaluated by various eras and cultures is a history of the sexual messages transmitted by social myths and the customs based upon such myths. The act of sex flows into the mythic imagination and, consequently, the mythology of a people largely determines its attitudes about sexuality. (Hightower, 1989, p. 19)

C. G. Jung focused on universal symbols and meanings among human cultures that appear in dreams, myths, and rites. For Jung (1968) a symbolic image "has a wider unconscious aspect that is never precisely defined or fully explained" (p. 4). Myths encapsulate many of these symbols, which are themselves archetypal images whose source is the collective unconscious.

Unlike Freud's modernist vision of sexuality in which dreams manifested repressed personal consciousness and cultures arose to suppress, restrict, or redirect libidinal energies, Jung (1989) viewed culture as a vehicle for personal transformation, not a mechanism for civil repression: "Only here, in life on earth, where the opposites clash together, can the general level of consciousness be raised" (p. 311). He articulated the concepts of the *Kollective* (transpersonal) unconscious and libido as a cosmic force. Both are central to the perspective of sexuality as embedded in myth and mystery and an instrument for transcendence—the transformation of the Self—the most fundamental of all archetypal images (Campbell, 1970; Progoff, 1969).

Archetypes, the content of the collective unconscious (Jacobi, 1970), manifest themselves in archetypal images: a psychological symbol, spontaneously produced, which appears in dreams, myths, and rites (Campbell, 1970). Archetypes are universal and hereditary primordial images that influence our behavior and interpretation of experience. Although meanings can be read into them and out of them, in themselves, these archetypes are antecedent to meaning (Campbell, 1970).

Many of these archetypal images manifest themselves in sexual symbols. As Ira Progoff (1969) notes, "Their importance, however, is not in the actual symbol. It is in what they represent or express of the deeper layers of the psyche" (p. 71). Sexual symbols arise from the unconscious and

represent something that transcends rational concepts but is partly manifested in the conscious. These include the Devil and its symbolic relation
to repressed homosexual feelings (Tejirian, 1990), and the Boy Androgyne
(Hopcke, 1989), symbolically represented in Greek mythic icons such as
Ganymede, the Renaissance art of Michelangelo and Cellini, and the early
20th-century Uranian poets and writers.

From this sexual/cultural perspective, sexuality, a manifestation of our
mythic-poetic heritage, is an instrument for transcendence: that which is
beyond language and thought (Singer, 1983). This integral relationship
between sexuality and spirituality, and the conceptualization of the body
as a organ of expression and the means for transformation, has seldom
been explored in relationship to homosexuality or pederasty.[12] The transhistorical and cross-cultural presence of the Boy Androgyne archetypal image
evidences its deepest embodiment in the human psyche.

In Greek mythology, for example, Ganymede, a Phrygian shepherd boy
possessed of unequaled male and female beauty, spends 2 months with
the Olympian Zeus, serving as his cupbearer and bedmate (Saslow, 1986).
Depicted in vase paintings and later in Renaissance art as an androgyne
being whisked away by an eagle, both myth and art suggest the transcendental potential of such relationships. This celebration of the adolescent
male was also practiced by mortals of Greek city-states ranging from Sparta's
military training, which centered on the "comradeship of warriors" (Marrou, 1956, p. 26), to the nudity of Athens' gymnasia, which focused on
athletics and aesthetics.[13]

Another myth is that of Calamus, a river god's son deeply in love with
Carpus. When his lover accidentally drowns, Calamus, plagued with grief,

---

[12]It is, however, widely referenced in Eastern heterosexual metaphysics (e.g., Elisofon &
Watts, 1971; Evola, 1983; John, 1978; Rajneesh, 1979b). Integrally related to spirituality, sex
is mythically transformed into eros through yoga. Sexual energy, conceived as a lower octave
of the divine energy, provides more to life than its procreative potential. Brachmacharya
Kundalini yoga has its origins in Sanskrit meaning "circular power" and refers to a person's
transformational life force—the serpent fire (Haich, 1972; Paulson, 1991; Rajneesh, 1979a,
1983; Sovatsky, 1985). The goal of Kundalini yoga is to awaken this natural force, located at
the base of the spine, drawing it from the base of the body out of the head. Brachmacharya
Kundalini yoga releases creativity, enhances mental abilities, and develops inner strength and
enlightenment by engaging in sexless eroticism through meditation. Another ritual for the
Kundalini release is maithuna in tantric yoga where sexual energy is sublimated by engaging
in orgasmless sex (e.g., Ajaya, 1979).

[13]The most extensive writings from extant Greek literature describing pederastic
relationships is found in the twelfth book known as the *Greek Anthology*, assembled by a
Byzantine scholar in the 10th century A.D. The twelfth book is composed of dozens of poems,
mainly written in the 1st century B.C., and expanded 2 centuries later and known as the
Musa paidike (Boy–Love Muse, or Boyish Muse). These include themes such as attraction and
rejection, the vanishing nature of youth (*anthos*), and the taunting of the older by the younger
(Englinton, 1964).

turns into a reed (*kalamos*). Whitman drew on this myth for his 19th-century homoerotic poetry. The mytho-poetics of the Boy Androgyne were evident a generation later during the Uranian Movement which extended nearly 80 years through 1930. Edward Carpenter, an English mystic who characterized himself as the moon reflecting the Whitmanesque sun, was a leader of this group of "calamites" or "uranian" poets. Describing themselves as the spiritual descendants of Aphrodite Urania—known as "Urnings" or the "third sex" (a term first used in 1864 by Karl Ulrichs)—they linked prophetic gifts with the cultivation of the androgynic youth (Conner, 1993; d'Arch Smith, 1970).

Noted for its elevation of the youthful male form as object of desire, the work of Ralph Chubb, rising near the end of this movement, is illustrative (Rahman, 1991). Embracing mysticism, Chubb developed a spiritual myth deifying the boy-god. In *Heavenly Cupid* (Chubb, 1934) he laid out his millennial theory of three spiritual dispensations: Adam & Lucider ("male principle"), Christ & Buddha ("female principle"), and the forthcoming millennium of the "boy principle." His spiritual myth was more fully developed in two later books, *Child of Dawn* (1948) and *Flames of Sunrise* (1954). Here the boy-god, Raphaos—"countenance of serenest innocence and beauty" (p. 76)—for whom Chubb is the prophet, ushers in this new millennium marked by a "race of angelic immortal naked boys, that is to say, Cupids, or neuters, perfect, bright, unblemish'd, translucent in body, full of celestial loveliness and wisdom of spirit" (p. 35).

Sex as Erotic Imagination

When conceptualizing culture largely in terms of language and text while viewing sex as a transcendental instrument, the erotic, particularly through the written word, is a dynamic instrument. For millennia, the Christianized West has perverted the erotic (Young, 1966); this sexual repressiveness has been coupled with linguistic ambiguities wherein the erotic rested in a shadowy existence of the mind's mist: "Sexual representation has been relegated to the categories of frivolous, bawdy, inarticulate, unspeakable. It is a source of humor that the language of sex is so imprecise, so polyvalent that it is 'hard' to know when we are talking about sex and when we are talking about business or politics or other weighty matters" (Patton, 1991, p. 374).

Although the erotic has been represented historically in texts (e.g., Thomas Mann's description of the wedding night of Jacob and Leah in the *Tales of Jacob*), "pornographers" responded to the vagaries of sexual language by displaying both the sexual language and the images in "pornographic" texts aimed at a mass market with an explicit intent to transform the unspeakable into the commonplace. Erotic literature, on the other hand, seeks to use the literary form to facilitate a sexual transformation of self and "to excite the reader sexually." Susan Sontag (1969) continues: "the physical sensations involuntarily produced in the reader carry with them something that touches upon the reader's whole experience of his humanity" (p. 47). Here, language is an aphrodisiac wherein words evoke images, sounds, and emotions to "articulate the mythos of animality" (Michelson, 1971, p. 40).

Erotic writers and philosophers such as Georges Bataille (1957), Marco Vassi (1970, 1972, 1975, 1993), and Peter Michelson (1971, 1993) have elaborated on how the erotic is "an important source of mythic self-knowledge" (Michelson, 1971, p. 19) with the power to transcend the ego through the disembodied word. In his provocative summary of modern erotic literature, Michael Perkins (1976), observed: "for human beings the most important sexual organ is above the neck. . . . One of the accomplishments of erotic literature is the literary transformation of an act which is innately mechanical into meaningful individual experience. By encrusting sexuality with symbolic meaning, erotic literature helps reclaim it for civilization" (p. 52).

For Vassi, greatly influenced by the iconoclastic Wilhelm Reich, the eroticization of life is essential for living; erotic literature can re-open that portal of essential human experience deadened by reproductive sex. Vassi, a proponent of "metasexual eroticism," wielded his pen to advance erotic scenes from the most mundane level to the transcendental—heightened sexual moments when the oneness of all was vivid. For Vassi, homosexuality was not simply an alternate lifestyle, it was a superior transcendental instrument of sexual expression. He argued provocatively:

> For what the man wants is to feel his own body. . . . What men need right now, more than anything, is the ability to be aware of their own feelings. And the only men who, as a self-identified group, are freeing themselves to feel are gays. There is a strong argument to be made for the notion that homosexuality should be the general sexual form of the future, with heterosexual unions forming a minority. . . . The majority, the heterosexuals who run the machines of civilization, will most likely grow more and more alienated from their animal sensibility. (Vassi, 1992, p. 275)

During the past generation, however, many homosexuals, led by assimilationists, have opted for heterosexual mimicry demanding their "place at the table" and, in Koestlerian fashion, becoming ghosts in the machine. But the ghost images from our "animal sensibility" and memic memories, premodern homoeroticism, and archetypal residue remain in literature.

Homoerotic writers like Jean Genet (*Our Lady of the Flowers*) or Samuel R. Delany (*The Tide of Lust*) along with pederastic erotic classics such as Jean Cocteau's *The White Paper*, Ronald Tavel's *Street of Stairs*, and Leo Skir's

Boychick are examples of literary works that transcend sexual boundaries while engaging Eros to transform the ego. In the early 1970s, for example, Skir wrote an autobiographical medieval dream story of a gay graduate student who falls in love with a young teen spotted in the shower of Brooklyn's St. George Hotel. There, too, is the more profound *Street of Stairs*, which takes place in Tangier. Here through the post-modernist narratives of three dozen characters, we can experience the love between Mark and the youthful Hamid as we explore thei(ou)r sensuality and violence that lurks beneath.

The erotic now extends beyond words to bytes (e.g., Morton, 1995; Tsang, 1996). As the power of language and text extends into cyberspace, multiple erotic positionalities intensify. Through the twin development of virtual realities and cyber technology, the body itself may be transcended as cyber-constructed subjectivities enter into an electronic playground wherein who one is becomes defined by who one chooses to be.

In the near future, entry into cyberspace will allow one to lose one's sexual identity and become, in the words of Vassi (1975), "a sexual entity" where one's cyber adventures can serve a sole purpose: "to exhaust all subjective aspects of the sexual act. . . . the many masks of libidinal displacement" (p. 62). Could it be this potential that the architects behind the Federal Communications Act of 1996 most fear?

AN EPILOGUE FOR EDUCATORS: PEDAGOGY AND PEDERASTY

The term *pedagogue* originates from the Greek servant (*paidagogos*) responsible for escorting his young master to school, protecting against sexual advances along the way to those who will embrace the youth with wisdom and affection. In recent contemporary curriculum discourse, we have displaced teacher with pedagogy as we move away from the technobabble of positivistic discourse. Generally, as curriculum thinkers, we have not examined the relationship between Eros and Logos, between teacher and student, between the Athenian gymnasium and the Freirian classroom. Distancing ourselves from discussing the perversity of pederasty perhaps evidences our lack of comfort with the homoerotic liaisons—imagined, desired, actual—within the schools. The legacy of pedagogical Eros extends from premodern to postmodern times, from the Greek gymnasium to the German *Wandervogelbewegung*.

The challenge of radical pedagogues is to re-examine the assumptions underlying the perversity of pederasty concept; I've written this essay not to advocate illegal activity, but with the hope that it will allow us to act in reconceptualizing Eros in relationship to Logos. As McWilliam (1997) has recently observed:

We need to re-conceive of pedagogical spaces as productive, not simply malevolent erotic spaces, and to find ways to do this without stepping away from the radical pedagogue's insistence on moral responsibility. In Cryle's (1994, p. viii) terms, we need to reconceive of an erotics of pedagogy "without being overwhelmed by the thematics of desire in its radically subjective forms." . . . The desiring body of the teacher need not continue to be mis-construed as mere malefice, to be eradicated in the service of pedagogical purity. Desire sustains many teachers who might otherwise join the swelling ranks of burnt-out educational radicals. . . . Nor has there been any real acknowledgment of the complicity of critical pedagogy itself in the prolif-eration of the "burnout radical teacher" phenomenon. Critical pedagogues must begin to speak about the potential productivity of desiring bodies for pedagogical work.

REFERENCES

Ajaya, S. (1979). Kundalini and the tantric tradition. In J. White (Ed.), *Kundalini, evolution and enlightenment* (pp. 99–105). Garden City, NY: Anchor Press.

Alcoff, L. (1988). Cultural feminism versus post-structuralism. *Signs 13*(3), 405–436.

Alexander, J., & Seidman, S. (Eds.). (1990). *Culture and society*. Cambridge, UK: Cambridge University Press.

Andriette, B. (1994). Intergenerational sex: Consent isn't the problem. In J. Sears (Ed.), *Bound by diversity* (pp. 207–212). Columbia, SC: Sebastian Press.

Ardener, E. (1985). Social anthropology and the decline of modernism. In J. Overing (Ed.), *Reason and morality* (pp. 55–70). London: Tavistock.

Aries, P. (1985). St. Paul and the flesh. In P. Aries & A. Bejin (Eds.), *Western sexuality: Practice and percept in past and present times* (pp. 36–39). Oxford, UK: Blackwell.

Austin-Broos, D. (1987). Clifford Geertz: Culture, sociology, and historicisism. In D. Austin-Broos (Ed.), *Creating culture* (pp. 141–159). Sydney: Allen & Unwin.

Ball, J. (1984). Memes as replicators. *Ethology and Sociobiology 5*, 145–161.

Barrett, S. (1984). *The rebirth of anthropological theory*. Toronto: University of Toronto Press.

Bataille, G. (1986). *L'erotisme or death and sensuality*. San Francisco: City Lights. (Original work published 1957)

Benedict, R. (1934). *Patterns of culture*. Boston: Houghton-Mifflin.

Beveridge, A. (1922). *The Babur-Nama in English*. London: Luzac.

Bieber, I. (1962). *Homosexuality: A psychoanalytic study*. New York: Vintage.

Blasius, M., & Phelan, P. (1997). (Eds.). *We are everywhere: An historical sourcebook of gay and lesbian poltics*. New York: Routledge.

Boas, F. (1938). *The mind of primitive man* (Rev. ed.). New York: Macmillan.

Boswell, J. (1980). *Christianity, social tolerance and homosexuality*. Chicago: University of Chicago Press.

Boswell, J. (1984). *Same sex unions in premodern Europe*. New York: Vintage.

Brongersma, E. (1986). *Loving boys: A multidisciplinary study of sexual relations between adult and minor males, Volume 1*. Elmhurst, NY: Global Academic Publishers.

Brongersma, E. (1991). Boy-lovers and their influence on boys: Distorted research and anecdotal observations. In T. Sandfort, E. Brongersma, & A. Naerseen (Eds.), *Male intergenerational intimacy* (pp. 145–173). New York: Haworth.

Brown, D. (1991). *Human universals*. Philadelphia: Temple University Press.

Burniston, S., Mort, F., & Weedon, C. (1978). Psychoanalysis and the cultural acquisition of sexuality and subjectivity. In Women's Studies Group (Ed.), *Women take issue* (pp. 109–131). London: Hutchinson.

Burns, K. (1956). The homosexual faces a challenge. Speech to the Third Annual Convention of the Mattachine Society. In M. Blasius & S. Phelan (Eds.), (1997). *We are everywhere: An historical sourcebook of gay and lesbian poltics* (pp. 285–289). New York: Routledge.

Campbell, J. (1970). Mythological themes in creative literature and art. In J. Campbell (Ed.), *Myths, dreams, and religion* (pp. 138–175). Dallas, TX: Spring.

Chodorow, N. (1978). *The reproduction of mothering: Psychoanalysis and the sociology of gender.* Berkeley: University of California Press.

Chubb, R. (1934). *Heavenly cupid: or, the true paradise of loves.* Newbury: Author.

Chubb, R. (1948). *Child of dawn, or the book of the manchild.* Newbury: Author.

Chubb, R. (1954). *Flames of sunrise: A book of the man child concerning the redemption of Albion.* Newbury: Author.

Clifford, J., & Marcus, G. (Eds.). (1986). *Writing culture: The poetics and politics of ethnography.* Berkeley: University of California Press.

Conner, R. (1993). *Blossom of bone. Reclaiming the connections between homoeroticism and the sacred.* New York: HarperCollins.

Crapanzano, V. (1980). *Tuhami: Portrait of a Moroccan.* Chicago: University of Chicago Press.

Croall, R. (1983). *Neill of Summerhill: The permanent rebel.* New York: Pantheon.

Cryle, P. (1994). *Geometry in the boudoir.* Ithaca, NY: Cornell University Press.

d'Arch, Smith, T. (1970). *Love in earnest: Some notes on the lives and writing of English "Uranian" poets from 1889 to 1930.* London: Routledge & Kegan Paul.

Dawkins, R. (1976). *The selfish gene.* Oxford, England: Oxford University Press.

Dawkins, R. (1982). *The extended phenotype: The gene as the unit of selection.* Oxford, England: Freeman.

de Lauretis, T. (Ed.). (1991). Queer theory. Special issue of *Differences, 3*(2).

Derrida, J. (1987). *The post card: From Socrates to Freud and beyond.* Chicago: University of Chicago Press.

Dilthey, W. (1976). *Selected writings.* Cambridge, UK: Cambridge University Press.

Douglas, M. (1973). *Natural symbols.* London: Barrie & Jenkins.

Dworkin, A. (1979). *Pornography: Men possessing women.* New York: Dutton.

Eagleton, T. (1968). The idea of a common culture. In T. Eagleton & B. Wicker (Eds.), *From culture to revolution.* London: Sheed & Ward.

D'Emillio, J. (1983). *Sexual politics, sexual communities.* Chicago: University of Chicago Press.

Englinton, J. (1964). *Greek love.* New York: Oliver.

Elisofon, E., & Watts, A. (1971). *Erotic spirituality.* New York: Collier.

Escoffier, J. (1992). Generations and paradigms. In H. Minton (Ed.), *Gay and lesbian studies* (pp. 7–26). New York: Haworth Press.

Evola, J. (1983). *The metaphysics of sex.* New York: Inner Traditions International.

Findlay, C., & Lumsden, C. (1988). *The creative mind.* London: Academic.

Foucault, M. (1978). *History of sexuality.* New York: Pantheon.

Foucault, M. (1980). *Power/knowledge.* New York: Pantheon.

Foucault, M. (1988). *Politics, philosophy, culture.* New York: Routledge.

Frazer, J. (1890). *The Golden Bow: A study in magic and religion.* London: Macmillan.

Freud, S. (1963). *Sexual enlightenment of children.* New York: Collier.

Fromm, E. (1961). *Marx's concept of man.* New York: Ungar.

Frye, M. (1997). Lesbian feminism and the gay rights movement. In M. Blasius & S. Phelan (Eds.), *We are everywhere: An historical sourcebook of gay and lesbian poltics* (pp. 499–510). New York: Routledge. (Original work published 1981)

Fuss, D. (1991). *Inside/Outside: Lesbian theories, gay theories.* New York: Routledge.

Gagnon, J., & Simon, W. (1969). *Sexual conduct.* Chicago: Aldine.

Geertz, C. (1973). *The interpretation of cultures.* New York: Basic.

Geertz, C. (1983). *Local knowledge: Further essays in interpretive anthropology.* New York: Basic.

Gerassi, J. (1966). *The boys from Boise: Furor, vice and folly in an American city.* New York: Macmillan.

Gessen, M. (1994). Intergenerational sex: Abuse and power. In J. Sears (Ed.), *Bound by diversity* (pp. 213–216). Columbia, SC: Sebastian Press.

Goodenough, W. (1981). *Culture, language, and society.* Menlo Park, CA: Benjamin/Cummings.

Gubar, S. (1987). Representing pornography: Feminism, criticism, and depictions of female violation. *Critical Inquiry,* (Summer), 712–741.

Haich, E. (1972). *Sexual energy and yoga.* New York: Aurora.

Hemphill, E. (1991). *Brother to brother: New writings by black gay men.* Boston, MA: Alyson.

Hearing Before the Subcommittee to Investigate Juvenile Delinquency of the Committee on the Judiciary (1956). United States Senate, Eighty-Fourth Congress, First Session, Pursuant to S. Res. 62 as extended, Investigation of Juvenile Delinquency in the United States, 16 November 1955. Washington, DC: US Government Printing Office.

Herdt, G. (1981). *Guardians of the flutes.* New York: McGraw-Hill.

Hightower, J. (1989). *Myth and sexuality.* New York: New American Library.

Holly, L. (1989). Introduction: The sexual agenda of schools. In L. Holly (Ed.), *Girls and sexuality: Teaching and learning* (pp. 1–10). Milton Keynes: Open University Press.

Hopcke, R. (1989). *Jung, Jungians and homosexuality.* Boston, MA: Shambhala.

Hooker, E. (1956). *The adjustment of the male overt homosexual.* Paper presented to the American Psychological Association.

Jacobi, J. (1970). *C. G. Jung: Psychological reflections* (Rev. ed.). Princeton, NJ: Princeton University Press.

John, B. (1978). *Love of the two-armed form.* Middletown, CA: Dawn Horse.

Jung, C. (1968). *Man and his symbols.* New York: Dell.

Jung, C. (1989). *Memories, dreams and reflections.* A. Jaffé (Ed.) & R. Winston & C. Winston (Trans.). New York: Vintage.

Kameny, F. (1965). Does research into homoeuxality matter. Reprinted in M. Blasius & S. Phelan (Eds.), (1997). *We are everywhere: An historical sourcebook of gay and lesbian poltics.* (pp. 335–339). New York: Routledge.

Kaplan, D., & Manners, R. (1972). *Culture theory.* Englewood Cliffs, NJ: Prentice-Hall.

Kinsey, A. (1948). *Sexual behavior in the human male.* Philadelphia, PA: Saunders.

Kinsey, A. (1953). *Sexual behavior in the human female.* Philadelphia, PA: Saunders.

Kluckhohn, C. (1954). *Mirror for man.* New York: McGraw-Hill.

Kroeber, A., & Kluckhohn, C. (1952). Culture: A critical review of concepts and definitions. *Papers of the Peabody Museum of American Archaeology and Ethnology, Volume 47.* Cambridge, MA: Harvard University Press.

Lacan, J. (1977). *The four fundamental concepts of psycho-analysis.* London: Hogarth.

Lance, H. (1989). The Bible and homosexuality. *American Baptist Quarterly, 8*(2), 140–151.

Lévy-Bruhl, L. (1936). *Primitives and the supernatural.* London: Allen & Unwin.

Licht, H. (1932). *Sexual life in ancient Greece.* London: Routledge & Kegan Paul.

Lumsden, C. (1989). Does culture need genes? *Ethnology and Sociobiology, 10*(3), 11–28.

Lumdsen, C., & Wilson, E. (1981). *Genes, mind, and culture.* Cambridge, MA: Harvard University Press.

Lumdsen, C., & Wilson, E. (1985). The relation between biological and cultural evolution. *Journal of Social Biological Structure, 8,* 343–359.

Manganaro, M. (1990). *Modernist anthropology: From fieldwork to text.* Princeton, NJ: Princeton University Press.

Marcus, E. (1992). *Making history.* New York: HarperCollins.

Marcus, G., & Fischer, M. (1986). *Anthropology as cultural critique.* Chicago: University of Chicago Press.

Marrou, H. (1956). *A history of education in antiquity.* New York: Sheed & Ward.

Mascia-Lees, F., Sharpe, P., & Cohen, C. (1989). The postmodernist turn in anthropology: Cautions from a feminist perspective. *Signs 15*(1), 7–33.

Martindale, B. (1997). *Un/popular culture: Lesbian writing after the sex wars.* Albany: State University of New York Press.

Mathers, E. (Trans.). (1972). *Comrade loves of the Samurai.* Rutland, VT: Tuttle.

McLaren, P. (1991). Decentering culture: Postmodernism, resistance, and critical pedagogy. In N. Wyner (Ed.), *Current perspectives on the culture of schools* (pp. 231–257). Boston: Brookline.

McNeil, J. (1976). *The church and the homosexual.* Boston: Beacon.

McWilliam, E. (1997). Beyond the missionary position: Teaching after critical pedagogy. *Teaching Education* [on line journal]. www.teachingeducation.com/vol9-1/mcwilliam.htm

Michelson, P. (1971). *The aesthetics of pornography.* New York: Herder & Herder.

Michelson, P. (1993). *Speaking the unspeakable: A poetics of obscenity.* Albany: State University of New York.

Miller, N. (1995). *Out of the past.* New York: Vintage.

Mitchell, J. (1975). *Psychoanalysis and feminism.* London: Pelican.

Moraga, C., & Anzaldúa, G. (Eds.). (1981). *This bridge called my back: Writings by radical women of color.* New York: Kitchen Table/Women of Color Press.

Morgan, L. (1963). *Ancient society.* New York: Meridan. (Original work published 1877)

Morton, D. (1993). The politics of queer theory in the (post)modern movement. *Genders, 17*, 121–150.

Morton, D. (1995). Birth of the cyberqueer. *PMLA, 110*(3), 369–381.

Morton, D. (Ed.). (1996). *The material queer.* Boulder, CO: Westview Press.

NAMBLA. (1997). The case for abolishing the age of consent laws. In M. Blasius & S. Phelan (Eds.), *We are everywhere: An historical sourcebook of gay and lesbian politics* (pp. 459–468). New York: Routledge. (Original work published 1980)

Neill, A. (1926). *The problem child.* London: Jenkins

Neill, A. (1953). *The free child.* London: Jenkins

Neill, A. (1960). *Summerhill: A radical approach to child rearing.* New York: Hart.

Ortner, O., & Whitehead, H. (Eds.). (1981). *Sexual meanings: The cultural construction of gender and sexuality.* Cambridge: Cambridge University Press.

Parkin, D. (Ed.). (1982). *Semantic anthropology.* London: Academic Press.

Paulson, G. (1991). *Kundalini and the chakras: A practical manual—evolution in this lifetime.* St. Paul, MN: Llewellyn.

Percy, W. (1990). *Greek pederasty.* New York: Garland.

Perkins, M. (1976). *The secret record.* New York: Morrow.

Petras, J. (1978). *The social meaning of human sexuality.* Boston: Allyn & Bacon.

Phelan, S. (1994). *Getting specific: Postmodern lesbian politics.* Minneapolis: University of Minnesota Press.

Plummer, K. (1991). Understanding childhood sexualities. In T. Sandfort, E. Brongersma, & A. van Naerssen (Eds.), *Male intergenerational intimacy* (pp. 231–249). New York: Haworth Press.

Preston, J. (1997). Goodbye to Sally Gearhart. In M. Blasius & S. Phelan (Eds.), *We are everywhere: An historical sourcebook of gay and lesbian politics* (pp. 511–521). New York: Routledge. (Original work published 1981)

Progoff, I. (1969). *Jung's psychology and its social meaning.* New York: Julian.

Rabinow, P. (1977). *Reflections on fieldwork in Morocco.* Berkeley: University of California Press.

Radcliffe-Brown, A. (1952). *Structure and function in primitive society.* London: Cohen & West.

Radicalesbians (1972). The woman-identified woman. In K. Jay & A. Young (Eds.), *Out of the closets* (pp. 172–177). New York: Harcourt-Brace. (Original work published 1970)

Rahman, T. (1991). Ephebophilia and the creation of a spiritual myth in the works of Ralph Nicholas Chubb. *Journal of Homosexuality, 20*(1/2), 103–128.

Rajneesh, B. (1979a). *The tantra vision.* Poona, India: Rajneesh Foundation.

Rajneesh, B. (1979b). *From sex to superconsciousness.* Poona, India: Rajneesh Foundation.

Rajneesh, B. (1983). *Tantra spirituality and sex.* Poona, India: Rajneesh Foundation.

Redfield, R. (1953). *The primitive world and its transformations.* Ithaca, NY: Cornell University Press.

Richerson, P., & Boyd, R. (1989). The role of evolved predispositions in cultural evolution: Or, human sociobiology meets Pascal's Wagner. *Ethnology and Sociobiology, 10*(1-3), 195–219.

Rohner, R. (1984). Toward a conception of culture for cross-cultural psychology. *Journal of Cross-Cultural Psychology, 15*(2), 111–113.

Sandfort, T. (1987). *Boys on their contact with men: A study of sexually expressed friendships.* Elmhurst, NY: Global Academic Publishers.

Sandfort, T., Brongersma, E., & van Naerssen, A. (1991). *Male intergenerational intimacy.* New York: Haworth Press.

Saslow, J. (1986). *Ganymede in the Renaissance.* New Haven, CT: Yale University Press.

Scroggs, R. (1983). *The New Testament and homosexuality.* Philadelphia, PA: Fortress.

Sears, J. (1997). *Lonely hunters: An oral history of lesbian and gay southern life, 1948–1968.* New York: HarperCollins-Westview.

Sedgwick, E. (1990). *Epistemology of the closet.* Berkeley: University of California Press.

Shepherd, J., & Reisman, J. (1985). Pornography: A sociological attempt at understanding. *Ethology and Sociobiology, 6,* 103–114.

Shweder, R. (1984). Anthropology's romantic rebellion against the enlightenment, or there's more to thinking than reason and evidence. In R. Shweder & R. LeVine (Eds.), *Culture theory: Essays on mind, self, and emotion* (pp. 27–66). Cambridge, MA: Cambridge University Press.

Singer, J. (1983). *Energies of love: Sexuality re-visioned.* Garden City, NY: Anchor.

Smith, B. (1983). *Home girls: A black femnist anthology.* New York: Kitchen Table/Women of Color Press.

Socarides, C. (1968). *The overt homosexual.* New York: Grune & Stratton.

Sontag, S. (1969). Pornographic imagination. In S. Sontag, *Styles of radical will* (pp. 35–73). New York: Farrar, Straus & Giroux.

Sovatsky, S. (1985). Eros as mystery: Toward a transpersonal sexology and procreativity. *Journal of Transperonal Psychology, 17*(1), 1–32.

Spiecker, B., & Steutel, J. (1997). Paedophilia, sexual desire, and diversity. *Journal of Moral Education, 26*(3), 331–342.

Streitmatter, R. (1995). *Unspeakable: The rise of the gay and lesbian press in America.* Winchester, MA: Faber & Faber.

Strossen, N. (1995). *Defending pornography.* New York: Scribner.

Teal, D. (1971). *The gay militants.* New York: Stein & Day.

Tejirian, E. (1990). *Sexuality and the devil: Symbols of love, power, and fear in male psychology.* New York: Routledge.

Tong, R. (1989). *Feminist thought.* Boulder, CO: Westview.

Toolin, C. (1983). Attitudes toward pornography: What have the feminists missed? *Journal of Popular Culture, 17*(2), 167–174.

Trivers, R. (1974). Parent–offspring conflict. *American Zoologist 14,* 249–264.

Tsang, D. (1996). Notes on queer 'n Asian virtual sex. In D. Morton (Ed.), *The material queer* (pp. 310–316). Boudler, CO: Westview.

Tyler, S. (1986a). Post-modern ethnography: From document of the occult to occult document. In J. Clifford & G. Marcus (Eds.), *Writing culture: The poetics and politics of ethnography.* Berkeley: University of California Press.

Tyler, S. (1986b). The poetic turn in postmodern anthropology: The poetry of Paul Friedrich. *American Anthropologist 6*(2), 328–336.

Tyler, S. (1987). *The unspeakable: Discourse, dialogue, and rhetoric in the postmodern world.* Madison: University of Wisconsin Press.

Tylor, E. (1871). *Primitive culture.* London: Murray.

Vance, C. (1982). Concept paper: Towards a politics of sexuality. In C. Vance (Ed.), *Diary of a conference on sexuality* (pp. 38–40). New York: Barnard College Women's Center, Faculty Press.

Vassi, M. (1970). *Mind blower.* Sag Harbor, NY: Second Chance Press.

Vassi, M. (1972). *The stoned apocalypse.* New York: Trident Press.

Vassi, M. (1975). *Metasex, mirth, and madness: Erotic tales of the absurdly real.* New York: Penthouse Press.

Vassi, M. (1992). Bodhi is the body. In D. Steinberg (Ed.), *The erotic impulse* (pp. 269–276). New York: Tarcher.

Vassi, M. (1993). *The Vassi collection.* Sag Harbor, NY: Permanent Press.

Walby, S. (1990). *Theorizing patriarchy.* Cambridge, UK: Blackwell.

Weeks, J. (1982). *Sex, politics and society: The regulation of sexuality since 1800.* London: Longman.

Weeks, J. (1985). *Sexuality and its discontents: Meanings, myths and modern sexualities.* London: Routledge & Kegan Paul.

Weinrich, J. (1986). A new sociobiological theory of homosexuality applicable to societies with universal marriage. *Ethnology and Sociobiology 8*(1), 37–47.

Wissler, C. (1923). *Man and culture.* New York: Crowell.

Wittam, C. (1972). Refugees from Amerika: A Gay Manifesto. In K. Jay & A. Young (Eds.), *Out of the closets* (pp. 330–345). New York: Harcourt-Brace. (Original work published 1969)

Wittgenstein, L. (1966). *Philosophical investigations* (G. Pitcher, Ed.). Garden City, NY: Anchor.

Young, W. (1966). *Eros denied.* New York: Grove.

Chapter 3

Who Am I?
Gay Identity and a Democratic
Politics of the Self

Dennis Carlson
Miami University

In the fall of 1995, a new float appeared in the homecoming parade at Miami University in Oxford, Ohio—a university known for its quiet conservatism. Wedged in between floats from Greek fraternities and sororities and from several other student groups on campus was a float representing the Gay, Lesbian, and Bisexual Alliance. In bold letters, the float proclaimed: "We're here, we're queer, and we have a float." What is perhaps most remarkable about this event is that it created hardly a stir on campus. Gays and lesbians—or "queers" as an increasing number of young politically aware students refer to themselves—were becoming part of the new campus community, a community that (at least on the surface) was organized around the theme of respecting diversity. If multicultural education in the public schools does not yet include gay people as part of the diversity that is to be acknowledged and respected within the new American community of difference, this has not been the case in higher education. Over the past decade, lesbian and gay studies programs and student and faculty groups have emerged on college campuses around the country; many colleges and universities appear to be making a real (albeit insufficient) effort to promote respect for, and protect the rights of, gay students. It is within such a context that the queer float in the homecoming parade needs to be interpreted. The float suggested, with irony, that being part of the officially diverse college community meant having the right to participate in one of the great rituals of college culture—homecoming.

The modern American college campus may be the most visible and best example we have of this new vision of multicultural community that is beginning, against continuing opposition, to emerge in the United States. It thus is a community that bears close watching; for in it I think we may see some of the important contributions but also limitations of dominant models of multicultural education and identity politics. Certainly, the new multiculturalism, with its visible inclusion of gays and lesbians, represents an important advance over earlier "normalizing" conceptions of community that repressed and silenced gayness. At the same time, I suggest in what follows that the new model of multicultural community may turn out in the long run to be less progressive than it now appears and less empowering for gays and lesbians, unless it is developed and pushed in some new directions (Carlson, 1995). Along these lines, I suggest that multiculturalism and identity politics need to be infused by a politics of the self that disrupts the underlying binary logic that governs identity formation in contemporary culture. For it is this binary construction of identity, and with it the representation of the subaltern Other as deficient and inferior, that provides a common thread that runs throughout histories of class, race, gender, and sexual orientation oppression in the modern era. Beyond this, binary construction of identity in Western culture has been closely linked to "truth games" or epistemic traditions governed by the *logos–mythos* binary, a binary that, beginning in classical Greek culture, has served to separate knowledge, reason, and authoritative truth (*logos*) from the world of illusion, mystification, and desire (*mythos*).

GAY AND QUEER IDENTITY POLITICS

In the homecoming parade I referred to, the word *queer* on the float representing the Gay, Lesbian, and Bisexual Alliance presumably was read by the vast majority of those who watched the parade as a newer or hipper synonym for *gay*. In this usage and reading, queer stands as a marker of identity. By asserting the right to be part of the homecoming parade, and proclaiming that they are here and not about to go away, the students on the float and the organization they represented were engaging in a form of identity politics—in this case performing or enacting a queer identity in a campus ritual, and thus disrupting that ritual's taken-for-granted valorization of heterosexuality.

We live in an age when democratic politics is, for the most part, identity politics; and it has proven to be a powerful tool in the empowerment agenda of marginalized identity groups. Through identity politics, those historically marginalized along various axes of identity formation (workers, women, African Americans and Hispanics, gays and lesbians, the physically challenged, etc.) have begun to find a voice and counter their historic disempowerment and cultural marginalization. Part of this project has involved the assertion of equal rights protection under the law, another part has been about challenging stereotypical and stigmatizing representations of identity in popular culture and asserting our own self-representations, and still another part has been about mobilizing and organizing a social movement to engage in political lobbying and provide a network and community of support. Finally, by locating purpose and meaning in identification with the values, lifestyles, and social projects of identity groups, identity politics has provided an answer to the great, troubling, existential question of the age: Who am I? It has done this by providing the self with an identity "habitus" (Bourdieu & Passeron, 1977), a community of common language and meaning that is also a cultural home—something inhabited and lived.

As with other versions of progressive identity politics in the United States, the modern (or postmodern) era of sexual orientation identity politics may be traced back to the 1960s and the emergence of the gay-rights movement. Like the civil rights and women's movement of the times, gay identity politics involved a three-pronged agenda: recognition, renaming, and re-representation. In Hegel's great story of the master and the slave, recognition as an equal, Hegel tells us, is the one thing that the slave ultimately wants from the master—no longer to be treated as a second-class citizen, as an inferior, as less than. By and large, the battle over recognition for gays and lesbians has been waged (again, in ways similar to other marginalized identity groups) through legal channels and campaigns for equal rights—what those on the Christian fundamentalist right call "special rights." Renaming is part of a process of reclaiming your own identity, to name yourself rather than accept the "master's" name for you. Thus, the civil rights movement of the 1960s asserted a "Black" and "Afro-American" identity in reaction to the dominant culture's usage of the identity markers, "Negro" and "colored," which came with their historical baggage of stigmatization and stereotypes. In the 1960s, "homosexuals" began to refer to themselves as "gay," or as "lesbians" and "gay men," as part of a project of reclaiming their identity from the medical profession and its pathologizing gaze. Among other things, gay implied that we were more than our sexuality; that we were people with a unique and historical culture that had been silenced and made invisible. Finally, re-representation implied for gay people a deliberate effort to challenge stereotypical and oppressive representations of gayness in popular culture through the promotion of an official ideology of "we're just like you" and positive media images.

This last project has turned out to be the most contradictory and illusive. For as gayness became widely accepted as a marker of identity by the 1970s, it inevitably became incorporated as the identity of the Other—both among many gays and lesbians and among straight Americans (Carlson, 1994). Gay people began to emerge as distinct cultural types in American popular culture—as the "Village People," drag queens, butch, take-charge dykes. In an industry known for character acting, Hollywood participated in integrating gayness into the mythical American sit-com community as another, but familiar, character. The commercialization of gay identity also affected the gay community, which became increasingly represented—even among gay people—as a world of high fashion, disco parties, and "buffed" bodies.

By the 1990s, the term *gay* had lost much of its radical connotation, and to a younger generation of politically aware lesbians and gays, *queer* began to surface as an identity marker of choice. Ironically, gay had also come to be associated with a particularly comfortable and accommodating lifestyle, in which one was closeted at work and in most social settings and out only in gay bars and among a small circle of gay friends. To be queer is to be out in a way that is more inclusive and less hypocritical—thus, outing popular or influential figures is justified as a way of breaking through this hypocrisy. As Corey (1992) put it: "To be out is really to be in—inside the realm of the visible, the speakable, the culturally intelligible" (p. 125). In this sense, queer identity is enacted through being out. Sedgwick (1990) remarks: "A T-shirt that ACT UP sells in New York bearing the text, 'I am out, therefore I am,' is meant to do for the wearer, not the constative work of reporting that s/he *is* out, but the performative work of coming out in the first place" (p. 4). Queerness also has challenged the gay credo, "we're just like you," and proudly and defiantly asserted the right and even importance of being different. It is a bold assertion from the margins, a declaration that we do not want to be normalized. It takes on a name that the dominant culture once used against us and inverts it, subverts it, and reappropriates it. It is the identity that homophobia is most fearful of, one that flaunts itself unashamedly. Queer identity politics hardly seems likely to replace gay identity politics, at least in the foreseeable future. However, it does begin to push gay identity politics in directions that are potentially consistent with the development of a new multicultural community of diversity in which differences are recognized rather than made invisible.

Aside from their obvious differences, gay and queer identities have both emerged out of, and given rise to, collective struggles of identity politics. In its various forms, sexual identity politics will no doubt continue to serve an important role in challenging heterosexism in the years ahead. We always have to do battle on the existing cultural terrain, and within that terrain gayness has been marginalized and oppressed. Furthermore, gay and lesbian identity politics has (from a purely strategic standpoint) helped advance the empowerment agendas of marginalized groups. In my own university teaching, I routinely find out or semi-out lesbian and gay students in classes; and perhaps partially because of this, I hear fewer put-downs of gay people as sick or sinful. As never before, gay people are becoming part of the fabric of the American campus community. Of course, this new visibility also means (ironically) that gay and lesbian students may be the victims of more harassment and made to feel oppression more than closeted students do.

This suggests that identity politics comes with dilemmas, and that it may not be able to take us too much farther before these dilemmas catch up with it. Foremost among these is a tendency to understand the self in terms of its identity or identities and thus in effect divide difference and self into neat, internally unified categories. The effect of such a reduction of self and others to categories of identity is the subversion of our right to be treated as unique persons rather than according to labels or categories. Sexual orientation matters, just as race matters, gender and class matter, and other differences among individuals matter; they should be taken into account in our relations with others, and in our hiring, recruitment, and admissions policies. To refuse to see or recognize the identity of those who have been oppressed or discriminated against because of that identity is to deny that oppression and discrimination exist. The problem arises when we become so aware of identity categories we no longer see anything in people but their identities (Taubman, 1993). Even more problematically, we may reduce individuals to one axis of identity that washes out all other differences. Thus, in progressive discourse we begin to talk about "Black people," "gay people," or "women" as if these were somehow subtypes of the human species. This may have the unwitting effect of reinforcing the otherness of marginalized groups and thus play into the hands of those looking for convenient scapegoats for society's problems. We need to bear in mind that this is similar to the kind of identity reductionism that prevailed in Nazi Germany, when those German citizens who just happened to be Jewish, among other things, were defined and oppressed entirely in terms of this one axis of difference. In the United States, it is similar to the reductionism that was used to legitimate slavery and Jim Crow laws, along with genocidal wars against Native Americans in the 19th century. In recent years, a similar kind of reductionism has characterized the discourse of some on the Christian right who seek to wage holy wars against the gay sexual infidel. Obviously, as I have already argued, there is a time and a place to affirm collective solidarity through the strategic use of identity categories. My fear, however, is that identity politics in its current form may not encourage us to distinguish between the strategic use of identity categories and their use to define and position the self.

Once identity is reduced to neat categories that can be represented in terms of identifiable lifestyles, images, and beliefs, it becomes open to manipulation not only by those on the political right but also by the new "market niche" commercialism of Madison Avenue. I noted earlier that one of the reasons the word *gay* began to lose some of its progressive potential as a basis for political mobilization by the 1980s was that it became increasingly commercialized. The invocation of a queer identity has often been presented as one way of dealing with this problem. Yet, there is evidence that the word *queer* is itself entering the domain of popular and thus commercial culture. Thus, within the publishing industry, there is a gay market of which queer readers now represent a small but growing niche, particularly among middle-class undergraduate and graduate students in liberal arts universities. Thus, the *Harvard Gay & Lesbian Review*, a journal of commentary and review with a highly educated, college-based readership, carried a series of ads on its back cover throughout 1995 and 1996 for a major trade publisher that were targeted at a queer readership. The headline on one ad merely presented the following definition: "*book-worm/*'buk-,wurm/ *n* 1. egghead 2. queer." Six novels were then briefly introduced presumably of interest to queer readers. These books included: a "queer theology" book, a retelling of classic folk and fairy tales for gay men, a true-life account of how "words can kill," a biography of famous lesbian and bisexual *literati*, a cultural history of the bond between lesbians and gay men, and pillow books of gay and lesbian love poems. Another ad in the series was headlined: "Queer Thing, reading." Here we have queer identity being produced commercially and sold back to queer readers in the academy. As this process of commercialization and commodification of queer identity continues, it no doubt will motivate the search for a new identity marker, one that is not so deeply colonized. However, this only points to the dilemmas inherent in attempting to use reductionistic identity categories in ways that are politically progressive rather than regressive.

Finally, for a democratic politics to be progressive, it has to provide some basis for building a broad-based democratic movement and power bloc, and identity politics does not take us far in that direction, despite what some have claimed. Laclau and Mouffe (1985) and other post-Marxist theorists argued that a counter-hegemonic, democratic power bloc could only be organized around the interweaving of a number of diverse social movements of identity, all committed to a "politics of difference" aimed at maximizing the autonomy and freedom of each to be self-producing and self-controlling. Beyond that, little appears to bind them together.

This is a form of radical democratic pluralism that has largely abandoned any notion of a public interest or good that is more than a combination of the empowerment agendas of various identity groups that might coalesce into a progressive power bloc. Without a public democratic discourse on change, progressive identity groups have tended to go their own ways, so to speak, developing their own discourses of empowerment. Empowerment only comes, from this perspective, through the articulation or reclaiming of a new symbolic order or epistemology that speaks to an identity group's unique experiences and ways of knowing the world. So it is that queer theory, in some of its forms, is organized around the desire for a gay way of knowing that is all our own. Gay people, so the argument goes, cannot construct empowering identities using heterosexual knowledge and ways of knowing (Honeychurch, 1996).

Although there is wisdom in the idea that oppressed groups need to see the world in a new way in order to break free from their oppression and, to some extent at least, articulate their own discourses of liberation, it is also the case that acting on their own, separated by their own language and cultures of difference, progressive identity groups cannot articulate a new way of understanding the world, what Gramsci (1971) called a "commonsense," that is the precondition for transformative change. Furthermore, it is not really possible to step outside of the dominant culture to forge some autonomous space and language of one's own. In the end, progressive politics must offer more than a collection of seemingly autonomous discourses of liberation or empowerment, and this means taking on the dominant commonsense—a commonsense governed by the logic of binary oppositions.

QUEER THEORY AND A POLITICS OF THE SELF

To this point I have used queer as a marker of identity associated with identity politics. However, queer is among the slipperiest of terms, and its meaning glides back and forth between affirming and disrupting identity categories—often in the same text. In its more subversive form, queer theory actually is one more variation on a poststructural theory of the self that is deeply suspicious of all identity categories, viewing them as (at least in part) regulatory mechanisms of the dominant culture, involved in locating the self within binary oppositional power relations and within the rigid boundaries or borders that police difference (Sedgwick, 1990; Seidman, 1996). The aim of queer theory and other poststructural theories of the self is to deconstruct the binary oppositions that govern identity formation, that is, to reveal the power relations that lie behind them and the "truth games" they organize and are organized by.

Particularly influential in redirecting the study of identity along these lines has been the later work of Foucault, and in particular his three-volume, incompleted history of sexuality in Western culture. According to Foucault, the modern homosexual subject did not exist before the late 19th century, when the homosexual was created by the medical profession as part of a project of defining, labeling, and treating sexual abnormalities. Foucault (1980) observes that: "As defined by ancient civil or canonical codes, sodomy was a category of forbidden acts; their perpetrator was nothing more than the juridical subject of them. The nineteenth-century [male] homosexual became a personage, a past, a case history, a life form" (p. 43). According to Sedgwick (1990), a leading queer theorist, by the end of the 19th century not only is the homosexual defined as a species or subspecies, but "so, as a result, is the heterosexual, and between these species the human species has come more and more to be divided" (p. 9). Sexual difference had become neatly describable in terms of a hetero–homo binary, with each term in the binary dependent for its meaning on its opposite, which it excluded. Hetero implied healthy, homo implied sickness; hetero represented control of sexual desire and impulses, homo represented the sexual outlaw controlled by his or her desires. All of this worked to support an elaborate system of motivating conformity to the highly repressive norms of modern culture. The stigmatization of the sexual Other served as a warning to those who might consider stepping outside the bounds of repressive sexual norms in other ways.

This suspicion of the power relations that lie behind identity formation provides, I think, an important corrective to the essentialistic, unproblematic affirmation of identity that one often finds in the discourse of identity politics. Multicultural education, because it has been so heavily influenced by identity politics, has tended to incorporate its unproblematic affirmation of identity categories. The gay and lesbian movement, by adopting the identity politics model, has been invested in the idea that gay people are a distinct subtype of the human species, born gay, so to speak. Multicultural education is then about teaching respect for gay people, similar to the way we teach respect for racial and ethnic groups. However, if we take a different approach, if we view categories of heterosexual and homosexual identity as historical productions that have served to regulate power relations of inequality, and, going a step further, if we recognize other major identity categories in modern culture (including gender, race, and class) as serving similar roles at least some of the time, then we can no longer unproblematically celebrate a multiculturalism that reduces the self to its identities. Such a multiculturalism may have the ironic effect of reinforcing inequalities by making the Other more visible as the Other.

Instead of merely affirming diverse identities, a democratic multicultural education needs to take on the process of identity formation itself, a process that too often involves establishing borders between self and Other and representing and positioning difference as the polar opposite of self. Despite evidence of acceptance of a growing diversity of identity groups in the United States, identity formation still tends to lead toward "alterity identity," that is, identity that depends on an alter-ego Other to define self, an Other who incorporates all that is excluded and devalued in the self. It is alterity identity, consequently, more than any particular identity, that should become the focus of concern in a critical and democratic multicultural education (Cole McNaught, 1996). Furthermore, the notion of alterity identity inevitably leads us beyond the study of identity in itself and toward a radical democratic critique of the simultaneous production of truth, knowledge, and self.

It leads us, that is, toward a critique of the *logos–mythos* binary that governs truth production in modern culture, a binary we may find already operating in the work of Plato and the classical Greek philosophers—those ancient precursors of modernism. Derrida (1981) suggested that Plato's primary project throughout his dialogues was the grounding of cultural authority on the construction of boundaries between the world of *logos* (understood as truth, knowledge, and reason) and *mythos* (understood as sophistry, falsehood, mystification, illusion, etc.). Western history, Derrida (1981) argues, "has been produced in its entirety in the ... difference between *mythos* and *logos*, blindly sinking down into that difference as the natural obviousness of its own element" (p. 86). And already in Plato, Derrida says, this is a gendered binary; *logos* is consistently presented as a masculine trait in Plato's dialogues.

In *Phaedrus*, for example, Plato invokes (ironically) an ancient Egyptian myth to distinguish between *logos* and *mythos*. It is a myth told by Socrates (speaking for Plato), of the minor messenger god Thoth, a god who among other things represents language and discourse. Thoth presents the many forms of language as gifts to Ra-Ammon, the father/sun god, for the use of all people. But Ra-Ammon, in his wisdom, accepts only some uses of language and rejects others as *pharmakon*, or drugs that lead people away from the truth. Among those he rejects are uses of language that do not adhere to or lead to "the" truth (i.e., fictions and poetry), texts that appeal to our emotions and personal feelings, texts that adhere to no formal logic, texts that deceive and trick, and so forth. Derrida suggests that this division of the forms and uses of language is, for Plato, gendered. It is a story used by Plato to assert the authority of patriarchal knowledge and the need to resist subversive uses of language associated with the feminine. It is not coincidental that in Egyptian mythology and in Plato's interpretation of this myth, Ra-Ammon is used to symbolize absolute, transcendent, authoritative truth, or *logos*. The conjunction between "father" and "sun" is particularly significant here, for the pure light of the sun is elsewhere a primary symbol for transcendent, authoritative truth in Plato's work. The effect, according to Derrida, is to assign the origin of *logos* to the paternal position, which legitimates patriarchal authority as not only guided by reason but also a manifestation of a transcendent absolute knowledge. Conversely, Plato associates *mythos* with the feminine, and with the world of poetry, fiction, and song—uses of language open to multiple readings and interpretations, and uses that may, like a *pharmakon*, impair our capacity to see the truth (Derrida, 1981, p. 76).

If the *logos–mythos* binary has been a gendered binary in Western culture, it is now becoming apparent that it has been involved in the construction of other identity binaries as well. Post-colonial scholars have helped us recognize that 19th-century European colonial discourse was involved in representing the European center as civilized, sane, rational, and fatherlike in relation to the colonized or native Other represented as savage, immoral, childlike, irrational, and operating at a lower or more primitive level of intelligence (McCarthy & Crichlow, 1993; Said, 1978). Beyond its linkages to the establishment of binary racial and gender identities, the *logos–mythos* binary may be implicated in the construction of a class binary that separates the "gifted" and "intellectually endowed" children of the middle class from the "manually oriented" children of the working poor who are presumed to be operating at a concrete developmental level. Sexual identity too falls under the spell of the *logos–mythos* binary. Gay people, like others assigned to the world of *mythos*, get represented as driven by desire and impulse rather than reason, with talents in the arts more than the "hard" sciences and math. In a sense, then, all marginalized identities have been represented in the dominant or logocentric culture of modernism as under the influence of what Freud called the "pleasure principle," whereas dominant groups have been represented as operating under the cool, dispassioned logic of the "reality principle." In the language of Cartesian dualism, marginalized identity groups represent the body and desire, whereas dominant identity groups represent mind and reason, which must rule over the body. Ultimately, this long history of separating *logos* from *mythos*, truth from non-truth, reason from irrationality, and mind from body must be interrogated in any investigation of identity formation.

In education, to shift the focus to the *logos–mythos* binary has some rather dramatic implications for how we understand the role schools have played throughout the 20th century in reproducing cultural and economic inequality. Critical educators have long argued that schools have not served to challenge inequality so much as legitimate it. But they have not been able to explain this theory of cultural and economic reproduction adequately, at least not without slipping into a functionist "correspondence principle" (Bowles & Gintis, 1976) or implying a conspiracy among dominant groups to make the schools serve their interests. Because public education has, throughout the 20th century, been governed by a rigidly logocentric rationality, and has been one of the leading defenders of logocentrism in society, it should not be surprising to find that it has also (and against the best efforts of many progressive educators) privileged those identity groups most associated with *logos* in the culture (i.e., male, middle class, White, and heterosexual) and conversely and simultaneously disempowered and silenced those most associated with *mythos* (i.e., female, working class and poor, Black, homosexual). This suggests that one of the most effective means of challenging and resisting the reproduction of unequal identities through the schooling process may be by moving toward a less logocentric curriculum and school organization.

But how can we begin moving beyond a logocentric curriculum and school organization and the "truth games" it promotes about student identity and self? Put somewhat differently, how can education promote the formation of a self that is less fixed and more open, without rigid identity boundaries or borders, and with greater freedom over its own self-production and growth? These questions take us well beyond identity politics and begin to lead in the direction of a new democratic politics of the self—something Foucault (1987) was exploring in his final work on the history of sexuality. The Graeco-Roman world did not have an ethic of sexual conduct that neatly divided sexual desires and practices into categories of sinful and non-sinful as the Christian age did, or categories of healthy and unhealthy, as the modern age does. Instead, individuals were governed by what Foucault called ethics and practices of freedom. This meant that in deciding how to interact and relate to others, rather than relying on a set of prescribed norms and prohibitions, and rather than positioning the other as the Other, that is, as an alterity identity, individuals sought to negotiate their relations in ways that protected the freedom and addressed the interests of all involved parties. This was an ethic and practice of self-regulation consistent with a goal of achieving balance in one's life and one's everyday relations with others, and keeping these relations as open as possible, which is also to say as unencumbered by power inequalities and normative expectations as possible so as to give the participants maximum freedom over the situation. To promote such practices of freedom or self-regulation, according to Foucault, Graeco-Roman culture encouraged a form of self-education and formal training in "care for the self." By this, Foucault (1987) had in mind practices or technologies of the self that involve self-reflection, and through which the self can "turn its gaze on itself"—with the purpose of recognizing itself; and in this recognition act "to improve one's self, to surpass one's self" (p. 5). Foucault identified a number of technologies of the self as associated with practices of freedom, including dialogue, listening, meditation, memory, self-examination, diary and journal keeping, and letter writing (Martin, Gutman, & Hutton, 1988).

Education, in this sense, is about learning practices of freedom in our everyday relations with others through an ethic of care for the self that leads inward. But it is a turning inward that ultimately leads outward again, to practices of the self that are based on new truth games, new power relations, new ethics, and a new ethos of everyday life. It refocuses our attention on the politics of everyday life and learning how to regulate and negotiate our relations with various others—including those who differ by class, race, gender, sexuality, and other identity markers—in ways that are non-oppressive and allow for the building of spontaneous alliances across differences within concrete, pragmatic contexts. Such an understanding of the self and others represents a significant shift in thinking about democratic culture and politics. It implies a much more active role on the part of individuals, outside the framework of a welfare state, in sustaining the conditions for freedom and democracy through local practices of self-regulation. A politics of the self based on practices of freedom does not or should not mean the end of identity politics, for collective identity is essential to the empowerment agendas of marginalized groups and helps provide an answer to the question, Who am I? Nevertheless, a politics of the self does begin to take seriously the ultimate goals of identity politics—to free the self to relate with others outside the same–other binary and thus not to be limited or privileged by race, class, gender, sexual orientation, or other markers of difference. Identity within such a context provides the self with a habitus and a subcultural language of difference, and thus with a unique perspective that enters into the public dialogue across differences, that is democratic community (Burbules & Rice, 1991). But the self does not lock itself into rigid oppositional identity politics and never mistakes its identities for itself. It seems to me that such a politics of the self is desperately needed within multicultural education if it is not to become a fragmented field of study that treats various minority and marginalized groups separately, each given its week or month in the curriculum, and if it is not to encourage young people to think about themselves and others according to reductionistic categories of difference in a new multicultural community. If the promise of multicultural education is to be realized, it must be committed to helping young people learn the technologies of self that will allow them to work together strategically across, as well as within, various identity boundaries to advance common democratic projects.

REFERENCES

Bowles, S., & Gintis, H. (1976). *Schooling in capitalist America.* New York: Routledge & Kegan Paul.

Bourdieu, P., & Passeron, J. (1977). *Reproduction in education, society, and culture.* London: Sage.

Burbules, N., & Rice, S. (1991). Dialogue across differences: Continuing the conversation. *Harvard Educational Review, 61,* 393–416.

Carlson, D. L. (1994). Gayness, multicultural education, and community. *Educational Foundations, 8*(4), 5–26.

Carlson, D. L. (1995). Constructing the margins: Of multicultural education and curriculum settlements. *Curriculum Inquiry, 25*(4), 407–432.

Cole McNaught, S. (1996). Alterity/identity: A postcolonial critique of educational policies and practices in the United States. Unpublished doctoral dissertation, Miami University, Oxford, Ohio.

Corey, F. (1992). Gay life/queer art. In A. Kroker & M. Kroker (Eds.), *The last sex; Feminism and outlaw bodies* (pp. 121–132). New York: St. Martin's Press.

Derrida, J. (1981). *Plato's pharmacy.* Chicago: University of Chicago Press.

Foucault, M. (1980). *The history of sexuality; Volume 1.* New York: Vintage.

Foucault, M. (1987). The ethic of care for the self as a practice of freedom (Interview, trans. J. Gauthier). In J. Bernauer & D. Rasmussen (Eds.), *The final Foucault* (pp. 1–20). Cambridge, MA: MIT Press.

Gramsci, A. (1971). *Selections from the prison notebooks.* New York: International Publishers.

Honeychurch, K. (1996). Researching dissident subjectivities: Queering the grounds of theory and practice. *Harvard Educational Review, 66*(2), 339–355.

Laclau, E., & Mouffe, C. (1985). *Hegemony and socialist strategy.* London: Verso.

Martin, L., Gutman, H., & Hutton, P. (Eds.). (1988). *Technologies of the self: A seminar with Michel Foucault.* London: Tavistock.

McCarthy C., & Crichlow, W. (Eds.). (1993). *Race, identity, and representation in education.* New York: Routledge.

Said, E. (1978). *Orientalism.* New York: Vintage Books.

Sedgwick, E. (1990). *Epistemology of the closet.* Berkeley: University of California Press.

Seidman, S. (Ed.). (1996). *Queer theory/sociology.* Oxford, UK: Blackwell.

Taubman, P. (1993). Separate identities, separate lives: Diversity in the curriculum. In L. Castenell & W. Pinar (Eds.), *Understanding curriculum as racial text: Representations of identity and difference in education* (pp. 287–306). Albany: State University of New York Press.

Chapter 4

Remember When All the Cars Were Fords and All the Lesbians Were Women? Some Notes on Identity, Mobility, and Capital

Erica Meiners
Simon Fraser University

> *I bought you drinks, I brought you flowers*
> *I read your books*
> *we talked for hours*
> *every day so many drinks such pretty flowers*
> *so tell me what have I, what have I, what have I done to deserve this?*
> > —"What Have I Done to Deserve This?" Pet Shop Boys

> *To treat one's body as a private possession (the basis of the discourse of sexual rights within a capitalist society) is to refuse the issue of inequality between owners.*
> > —Connell (1996, p. 392)

A GENESIS

I am having a few beers with a friend, Eve. With a measure of angst, Eve tells me that she thinks she's a post-lesbian, she must be really queer indeed. She wants to leave her live-in lover, Grace, and start up with men. She adds that she watches boys on public transit now and it generates a kind of illicit pleasure. What frames her confession is that Eve was an LKG—Lesbian Knowledge Goddess—to siphon Laurie Fuller's phrase.[1] For the last 10 years or so Eve was a queer-about-town, out-loud-proud, involved in community

---

[1]Fuller, Laurie (1996). *Disrupting Whiteness: Race, Queerness and Pedagogy*. Doctoral Dissertation, University of Madison–Wisconsin.

activities and activism, more often than not with a most lovely girlfriend in tow. What tempted Eve? Why this fall from Grace? Drama! Drama!

An apostrophe is required here to massage the reader's ongoing faith in the integrity and authority of the author: Although the author occupies what others might perceive as a closet, really it is an elevator and she's just the nonunion operator.

The next day I tried to map the ontological and cartographic dilemmas of queerness and/or post-lesbianism. Does one come out as a post-lesbian or go back in? If the latter, where is the out from to go back in to? If she outs from the closet into the bedroom, would she now be escorted by protocol to the patio? Or has "queer" moved all the players into an over-priced loft with no walls and bad art? Does one self-identify as a "post" at lesbian potlucks? As a heterosexual in recovery in straight bars? What if she ends up again with women? Will she be a born-again lesbian? What about a queer bisexual post-lesbian heterosexual in 12-step recovery, with the fixed categories White, unemployed, short, attached? (Of course none of these labels addresses that Eve has always been a top and what, exactly, she is planning to do with which boys, remains to be seen.)

To dodge possibly accurate accusations of neoconservatism, I want to articulate that these gyrations about essence, identifications, self/de-con-structions, and/or variations on Locke-ian boundaries of personal identity are not restricted to the previous example: Eve's fall from Grace and subsequent banishment from the garden of Eden. The Vancouver Lesbian Center had extensive debates over the last 2 years on who can constitute a body using the services of a lesbian center: transgendered bodies, men who identify as lesbians, only women born lesbians, only women identified lesbians, and so on. Identity is conflated with versions of biology and placed against identifications in defining who can constitute the real lesbian. The February 18, 1997, issue of the *Advocate*, a White gay upscale North American magazine, ran a cover story on Joann Loulan, author of *Lesbian Sex* and *Lesbian Passion*, who is now in love with a feminine man. In an article discussing the complexities involved in Loulan's confession of not just straight sex but straight desire, a Vancouver GLBT[2] paper's lesbian columnist also admitted to having an affair with a man. She asserted her lesbian-ness despite this indiscretion, adding the comment, "After all, having the occa-sional Gardenburger does not a vegetarian make" (Filipenko, 1997, p. 7).[3]

---

[2]Gay, Lesbian, Bisexual, Transgendered.

[3]A related note on naming sexual practices: The Simon Fraser University MA work of Ibanez-Carrasco (1993) and to a lesser degree Luinenburg (1994) articulates that individuals across ethnic, cultural, and socioeconomic spaces engage in same-sex relations but do not classify these practices as homosexual. This could be interpreted as a denial or internalized homophobia, however these nonacknowledgments of same-sex acts as participation or identification within a homosexual community (e.g., lesbian or gay) can also illustrate that sexualities are always co-inscribed by cultural, economic, social, and/or racial discourses.

These outings of innings, straightening of seemingly kinked desire, morphing bodies and quibbles on queerness, pose quandaries for GLBT: where, when, and whether to draw boundaries for a community? Who is acceptable in these new Nations, who isn't, and who gets to mark the territories? Which practices, identity markers, or identifications, count? And how soon will these boundaries be out-of-date (more essentially, who cares, and why)? An article by Maria Pallotta-Chiarolli (1996–97), "To be, or not, or both, or neither" in an Australian queer magazine comically highlights a pre-occupation with fixing sexual identifications that do not neatly map:

> At the Parade and at the dance, gays and lesbians stare. They want to figure it out. Put them in a neat box. Is he gay? Is he straight? Are they together? Are they friends? Is she a femme dyke? Is she a post op transsexual success story? Is he a leatherman? What on earth is she then? His SM slave? (p. 25)

Queer appeared to pose possible solutions to this categorical angst. As an identity marker, queer is posited as a way to disrupt and simultaneously expose the construction of the reified binaries of heterosexual and homosexual and the static, constructed gender assignments male and female. In seeming contrast to GLBT identities, queer points to the fluidity and multiplicity of sexualities. *Queer theory*, a term applied across disciplines, addresses issues that gay and lesbian theorizing covers and also works beyond the parameters of identity and identifications set by gay, lesbian, or bisexual work. Folded into discourses of post-structuralism and postmodernism, interdisciplinary queer theory questions the foundations and formations of sexual identities or sexual identifications.[4]

There is an influx in theorizing about/on/for queer on the 1990s academic theory market. Although I do not profess to be the mistress of the totality of discourses on queerness or queer theory, in this discussion I look at some implications of contemporary moves in queer theorizing. As Cindy Patton (1996) suggests in her work examining the successful appropriation of progressive discourses and identity markers by the republican right in American politics, a persistent analysis is required of some of the social spaces progressive discourses occupy.

> My reading of the new right rhetoric suggests that while we are deconstructing identity, the new right is deconstructing the social space that our identities predicate. Defending social space (if this is indeed desirable) while avoiding the problems of identitarian politics requires a broader critique than so far has been argued by critics of essentialized identity: if, as many argue, identity is performative or a performance, then identity is necessarily always in context or in practice. In order to be useful and not merely nihilistic

---

[4]de Lauretis, 1991; Sedgwick, 1993; Abelove, Barale, and Halperin, 1993.

(not that I object in principle to regular doses of nihilism), the deconstruction of identity must be accompanied by an analysis of the social spaces posited by or through identity.[5] (p. 227)

I highlight this quote and apply it to my discussion on queer theory because it addresses the need for continued, situated analysis of how identities and identifications work and are worked. As Patton suggests, constant evaluations of the fields in which "progressive" discourses circulate are required. By looking at some recent turns in queer theory to understand what varied (and possibly unintentional) epistemologies and ideologies these splitting theories may inform, I do not trivialize or dismiss the continued work done by GLBT activists and/or queer bodies who in effect have made this body of writing possible. As a related qualifier, this is not a discussion about the politics of visibility: being out or being in.[6] To interpret from my discussion that I advocate the invisibility of GLBT and/or other identities or that I dismiss the possibilities that terms such as *queer* can offer, reduces the complexities of this analysis.

In the first section of this chapter, I cover an analysis of some of the implications of the traveling metaphors within a specific stream of queer theorizing: post-al queer theory. Incorporating Patton's framework of thinking about the social spaces posited by or through identity, I examine post-al interpretations of queer, and how queer circulates with other identity categories. I also offer additional interpretations of what ideological and economic shifts these fluid constructions of queer subjectivities serve. In conjunction to Patton's work in "Refiguring Social Space" I use works from theorists that look at queer theorizing from other perspectives: Rosemary Hennessy, Donald Morton, and Evelynn Hammonds.

In addition, I don't want to lose sight of Eve—the maiden at stake. As this chapter is subtitled, "some notes on identity, mobility, and capital," in the second section of this discussion, in the doubled interests of tainting economic theory and economizing on the production of queer theory, I encourage Eve to come out as a Post-Fordist. In this section, I provide a definition of Fordism and Post-Fordism, terms I borrow from cultural and economic geography.

As an aside on my methodological stance, I inject humor into this discussion, with apologies if pressed. At times, a comical mode is the most useful tactic to adopt when one does not own the terms of discussion. (I

---

[5]For a related analysis in a Canadian context I direct readers to, for example, Himani Bannerji's ongoing work critiquing political constructions and deployments of multiculturalism in Canada.

[6]Foucault (1977): "What placements are determined for possible subjects? What are the modes of existence of this discourse? Where does it come from, how is it circulated, who controls it?" (p. 239).

too do not object in principle to regular doses of nihilism.) Writing about sexualities and identities and the practices of identifications is fragmented and partial. Pens and tongues often slip over points. Toni Morrison (1993) and Michel de Certeau (1987) have noted that humor or irony as a destabilizing tactic can seduce and subvert readers to dis-place readings, render particular every/any reading, and can place the writer at a safer distance from the text. Writing cultural history or cultural theory in the comic mode is the preference for historian Caroline Bynum Walker (1991):

> If tragedy tells a cogent story, with a moral and a hero, and undergrids our sense of the nobility of humanity, comedy tells many stories, achieves a conclusion only by coincidence and wild improbability . . . in comedy, the happy ending is always contrived. Thus a comic stance toward doing history is aware of a contrivance, of risk. A comic stance knows there is, in actuality, no ending, (happy or otherwise). (pp. 24–25)

I too, have no interest in telling a whole story—or perhaps even a true one for any/every body—yet I have no intent to fragment or dull the realities of systematic violence: racism, heteronormativity, poverty, etc. My multiple plays with Eve: Eve as an icon; Eve as signifying a project of re-mythologization; Eve as always technologically mediated; Eve as natural as a Ford, are intended, not to be superficially irresponsible, but to add another layer to this discussion to provoke some thoughts about the spaces, implications, and anxieties of naming.

CONSUMING SUBJECTIVITY—SOME QUERIES ON THE POST-AL QUEER

> *hey you*
> *who me?*
> *yes you—get into my car . . .*
> *we're going riding on the freeway of love*
> —"Freeway of Love," Aretha Franklin

Questioning the elitism in queerness and queer theorizing is not new. Before assessing the implications of metaphors of mobility in desire, I want to stress that scholars have pointed to the Whiteness of queer theory as an extension of the Whiteness of mainstream GLBT theorizing. Evelynn Hammonds (1991) asks in her article, "Black (W)holes and the Geometry of Black Female Sexuality": "Does a shift from lesbian to queer relieve my sense of anxiety over whether the exclusionary practices of lesbian and gay studies can be resolved?" (p. 128). Hammonds questions the utility of placing new terms on inequitable foundations.

Teresa de Lauretis (1991), introducing the first edition of *differences* on queer theory, poses a number of possibilities on how queer theorizing can work difference differently, and address other social movements, not just heteronormativity. As Hammonds writes in her response to de Lauretis's theoretical posings, this disruption is located within specific White northern bodies located within late capitalist economies and often does not address the implicit metaphorical threads binding practices, definitions, and identifications of sexualities to (Other) identity markers, specifically race. Hammonds (1991) writes:

> The canonical terms and categories of the field: "lesbian" "gay" "butch" "femme" "sexuality" and "subjectivity" are stripped of context in the works of those theorizing about those very categories, identities, and subjects positions. Each of these terms is defined with white as the normative state of existence. (p. 128; see also hooks, 1992)

The terms that operate within discourses on queer sexualities are always and already situated within another set of social relations: Whiteness.

One trajectory of recent work in queer theory embraces mobility in practices and pleasures and degrees of difference(s) in context(s). These discourses are attempts to shift away from Hammonds' canonical terms of the field and their associations with eurocentric values. Emphasizing mobility in desire, being queer is about perpetual desires in motion and body-morphing, not necessarily about the identity or identification a body occupies. I borrow the term *post-al* from Donald Morton to refer to this stream of queer theorizing. In his essay "Queerity and Ludic Sado-Masochism: Compulsory Consumption and the Emerging Post-al Queer," Morton (1995) points to the work of these post-al queer theorists:

> What we are witnessing today is the emergence of the "post al" queer which Queer Theorists represent as a set of social practices and a form of subjectivity that are said to be progressive because in addition to being supposedly non-natural, non-essentialistic, and textuo-socially "constructed" they are differential and non-exclusionary and therefore "changeable." ... In broad terms, for Queer Theory the queer subject is constructed by the processes of signification—"homosexuality is textuality" one queer critic has declared. (p. 190)

Travel metaphors are emphasized in recent post-al interpretations and applications of queer theory by theorists looking at the body and desire: Sexual desire is often characterized by movement or as something to move: becomings; intensifications; outside belongings; cruising machines; unfixing desire.[7] Risking overgeneralization, one interpretation of the goal of

---

[7]See also Rosemary Hennessy's (1996) analysis or Morton's (1995) analysis of the uptake of S/M and fist-fucking by post-al theoretical agendas.

this queer theorizing or thinking on queer desires is, as Probyn (1995) writes, "to queer oneself through movement" (p. 15). Queer is implicitly positioned as a more progressive and a non-exclusionary interpretation of the fluidity of sexualities. Deleuzian nomadism and fluidity are romanced, and certain travel metaphors (flight and migrancy, not deportation or homelessness) abound. Bodies and identities are in a constant state of becoming and are consuming desiring machines. Following the situatedness of this theorizing on queerness for White bodies living in industrialized states: everybody who is anybody has a frequent-flier plan.

Assignments of post-al queerness, in this psychoanalytic or post-structural turn, are based not on who one does or who one is, but what one does and how or where one does it. Although I am not negating that sexuality is a construction and in construction,[8] as Connell (1996) states, the goals of the 1960s radical liberation sexual theorists have shifted. A more complex and global understanding of the place of theorizing on/about/for sexualities is required. "We can no more liberate the libido than we can liberate the square root of minus one. There is no Thing there to liberate . . . the goal cannot be the liberation of 'sexuality' from social constraint. The only thing that can be liberated is people" (Connell, 1996, pp. 284, 390).

Although I concur with Connell that there is no libido to liberate, only bodies, I do not disagree with the analysis of post-al theorists. As Probyn (1995) states: "Freeing desire from its location, its epistemological stake in the individual necessitates rethinking the role of images, images and motion" (p. 9). This querying of the object(s) of desire and pushing boundaries and understandings of how, why, and when sexualities are constituted is important, but I want to look at some discursive and material implications of these post-al moves and some social spaces these discourses occupy. What can queer come to mean if it is structured as a kind of freefalling play for certain bodies? Who benefits from these discourses, who does not, and why? Into what other ideological frameworks does the theoretical construction of the post-al queer body as consuming desiring machines fit?

In this post-ality move to locate sexuality as meaningful in contexts and desire as always a state of becoming and in motion, acts and identities can become ahistorical and decontextualized. Interpretations become unclear of what is the queer enough difference that makes a difference queer. So Eve was a queer lesbian and now she is a queer straight White girl. Is queer

---

[8]This understanding of sexualities as always in construction and a construction does not negate that that some identity categories or identifications are marked on a body: i.e., race; disability. To posit identity and/or identifications as simply a choice is again simplistic, reductive. For example see: Smukler (1994), Lorde (1982b), Allison (1995).

merely a self-applied avant-garde modifier used to modify more supposedly static identities and identifications? If so, queer functions to erase economic and political inequalities. In contemporary culture, there are different political and social privileges afforded to queer lesbians and queer straights. If queer is a modifier applying to the more avant-garde or perverse sexual practices, how (and whether) to distinguish between any Dick or Harry who identifies as heterosexual yet considers his practices—for example child prostitution, S/M, or fetish gear—as queer, and those bodies who term their same-sex desire and sex as queer? Is the queer difference in this comparison one of degree, or kind, or does this difference not matter? What about recent work positing excess—piercing, tattooing, and addiction—as forms of queer desire?

So Eve can be queer, but anybody can be queer because every body is queer.

Without displacing economic, social, political, and racial constructions of sexualities, the post-al queer is applied as qualifier to supposedly more static identity markers: race, ability, gender. In this vein of theorizing, queer becomes a modifier available to anybody that can self-identify his or her practice(s) as such. The utility of the term *queer* to deconstruct typically eurocentric foundations of (White)(hetero)sexualities seems diluted, as it is positioned as an outside to static definitions of Other identity categories. Also, post-al definitions of *queer* do not forge or invite coalitions with those bodies who do not identify predominantly or primarily through a lens of sexuality but through, for example, their employment practices or through membership in a religious or ethnic community.

As Hammonds and Patton point out, a deeper analysis is required that works to dis-place and denaturalize the reified binaries of homo and hetero, and to expose the social, economic, and political privileges embedded in these positionings. In addition, an exploration of the relationships between these constructed sexualities and other identity positionings, such as race, is required. Without this corresponding work, the post-al queer theory move to focus on practices and pleasures or mobile difference(s) in context(s) as a marker of queerness introduces a slippery slope. The modifier *queer*, to appropriate Patton's (1996) term, can play as a "dis-identification," or a type of "logofellatio" (p. 219).[9]

Patton's work examining how progressive left discourses about race and racism are too easily successfully assimilated or appropriated by right-wing agendas demonstrates that negotiations about context, history, and coalitions are critical to sustaining some long(er)-term political agendas for social change. Although it may be argued that long-term assessments are

---

[9]Patton uses this term in reference to her analysis of how identity politics, specifically discourses on race, function in contemporary American politics.

a luxury, that responses to oppressions in contemporary political spheres are reduced to de Certeau-ian tactics, this response is naive.[10] In order not to engage in (the dreaded) "repetition" that Patton mentions, fields and terms of discussion need to be cautiously and carefully altered. Although I like and enjoy disruptions, in order for sustained changes to structures and foundations, more rigorous coalition-based work needs working out. To have coalition work that is not based on simplistic notions of identity politics, a more complex understanding of identities and identifications (even if these are considered performative and temporal) is required.

> [R]ecovering a progressive political project requires understanding the limi-
> tations of performative personae as well as evaluating the role of the field.
> . . . One of the crucial analytic issues then, is considering how to think about
> the space in which performative identities are at play, how to interrogate
> identity as it is situated in fields of power. Power must not be treated mono-
> lithically or viewed as isomorphic or continuous across the various forms of
> space ('culture' 'political' 'social') which identities inhabit, however perfor-
> matively. (Patton, 1996, p. 227)

Patton (1996) posits a practice of "queering social theory" (p. 228) that involves looking at the structures that produce, maintain, and manage social relations, and attempting to understand how these structures work and are worked by bodies. In a similar move Hennessy (1996) also points to the need to "queer-y social theory" (p. 143). In contrast to post-al queer theory, Hennessy and Patton stress the need to challenge, assess, and understand structures that allocate spaces for specific identity positionings, and they point to the necessity of continually evaluating, in contexts, the use of any progressive or liberatory discourse. This queery-ing of theory points to the need to do more than perform deviance or queer disruptions and asks for a more rigorous and contextual assessment of the implications and constructions of identity positionings.

Aspects of academic theory, research, and scholarship are working Patton's analysis. Historians and critical theorists, exploring the social, economic, and political genealogies of desire, sexuality, and the body, continue to illustrate that the normal is always just passing.[11] These theorists, writers, artists, and others attempt to undo the binaries of hetero and homo by positing that there is nothing straight, original, or natural about the self,

---

[10]Debates about gay pedophilia within GLBT and straight communities continue to demonstrate that the terms and the fields in which terms circulate obscure the complexities of the issues. These debates require unpacking (mis)conceptions about the asexuality of children, heteronormativity—not just homophobia—power relations and the production of sexualities, and unequal access to terminology. Most public discussion are confined to superficial assessments about morality, and/or appropriate ages for consent.

[11]For example, see varied works by Tsing (1995) and Walker (1991).

the body, or any social order. To steal Suzanne de Castell's word, "in-ver-sions" of the everyday or, more problematically anthropological exposures of the sameness of an Other, demonstrate the queer-ity of what passes for natural desires.[12] Although often doing little to illustrate connections be-tween the racialization or class-ification of a body's sexualities, these works develop the argument, working the inside out, so to speak, that social structures manufacture straightness.

I take a detour from this theorizing to return to Eve's ongoing onto-logical angst. Still keen to be of assistance, I looked in a critical *Dictionary of Human Geography 3rd Edition*. As Eve is hardly original in her fall, looking to a dictionary of human geography for an entry for *queer* or *post-lesbianism*, is a natural option to find possible solutions for spatial and ontological queries. No entries were found, but on the page where post-lesbian should (or could or would have been) is a productive and possibly relevant eco-nomic term: Post-Fordism. Why not Eve as a Post-Fordist? Why not Post-Fordism as the most avant-garde, cutting edge identity position to assume? (she's hot—she's a post-fordist . . .) Or, less facetiously, might this economic and geographic term (in context, of course) be more politically and eco-nomically appropriate(d) than *queer*?

As I stated earlier, this discussion is also focused on assessing some implications of naming. As Marilyn Frye (1983) points out, the erasure and the lack of available terms for identities or identifications within any given framework is meaningful. "If a conceptual scheme excludes some-thing, the standard vocabulary of those whose scheme it is will not be adequate to the defining of a terms which denotes it" (p. 154).[13] Frye acknowledges in her project of attempting to understand and render po-litically meaningful these cognitive gaps and negative spaces, that she is always flirting with meaninglessness and incoherence. Rather than making the theoretical, political, and discursive moves that Frye has executed in her work on lesbianism or that Hammonds advocates, I opt for recycling theory. Recycling is defined in *Webster's Ninth New Collegiate Dictionary* (1983) as: "to adapt to a new use" (p. 985). If as Patton articulates, recovering a progressive political project requires thinking differently about the spaces performative identities are at play, I stress that a re-covering of Post-Fordist theory might be a possibility to queery social theory. After careful reading of the spaces surrounding the in/visible gap in the *Dictionary of Human Geography*, in the (at least) doubled interests of tainting economic theory

---

[12]As Tsing (1995) states in her ethnography on marginality-in-out-of-the-way places, bodies and social relations are invented. "As people preen and squabble over the correct rules of propriety, their inventedness becomes obvious" (p. 258).

[13]bell hooks (1992) also points to the erasure of Black women with and in feminist theory as symbolic, and locates this silencing as essential to think through.

and economizing on the production of post-al queer theory, I want to encourage Eve to come out as a Post-Fordist.

Although I enjoy this text-play, my turn to economic and cultural geography is not as accidental as I construct it to be. I use these predominantly economic terms intentionally to flesh out another context to post-al queer theorizing. I highlight Fordism for several reasons. First, it functions as a simplistic vehicle to make a superficial critique of the aforementioned romanticization of mobility of the Deleuzian desiring machines and the ever-morphing *Volatile Bodies* (Grosz, 1995). With cars, as for bodies, questions of mobility are directly related to economic and identity privileges: who is permitted to drive, who has access to which forms of transportation, who is moved by choice and who is not, and so on. I also deploy Fordism because of the social contract or scaffolding relationships the theoretical term *Fordism* acknowledges between the production of the identities of workers and the production of consumers for goods. Finally, Post-Fordism poses questions (similar to critiques of post-colonialism) about the use of and allocation of the marker *post.* After a brief outlaying of some characteristics of Fordism and Post-Fordism, I return to a discussion of identities and identifications to make some queer connections.

SHIFTING GEARS—THEORIZING ON FORDS

'Have you driven a Ford Lately?'

—ad slogan

Fordism is a term used predominantly in economic or cultural geography, and for my (albeit superficial) analysis I borrow heavily from the *Dictionary of Human Geography 3rd edition,* and also related works by other cultural and social geographers.[14] Fordism is affiliated with an analysis of labor, the productions of goods, and the resulting social and cultural shifts that occurred in conjunction to changes in labor practices and the workplace. Derived from Henry Ford, the man associated with the development of the assembly-line production of cars (Fords) in Detroit, Michigan, Fordism is associated with particular developments in the workplace, most notably the assembly line. In assembly-line production, which Ford borrowed and refined from meat-packing plants, the product and/or parts move while the worker remains static, fulfilling a singular repetitive task. Fordism is also associated with a "scaffolding" relationship that the Ford corporation

---

[14]See works by Pile and Thrift (1995), Harvey (1989), and Gramsci (1971). Due to spatial constraints I only sketch some aspects of these terms as they pertain to my discussion, and I do not chronologically or historically place these terms.

attempted to develop between the product the assembly-line plants were producing and the workers that were producing those products. The product, a Ford, should be available, affordable, and *desired* by the workers.

I emphasize this scaffolding or the social, cultural, and political developments that occurred in conjunction to the changes in workplace practices, because these corresponding relationships are an essential component of both Fordism and Post-Fordism. As I argue in the following section, this conception of scaffolding is related to post-al queer theorizing. Initially, cars were only available to a privileged few, but with the assembly-line mass-production of Fords (and other products), productivity increased. To simplify drastically a complex process, cars became cheaper, therefore more widely available. The social contract the corporation attempted to instill in workers connected the supply—the availability of the product—to the means of acquisition—a paycheck. "Work rationalization and rational consumption, for Ford, must go hand in hand" (Yanerella & Reid, 1996, p. 197).

This commodification process instills 'need' and 'desire' for goods into a consuming subject. This linkage, of manufacturing desire and need between a product and a worker, lent support to the development of political and social systems of regulation. These systems of regulation developed into labor regulations, social and political institutions in the United States addressing social welfare functions, and more intimate restructuring of work, worker, and the like. Capital then had an impact in forming identities (determining needs, wants, and desires) and capital also worked to shape social institutions. See Harvey (1989), Pile and Thrift (1995), Gramsci (1971), and Johnston, Gregory, and Smith (1994) entries for Fordism. Gramsci (1971) observes in "Americanism and Fordism" that these changes in the workplace also regulated monogamous heterosexual relationships and implicitly enforced definitions of the family. Emily Martin (1994) noted in *Flexible Bodies: The Role of Immunity in American Culture from the Days of Polio to the Age of AIDS*, that Henry Ford sent investigators into his workers' homes to regulate morality, in the name of productivity.

> Over one hundred investigators visited workers' homes and admonished them to practice thrifty and hygienic habits and avoid smoking, gambling, and drinking. These early social workers decided which workers 'because of unsatisfactory personal habits or home conditions' were not eligible to receive the full five dollar wage that Ford offered. (p. 30)

Martin's example of "early social workers" illustrates that domestic practices required regulation to produce efficient laborers and consumers.

In a related interpretation of Fordism, *Ford* functions metonymically as a signifier for American culture, entrepreneurship, and consumerism, as

Gramsci implies in "Americanism and Fordism." Fords (along with Coca Cola, Nike, and other American cultural icons) symbolize Americana.[15] This signification is attributed to the systems of production of a product as well as the circulation of a product. (Max Weber, after visiting a Chicago meat slaughterhouse/packinghouse plant in the 1870s, is reported to have stated that the assembly line process was "the crystallization of the American Spirit" [Yanerella & Reid, 1996, p. 194].) Fords, more specifically than Nike or Coca Cola, have roots in White working-class labor practices, thus doubly imbedding Ford, both as icon and product, within North American definitions of boot-strapism and meritocracy. Current Ford advertising slogans—Have you driven a Ford lately?—attempt to move purchasers away from the popular conception that a Ford is a staid, standardized, typically not exotic American vehicle. This conception of an American exists at the construction of an-Other: exotic and foreign. Fordism, along with signifying a system of production also represents implicit norms of American culture, good citizenship, and stereotypical assumptions about American values (see Yanerella & Reid, 1996).

Post-Fordism—and my frame of reference here is still predominantly cultural and economic geography—typically follows Fordism and covers roughly the same aspects: an analysis of labor, the productions of goods, and the resulting social and cultural shifts that occur in conjunction with changes in the labor practice. As a definition, I draw directly from Johnston et al. (1994):

> [Post-Fordism] is characterized by the application of production methods considered to be more flexible those of the Fordist era. These many include more versatile, programmable machines, labour that is more flexibly deployed (in terms of both quantity and tasks performed) vertical disintegration of large corporations and a closer integration of product development, marketing and production. Accompanying these changes in production and industrial management is a new set of enabling institutions to re-structure labour-management relations, labour training, competition law, and financial markets. (SEE ALSO FLEXIBLE ACCUMULATION) (p. 459)

The *post* in Post-Fordism is to represent the disintegration of the static assembly-line production of goods (a center of production) or perhaps just the redistribution of access to a center. As definitions of labor and worksites shift, the placement and expectations of a laborer are also altered. This shift denotes sexual, corporeal, and geographical changes in the laboring body. Geographical understandings of community, regulations about sexuality as it pertains to labor and consumption, and conceptions

---

[15]Of note of course is that these are not all U.S.-owned companies, thus posing interesting questions of facades of representations.

of what labor entails and who laborers can be, are all seemingly open for reconfiguration in this post phase. However, a market for goods is still required, as Post-Fordism is not about de-industrialization or a decrease in the production or consumption of products. Mechanisms to instill need and desire for products in bodies are still required. The social contract that Fordism ensured, between product and worker, is no longer available, necessitating alternate means of binding product to consumers (not necessarily the laborers) or reconstructing bodies as consuming subjects. More flexible forms of production signal a shift in the corresponding mechanisms that regulate forms of accumulation or consumerism.

WHY QUEER? WHY FORDS?
WHAT IS THE GIRL TO DO?

> *I'm gonna drive you in queer cars*
>
> —2 nice girls

In case connections between Fords and Other bodies have been missed, I want to make links between my simplistic overview of Fordism/Post-Fordism to my analysis of post-al queer theory. To begin, I want to re-emphasize my topographical critique of mobility by reading Fords as bodies to re-articulate that transportation is not equally available to all. Mobility is always constrained by sets of social, political, and economic relations. As Hammonds points out, discourses on/of queerness are still facilitated by metaphorical relationships to Whiteness. Forms of transportation, whether material, epistemological, or sexual, are produced and facilitated by Others. Fords and post-al queer theory, or other pieces of discursive or material technology, are meaningful in particular sets of social, political, and economic spheres. These technological apparatuses (to appropriate de Lauretis's assessment of gender) shape and influence the spheres in which they operate, but they do not exist independently from these preexisting sets of relations. Neither the mass production of Fords nor post-al queer theory produces liberatory or more equitably accessible vehicles.

The relationship between Fordism and Post-Fordism is also significant to contemporary discourses on queerness/identity politics. The assumption in articulating that any state or body has moved from Fordism to Post-Fordism is that a significant shift has occurred: a radical disintegration of the means, mode, and mechanisms of production. However, does this signifier of *post* act as Zavarzadeh (1995) suggests, to create "a history without a middle" (p. 22)? As in postcolonialism or postmodernism, there is an implicit assumption of progress with the marker of post. Often contextual, historical, economic, and political factors that facilitated or profit from the marking of a post are obscured. Queer can serve the same function as post, implying a radical shift in the possibilities available for the means, modes, and mechanisms of sexualities, but these possibilities are only afforded to few. Whose mobility this theorizing facilitates is starkly highlighted when Eve's fall from Grace is juxtaposed next to less metaphorical constructions of sexual mobility, namely the sex-tourism trade. Following Patton's push to continue evaluating progressive political projects, I am asking what is the cost of this often-marked-as-progressive decentralization? Who benefits? Hennessy notes in her analysis of some American gay and lesbian positive workplaces that although these progressive practices and/or discourses allocate needed support and resources at the local level, they need to be evaluated more globally.

> Gay-friendly corporations like Levi Strauss, for example, re-inforce the gender flexible subjects their advertising campaigns promote through gay window-dressing strategies by way of public relations programs that boast of their progressive policies for lesbians and gays. Levi Strauss gives health insurance benefits to unmarried domestic partners of their employees, has created a supportive environment for employees who test HIV positive, and has a Lesbian and Gay Employees Association. . . . Levi Strauss closed its San Antonio plant in 1990, laying off 1,150 workers, 92% Latino and 86% of them women and moved its operations to the Caribbean where it can pay labourers $3.80 a day. . . . Displaying the gay-friendly politics of progressive US corporations often deflects attention from the exploitative international division of labour they depend on in the interest of company's bottom line—profits. (Hennessy, 1996, p. 175)

As Hennessy's example illustrates, corporations talk about progressive policies yet move to countries with more exploitable labor sources (humanware) and less environmental regulations.[16]

In addition, I fixate on Fordism and Post-Fordism because I see the construction of the relationships between products and workers, or consumers, as a key component to looking critically at post-al queer theory. As my Reader's Digest-summary of Post-Fordism illustrates, with any social practice or social shift, complex forms of scaffolding are required. The continued need for capital to produce commodifiable or consuming subjects necessitates complex and ever-morphing ways of manufacturing rela-

---

[16]Thanks to Jodi Jensen for informing me of the tensions that occurred in '91 when a boycott of Levi's products was structured in response to these relocations. The corporation had progressive policies and these policies, in some interpretations, enabled the corporation to retain a good public image throughout a boycott and perhaps functioned to weaken the boycott. Whether Levi Strauss Corporation intentionally orchestrated it or not, coalition work between marginalized groups (i.e., gays/lesbians and Latino workers) was difficult as these groups were placed against each other for resources (Jensen, personal communication, 1997).

tionships with consumers. As the example from Hennessy notes, the gender bending in advertising campaigns for Levi products is linked to the window-dressing PR campaigns about Levi's progressive corporate policies for gay and lesbian identities.[17] Whereas Fordism promoted heterosexual monogamy in the single body of laborer and consumer, the fragmentation of a static centre of production in Post-Fordism requires a corresponding fragmentation and fluidity in the seperate body of the laborer and the consumer. Trying not to reduce this analysis to pure economic determinism, I ask, is the fluid queer subject posited by some queer theorists "the model consuming subject for the regime of late capitalism" (Morton, 1995, p. 194)? Whereas most theorizing with queer theory is focused on the identity disruptions and identificatory dis-locations that post-al interpretations of queerness can offer, I want my framework of Fordism/Post-Fordism to query these questions to ask, what larger ideological and economic shifts does queer theory serve? Is the post-al production of a consuming queer subject a form of scaffolding?

Morton (1995) articulates a response to this question, illustrating that these fluid mobile bodies work well within fluid capital:

> Queer it is often argued, refers to a space of utter flexibility and fluidity that includes all kinds of differences (homosexuals, bisexuals, transsexuals, . . .) not the space of a particular difference. . . . Ultimately the queer subject is not also a specifically sexed, raced, gendered . . . subject but the subject of sensation. . . . Queer theorists urge the subject to "affirm" and celebrate it own "shiftingness" as a form of "self deconstruction" which is a form of performative "self invention." . . . this newly celebrated fluidity is nothing more than a new level of adaptability to late capitalisms shifting exchange values. (p. 196)

Both Hennessy and Morton strongly link post-al queer theorizing to late Western industrialized capital (or loosely what I am referring to in this paper as Post-Fordism), and posit this theorizing as a form of neoconservativism. Post-al queerness aids in the production of the perfect commodifiable subject: a consuming, desiring machine.

Although I find aspects of this analysis convincing, I do not want to reduce my analysis of post-al queer theory to a fragmentation that Morton seems to resort to in his work. To posit post-al queer theorizing as fodder for late capitals cannon is simplistic, and this kind of neo-marxist economic determinism negates other equally valid critiques of whose mobility this theorizing can serve, such as colonial ideologies or misogynist paradigms. However, I highlight and salvage parts of this conception of the ways in

---

[17]Also think of the progressive politics of the Body Shop, which are forefronted while the cosmetics industry still promotes very specific versions of White femininity; the colorful White androgyny in the advertising of GAP, Bennetton, etc. See Perkins (1996).

which capital in part produces, manages, and maintains commodifiable subjects. Perspectives on post-al queer theorizing, such as Hennessy (1996) and Morton (1995) offer, are not sexy and are often ignored or inserted as a small qualifier by post-al scholars. In my interpretation, a dismissal or ignorance of the relationships between capital and identities, or how visibility is always achieved at a price, weakens any theorizing on queer nations, queerness, or queer bodies. "What is the consequence of a theory that does not allow this kind of question?" (Hennessey, 1996, p. 153).

As I have tried to address in this discussion, most post-al queer theorizing does not, as Patton suggests queery social theory. An understanding of the production of scaffolding, merging aspects of psychoanalysis, marxism, and post-al theorizing can be an effective combination to queery social theory rather than posit a modifier of queerness. A fusion of these differing intellectual perspectives can offer a more global perspective and pose important pedagogical questions to progressive left theorists interesting in coalition work that queeries social theory, such as: What does it mean for specific bodies to mourn for reified mechanisms of (hetero)sexuality that fostered sets of social, cultural and economic institutions?; What would a socially responsible form of collective mourning entail that could lead to the opening up of differing sets of possibilities of identifications, identity positionings, and social relations?; How should one acknowledge and situate these processes globally, economically, and in conjunction to other sets of identity positionings and identity relations?

These questions exist in conjunction to evaluations of who benefits from progressive discourses and why, and ongoing longer-term assessments of how, why, and where identifications function and identities are re/de/formed. The tenacious analogy in this chapter about identities as always being mediated—Eve is always, as natural as a Ford—is intended to highlight the necessity of persistent work evaluating, as the previously cited works by Hammond and Patton point to, the goals and the spaces of theoretical moves.

More essentially, to return to the fading heroine, what can this deconstruction of queerness offer to her ontological quandaries? I suggest to Eve that a modifier of Post-Fordist is more applicable than queer. But, would a more fruitful exercise, Eve's way out (so to speak) be to persuade her that in fact, there is no out or in—only in context; that states of grace are always bound: culturally, socially, economically, politically?

A 'POST' (ON) SCRIPTS

So Eve called me a few weeks ago to go for dinner with her new date. What's his name—Bob, Dave, Doug, no Adam—that's it. We go to a drive-in restaurant.

Adam—well, he's okay, no sense of humor and fairly uptight. He's a farmer, drives a Ford truck, for Christ's sake. We chat and I am asking him about the harvest and planting because it seems to keep the conversation flowing, when out of nowhere this lady pulls up beside us in a convertible with the top down. She leans over and starts talking to us. Adam's face is shifting colors—he looks about ready to explode. He tells this lady to leave and that she isn't invited and she just smiles at him. She introduces herself as Lilith and sets her tractor beam on Eve. I am wishing I'd worn some sexier clothes. Eve is hanging out the passenger window and Lilith is chatting up Eve. It seems she and Eve have a lot in common, after all this is a small town. They've both been with Grace.

So right before the apple pie a la mode, Eve gets out of Adam's car and gets in beside Lilith. Eve says she will be back soon, and that she just wants to take a spin in a faster car.

ACKNOWLEDGMENTS

The author acknowledges the varied feedback from: Celia Haig Brown, Suzanne de Castell, Kate Eichhorn, Fransisco Ibañez-Carrasco, Jodi Jensen, and Laurie Fuller. Despite these contributions, all errors of fact or fiction, are mine.

REFERENCES

Abelove, H., Barale, M., & Halperin, D. (Eds.). (1993). *The lesbian and gay studies reader.* New York: Routledge.

Allison, D. (1995). *Skin: Talking about sex, class and literature.* New York: Dutton.

Bannerji, H. (Ed.). (1993). *Returning the gaze: Essays on racism, feminism, and politics.* Toronto: Sister Vision Press.

Boundas, C., & Olkowski, D. (Eds.). (1994). *Gilles Deleuze and the theatre of philosophy.* New York: Routledge.

Burger, P. (1984). *Theory of the avant-garde.* (Trans. Michael Shaw). Minneapolis: University of Minnesota Press.

Connell, R. (1996). Democracies of pleasure: Thoughts on the goals of radical sexual politics. In S. Seidman & L. Nicholson (Eds.), *Social postmodernisms: Beyond identity politics* (pp. 384–397). New York: Cambridge University Press.

de Certeau, M. (1984). *The practice of everyday life.* Berkeley: The University of California Press.

de Lauretis, T. (1991). Queer theory: Lesbian and gay sexualities: An introduction. *differences: A Journal of Feminist Cultural Studies, 3,* iii–xviii.

Deleuze, G. (1989). *Masochism.* New York: Zone Books.

Filipenko, C. (1997, March). Sexual purity. *the buzz,* p. 7.

Foucault, M. (1977). *Language, counter-memory, practice.* Ithaca, NY: Cornell University Press.

Frye, M. (1983). *The politics of reality: Essays in feminist theory.* New York: The Crossing Press.

Fuller, L. (1996). *Disrupting whiteness: Race, queerness and pedagogy*. Unpublished doctoral dissertation, University of Madison–Wisconsin.

Gramsci, A. (1971). Americanism and Fordism. In Q. Hoare & G. N. Smith (Eds. & Trans.), *Selections from the prison notebooks*. New York: International Publishers.

Hammonds, E. (1991). Black (w)holes and the geometry of Black female sexuality. *differences: A Journal of Feminist Cultural Studies, 3*, 126–144.

Harvey, D. (1989). *The condition of postmodernity: An enquiry into origins of cultural change*. New York: Oxford University Press.

Hennessy, R. (1996). Queer visibility in a commodity culture. In S. Seidman & L. Nicholson (Eds.), *Social postmodernisms* (pp. 142–186). New York: Cambridge University Press.

hooks, b. (1992). *Black looks: Race and representation*. Boston: South End Press.

Ibañez-Carrasco, F. (1993, April). *An ethnographic cross-cultural exploration of the translations between official safe sex discourse and lived experiences of men who have sex with men*. Unpublished masters' thesis, Simon Fraser University.

Johnston, R. J., Gregory, D., & Smith, D. (Eds.). (1994). *Dictionary of human geography* (3rd ed.). Cambridge, England: Blackwell.

Kelly, M. (1994). *Critique and power: Recasting the Foucault Habermas debate*. Cambridge, MA: MIT Press.

Lather, P. (1991). *Getting smart*. New York: Routledge.

Lorde, A. (1982a). *Sister outsider*. Freedom, CA: The Crossing Press.

Lorde, A. (1982b). *Zami: A new spelling of my name*. Freedom, CA: The Crossing Press.

Luinenburg, O. (1994). *Lesbians and safer sex discourses: Identity barriers, fluid practices*. Unpublished master's thesis, Simon Fraser University.

Martin, E. (1994). *Flexible bodies: The role of immunology in American culture from the days of polio to the age of AIDS*. Boston: Beacon Press.

Morrison, T. (1993). *The bluest eye*. New York: Penguin.

Morton, D. (1995). Queerity and ludic sado-masochism: Compulsory consumption and the emerging post-al queer. In Zazarzadeh, Ebert, and Morton (Eds.), *Post-ality: Marxism and postmodernism* (pp. 189–215). Washington, DC: Maisonneuve Press.

Morton, D. (1996). Changing the terms. In D. Morton (Ed.), *The material queer* (pp. 1–34). New York: Westview Press.

Pallotta-Chiarolli, M. (1996/1997, Summer). To be, or not, or both, or neither. *Screaming Hyena, 8*, 25.

Patton, C. (1996). Refiguring social space. In Seidman and Nicholson (Eds.), *Social postmodernisms: Beyond identity politics* (pp. 216–249). New York: Cambridge University Press.

Perkins, C. (1996). *"Any more colorful and we'd have to censor it": speaking of "race," subjectivity, and institutionalized violations*. Burnaby: The Production House.

Pile, S., & Thrift, N. (Eds.). (1995). *Mapping the subject: Geographies of cultural transformation*. New York: Routledge.

Probyn, E. (1995). The politics of departure. In E. Probyn & E. Grosz (Eds.), *Sexy bodies: The strange carnalities of feminism* (pp. 1–18). New York: Routledge.

Probyn, E. (1996). *Outside belongings*. New York: Routledge.

Sedgwick, E. (1993). *Tendencies*. Durham, NC: Duke University Press.

Smith, D. (1990). *The conceptual practices of power: A feminist sociology of knowledge*. Toronto: University of Toronto Press.

Smukler, L. (1994). *Normal sex*. New York: Firebrand Books.

Tsing, A. L. (1995). *In the realm of the diamond queen: Marginality in an out-of-the-way place*. Princeton, NJ: Princeton University Press.

Walker, C. B. (1991). *Fragmentation and redemption*. New York: Zone Books.

Warner, M. (Ed.). (1993). *Fear of a queer planet: Queer politics and social theory*. Minneapolis: University of Minnesota Press.

Yanerella, & Reid (1996). From trained "gorilla" to "humanware": Repoliticizing the body–machine complex between fordism and post-fordism. In Natter & Schutzki (Eds.), *The social and political body* (pp. 181–219). New York: Guilford.

Zavarzadeh, M. (1995). Post-Ality: The (Dis)Simulations of cybercapitalism. In E. Zavarzadeh & D. Morton (Eds.), *Post-ality: Marxism and postmodernism* (pp. 2–75). Washington, DC: Maisonneuve Press.

Chapter 5

Queering/Querying Pedagogy? Or, Pedagogy Is a Pretty Queer Thing

Susanne Luhmann
York University

How can one imagine a queer pedagogy? As of yet, it is unclear what such a pedagogy might look like or for whom this queer pedagogy would be. What would be its ambitions, and where would it take place? Is a queer pedagogy about and for queer students or queer teachers? Is a queer pedagogy a question of queer curriculum? Or, is it about teaching methods adequate for queer content? Or, about queer learning and teaching—and what would that mean? Moreover, is a queer pedagogy to become the house pedagogy of queer studies or is it about the queering of pedagogical theory?

In this chapter, I approach some of these questions, first by examining what queer theory offers to pedagogies that wish for emancipatory teaching and learning practices, and second, by thinking through the pedagogy of queer theory. The pedagogy at work is one where the desire for knowledge interferes with the repetition of both heterosexual and lesbian/gay normalization. By way of exploring what queer theory and pedagogy have to offer, I suggest that a queer pedagogy exceeds the incorporation of queer content into curricula and the worry over finding teaching strategies that make this content more palatable to students. I also suggest a queer pedagogy that draws on pedagogy's curiosity toward the social relations made possible in the process of learning and on queer critiques of identity-based knowledges. Finally, I consider how a post-identity pedagogy becomes thinkable.

With the dual suggestions that queer theory always assumes a pedagogy and that pedagogy is a pretty queer thing, consider the terms *pedagogy* and *queer.* Both suffer a reputation and are reminiscent of older slanderous meanings. Better known than the term *pedagogy*, the *pedagogue* connotes, rather unflatteringly, the pedantic and dogmatic schoolteacher. *Queer*, used homophobically, is meant to shame people as strange and to position them as unintelligible within the discursive framework of heteronormative gender dichotomies and binary sexualities. Both queer and pedagogy—though from different social positions—are marked by repudiation. Recently, however, both have been refurbished to serve critical functions. Pedagogy, when attached to signifiers such as *feminist, anti-racist, radical,* or *anti-homophobic,* is critical of mainstream education as a site for the reproduction of unequal power relations. Similarly, queer turns critically against the practices of normalization at stake in the study of sexuality. At the same time, both terms are under threat from their earlier reputations, and they share the common fate of reduction—of being rendered superfluous, and not taken seriously. Even in their more recent usage as critical terms, both queer and pedagogy run risk of serving as little more than convenient terminological abbreviations that suffer from over-determination and under-definition. For example, even teachers dedicated to critical pedagogy when speaking about their pedagogy might refer to little else than their teaching style, their classroom conduct, or their preferred teaching methods. In similar fashion, even in queer circles queer is often used as a mere alternative, or more convenient short-form to the lengthy "lesbian, gay, bisexual, transgendered, and transsexual."

There may, however, be more substantial issues at stake in the desires of radical pedagogies and queer theories. In spite of their intentions to serve as forms of critical or subversive intervention in oppressive classroom relations, heteronormative sexualities and gender regimes, respectively, with their confident claims of subversion and provocative interference with the production of normalcy, risk overlooking the normalization at stake in their own practices. Although the direction of my argument is to think about interventions in normalcy, I have grown more cautious, and now worry about the limits of subversive practices. Accordingly, I suggest that a queer pedagogy must learn to be self-reflective of its own limitations.

QUEERING PEDAGOGY: OR, WHAT HAPPENS WHEN QUEER THEORY IS BROUGHT TO BEAR ON PEDAGOGY?

Immense moral panics erupt over the discovery that lesbians and gays educate our children. Intense, sometimes even violent, contestations occur over the curricular inclusion of the study of sexuality in general, and of lesbian and gay content in particular. For many, this is at once evidence of the repressed state of sexuality within the realm of education and of the marginalization of lesbian, gay, and bisexual subjects in the classroom. If the topic of sexuality is repressed and the problem is marginalization, then the scarcity of material that engages the issues of sexuality in the discussion of education in general, and of pedagogy specifically, is unsurprising. Writings concerned with the experience of being queer in the classroom do the important work of documenting the injurious effects that heterosexism and homophobic discourse and practices have on non-straight teachers and students alike (Epstein, 1994; Harbeck, 1992; Khayatt, 1992). As engaged critiques of heterosexual solipsism and privilege, these writings give emphatic testimonial to the alienating and discriminatory experiences within the educational system; these texts challenge the inequality, invisibility, and marginalization of lesbian and gay subjects and call for representational equality. Citing the injurious effects of representational absence, lesbian and gay content is figured as a remedy against homophobia and a prerequisite for the self-esteem and safe existence of queers in the classroom.

This approach is grounded in a set of assumptions common to lesbian and gay politics that follow from the notion that homophobia is little more than a problem of representation, an effect of lacking or distorted images of lesbians and gays. Many view the solution as learning to protest the portrayals of lesbians and gays as sick, sexually perverted, unhappy, and antisocial. Against erasure or distortion, the mainstream lesbian and gay strategy demands accurate—meaning positive—representations of lesbian and gay life. Here, two implicit assumptions about learning are at work. One targets the learning of heterosexuals. This story of learning sees homophobia as a problem of ignorance, of not knowing any lesbian and gay folks. According to the proponents of lesbian and gay inclusion, with representation comes knowledge, with learning about lesbians and gays comes the realization of the latter's normalcy, and finally a happy end to discrimination. According to another story of learning, which worries about queer classroom audiences, even if homophobia cannot be eradicated through the curricular representations, at least such images offer role models and self-esteem to lesbian and gay students.[1]

Critics identify this demand for equal cultural and political representation with assimilationist politics. Such a strategy, according to its critics, looks to expand the definition of *normal* to include lesbians and gays, rather than attacking and undermining the very processes by which (some)

---

[1]However, what counts as accurate representation and who qualifies as a positive role model is highly contested within lesbian and gay communities, to which the reoccurring controversies over lesbian characters in cinematic productions or the visibility of particular sexual constituencies in public gay pride events testify.

subjects become normalized and others marginalized.[2] In difference to the repressive hypothesis of sexuality[3] and to strategies that focus on the goal to overcome lesbian and gay marginalization, queer theories and practices refuse to see gay sexualities as purely marginal or even repressed by an overbearing stable heterosexuality. Instead, queer theorists insist that the homo/hetero opposition is central to Western societies and constitutive of Western culture, modes of thinking, and concepts of the modern self. Hence, Sedgwick's (1990) critique that "an understanding of virtually any aspect of modern Western culture must be, not merely incomplete, but damaged in its central substance to the degree that it does not incorporate a critical analysis of modern homo/heterosexual definition" (p. 1). The queer insistence is that non-straight sexualities are simultaneously marginal and central, and that heterosexuality exists in an epistemic symbiosis with homosexuality.

In the introduction to *Inside/Out. Lesbian Theories Gay Theories*, Diana Fuss (1991) describes binary distinctions such as hetero–homo and inside–outside as indispensable figures for meaning making. Only through a drawing of (identity) borders do both self and other come into being. Thus, difference is the necessary condition for identity. As Michel Foucault (1978/1990) argued in his *History of Sexuality*, the making of the bourgeois self relies on the heterosexual/homosexual binary. Only homosexuality as an "indispensable interior exclusion" (Fuss, 1991, p. 3) makes the articulation of heterosexuality possible. Heterosexuality only becomes intelligible through the difference to its other—homosexuality. At the same time, it is always threatened in its epistemic arrogance by the latter. Thus the relations between hetero and homo are irresolvably unstable. Their definitional interdependence poses a threat to heterosexuality's distinctness. Heterosexuality recuperates itself from this threat of collapsing into homosexuality through various forms of normalization ranging from violence such as gay bashing, to insistence on social and legal inequality, to gestures of toleration of lesbians and gays as "different but equal." These normalizations restrain the potentially disruptive force that homosexuality poses. Sedgwick (1990) alerts us to the inherent contradiction that underlies this

---

[2]Symptomatic of this strategy is a sole focus on lesbians and gays; more unruly sexual/gendered identities such as bisexual, transgendered, intersexual, and transsexual rarely figure in equal rights politics. Neither have they made it into the pedagogy literature. For example, Linda Garber (1994) in her introduction to *Tilting the Tower. Lesbians Teaching Queer Subjects* does nothing but acknowledge the absence of queer subjects in excess of lesbian and gay. Thus, the reduction of queer to a short-form for lesbian and gay points to more than a terminological glitch.

[3]In the *History of Sexuality*, Foucault (1978/1990) makes the important claim that, contrary to common assumption, sexual matters were not repressed in the 19th century in the West. Instead, Foucault argues that this period witnessed a "discursive explosion" (p. 17) covering all aspects of sexuality, thereby producing sexuality as we know it today.

structure: on the one hand, homosexuality and heterosexuality are supposed to be inherently different; on the other hand, the former is configured as a corruptive force that threatens the latter.

Queer, as a term, signals not only the disruption of the binary of heterosexual normalcy on the one hand and homosexual defiance on the
other, but desires "to bring the hetero/homo opposition to the point of
collapse" (Fuss, 1991, p. 1). But how does the subversion of such central
strategies of normalization become possible? The most visible disruption
comes perhaps in the form of queer sexual street activism and queer
self-fashioning, the proliferation of queer sexual practices and identities
that seek to transgress and subvert heteronormative sex/gender dichotomies. The rebellious queer avant garde of sexual outlaws and perverts,
bisexual, intersexed, transgendered, transvestite, pre/post-op transsexual
(female to male, male to female), to name just a few, has produced a
strange array of queer identities and identifications. These take to task the
normalizing demands for stable and binary gender identities and sexual
object choices central to the dominant heterosexual order. Instead, queer
aims to spoil and transgress coherent (and essential) gender configurations
and the desire for a neat arrangement of dichotomous sexual and gendered
difference, central to both heterosexual and homosexual identities.[4] But
beyond suggesting gender fluidity, queer theory also insists on the complications of the two: without gender, sexuality is nothing.

The unsettling implications of queer theories not only threaten the
notion of (heterosexual) normalcy but also demand a self-reflexivity of
lesbian and gay theories. This demand disturbs fragile formulations of
lesbian and gay self certainty and, therefore, it is frequently rebuked.[5] De

---

[4]If heterosexuality commonly assumes a congruence among a sexed body, its gender
identity, and its (different sex) object choice, homosexuality's only variation is that the object
choice is same sex. Thus both heterosexuality and homosexuality build on clearly identifiable
sex/gender systems. Even narratives that explicitly target the system of compulsory
heterosexuality may not question, but reinforce, congruencies and stabilities of bodies and
genders. For example, the radical feminist concept of the woman-loving-woman posed female
same-sex relations as the epitome of femaleness (analogously, gay male desire was understood
as the clearest expression of maleness; Rich, 1980; Sedgwick, 1990).

[5]The frequent charge that queer elides lesbians and/or feminism can serve as an example
here (Case, 1995; Jeffreys, 1994; Zita, 1994). However, de Lauretis (1991) rightly observes
that the threat to lesbian is not prevented in the mantra of "lesbian and gay," which, although
naming the differences, might evacuate them as taken for granted. Contrary to the fears that
lesbian is under the siege of queer, in recent years publications in the field of lesbian studies
have been burgeoning (see, e.g., Hart, 1993; de Lauretis, 1991; Doan, 1994; Jagose, 1994;
Martindale, 1997; Meese, 1992; Roof, 1991). This seems to suggest that, rather than making
lesbian scholarship obsolete, queer and lesbian coexist and facilitate each other. Queer
unsettles and questions the genderedness of sexuality, whereas lesbian inquires into its
gendered specificity (de Lauretis, 1991). Queer seems not so much to threaten lesbian theory;
however, its relationship to feminism is conflicted. See Martin (1994) for a lucid critique of

Lauretis (1991) writes: "Queer theory conveys a double emphasis—on the conceptual and speculative work involved in discourse production, and on the necessary critical work of deconstructing our own discourses and their constructed silences" (p. iv). Queer theory's productivity lies in this double impulse of production and deconstruction, in its "both . . . and" structure. Queer theory antagonizes identity while at the same time claiming in-your-face visibility (de Lauretis, 1991). And, when posed as a pedagogy, beyond suggesting the limitations of transformation of content, of queering curriculum, the questions asked here render suspect the very basics of pedagogy and its appeal to rational subjects capable of toleration or consolation through accurate representations.

The queer insistence on undermining idyllic stabilities of normalcy might be an important point of entry from which to employ queer theory for thinking through a queer pedagogy. Beyond proudly reclaiming a marginal space, against merely adding authentic or likable portrayals of lesbian/gay icons to an otherwise straight—and already overcrowded—curriculum, against claiming normalcy for lesbians and gays, queer theory looks at the process of subject formation (ironically) by asking: How do normalcy and abnormalcy become assigned subject positions? How can they be subverted? How can the very notion of a unified human subject be parodied and, jointly with other discourses, radically deconstructed into a fluid, permanently shifting, and unintelligible subjectivity? Queer contests authority and hopes to resist ideological appropriation. It transgresses the boundaries between queer and straight, partly by deciphering queer content and subtexts in ostensibly straight narratives, partly by pointing to the overlap between heterosexual and homosexual practices.

With the difficult suggestion that knowable subjects are merely another form of subjection to normalization, queer shatters the hopes associated with representational inclusion of lesbians and gays in curricula as a viable strategy against homophobia or as a strategy of subversion. "Subversiveness" in the words of Judith Butler (1993) "is the kind of effect that *resists calculation*" (p. 20). Something is potentially subversive when reading or understanding is rendered impossible. "Subversive practices have to over-

---

how feminism gets constructed as anachronistic in queer theory. Moreover, a queer claim to being the nexus of difference might prove problematic. In this claim, queer supersedes the dissection into artificially distinct identities. Instead, queer is supposed to speak to the fluidity and interconnectedness of race, gender, and class, of sexual practices and bodies. But queer practices have yet to live up to claims such as the following, which understands queer as the mark of an "oxymoronic community of difference [able] to teach the world how to get along" (Sloan in Duggan, 1992, p. 19). Although queer theory has the potential to theorize these important interconnections, future scholarship will have to deliver more than a declaration of intent. (See *The Lesbian and Gay Studies Reader* for theorizations of the intersection of race and sexuality; also Abou-Rihan, 1994; McClintock, 1995; Ross, 1994).

whelm the capacity to read, challenge conventions of reading, and demand new possibilities of reading" (Butler, 1993, p. 20). Subversiveness, rather than being an easily identifiable counter-knowledge, lies in the very moment of unintelligibility, or in the absence of knowledge. If subversiveness is not a new form of knowledge but lies in the capacity to raise questions about the detours of coming to know and making sense, then what does this mean for a pedagogy that imagines itself as queer? Can a queer pedagogy resist the desire for authority and stable knowledge; can it resist disseminating new knowledge and new forms of subjection? What if a queer pedagogy puts into crisis what is known and how we come to know?

QUERYING PEDAGOGY

The hope for lesbian/gay content as a remedy against homophobia is also thrown into relief by experiences within queer studies: Even in designated queer studies classrooms heterosexism and homophobia reemerge and threaten to overwhelm queer subjects, as Mary Bryson and Suzanne de Castell (1993) teach us in "Queer Pedagogy: Praxis Makes Im/Perfect." Neither an explicit ethic of anti-homophobia nor goals such as the exploration of queer subjects can ensure the classroom as a safe space for queer students or teachers.

In the face of homophobic resistance to a queer curriculum, the call for queer pedagogy as a method adequate for queer content emerges.[6] I suggest that the call for lesbian and gay material, as well as for methods of instruction appropriate for queer content, is reflective of wishful assumptions about pedagogy, about what pedagogy is and what pedagogy can do.

Pedagogy has often been understood as referring to teaching methodology or instruction (the "how-to" of teaching). More recently, flagged by signifiers such as *feminist, radical,* and *anti-racist,* pedagogy has been highly critical of mainstream education and of its tendency to reproduce racial, gendered, and class-based power relations in its institutions, ideologies, and practices. Common to what has been referred to variously as radical or critical approaches to pedagogy is the desire to intervene in the reproduction of power dynamics and to make education part of a process of political empowerment and liberation of students. Central to this work has been a focus on both curricular and instructional changes that aim toward more inclusive learning environments by way of transforming the discursive frameworks of curricula and the structures of social interactions within classrooms.

---

[6]This is not the direction of Bryson and de Castell's argument; instead they are skeptical of the -deconstructive approach toward lesbian identities suggested by queer/postmodern theories.

The concept of pedagogy at stake in my argument, although sympathetic to these goals, takes a different turn. Instead of focusing on the common concerns of teaching, such as what should be learned and how to teach this knowledge, pedagogy might begin with the question of how we come to know and how knowledge is produced in the interaction between teacher/text and student. This orientation to pedagogy exceeds education's traditional fixation on knowledge transmission, and its wish for the teacher as the master of knowledge. The teacher–student relationship at the heart of the transmission model of learning reminds Jane Gallop (1982) of pederasty, where "[a] greater man penetrates a lesser man with his knowledge" (p. 63).

Although few progressive educators today would agree with such a transmission model of learning and teaching, I suggest that it returns like the repressed in the prevalent preoccupation of teachers with methods, or the how-to of teaching. The rationale behind this search for an adequate method is that the teacher's pedagogical skills—her instructional talents, as well as behaviors—will reflect in the students' progress of learning. Learning then is relegated to the teacher's effort and to good teaching, an assumption that gives way to some (fantasmatic) investments in the role of the teacher in the learning process.

To think about learning primarily as a problem of instructional techniques is surely preferable to seeing learning as a problem solely of the intellectual (or moral) capacities of the student. But both approaches to learning—as limited only by either students' or teachers' capabilities—are still invested in a notion that knowledge and its transmission can, and should, be mastered. Such a story is strangely reminiscent of the dynamics of gender and sexuality disrupted by queer theory. It is precisely in this wish to master that meaning must break down.

As an alternative to the worry over strategies for effective knowledge transmission that reduce knowledge to mere information and students to rational but passive beings untroubled by the material studied, pedagogy might be posed as a question (as opposed to the answer) of knowledge: What does being taught, what does knowledge do to students? How does knowledge become understood in the relationship between teacher/text and student (Lusted, 1986)? The shift is one of pedagogic curiosity, from what (and how) the author writes or the teacher teaches, to what the student understands, or what the reader reads. Accordingly, pedagogy then begins to shift from transmission strategies to an inquiry into the conditions for understanding, or refusing, knowledge (Felman, 1987; Lusted, 1986). Hence, Felman's (1987) suggestion that "teaching is . . . not the transmission of ready-made knowledge. It is rather the creation of a new condition of knowledge, the creation of an original learning disposition" (p. 80).

Such an approach, rather than assuming the student as ignorant or lacking knowledge, inquires into, for example, how textual positions are being taken up by the reading or learning subject. This inquiry is made more difficult in its refusal to assume that these positions are determined solely by the text, or by what is taught. Instead, Walkerdine (1990), for example, reminds us that textual positions are "not just grafted on to a cognate and waiting subject, who can easily be changed. Rather, the positions and relations created in the text . . . relate to existing social and psychic struggle and provide a fantasy vehicle which inserts the reader into the text" (p. 89). The questions thus become: How does the reader insert herself into the text? What kind of identifications are at stake in this process? What structures these identifications? How do identifications become possible, what prevents them, and ultimately, makes learning (im)possible?[7]

Moreover, an attention to what students hear or read takes a new interest in the refusal to understand. Understanding all learning as remembering and recollecting, Felman (1987) pointed out that ignorance, or forgetting, is tied to repression, as "the imperative to forget. . . . Ignorance . . . is not a passive state of absence, a simple lack of information: it is an active dynamic of negation, an active refusal of information" (p. 79). Rather than posing ignorance and knowledge in an exclusionary opposition, in psychoanalytic thinking, ignorance constitutes knowledge. Ignorance is not the opposite to knowledge but an opposition to knowing. Instead of a lack of information, ignorance is a form of psychic resistance, a desire not to know, which perhaps can be described as a position of "I do not want to learn anything else, because I already know too much." Teaching, so Fel-

---

[7]Here I am not arguing that we do not need diverse representations, nor do I justify exclusive curricula. I only want to suggest the limitations of representational strategies. The argument of the interminable instability of reading practices is lent support from a variety of vantage points. For one, the historical absence of lesbian, gay, and bisexual images in mainstream cinematic productions has, at least for some viewers, led to reading practices by which queer subtexts are inserted or actively produced in the viewing of seemingly heterosexual film narratives. Secondly, even the most palatable portrayals of lesbians and gays that clearly play to heteronormative sensibilities, at times fail to find tolerance and acceptance in heterosexual audiences. This suggests the susceptibility of any kind of representation to a multiplicity of possible readings, ranging from the antagonistic to the empathetic. Considering the instability of reading practices less as danger than as potential has a variety of implications. It suggests moving from a primary concern with curriculum (i.e., accurate representations) to an interest in reading practices. How do we insert ourselves in the text? What positions do we refuse? Which ones are desirable? What I am suggesting along with Britzman (1995) is a proliferation of possible identifications rather than shutting down sites of identification. (See Martin's [1996] "The Hobo, the Fairy and the Quarterback" for a wonderful example of a reading practice that traces structures of identification.)

man concludes, is engaging with these resistances to knowledge more so than correcting a lack of knowledge. Contrary to a traditional assumption of a passion for knowledge, Felman (1987) suggests that pedagogy reckons with the "passion for ignorance" and she poses the curious question: "what can ignorance tell us?" (p. 79). In this question, the desire for ignorance is performative rather than cognitive. It is indicative of the incapacity—or the unwillingness—to acknowledge one's own implication in the material studied. Rather than assuming that the information studied does not pose a problem to the student, questions to ask are: What does this information do to one's own sense of self? What does the knowledge ask me to reconsider about myself and the subject studied? Similarly, Alice Pitt (1995) points out: "Learning about content is not the same thing as learning from it. In other words . . . learning is something more than a series of encounters with knowledge; learning entails, rather, the messier and less predictable process of becoming implicated in knowledge" (p. 298).

These questions of implication (similar to the implication of the homo/hetero divide posed by queer theory) raise the difficulty that students might not be able to bear the implications of knowledge. (Perhaps more crucially, it asks of educators dedicated to radical or emancipatory pedagogies: can we bear the knowledge that students may not be able to bear what we want them to know?) This is more than a problem of addressing ignorance as an ideological disagreement or as residue of ideological blindness. To understand ignorance not as a lack of (political) consciousness but as a resistance to knowledge might allow teachers to become more curious about the question of resistance. Instead of dismissing the resisting student as ignorant, troublesome, or politically naive, we might begin to ask about the conditions and limits of knowledge, and of what one can bear to know. Where is the resistance to knowledge located? Where does a text stop making sense to the student? Where does the breakdown of meaning occur? (How) can the teacher work through the refusal to learning? What is there to learn from ignorance?

QUEER PEDAGOGY: INCITING THE (SOMETIMES REFUSED) SOCIALITY OF LEARNING

My discussion of pedagogy suggests ignorance and knowledge not as mutually exclusive but as implicated in and constitutive of each other. This move is comparable to how queer theory rethinks gender/sexual binaries. Both queer theory and pedagogy argue that the process of making (sense) of selves relies on binaries such as homo–hetero, ignorance–knowledge, learner–teacher, reader–writer, and so on. Queer theory and pedagogy place at stake the desire to deconstruct binaries central to Western modes of meaning making, learning, teaching, and doing politics. Both desire to subvert the processes of normalization. Thus queer theory and pedagogy, in difference to a repressive hypothesis of sexuality and power, suggest that the construction of the norm actually requires and depends on its abject other to become intelligible. The norm and its negated other are implicated and mutually constitutive of each other. Normalized identities such as straight and stable gender identities work through, invoke, produce, constitute, as well as refuse its other. Queer tries to interrupt these modes of making selves and making sense by refusing stable identities and by producing new identifications that lie outside binary models of gender and sexuality.

Hence, what is at stake in a queer pedagogy is not the application of queer theory (as a new knowledge) onto pedagogy, nor the application of pedagogy (as a new method) for the dissemination of queer theory and knowledge. Instead, at stake are the implications of queer theory and pedagogy for the messy processes of learning and teaching, reading and writing. Instead of posing (the right) knowledge as answer or solution, queer theory and the pedagogy I have outlined here pose knowledge as an interminable question.

Accordingly, a queer pedagogy looks with skepticism at the processes of how identities are constructed and, according to Britzman's (1995) essay "Is There a Queer Pedagogy? Or, Stop Reading Straight," becomes concerned with normalcy's immanent exclusions. If queer pedagogy, as Britzman suggests, is foremost concerned with a radical practice of deconstructing normalcy, then it is obviously not confined to teaching *as, for,* or *about* queer subject(s). Moreover, the refusal of *any* normalization, be it racist, sexist, or whatever, necessarily has to be part of the queer agenda. To return to de Lauretis' point, queer theory must persist in self-critiques and hence reflect on how normalization may also constitute lesbian and gay studies. Rather than exploring, presenting, and manifesting self-esteemed queer subjects, a queer pedagogy aims at the infinite proliferation of new identifications. In this way, learning becomes a process of risking the self, much like Foucault (1982) suggests: "the target . . . is not to discover what we are, but to refuse what we are" (p. 216). Still, the tricky question of how to engage in such self-critical practices without losing track of the wider practices of social injustices persists. Or, as Britzman (1995) poses the question, how can we "exceed such binary oppositions as the tolerant and the tolerated, the oppressed and oppressor yet still hold onto an analysis of social difference that can account for how dynamics of subordination and subjection work at the level of the historical, the structural, the epistemological, the conceptual, and the social, and the psychic?" (p. 164).

Mireille Rosello's equation of studying lesbian and gay material with learning a foreign language gets at some of the issues at stake for a pedagogy that is curious about the conditions of learning and how such learning might incite the proliferation of new identifications. Rosello's (1994) essay, " 'Get out of here!' Modern Queer Language in the 1990's," draws an odd—a queer?—parallel between teaching, or being a student of, lesbian and gay studies, and the experiences of learning another tongue. Inspired by a conference address that urged graduate students to come out of their disciplinary closets and listen to what others in other fields have to say, Rosello rethinks the process of coming out. Instead of the (repetitive) moment of public self-constitution by way of confessional truth-telling, coming out, in Rosello's terms, becomes a problem of dialogue. Rosello asks, "is it possible to imagine 'coming out' . . . as the form of *listening* that partakes in the learning of another, 'foreign' language?" (p. 154); is it possible to shift the attention from *speaking* one's identity, from one's declaration of *being gay*, to *listening* to someone *speaking* gay?

Rosello's shift of address from speaking one's identity (be it through curricular presentations or personal confessionals) to listening to or reading lesbian and gay writing, suggests a move from identity to dialogue. Her interest is in the dynamics at stake in the classroom, both in teaching queer studies and in speaking a foreign language.

Language instruction, Rosello argues, must assume rather than condemn students' ignorance and take into consideration the specific dynamics at stake, namely that students enter the class with different levels of knowledge. Some might have grown up bilingual or have been exposed to another language prior to formal instruction, or may be more flexible in acquiring another tongue. The interesting moment in classroom interaction occurs when these differences meet and their meanings require negotiation. Significantly, these skill differentials are less identity-bound than commonly assumed. Rosello suggests that the refusal of knowledge might be related to the "infantilizing process" that occurs at the moment when an adult learns another language (p. 155). If translated for queer teaching, students' ignorance or homophobia becomes grounded within the wider field of culture rather than tied to a student's sexual identity.

The language analogy[8] might be further productive in disentangling teaching and learning queer studies from the notion of identity, deconstructing both the normalcy and its difference without disavowing moments of identification. The process of language acquisition acknowledges that all languages are acquired, that there is no "natural" language, that a straight person can learn a gay idiom, and that gays speaking straight are bilingual, who, like "bilingual children of immigrants . . . can be both

---

[8]Rosello insists that she is not suggesting a linguistic replacement for the earlier ethnic model of gay identity; rather, she argues that her comparison works strictly as an analogy. For an ethnic model of gay identity, see Epstein, 1992.

alienated and empowered by their double origin" (Rosello, 1994, p. 160). By the same token, this analogy does not dismiss altogether hierarchical and political struggles over language and language instruction. Although languages are habitually taught by native speakers or by those with a native-like fluency, even native speakers are never a unified homogenous group. How a language is spoken varies greatly according to regional and geographically varying dialects.

According to Rosello, language instruction, much like teaching lesbian and gay material, has its most dangerous and powerful moment in the recognition of ignorance, or the students' refusal to see anything else but a superfluous language and an unimportant skill. Rosello's analogy of speaking and teaching gay avoids a judge-like mentality full of indignation about students' ignorance. Instead, it offers a new set questions: Why do some students acquire near-native fluency, whereas others never identify the value of learning another language? How does learning, speaking, and listening to a new language affect how one relates to one's mother tongue, one's own culture? Who do I become through listening to and speaking another language? How is this process a form of risking one's self, for example in the moment when I am neither understood nor understand what is being said? How does the self respond to this breakdown of mastery of self? What kind of defense mechanisms are elaborated? What does this other language foreclose, or open up? What is at stake in not understanding? Who can I become through speaking and listening to another language?

What becomes common to queer theory, pedagogy, and Rosello's language analogy, is the curiosity toward how subjects fashion themselves in the highly social processes of learning. The making of selves begins with an other—the other in the text, in speech, the teacher, the student. The queer pedagogy that I imagine engages students in a conversation about how textual positions are being taken up or refused, for example when reading lesbian and gay texts or when listening to somebody speaking gay. What happens to the self in this dialogue? What does the student actually hear and how does he or she respond to the text? Can queer teaching, rather than assuming and affirming identities, take on the problem of how identifications are made and refused in the process of learning?

Such queer pedagogy does not hold the promise of a successful remedy against homophobia, nor is it a cure for the lack of self-esteem. This pedagogy is not (just) about a different curriculum or new methods of instruction. It is an inquiry into the conditions that make learning possible or prevent learning. It suggests a conversation about what I can bear to know and what I refuse when I refuse certain identifications. What is at stake in this pedagogy is the deeply social or dialogic situation of subject formation, the processes of how we make ourselves through and against others. As an inquiry into those processes, my queer pedagogy is not very heroic. It does not position itself as a bulwark against oppression, it does not claim the high grounds of subversion but hopefully it encourages an ethical practice by studying the risks of normalization, the limits of its own practices, and the im/possibilities of (subversive) teaching and learning.

ACKNOWLEDGMENTS

Earlier versions of this chapter were presented at The Fifth Annual National Lesbian, Gay and Bisexual Graduate Students Conference at the University of Southern California, Los Angeles, in April 1995; The Canadian Lesbian and Gay Studies Conference at the Learned Societies Conference, Université du Québec, Montréal, in June 1995; and the Explorations Series of the Toronto Center for Lesbian and Gay Studies, in April 1996. The author thanks the following for insightful readings of the various drafts of this text as well as for invaluable editorial suggestions: Deborah Britzman, Sheila Cavanagh, Nadia Habib, Rose-Marie Kennedy, Alice Pitt, and especially Heather Cameron who read them all.

REFERENCES

Abou-Rihan, F. (1994). Queer marks/nomadic difference: Sexuality and the politics of race and ethnicity. *Canadian Review of Literature, 21*(1–2), 255–262.

Britzman, D. (1995). Is there a queer pedagogy? Or, stop reading straight! *Educational Theory, 45*(2), 151–165.

Bryson, M., & de Castell, S. (1993). Queer pedagogy makes im/perfect. *Canadian Journal of Education, 18*(3), 285–305.

Butler, J. (1993). Critically queer. *GLQ, 1*(1), 17–32.

Case, S. E. (1995, April). *Toward a butch-femme retro future.* Unpublished keynote address presented at the fifth annual national lesbian, gay, and bisexual graduate student conference, University of Southern California, Los Angeles.

de Lauretis, T. (1991). Queer theory: Lesbian and gay sexualities: An introduction. *differences, 3*(2), iii–xviii.

Doan, L. (Ed.). (1994). *The lesbian postmodern.* New York: Columbia University Press.

Duggan, L. (1992). Making it perfectly queer. *Socialist Review, 22,* 11–31.

Epstein, D. (1994). *Challenging lesbian and gay inequalities in education.* Philadelphia: Open University Press.

Epstein, S. (1992). Gay politics, ethnic identity: The limits of social constructionism. In E. Stein (Ed.), *Forms of desire: Sexual orientation and the social constructionist controversy* (pp. 239–293). New York: Routledge.

Felman, S. (1987). *Jacques Lacan and the adventure of insight. Psychoanalysis in contemporary culture.* Boston: Harvard University Press.

Foucault, M. (1978/1990). *The history of sexuality. Volume one: An introduction.* New York: Vintage Books.

Fuss, D. (1991). Inside/Out. In *InsideOut: Lesbian theories, gay theories* (pp. 1–13). New York: Routledge.

Garber, L. (Ed.). (1994). *Tilting the tower. Lesbians teaching queer subjects.* New York: Routledge.

Gallop, J. (1982). *The daughter's seduction: Feminism and psychoanalysis.* Ithaca, NY: Cornell University Press.

Harbeck, K. M. (Ed.). (1992). *Coming out of the classroom closet: Gay and lesbian students, classroom and curriculum.* New York: Harrington Park Press.

Hart, L. (1993). Identity and seduction: Lesbians in the mainstream. In L. Hart & P. Phelan (Eds.), *Acting out: Feminist performances* (pp. 119–140). Ann Arbor: University of Michigan Press.

Hart, L. (1994). *Fatal women. Lesbian sexuality and the mark of aggression.* Princeton, NJ: Princeton University Press.

Jagose, A. (1994). *Lesbian utopics.* New York: Routledge.

Jeffreys, S. (1994). The queer disappearance of lesbians: Sexuality in the academy. *Women's Studies International Forum, 17*(5), 459–472.

Khayatt, M. D. (1992). *Lesbian teachers: An invisible presence.* Albany: SUNY Press.

Lusted, D. (1986). Why pedagogy? *Screen, 27*(5), 2–14.

Martin, B. (1994). Sexualities without genders and other queer utopias. *diacritics, 24*(2–3), 104–121.

Martin, B. (1996). The hobo, the fairy, and the quarterback. In *Femininity played straight: The significance of being lesbian* (pp. 33–44). New York: Routledge.

Martindale, K. (1997). *Un/Popular culture: Lesbian writing after the sex wars.* Albany: State University of New York Press.

McClintock, A. (1995). *Imperial leather: Race, gender, and sexualities in the colonial contest.* New York: Routledge.

Meese, E. (1992). *(Sem)erotics. Theorizing lesbian: Writing.* New York: New York University Press.

Pitt, A. (1995). *Subjects in tension. Engaged resistance in the feminist classroom.* Unpublished doctoral dissertation. Ontario Institute for the Study of Education/University of Toronto, Toronto, Canada.

Rich, A. (1980). Compulsory heterosexuality and lesbian existence. *Signs: Journal of Women in Culture and Society, 5*(4), 631–640.

Roof, J. (1991). *A lure of knowledge. Lesbian sexuality and theory.* New York: Columbia University Press.

Rosello, M. (1994, March–June). "Get out of here!" Modern queer languages in the 1990s. *Canadian Review of Literature, 21*(1–2), 149–168.

Ross, M. S. (1994, March–June). Some glances at the black fag: Race, same-sex desire and cultural belonging. *Canadian Review of Literature, 21*(1–2), 193–214.

Sedgwick, E. K. (1990). *Epistemology of the closet.* Berkeley: University of California Press.

Walkerdine, V. (1990). *School girl fictions.* London: Verso.

Zita, J. (1994). Gay and lesbian studies: Yet another unhappy marriage? In L. Garber (Ed.), *Tilting the tower: Lesbians teaching queer subjects* (pp. 258–276). New York: Routledge.

Chapter 6

Queer Texts and Performativity: Zora, Rap, and Community

Rinaldo Walcott
York University

There is a curious tension that troubles the interminable relation between social justice and education and between knowledge and pedagogy. On the one hand, transformative pedagogies preoccupied with teaching about social injury and discrimination have taken these dynamics as the sum total of lived experiences. And yet, because people do not live their lives as stereotypes, their lives in this version are reduced to fighting these creations. Here, pedagogical efforts become a game of hide and seek: stereotypes are found and then reconstituted into role models. On the other hand, when pedagogies founded on role modeling are dominant, new tensions emerge. Whereas stereotypes are assumed to be capable of deconstruction, role models seem to take on a rather magical stability and then learning seems to be no problem for the learner.

However, for there to be learning there must be a problem. This chapter explores questions that unmoor the texts of pedagogy from foundational claims. I ask how the dynamics of popular culture, queer theory, and the instability of reading might open some questions into the dynamics of identification, community, and new desires. What does it mean to live with and in social difference? How do communities already complicate themselves in their willingness and in their failure to experiment with new forms of life?

To reconceptualize the work of living a life and engaging in the question of the social, I draw on textual examples that refuse to stabilize boundaries of identification and endorse demands for the proper body. What does it mean to live with social difference? The instability of identities and the resulting possibilities of a host of identificatory moments suggest more complex readings than social justice and corrective pedagogies often allow. Alexander Doty's (1993) notion of queer reading practices offers some commentary on reading beyond the assumed in the hope that something more of all our identities might be unleashed. Doty's notions of a queer reading and making texts queer bridge my readings of what might appear to be a number of disparate texts. I read Zora Neale Hurston's (1990) *Moses Man of the Mountain* alongside rap music and ideas concerning the question of community. The readings are done in an attempt to make more complicated the notion of Black community and to bring into discussion texts that often do not mingle. Interpretations of Blackness might be rendered suspect and dangerous in the contexts of education when the performative sign of Blackness is read as singular. Making texts queer points to the performative aspects of texts and bodies. Making texts queer reveals the act of identification, which in this context is always a verb—always in process.

Doty's notion of making things queer is elaborated in the context of Nathaniel Mackey's (1995) observations in "Other from Noun to Verb." Mackey argues that performativity in Black cultures is a concern with the constant *verbing* of art and life. Mackey's re-reading of LeRoi Jones (Amiri Baraka)[1] is important in that he is intent on demonstrating the continual rewriting and reinventing of various cultural forms in Black diasporic communities. Mackey's reading allows us to highlight actions that point to the performative as a method of living with instability and continual revision. Black performance studies, or in this sense the *verbing* of life, has much to offer discourses of education that attempt to undo the bad behaviors of what is loosely called the dominant culture.

Andrew Parker and Eve Kosofsky Sedgwick (1995) write: "But if a spatialized, postmodernist performative analysis like the present one can demonstrate any one thing, surely it is how contingent and how radically *heterogeneous*, as well as how contestable, must be the relations between any subject and any utterance" (p. 14). What Parker and Sedgwick suggest is the contingency of meaning as it moves across different spheres. To access that contingency and glean some sense from it, meaning has to be taken as embedded in various utterances that cannot and do not guarantee the revelation of any one historicity (Butler, 1993). What performative utterances offer are the traces of the various references, citations, and repetitions that constitute "dramatic and contingent constructions of meaning" (Butler, 1990, p. 136). The significance of contingent meanings resides in how they allow for better discussions of questions of community and freedom.

---

[1]See Jones (1963), *Blues People: The Negro Experience in White America and the Music that Developed from It*, in particular chapter 10, "Swing—From Verb to Noun."

Performativity signals and thus puts into public space crucial questions concerning both the limits and excesses of community. Harris (1990) makes this point central in his discussion and response to the *fatwa* placed on Salman Rushdie: "A love of Justice born of a voyage in space cannot be real until it gains cross-cultural resonance within a theatre of the creature where the ceremony of politics may perceive its obsessions undercut and transformed: a ceremony that so enacts, and re-enacts itself, that it *sees* within and through its own *blind* one-track logic and circumscription of history" (p. 11).

Harris posits that notions of community as sacred have become the grounds upon which freedom is impinged. When culture is conceptualized as something to be disturbed, the only positions offered are reverence and conservation. It is only through cross-cultural resonance(s) that any hope for justice might be possible at the dawn of the 21st century. But as we shall see, culture is not a sacred temple. Indeed, following Harris it is only through cross-cultural resonances that the possibility of something more is made evident. The recognition and highlighting of the act, the performance, the verbing of being becomes increasingly the element that must be addressed.

So what can the study of performativity reveal? What can ideas of performativity offer to educational research and theory? N-Trance, a rap group, did a version of the Bee Gees "Stayin' Alive." Alongside rap's danceability, the lyrics of the N-Trance version suggested a meaning of hypermasculinity, toughness, authenticity, and the staying power of rap as popular music. What is interesting about performance and performativity in relation to N-Trance's cover is that N-Trance used one of the songs or anthems of gay bars to reproduce authentic notions of hetero-masculinity. At stake here is "realness." In N-Trance's accompanying heteronormative video, the new meanings could not, however, jettison the queer traces that allowed for other kinds of readings and meanings of the song. N-Trance's version of "Stayin' Alive" has cross-cut both homo and hetero communities, with dance floors serving as evidence to the different readings and meanings of the song.

But much more is revealed in thinking through the performativity of music. Careful readings of N-Trance, the Bee Gees, and their respective publics can allow us to recognize that music and in particular, "Stayin' Alive" has always had cross-cultural resonances. We can refuse the idea that communities, identities, and identifications do not cross-cut each other. Recognizing that the audiences of disco were multiply constituted and derived much of their innovation from popular gay dance cultures (both Black and White; Currid, 1995) allows for understanding the different meanings of N-Trance's version of "Stayin' Alive." Those different readings help us address the problem of constituting discreet and stable concepts of community. N-Trance's version highlights the instability of community.

The cross-cutting resonances of popular culture have the potential to usher in new and hopeful communities of difference premised on the identifications that audiences make. By excavating the connections between N-Trance's "copy" of the Bee Gees and the Bee Gees' "copy" of Black and White gay cultures, and reading these as crucial moments of what Deleuze and Guattari (1987) term the *rhizomatic*, our reading practices are placed at stake. Social justice pedagogies need to develop reading practices that point to the more complex manifestations of identities inhabiting the classrooms in which the pedagogy is deployed. This would mean jettisoning the bipolar positions that stake out stable identities in need of affirmation and "bad" identities in need of downsizing.

Staying alive is a crucial and important priority for those of us who recognize that the pandemic HIV/AIDS cross-cuts and creates new figurations of communities. What the fluid traces of HIV/AIDS suggest is how interconnected we all are.[2] Bodies then are not discreet entities, but are connect in space and time: they in effect reveal cross-cultural *resonances*. Hayden White (1995) suggested that it may not be death, but

> rather the leakage of the body that is the source of ontological anxiety . . . The body leaks, even when it has not been perforated, punctured, or otherwise penetrated. This is the physico-ontological truth on which the fortunes of the redemptive religions and the medical professions, but also and above all the cosmetic industry, depend. The care, control, disposal, and cultivation of the body's effusions provide the basis of all "culture." (p. 234)

White's insight is important because it attests to the various ways in which the performativity of bodies is regulated and controlled, the ways bodies are continually commanded to perform in relationship to other bodies and bodies of discourse. In this historical moment, the insistence on stable boundaries seems to be a disavowal of HIV/AIDS and, of course, the elaboration of safer sex practices.

Performance studies call into question the old categories of *us* and *them* in their focus on different kinds of formations, identifications, limits, possibilities, and excesses. Considering performance calls attention to the traces that link or suggest cross-cultural resonances as sites for beginning new kinds of conversations, dialogues, and pedagogy. Thus we might begin to understand how it is that every body performs, but only certain of these performances are noticed or read as such. Bringing into discussions, dialogues, and pedagogy the verbing of the noun, or rather the performance

---

[2]"Sunday, the Rabbi Got AIDS" (Beiser, 1995) is one of those politico-tragic stories that continually points out the ways in which we are interconnected.

of performativity, signals a resistance to a static conception of identity, community, and politics.

Sylvia Wynter (1990), in "Beyond Miranda's Meanings: Un/silencing the 'Demonic Ground' of Caliban's 'Woman,' " suggests that we need to "point toward the epochal threshold of a new post-modern and post-Western mode of cognitive inquiry; one which goes beyond the limits of our present 'human sciences', to constitute itself as a new science of human 'forms of life' " (p. 356). The importance of queer theory to opening new positions in cultural studies suggests the need to understand and analyze HIV as both a form of life and one that therefore lives across communities.

HIV forces us to come to terms with the multiple intersectionalities of human forms. HIV's cross-cutting produces a crucial moment of politicality where identification beyond imagined categories can happen. These identifications point to human forms that Wynter suggests are different from Western and humanist notions of *mankind*, which impose the categories of sex, gender, race, sexuality, and other signifiers of difference as the present structure of governance. Such a structure represses how we cross-cut each other and how that cross-cutting might aid in something more. The working through of this repression might lead to a different conversation, one concerned with the survival of the species beyond the present order of governance.

THE POLITICS OF COMMUNITY: AFTER THE CATEGORY OF THE SAME

> That is to say, there is no original or origin of identity. What holds the place of an "origin" is the sharing of singularities. This means that this "origin"—the origin of community or the originary community—is nothing other than the limit: the origin is the tracing of the borders upon which or along which singular beings are exposed. (Nancy, 1991, p. 33)

Attempts to move beyond present orders of governance are often met with identity and community fortresses. Douglas Crimp (1993) in "Right On, Girlfriend!" argues for understanding community as a process of identifications with other political struggles and movements. He details how the emergence of the use of the word *queer* as both identity and as a practice of identification was a response both to a liberal human rights gay agenda and a gay separatist politics. Crimp argues that both of the positions (separatist and liberal) grew out of an inability to deal with anti-racism, feminism, and imperialism within gay liberation circles. His observations concerning singularity and gay community are analogous to the ways in which the discourse of Black community often reproduces similar positions (integrationist [read liberal] or separatist). The concept of community as singular means that only two positions are possible—in or out.

Hip-hop culture does not escape these bipolar arguments despite its constitution as a collage form. Membership in the hip-hop community is seen by some as the birthright of Black youth, an epidermal belonging (see Allinson, 1994). As Crimp (1993) writes:

> Political identifications remaking identities are, of course, productive of collective political struggle, but only if they result in a broadening of alliances rather than an exacerbation of antagonisms. And the latter seems often to result when, from within a development toward a politics of alliance based on relational identities, old antagonisms based on fixed identities reemerge. Activist politics then faces the impasse of ranking oppressions, moralism, and self-righteousness. (p. 317)

For Crimp, intersectionality might be understood as an elaboration of what he calls relational identities. It is in recognizing the intersectionalities of identities that political identifications occur. N-Trance's "Stayin' Alive" brings all these social identities (PWA, race, gender, class, and sex) into collision. Two lines from the N-Trance song—"Move to the side/Ev'rybody wants to stay alive"—open multiple and conflicting readings of the stakes of sociality.

These new or possible political identifications might be characterized as the "third space" (Bhabha, 1990), a contingent intersection of becoming and possibilities. The third space that I am suggesting is one that attempts to come to grips with the intersectionality of identifications, as well as account for what kinds of identifications might emerge in the context of important political moments. Education is obviously a site of an important political moment and the classroom a space where explorations into relational identities might occur. To elaborate further this idea of relational identities as the basis for founding community, I turn to Zora Neale Hurston's musings on this subject.

Moses Man of the Mountain

In Hurston's (1990) *Moses Man of the Mountain*, the Exodus narrative is rewritten and in the process, questions of race, leadership, and community are complicated. Hurston sets up the terrain for moving beyond notions of Black sameness to address questions of community. Hurston does not sentimentalize what community is but questions what Black community might mean. She attempts to articulate something beyond the sign of phenotype for the politics of community.

Deborah McDowell (1990), in her foreword "Lines of Descent/Dissenting Lines," reads Hurston's *Moses* not as a failed and flawed project as is usually done, but as a critique of male leadership and its desire to censor women from public roles in politics. Like McDowell, I am quite willing to read Hurston's project as being more successful than flawed in light of the debate in Black communities concerning questions of leadership and community. In fact, one might argue that the questions of Black leadership and community are two sides of the same coin.

The story of Moses, as imagined by Hurston, follows the Biblical story's outlines but considers the question of identity as central to the narrative. Who Moses is to himself, his Ethiopian wife, to the Egyptian court and his royal title, and to the Hebrews becomes the central dilemma of both community and self. Hurston's emphasis on identity allows her to explore the complex process of making community through a process of identifications. The effect is to unmoor us from identity and origins as fixations for politics.

By obfuscating exactly who Moses is, Hurston launches a critique of male leadership and the male vision of community. She makes clear that whether Moses is or is not Egyptian should not be of paramount importance. Rather, his actions, or put another way, his "unworking" of community and his eventual rejection of courtly allegiances as a "community given"[3] in favor of a community that one makes and needs is what matters politically and ethically. I believe that such a position is crucial for reading Hurston's text as a radical vision of community and for considering present dilemmas in community.

Moses is made aware of who he is when confronted by his Ethiopian wife as being a Hebrew. That confrontation or outing is the mechanism around which community as given and community as needed revolves, forcing a number of very important issues into play. The most crucial among them is the politics of passing.[4] Passing here immediately signals the relations of privilege and disadvantage according to which social identity is claimed. The instability of identity, knowledge, and community is immediately made evident. Could Moses have been passing all this time, even as he became a great man in Egypt? What flaws or oversights led to his getting away with passing for so long? And, if Moses was not passing, what does it say about a community who condemns and abandons one of its own?

Moses's Ethiopian wife says to him: "What a filthy trick you have played on me and my country! She says she remembers when you were born and

---

[3]Jean-Luc Nancy (1991). *The Inoperative Community.* In the essay "The Inoperative Community," Nancy outlines a critique of community as given and argues for the making of community as a process.

[4]See Adrian Piper (1992) "Passing for White, Passing for Black" for the complex issues involved in passing as both a sense of self-denial and as a subversive strategy; Valerie Smith (1994) "Reading the Intersection of Race and Gender in Narratives of Passing."

how you were put to the river in an ark and that is how the Princess got hold of you in the first place" (Hurston, 1990, p. 65). Expressed is the terrifying fear of passing, the instability and mutability of identity, in the face of the assertion of origins. That Moses passed for so long opens up the question of what exactly constitutes truth and community. The myth that Miriam had weaved over the years to protect her own culpability in regard to having neglected her duty becomes the truth that is used to render Moses an outsider to the courtly Egyptian community. On the other hand, he is now positioned as, or forced to be, a political activist, leader, and maker of community. Moses then is the symbolic transgressor of social codes and modes of the ruling order of identity and community.

Moses' banishment and his refusal of courtly community lies alongside his choice of community among the Hebrews. His choice, however, is not an uncomplicated one, for it finds him in a leadership role. Thus a number of other questions come into play. Does it matter who leads, or is political action what matters? How important is it that Moses is a man making choices about community and fashioning a new community? In a word, what levels of *trust* exist for the building of community beyond the repetitions or replications of the same?

Hurston's (1990) critique of nationalism is ushered in through an obfuscation of origins that points to some very important issues. June Jordan (Christakos, 1992) states regarding origins: "The journey away from the original, from our origins and our preoccupation with our origins, I think will mark a kind of maturity" (p. 35). Hurston articulated a desire for that maturity well in advance of current debates concerning the essentializing nature of some forms of Black politics. That both the Hebrews and the Egyptians could not trust in Moses' origins and thus could not trust in his politics are important for understanding why discourses that locate liberation in biologically essentialist terms continue to generate heated debate. The question always remains, on what grounds do we trust? The fact that Hurston's work precedes the current debates on the nature of community and Black community should not be taken lightly, for it tells something about the dialectic and desires of the dark diaspora for complex renderings of community as constituting much more than a Black sameness.[5]

The desire to create community that exceeds an epidermal schema is a desire that refuses an understanding of the self as only victim. Hurston (1939) in *Moses* articulates the desire for community as such:

---

[5]For example, debates concerning rap and celebrating rap often articulate masculinized nationalist manifestos claiming a single liberation agenda for a singular Black community. See in particular Jeffrey Louis Decker (1994).

You can't have a state of individuals. Everybody just can't be allowed to do as they please. I love liberty and I love freedom so I started off giving everybody a free rein. But I soon found out that it wouldn't do. A great state is a well-blended mash of *something of all of the people and all of none of the people*. (p. 278, emphasis added)

Hurston has Moses utter the ambivalence of nationhood in a manner that suggests both a oneness and a desire for multiplicity that remains a part of the question of how to understand the ethical relations of community. Moses' dilemma is ethical. Hurston articulates through Moses what Georgio Agamben (1993) calls singularities. Agamben writes: "What the state cannot tolerate in any way, however, is that the singularities form a community without affirming an identity, that humans co-belong without any representable condition of belonging (even in the form of a simple presupposition)" (pp. 85, 87). Moses' desire for community is not founded on the repetition of foundational identity claims, but in the working out of what it might mean to possibly live together. It is by obfuscating the identity of Moses, "The Great Deliverer" that Hurston is able to address the crucial and fundamental questions of identity, politics, and community.

It is in negotiating the differences that Moses represents that the limits of community as given are exposed as a desire for trust. Thus Hurston is able to question whether, as McDowell (1991) puts it, "liberation is ever achieved through a single charismatic leader" (p. x). That Hurston "dramatizes and critiques the terms and problematics of liberation" (McDowell, 1991, p. x) is central to the project that she articulates. In the patriarchal descent of power that Hurston plots, Moses says to Joshua: "No man may make another free. Freedom was something internal. . . . All you could do was to give the opportunity for freedom and the man himself must make his own emancipation" (Hurston, 1939, p. 282). By putting these words into the mouth of Moses, Hurston utters the move away from social identity to identity as constituted through one's political acts and actions.[6] Liberation might ultimately be more psychological. This does not deny the political economy of exploitation and denigration of one's humanity but it does force the question of the stakes of living as if.

---

[6]For analytic purposes, separating social identities (gender, race, sexuality) and political identities is important. Yeatman (1995) argues via Hanna Arendt that political identities (what one does and its effects on others) should be understood as different from social identities (gender, race, class) because social identities hold no necessary guarantees for a progressive politics. This is not an attempt to deny the histories of social identities and the movements they have spawned for justice, but to articulate the uncoupling of what has come to be the assumed causal link between particular social identities and progressive politics (e.g., that women or Black people would work against oppressive forces because of being Black or being a woman).

Hurston's overt political allegory (*Moses*) forces us to ask some questions concerning the nature of community as rooted in foundational identity claims. On what terms is community made and in the name of what do we join our singularities in an effort to produce narratives of community that remain conscious of our differences? The story of Moses suggests that a shared oppression is not the sole ground of community. Indeed, the purpose of the Hebrews' exile into the desert for 40 years raises the problem of what may have been decolonizing of the mind. As Moses says to Joshua, "What we been trying to do all these forty-odd years was to channel the intentions of men. We got to fix their intentions" (Hurston, 1990, p. 279). Hurston points out that concepts and practices of nation and community are often coterminous with relations of oppression.

Often conceptions of Black community are too narrowly constituted through what Gilroy (1993) calls "the condition of being in pain" (p. 203). This conception of community does not assess community as a shared experience of its unworking (Nancy, 1991), so that new ways of living and thinking community might be had. One reason that music aids in the construction of complex communities of difference, even if only momentarily, is because the ambivalence of language is always opened up for different performances, utterances, and revisions.[7]

A Queer Hip Hop?

So how does rap music and hip-hop culture take us to or allow for a desiring of new publics and communities that move us beyond easy notions of sameness? Both lyrically and musically, rap artists and their publics have begun to move beyond the too easy confines of family. The discourse of family was not so clearly evident in early rap, but became important to rap in the mid-1980s. Public Enemy's nationalist work best exemplifies the framework of rap that used discourses of the family as its unifying theme. What needs to be acknowledged is how the desire for family in the Reagan–Bush era of attacks on the most disadvantaged and disenfranchised Americans could have and did impact on how the hip-hop nation imagined itself, who was in and who was out. By the 1990s, rap and hip-hop culture has not only continued to strive and break new ground, but it has continued to produce new networks that question narrow parameters of hip hop while articulating the instability of family, community, and nation.

The Disposable Heroes of Hiphoprisy (DHH; 1992) on the album *Hypocrisy is the Greatest Luxury*, articulate the desire for complex notions of community. DHH's "Language of Violence" narrates the story of how a

---

[7]One only has to witness drag queens perform and reformulate heterosexual love songs to see how the instability of meaning is rendered contextual.

group of boys violate another by naming him faggot, sissy, punk, queen, queer, and then physically abusing him after school. One of the boys in the mob is convicted of the crime and encounters a similar but different terrain of violence in prison. DHH are not just recounting a revenge fantasy or a moral tale in their song.

Michael Franti, the songwriter and lead rapper, claims that they did not set out to write a song that would be read or interpreted as a statement on homophobia. Various mainstream media representations have sanitized any affirmative queer references from hip hop[8] and instead promoted hip hop, which most exemplified a "fear of a queer planet." DHH bring to the discourse of hip-hop culture the unthinking of rap music as confined to a politics that articulates race as singular. In their song, race and sexuality are intersectional. It is this type of music that opens up how rap and its artists are (un)thinking community in increasingly complex ways.

In my appropriation of Doty's (1993) notion of a queer reading and making a text queer, the utterances in this genre of rap are "the recognition and articulation of the complex range of queerness that has been in popular culture texts and their audiences all along" (p. 16). Thus what projects like DHH's *Hypocrisy is the Greatest Luxury* do is not only map new publics for rap and hip hop, but acknowledge the silence and reveal the traces already there. In queer spaces like dance clubs, rap can often get most people dancing because queer listeners can rewrite the lyrics of many rap songs. Queer men often eroticize hypermasculine rappers in a sexualized dance economy that undermines reading some rap songs as only heteronormative.

In Isaac Julien's (1994) film, *Darker Side of Black*, an exploration of the nihilistic and heterosexist postures of rap and dancehall, there is a fleeting moment when the queering of rap is evident. Julien's camera cruises the streets of Manhattan and an interviewer questions young people all fashioned in the styles that mark them as members of the hip-hop nation. What ultimately distinguishes them is their political positions, utterances, and their sexual practices. Cinematically, Julien queered hip hop and dancehall by uncovering authoritative queer hip hoppers (banjee boys) who find the music pleasurable and who resist heteronormativity in the music and culture.

---

[8]Nelson George (1988) offers an analysis of the relationship among disco, queer culture, and other Black musics. For example, showing one's underwear at the pant waist can be read as related to queer club culture. Additionally, leather, latex, and sequins have been appropriated from queer culture to become an important part of dancehall culture. These are indications of the interconnectedness of popular queer culture and expressive popular cultures. One of the interesting things about some club cultures is that dialogues across social and political identities often take place. Those dialogues, although often nonverbal, manifest themselves in various adaptations of styles and fashion.

If the evidence appears to be too ephemeral, we might want to consider Jose Esteban Munoz's (1996) definition of queer ephemeral:

> Ephemera, and especially the ephemeral work of structures of feeling, is firmly anchored *within* the social. Ephemera includes traces of lived experience, maintaining experiential politics and urgencies long after these structures of feeling have been lived. Queerness, too, can be understood as a structure of feeling. Since queerness has not been let to stand, unassailed, in the mass public sphere, it has often existed and circulated as a shared structure of feeling that encompasses same-sex desire and other minoritarian sexualities but also holds other dissident affective relationships to different aspects of the sex/gender system. (pp. 10–11)

Social and corrective pedagogy might need to work at the level of the ephemeral to demonstrate how we are all bound together. Thus moving beyond bipolar understandings of the social, we might begin at some level to address the real of people's lives. I am making a case for the always already queer presence, absented but not gone. The most difficult task for social corrective pedagogies might be to account for our interconnectedness outside the discourse of victims and victimizers.

What I am suggesting is neither a simple theory of permutation of hip hop by queer bodies nor an indication of some withdrawal from taking political stances in the context of the larger question of justice. Instead, I am interested in how we ethically arrive at the so-called place of justice. Therefore, Doty's (1993) insistence that a queer reading can be done of any text helps to uncover rap's queer readers, audiences, traces, and pedagogies, and a similar reading practice can hold true in the classroom. I would venture to say that a fundamental part of the fiction of community that gave rise to rap as popular urban Black song/sound in the 1980s was dependent on creating and producing the hip-hop nation as uncomplicated and simple and therefore repressing any queer evidences. Thus the pathologizing of the Black working class, the uncomplicated and narrowly argued positions concerning rap music, constituted a one-dimensional ghettocentric Blackness and led to the denial of a much more complex history of rap music and Black communities.

For example, one of the most sampled musicians by rap artists is George Clinton, whose mothership was taking off from earth quite similar to Noah's ark—all species were on board. What I am trying to get at here is that the foundations of rap music and its publics/communities have historically been complex creations. Clinton's songs often have coded in them (especially his mothership songs) the Exodus narrative or a variant or derivative of that narrative. Exodus re-presents Black desire for liberation, but in Clinton's and Hurston's hands liberation and community become complex projects of love and loss.

Hurston and Clinton both signal a desire for community that is constituted through one's relation to the political actions of those with whom one might or might not share certain historical experiences. Understanding historical experience as a potent ingredient in desires for community cannot be understated, because it is what often complicates discussions and leads to assumptions concerning communities of the same.

In fact, in terms of Black historical experience and memory, the idea of community has become sacred. Nancy (1991) writes that "community itself now occupies the place of the sacred. Community is the sacred" (p. 35). Community as sacred often denies or occludes Black differences. Hurston and the others refused to bow down or be abandoned to the concept of community, for as Nancy (1991) states, "[c]ommunity is given to us with being and as being, well in advance of all projects, desires, and undertakings" (p. 35). Instead, Hurston and the others are intent on the project of unworking community so that "a community consciously undergoing the experience of its sharing" might be made as the community needed (Nancy, 1991, p. 40). In such a scenario, community might well exceed its limit to include those who do not share common experiences but share common identifications.

These thoughts on community gesture to community as a process that is never complete or finished. Such claims have profound effects for a pedagogy of social justice invested in singular social identities and disuniting identities into single categories as either victim or victimizer. The Hebrews' continued suspicion of Moses despite his having led them out is a clear example of community as process. I have continually gestured to the problem of origins and their relationship to creating homogenizing community. June Jordan (Christakos, 1992) states on the question of origins: "[t]he journey away from [the] original, from our origins and our preoccupation with our origins, I think will mark a kind of maturity" (p. 35). Jordan is not eschewing common or similar historical experiences, but she is calling into question the pinning down of experience to originary moments. I take her injunction seriously because I think that her comments inaugurate a new way to think about the project of community that Hurston and those engaged in the pleasures, desires, and play of the hip-hop nation would find refreshing. The implications of constituting community beyond Black sameness (re)presents a dangerous crossroads full of possibilities.

Liberal pedagogies of the oppressed continue to reproduce a bipolar paradigm where understanding is central to the imagined outcome. Those of us who question the limit and indeed the obscenity of understanding are trying to articulate ways of working with difference and oppression that are not dependent on stable identity categories. In unhinging the discourse of understanding from social justice pedagogies, what becomes apparent are the ways in which we are all implicated in both the up and downsides of social (dis)order. What is ultimately at stake is a shift in reading practices that might lead to an appreciation of complex, shifting identities and facilitate a discussion of life's horrors—a discussion that is not stuck in the fictive, stable categories we imagine, but never perform as identity. Our reading practices might aspire to continually subvert Us–Them positions and scenarios.

REFERENCES

Agamben, G. (1993). *The coming community* (M. Hardt, trans.). Minneapolis: University of Minnesota Press.
Allinson, E. (1994). It's a Black thing: Hearing how Whites can't. *Cultural Studies, 8*, 3.
Beiser, V. (1995, December 5). Sunday, the rabbi got AIDS. *The Village Voice*, 27–30.
Bhabha, H. (1990). Interview with Homi Bhabha: The third space. In J. Rutherford (Ed.), *Identity community, culture, difference* (pp. 207–221). London: Lawrence & Wishart.
Butler, J. (1990). *Gender trouble: Feminism and the subversion of identity.* New York: Routledge.
Butler, J. (1993). *Bodies that matter: On the discursive limits of "sex."* New York: Routledge.
Christakos, M. (1992). The craft the politics requires: An interview with June Jordan. *Fireweed, 36*, 26–39.
Crimp, D. (1993). Right on, girlfriend! In M. Warner (Ed.), *Fear of a queer planet: Queer politics and social theory* (pp. 300–320). Minneapolis: University of Minnesota Press.
Currid, B. (1995). "We are family": House music and queer performativity. In S. Case, P. Brett, & S. Foster (Eds.), *Cruising the performative: Interventions into the representation of ethnicity, nationality, and sexuality* (pp. 165–196). Bloomington: Indiana University Press.
Decker, J. (1994). The state rap: Time and place in hip hop nationalism. In A. Ross & T. Rose (Eds.), *Microphone fiends: Youth music & youth culture* (pp. 89–121). New York: Routledge.
Deleuze, G., & Guattari, F. (1987). *A thousand plateaus* (B. Massumi, trans.). Minneapolis: University of Minnesota Press.
Doty, A. (1993). *Making things perfectly queer: Interpreting mass culture.* Minneapolis: University of Minnesota Press.
George, N. (1988). *The death of rhythm & blues.* New York: Plume.
Gilroy, P. (1993). *The black atlantic: Modernity and double consciousness.* Cambridge, MA: Harvard University Press.
Harris, W. (1990, Summer). In the name of liberty. *Third Text, 11*, 7–15.
Hurston, Z. (1990). *Moses man of the mountain.* New York: HarperPerennial. (Original work published 1939)
Jones, L. (1963). *Blues people: The negro experience in white America and the music that developed from it.* New York: Morrow Quill.
Julien, I. (1994). *The darker side of black* [film]. London: Black Audio Collective and Normal Films.
Mackey, N. (1995). Other: From noun to verb. In K. Gabbard (Ed.), *Jazz among the discourses* (pp. 76–99). Durham, NC: Duke University Press.
McDowell, D. (1990). Foreword: Lines of descent/dissenting lines. In Z. N. Hurston, *Moses man of the mountain* (pp. vii–xxii). New York: HarperPerennial.
Munoz, J. (1996). Ephemera as evidence: Introductory notes to queer acts. *Women and Performance, 8*(2), 16.
Nancy, J. (1991). *The inoperative community* (P. Connor, L. Garbus, M. Holland, & S. Sawhney, trans.). Minneapolis: University of Minnesota Press.

Parker, A., & Sedgwick, E. (1995). Introduction: Performativity and performance. In A. Parker & E. Sedgwick (Eds.), *Performativity and performance* (pp. 1–18). New York: Routledge.

Piper, A. (1992). Passing for white, passing for black. *Transition, 58*, 4–32.

Smith, V. (1994, Summer/Fall). Reading the intersections of race and gender in narratives of passing. *Diacritics*, 43–57.

White, H. (1995). Bodies and their plots. In S. Foster (Ed.), *Choreographing history* (pp. 229–234). Bloomington: Indiana University Press.

Wynter, S. (1990). Beyond Miranda's meanings: Un/silencing the "demonic ground" of caliban's "woman." In C. B. Davies & E. Fido (Eds.), *Out of the kumbla: Caribbean women and literature* (pp. 355–370). Trenton, NJ: Africa World Press.

Yeatman, A. (1995). The personal and the political: A feminist critique. In P. James (Ed.), *Critical politics: From the personal to the global* (pp. 35–56). Melbourne, Australia: Arena Publications.

Chapter 7

(Queer) Youth as Political and Pedagogical

Nelson Rodriguez
Pennsylvania State University

> *Young people and their culture play a particularly important role in the neo-conservative strategy . . . countersubversives need demonized enemies to justify their own repressive and authoritarian desires.*
>
> —Lipsitz (1994, p. 19)

On October 8, 1996, the Associated Press releases the following regarding a middle/high school in Elizabethtown, Pennsylvania:

> Defying warnings from school officials, more than 250 middle and high school students marched out of classes Tuesday to protest their school board's new "pro-family" resolution. The resolution, passed September 17, says, "pro-homosexual concepts on sex and the family will never be tolerated or accepted in this school." Students also objected to its description of the two-parent family as "the norm." "Why should gays be less important?" said Dave Fritz, a sophomore who joined the demonstration. "Why should kids with one parent be discriminated against?" The high school's 1,168 students had been told they would be disciplined if they protested. School officials, in classes Tuesday morning and in letters the day before, urged them not to join the demonstration. Some of the students carried signs saying, "We were taught to fight for what we believe in," and "What does my parents' marital status have to do with my education?" More than a dozen parents attended in support. The board's resolution matches one sent to districts by the Concerned Women for America, a conservative Christian group, in response to a National Education Association resolution on diversity, racism, sexism and sexual orientation. (Associated Press, 1996)

Attempting to establish itself around the name S.T.R.A.I.G.H.T., a soon-to-be university organization has this to say about its mission statement:

> A new student organization is in the process of being formed at this campus. It's called STRAIGHT, which stands for "Students Reinforcing Adherence In General Heterosexual Tradition." The agenda of this group will be to promote, encourage, and preserve heterosexuality. In addition, STRAIGHT will promote education and pride in the tradition and appropriateness of heterosexuality in society. . . . STRAIGHT is not a religious organization; however, Judeo-Christian beliefs, as well as sociological and biological principles, do constitute a fundamental part of the support for STRAIGHT's beliefs. (STRAIGHT Flyer, 1996)

What thread runs through these seemingly disparate events? To rephrase the question in more politically charged terms: What broader public "moral crisis" connects these historically specific dramas? At a time in U.S. history when gays and lesbians are arguably gaining more visibility, acceptance, and perhaps even power, there becomes a necessity on the part of the "moral right" to guard its self-appointed power and privilege from the encroaching contestations of a particular group who dares assert its individual and collective identity against a pervasive heterosexism and homophobia that threatens the very stuff of democracy itself. Indeed, what connects these two events is the right's fearful recognition that the gay community is becoming more and more vocal, assertive, and successful about its right to equality, respect, and human dignity; consequently, the right must scurry to find foundationalist antidemocratic arguments to preserve their narrow notions of sexuality and family in a world that's become increasingly fractured and hybridized and where "no cultural practice has any necessary or a priori meaning" (Raymond, 1994, p. 129). In addition, the moral right understands on some level the inherent fragility of sexual borders themselves; the pedagogical lie of "stability in sexuality" is perhaps even apparent to them. In her essay, "The Construction of Heterosexuality," Janet E. Haley (1993) captures the instability of any sexual class and hence the need for neoconservatives to work that much harder to secure the insecurable, that is, to secure their vulnerable sexual border by demonizing sexual practices that fall outside of its hegemonic project: "The . . . class of heterosexuals is a default class, home to those who have not fallen out of it. It openly expels but covertly incorporates the homosexual other, an undertaking that renders it profoundly heterogeneous, unstable, and provisional" (pp. 85–86).

Something else, though, links these two events. Brought together by *who* the participants of these events are—namely, youth—the events help show that "youth" is a political site. In the first instance, for example, middle and high school students contest the heterosexism of the curriculum as well as the authority that legitimates some histories and cultures and derails others. To be sure, as the student protesters recognize on some level, "schools do not merely teach academic subjects, but also, in part, produce student subjectivities or particular sets of experiences that are in themselves part of an ideological process" (Giroux & McLaren, 1996, p. 317). In the second event, youth again can be seen as political, but this time in a different way. That is, here we see how a particular site becomes the means by which discourses of the right are promulgated. Indeed, in this second instance, the ideological work of the group S.T.R.A.I.G.H.T. cannot be separated from the broader public ideological conversation of the right on such political issues as heterosexual-only marriages, heterosexual-only families, heterosexuality as "norm."

But as soon as we configure youth as a political site, it becomes impossible not to discuss as well the site of youth *as pedagogical,* which is to say that pedagogy and politics are intertwined. Indeed, the ways in which youth politically use and appropriate their bodies, language, culture, and myriad public spheres to contest dominant cultural practices, as well as dominant representations and ideologies, suggests that they are engaging in a pedagogical enterprise that wishes to educate us about, among other things, this important point: "[al]though dominant cultural practices are not free-floating and are extremely difficult to subvert, . . . any particular practice can be (re)appropriated by a subcultural group and 'rearticulated' according to its own specific political meanings and values. . . . [Hence], oppression is never one-sided, and struggles over meaning are ongoing in every culture" (Raymond, 1994, p. 129). As we see shortly, a teenager who attends a heterosexual ritual such as a prom with someone of the same sex is precisely engaging in the kind of political and pedagogical practice that aims to subvert hegemonic culture. Of course, in addition to engaging in counter-hegemonic political/pedagogical practices that rupture dominant culture, dominant practices, and dominant assumptions, youth, as are other subcultural groups, are vulnerable to being appropriated themselves to perform pedagogically and politically in the service of the dominant ideology and culture. The university-based group, S.T.R.A.I.G.H.T., in my estimation, is such an example.

In this chapter, I argue that teachers, teacher educators, and educational administrative leaders must move beyond thinking about youth as only a social category in need of management and "discipline," for "within such a tradition, management issues take precedence over understanding and furthering schools as democratic public spheres" (Giroux, 1996, p. 16). To open space for theoretical discourses about the category *youth* as a political and pedagogical site is also to open the possibility for educating youth in critical languages that enable them to connect their own ideological work to a broader democratic vision; in addition, it enables them to recognize and combat ideologies that attempt to exploit them in the service of homogenizing thought and eradicating difference. From this perspective, schooling partly entails having students engage in the "construction of ideologies that vie with dominant ideology for hegemony" (Raymond, 1994, p. 129). As a way to focus my argument that the site of youth must be understood as political and pedagogical, I concentrate in the first half of this chapter on queer youth. A subculture within a subculture, the pedagogical politics surrounding queer youth demonstrate how an understanding of youth as political and pedagogical can serve in the ongoing formation of a radical democracy, one that takes seriously the issue of difference in the attempt to challenge the violence of normativity.

Layered over the notion that (queer) youth must be understood as political and pedagogical, I also make a second, but related, argument: The political and pedagogical practices and struggles of subcultural groups such as youth need to be linked to the practices and struggles of other (subcultural) groups, and schools and colleges of education need to provide the critical, theoretical, and pedagogical space for imagining how such coalitions might take place. However, to discuss the site of youth *critically*, as well as the politics of coalition building, within the anti-intellectual location of the school or college of education is to confront a discipline that has historically conceived of educational reform solely in terms of practical considerations. As educational and cultural theorist Henry Giroux (1995) explains: "While other disciplines have appropriated, engaged, and produced new theoretical languages in keeping with changing historical conditions, colleges of education have maintained a deep suspicion of theory and intellectual dialogue" (p. 128). Part of the problem with schools and colleges of education being wedded to practical considerations stems from their inability to recognize that "considerations of the practical cannot take place without a detour through theory" (Giroux, 1995, p. 135) and furthermore that theory itself must take a detour through the practical and/or experience. In an attempt to challenge this critical, theoretical lacuna so pervasive in the field of education today, I conclude this chapter by examining how teacher educators and their students might theoretically analyze a particular scene from the cultural text, *The Celluloid Closet*, by drawing on recent advances from the field of queer theory.

A documentary that traces the historical representations of gays and lesbians in Hollywood film, a critical analysis of *The Celluloid Closet* does more than simply bring theory into the classroom. Indeed, an analysis of this film with youth would emphasize that the politics of social positioning—that is, how one's individual and collective identity is constructed, understood, and enacted—has much to do with mainstream representational politics. For this reason, (queer) youth must be able to recognize critically, resist, and turn inside-out any representational politics of exploitation. Thus, I use *The Celluloid Closet* not only to contribute critically, theoretically, and politically to the field of education itself, given such pervasive absences, but also to consider how teacher educators and their students might construct curricula based on the notion of educating youth about how an understanding of the political and pedagogical nature of other subcultural groups, such as gays and lesbians in terms of their representation in media culture, can enable youth to envision a politics of coalition building that cuts across social axes and indeed links the individual to a broader democratic community and project.

Finally, I have specifically chosen a film about gays and lesbians in history for use in a classroom setting for the following reason: although the gay community has seen a hint of acceptance in the wider society, educational institutions at all levels still suffer their students, faculty, and staff to a highly heterocentric culture. As Gerald Unks (1995) notes, for example, about the high school:

> The high school—the center of most adolescent life and culture—stands staunchly aloof and rigidly resistant to even a suggestion that any of its faculty or student body might be homosexual or that homosexuals deserve anything but derision and scorn within its walls. High schools may be the most homophobic institutions in American society. (p. 5)

Perhaps most damaging about such pervasive heterocentrism, and the silence that often accompanies it, is the way institutions such as schools end up being driven by overriding ideologies such as heterosexism, the latter ideology being one that denies difference, that is, one that "denies, denigrates, and stigmatizes any nonheterosexual form of behavior, identity, relationship, or community" (Unks, 1995, p. 5). Indeed, combining heterosexism with schooling is an insidious way of educating youth to promote "sexual fascism"; no doubt it is part of the moral right's "hidden curriculum." Before turning to *The Celluloid Closet*, however, as a tool to be used pedagogically to rupture schooling's engagement in the politics of the social construction of not seeing, let us first examine briefly the politics and pedagogy of (queer) youth and (queer) youth politics and pedagogy. This brief theoretical detour sets the stage for how teacher educators and their students might use cultural texts *politically and theoretically* in the classroom as a way to negotiate the intersection among identity politics, representation, and pedagogy.

THE POLITICAL AND PEDAGOGICAL SPACE OF (QUEER) YOUTH

What typically is pegged as "disruptive behavior" or consigned to the bizarre or written off as juvenile, youth cultural practices instead are often highly political and pedagogical in the sense that, in many cases, they challenge inequitable status quo patterns and can even potentially overturn dominant legislation and policy. Indeed, the reverberations of youth resistance often force lawmakers to confront and have to rethink and rework taken-for-granted dominant ideologies. The case of Aaron Fricke, a 1980 gay high-school senior, is such an example. Wanting to attend his high-school prom with another male youth, Fricke was refused permission by principal Richard Lynch, the latter arguing that Aaron's attendance with another male would place both Aaron and his classmates in danger. Ultimately, though, "the Rhode Island District Court determined that the school's claim that Fricke's attendance at the dance posed a threat to security was not sufficiently compelling to override Fricke's first amendment rights to free speech and association" (Raymond, 1994, p. 115). What we see, then, with this isolated moment of youth resistance, is the way it challenges not only a particular school's authority, and "the Law" that circulates and governs such an institution, but that Fricke's resistance is even felt on a broader level as it forces the authority of the state of Rhode Island to confront and negotiate a "clash in ideologies." But Fricke's cultural work connects to even broader terrain. That is, his resistance contests what Judith Butler (1990) calls the *heterosexual matrix*, "that grid of cultural intelligibility through which bodies, genders, and desires are naturalized" (p. 151). To be sure, Fricke's attendance at "a paradigmatic heterosexual ritual like a prom [with another male] cannot but call into question our normative assumptions about dating, romance, and the nature of desire" (Raymond, 1994, p. 116). It may be argued, however, that Fricke's oppositional work in the form of attending a prom with another male is what Cornel West calls an example of "thin opposition" (Raymond, 1994, p. 115) in the sense that, whereas there has been a confrontation with a dominant cultural practice, structurally, all still remains sound. In fact, some may argue that Fricke's attendance is precisely an example of the operations of hegemony, for "hegemonic practices generally have enough 'give' to enable them to tolerate some deviance and remain structurally sound" (Raymond, 1994, p. 116).

I would agree that Fricke has not *overturned or gotten outside* of the notions and practices of the heterosexual matrix. It is not possible to step fully outside of such a matrix, for that would entail, among other things, stepping outside of language itself and engaging in an act of linguistic willed amnesia. However, this still does not cancel out how Fricke's movement into cultural visibility has been a political and pedagogical act that may be added to other similar counter-cultural practices that, taken together, can create the conditions for rewriting, in this case, "our inherited sexual vocabularies [and practices] . . . [thus] turning them inside out, giving them a new face" (Fuss, 1991, p. 4). There is an irony, however, surrounding Fricke's "pedagogical practice," precisely because it has taken place within an institution that supposedly is in the service of promoting democracy. Indeed, despite what his pedagogy has to say about schooling's pivotal role and ethical responsibility in the production of critical citizens and in expanding and deepening democracy itself, few teachers rarely take up the important consequences of such pedagogical work as part of *their* pedagogy in the classroom. But I see this lack more the fault of schools and colleges of education than of teachers themselves. Let me be more specific here.

Fricke is engaging in a form of pedagogy that takes seriously identity politics. He understands that his identity is not inherently oppressive but that instead, culture and cultural practices have been used to pedagogically position him as Other. A discussion of identity politics in the classroom, thus, would investigate the ways in which language and media culture, for example, must be studied in an attempt to examine how the terrain of culture either prevents or enables the possibilities for critical agency and human dignity. Erica Rand (1995) in her text, *Barbie's Queer Accessories*, offers us a sense of how culture—in particular popular culture—is a politically pedagogical site that has enormous power in constructing gay and lesbian identity and socially positioning gays and lesbians as outsiders:

> People . . . glean their sense of possibility and self-worth partly from available cultural products—objects, narratives, interpretations. Surely, for instance, the feelings of despair, self-loathing, and helplessness that often attend coming out to oneself stem partly from living in an environment filled with pop songs, music videos, movies, books, television shows, and ads that presume or articulate the naturalness and greater value of heterosexual desire. The world will not change if Brandon and Dylan become lovers and join ACT UP 90210, but it matters that we already know that they won't no matter how soulfully they looked into each other's eyes during the first few seasons. (p. 5)

For teachers to enact a pedagogy that takes seriously the question of identity politics, or to enact other pedagogies that take up critically such issues as race, class, and gender, they must encounter and engage a curriculum during their training in college that enables them to acquire the critical languages and methodologies "that will allow them not only to critically analyze the democratic and political shortcomings of schools, but also to develop the knowledge and skills that will advance the possibilities for generating and cultivating a deep respect for a democratic and ethically-based community. In effect, this means that the relationship of teacher education programs to public schooling would be self-consciously guided by political and moral considerations" (Giroux & McLaren, 1996, p. 311). Indeed, with such training, teachers will be able to create the pedagogical conditions for enabling youth to understand how their own social location *as youth* can be used, as we saw in Fricke's case, *to insert themselves into, and by all means make themselves felt in, the political realm.*

Although it is important to understand youth as a site that is able productively to disrupt and make change in the sociopolitical order, it is also necessary to recognize the political and pedagogical site of youth as *contradictory.* Teacher educators and their students must not glorify the site of youth simply because of its inherent oppositional nature. George Lipsitz (1994) in his essay, "We Know What Time It Is: Race, Class, and Youth Culture in the Nineties," discusses how youth cultures, in particular hip hop, have been able to create and use culture to build coalitions across race and ethnic lines. However, these very same cultural practices can be exclusionary in terms of their sexism, misogyny, and homophobia. As Lipsitz notes, "One ugly aspect of the popularity enjoyed by hip hop among suburban youth has been its symbolic value to them as a franchise on an imagined male power created through the degradation of women" (p. 24). In order for youth not to truncate the emancipatory possibilities their cultural practices can offer, that is, not engage in misguided forms of oppositional resistance that reify dominant practices, teacher-educators and their students must create the pedagogical conditions that enable youth to imagine forms of organized political struggle and resistance that cut across social axes. From this perspective, youth involve themselves in forms of border crossing that enable them to rethink and rewrite themselves progressively based on their encounters with other identities, histories, languages, and cultural practices. In an attempt to consider how we teacher educators and other cultural workers might create with our students a critical pedagogy that enables youth to understand critically the politics of solidarity-building, let us now take a brief detour through *The Celluloid Closet.*

YOUTH, REPRESENTATION, AND THE POLITICS
OF SOLIDARITY-BUILDING

Thus far my argument has been (in a nutshell) that the site of youth offers enormous possibility in challenging the logic of dominant culture. In confronting, for example, *processes of legitimation,* youth can often expose the socially constructed nature of what has come to seem self-evident and apparently inevitable. With the case of Fricke, for instance, he challenged, by his very presence with another male at a prom, the belief that proms are somehow transcendentally heterosexual cultural practices. He did so by bringing forward one way in which dominant power legitimates and sustains its domination over others: by making particular beliefs and practices seem *natural and universal.* It is this kind of fronting with the logic of dominant culture, and how such confrontations can possibly deepen and extend democracy "in the present conjuncture, characterized as it is by an increasing disaffection towards democracy" (Mouffe, 1996, p. 5), that necessitates a discussion of youth as political and pedagogical within schools and colleges of education.

However, as I have begun to suggest, it is important that youth not reify dominant practices while engaging in oppositional work. Indeed, as Lipsitz helped clarify earlier, it is possible to engage in forms of antiracist cultural work yet at the same time engage in and sustain sexism and homophobia. One approach teacher educators and their students might take in order to construct a critical pedagogy that attempts to grapple with the dilemma of youth vis-a-vis the problematic of opposition/reification, is by building such a pedagogy around a critical engagement with the politics of cultural representation but within the project of solidarity building. To put this another way: having youth recognize, for example, that homophobic representations in culture engender undesirable consequences not only for gays and lesbians but for so-called straights too, youth can then begin to consider the importance and necessity of constructing a politics that connects *particular* interests and struggles to a broader democratic project. It is with this understanding that oppositional work *without* reification becomes more and more possible. Drawing on the critical, theoretical discourse of Judith Butler, in particular her notion of *gender performativity*, I now engage the nexus between homophobic representation and "doing gender," by examining a particular scene from *The Celluloid Closet*, a clip from the 1991 movie, *Fried Green Tomatoes*. It is my aim that, by drawing on Butler's critical theory, by engaging this nexus, and by examining this scene, I will illustrate how it is possible to build a critical pedagogy that attempts to argue for the significance of discussing with youth the necessity of *recognizing the importance to them of another group's struggles*.

Produced and directed by Rob Epstein and Jeffrey Friedman, and based on the book by Vito Russo, *The Celluloid Closet* (1995) chronicles gay and lesbian representation in Hollywood film from the mid 1890s to the early 1990s. The documentary itself is constructed around a series of clips from a variety of movies such as *Behind the Screen* (1916), *The Gay Divorcee* (1934), *Rope* (1948), *Rebel Without a Cause* (1955), *Ben-Hur* (1959), *Some Like It Hot* (1959), *The Boys in the Band* (1970), *Freebie and the Bean* (1974), *Cruising* (1980), *Making Love* (1982), *The Color Purple* (1985), *Thelma and Louise* (1991), *Fried Green Tomatoes* (1991), and *Philadelphia* (1993), among others. With the aid of many analysts, most of them drawn from the movie industry itself, including Lily Tomlin, *The Celluloid Closet* attempts to *problematize* the numerous representations of gays and lesbians for either their explicit or implicit homophobia, and for their practices and politics of demonization, stereotyping, and erasure. For example, Lily Tomlin discusses the politics surrounding the emergence of "the sissy" in the film, *The Gay Divorcee*

(1934). The sissy is considered Hollywood's first gay stock character. It was a convention that was completely accepted, for it enabled the issue of homosexuality to remain supposedly out of sight, that is, to remain safely at a subliminal or subtextual level. The sissy also, as Tomlin notes, "made everyone feel more manly or more womanly by occupying the space in-between. He did not seem to have a sexuality, so Hollywood allowed him to thrive."

An interesting implication of Tomlin's analysis that especially concerns us here is the importance of not underrating the power of culture to aid in the belief in the notion of discrete genders, or in the idea of tradi-tional/natural gender roles, or even in the idea of gender at all. Judith Butler (1990), in her now-famous book, *Gender Trouble: Feminism and the Subversion of Identity*, takes issue with the articulation of gender as "natural" or "given," or as somehow removed from the issue of power. It is worth citing her at length on this:

> Discrete genders are part of what "humanizes" individuals within contem-porary culture; indeed, we regularly punish those who fail to do their gender right. Because there is neither an "essence" that gender expresses or exter-nalizes nor an objective ideal to which gender aspires, and because gender is not a fact, the various acts of gender create the idea of gender, and without those acts, there would be no gender at all. Gender is, thus, a construction that regularly conceals its genesis; the tacit agreement to perform, produce, and sustain discrete and polar genders as cultural fictions is obscured by the credibility of those productions—and the punishments that attend not agreeing to believe in them; the construction "compels" our belief in its necessity and naturalness. (pp. 139–140)

As Butler argues, gender is not a fact. Instead, what makes for the idea of gender or, still yet, what creates the effect of gender uniformity is "a compulsory repetition of prior and subjectivating norms, [and it is] social constraints, taboos, prohibitions, threats of punishment [which] operate in [this] ritualized repetition of norms" (Butler, 1993, pp. 21–22). What this means in terms of the intersection among power, gender construction, and subjectivity, is that subject formation cannot be understood outside of the matrices of gender and power. Indeed, the subject is produced, according to Butler, *retroactively* in the repetition of (gender) norms, and this entire scene of identity formation and gender performativity takes place within a complex matrix of power. One aspect of this matrix, that is, one way in which power works to force or sustain a compulsory repetition of (gender) norms, is by deploying implicitly or explicitly "the grammar" (linguistic, visual, aural, etc.) of prohibition or taboo in opposition to the axis of homosexuality as a way to maintain under duress dominant or traditional gender roles or practices.

This relation among homosexuality, doing gender "right," and the deployment of the grammar of prohibition often emerges in complex configurations in popular culture as a form of "cultural pedagogy." Which is to say that these configurations are political in the sense that they work to "educate" us about "how to behave and what to think, feel, believe, fear, and desire—and what not to" (Kellner, 1995, p. 2). In terms of gender, then, popular culture profoundly and powerfully shapes our view of what constitutes (in)appropriate gender roles. Film critic, Richard Dyer, in *The Celluloid Closet*, makes this point well when he tells us that, "[our] ideas about who [we] are don't just come from inside [us]; they come from the culture. And in this culture, they come especially from the movies. So we learn from the movies what it means to be a man or a woman; what it means to have sexuality." If, as Dyer notes, we learn from the movies what it means to be a man or a woman, then by what specific mechanism(s) does this process of gendering occur, say, within popular culture? Again, to repeat, as I have begun to argue, it is in part through the juxtaposition of the axis of gender to that of homosexuality that a "radical" fabrication of discrete genders and/or "natural" gender roles takes hold and is sustained, often through the deployment of the grammar of prohibition or taboo.

In *The Celluloid Closet*, this mechanism of contiguity, as well as its effects, can be located in a brief clip from *Fried Green Tomatoes*. In this scene, two young, attractive women are presented one evening sitting and talking by a lake. Both women have been drinking. Analyzing critically this scene, writer Susie Bright shares her frustration at how the movie remains explicitly silent about the passion and homoeroticism these women feel for each other. As she notes: "The passion that these two women feel for each other was not presented in an open way in the movie. . . . I get so angry about what Hollywood will do with an original story or script to get rid of the lesbian element that I feel like standing up in the theater and shouting, 'These characters are dykes and this movie isn't saying so.' " I agree with Bright that the two characters are lesbians and Hollywood isn't saying so, at least not explicitly. The suggestive eye contact, the sexual energy present, the anxiety over the idea of parting (because one of the them intends on marrying), and a quick kiss on the cheek by one of the women to the other, all suggest that indeed there is a homoerotic (sub)script struggling to make its way into mainstream visibility in this scene. What this struggle *to come into history* suggests, then, within the context of Bright's criticism, is that homophobic representations do not only occur at an explicit level. Indeed, representation also becomes homophobic when it endorses or participates in a politics of silence or erasure regarding the existence of other sexualities as a way to maintain the belief, erroneous as it is, that somehow humanity and heterosexuality are synonymous.

In addition to making use of homophobic representation to maintain a heterosexist worldview, popular culture often deploys these very representations to uphold the notion of discrete, natural, and/or traditional gender roles, as well as to generate the belief in the *necessary* fulfillment of these roles. For example, in light of Bright's important criticism that Hollywood is engaging in a form of homophobia by remaining silent yet suggestive about the lesbian issue in *Fried Green Tomatoes*, consider now the following dialogue between the two women as "feeding off of" such homophobic representation in the attempt to reinscribe what constitutes doing one's gender "right," especially for women:

What's your mother going to say when she sees us both drunk?

You gotta stop worrying about what people think.

I know.

I mean you've always done the right thing. You took care of your daddy, the preacher, when he took sick. You take care all the kids over the church school. You go on an take care of your mamma . . .

I know, and I'm going to marry the man I'm supposed to.

You gettin' married?

Not validating in an open, honest, and positive way the love, passion, and desire these women feel for each other, yet at the same time suggesting that they are on the verge of transgressing "normal" sexual roles, and finally, by inserting the language of determinism or inevitability regarding marriage, Hollywood produces a scene that explicitly reinforces adherence to expected gender norms for women (i.e., caretaker, wife/marriage, mother/ children, etc.) by suggesting (because of its silence) as taboo that which it refuses to endorse openly: homosexuality as a viable, rewarding, and meaningful alternative to compulsory heterosexuality. Interestingly, this process of reinscription of gender norms through the grammar of taboo attempts to secure itself even more, as we see in the scene from *Fried Green Tomatoes*, by hegemonically compelling social actors to engage in the fulfillment of the quintessential heterosexual social contract: marriage. Which is to say that the cultural practice of marriage, although it does *not* guarantee that heterosexual men and women will reinscribe gender norms, significantly *is* nevertheless bound up with the forcible reiteration of such norms. As Judith Butler (1993) notes: "Gender norms operate by requiring the embodiment of certain ideals of femininity and masculinity, ones which are almost always related to the idealization of the heterosexual bond" (p. 22).

If homophobic representation crisscrosses with gender norms to the extent that the former contributes to the credibility in the fulfillment of the latter, then I conclude with this question and answer: who suffers, and hence, should care? This chapter has argued that the answer is certainly not only gays and lesbians.

REFERENCES

Butler, J. (1990). *Gender trouble: Feminism and the subversion of identity.* London & New York: Routledge.

Butler, J. (1993). Critically queer, *GLQ: A Journal of Lesbian and Gay Studies, 1,* 17–32.

Epstein, R. (Producer and Director), & Friedman, J. (Producer and Director). (1995). *The celluloid closet* [Film].

Fuss, D. (1991). Inside/out. In D. Fuss (Ed.), *Inside/out: Lesbian theories, gay theories.* New York & London: Routledge.

Giroux, H. (1995). Is there a place for cultural studies in colleges of education? *The Review of Education/Pedagogy/Cultural Studies, 17*(2), 127–142.

Giroux, H. (1996). *Fugitive cultures: Race, violence, and youth.* New York & London: Routledge.

Giroux, H., & McLaren, P. (1996). Teacher education and the politics of engagement: The case for democratic schooling. In P. Leistyna, A. Woodrum, & S. A. Sherblom (Eds.), *Breaking free: The transformative power of critical pedagogy.* Cambridge, MA: Harvard Educational Review.

Haley, J. E. (1993). The construction of heterosexuality. In M. Warner (Ed.), *Fear of a Queer planet: Queer politics and social theory.* Minneapolis & London: University of Minnesota Press.

Kellner, D. (1995). *Media culture: Cultural studies, identity and politics between the modern and the postmodern.* London & New York: Routledge.

Lipsitz, G. (1994). We know what time it is: Race, class, and youth in the nineties. In A. Ross & T. Rose (Eds.), *Microphone fiends: Youth music and youth culture.* New York & London: Routledge.

Mouffe, C. (1996). Deconstruction, pragmatism and the politics of engagement. In C. Mouffe (Ed.), *Deconstruction and pragmatism.* London & New York: Routledge.

Rand, E. (1995). *Barbie's queer accessories.* Durham & London: Duke University Press.

Raymond, D. (1994). Homophobia, identity, and the meanings of desire: reflections on the cultural construction of gay and lesbian adolescent identities. In J. M. Irvine (Ed.), *Sexual cultures and the construction of adolescent identities.* Philadelphia: Temple University Press.

Unks, G. (1995). Thinking about the gay teen. In G. Unks (Ed.), *The gay teen: Educational practice and theory for lesbian, gay, and bisexual adolescents.* London & New York: Routledge.

Chapter 8

Appropriating Queerness:
Hollywood Sanitation

Shirley R. Steinberg
Adelphi University

Sitting in my therapist's office last month, I suddenly declared that I thought I was a misplaced drag queen. In her low-key way, my counselor seemed a bit taken aback—we didn't pursue the random thought—I mean, where would we have gone? To drag, to queen, to where? As a seemingly heterosexual mother and wife, a "drama person," and as a Jewish woman, I have enough to cover in therapy—so we didn't go there. However, I have always been drawn to gayness, to queerness, and to dragness in particular. I was never a fag hag, more like a fag wannabe, especially as a younger woman. At this point in my life, however, I am content with being a friend and voyeur into lifestyles of which I can only dream. These thoughts have not been lost on some film directors in the past decade, to the point that gay/queer/dragness has become a focus of mainstream Hollywood films. Using my own positionality as a wannabe, I offer these thoughts to discuss and problematize the new trend in cinema outing.

The film, *The Celluloid Closet,* is an excellent documentary on the past 100 years of gayness and lesbianness in films. As the film begins, we are informed that Hollywood "has taught us how to think like and about gay people." Although discussions of stereotyping, homophobia, and outing are lengthy in this film, I question the lack of attention in the film to Hollywood's heterosexual agendas and/or exploitations in the name of sexual diversity. This implied pedagogy, or pseudo queer theory, is ignored in the discussion of films dealing with issues of homosexuality, lives of homosexuals, and queerness. Although I agree, indeed, that teaching has taken place and the viewer is left with a curriculum of thinking about gayness, I am concerned that this curriculum is a liberal attempt to cover up, sanitize, and Disney-fy queerness. This cleansing, then, becomes a reinscription of homophobia and heterosexism.

Since the beginning of cinematic history, homosexuality has been implied, and occasionally overt, in films. Flirtatious scenes can be identified as either gay or straight. In older movies, we are empowered as viewers to choose an interpretation to fit the image. However, in the 1940s and 1950s, Hollywood was commanded to clean up its act in the form of the Hays Code. In order to prevent "sleazy" and suggestive or compromising scenes, the code censored producers' and directors' film work. Restricted through the code were the following:

- open-mouthed kissing
- lustful embraces
- sex perversion
- seduction
- rape
- abortion
- prostitution and white slavery
- nudity
- obscenity
- profanity

For more than 20 years, the code was followed and "ugly sex situations" were avoided in the cinema (*The Celluloid Closet*, 1995). However, as the Legion of Decency, the Catholic Church, and conservative politicians lost their stronghold, the code was disregarded in the 1960s and forgotten by the 1970s. The once-forbidden scenes were plentiful in films—all except those showing "sex perversion" (i.e., homosexuality). For mainstream films, gayness remained, and remains, a taboo—June and Ward Cleaver can allow the Beaver to view stalker/slasher films, but never films dealing with same gender sexual situations. During the Hays days, some films inserted subtexts that could be deconstructed by gay viewers to their own desire. However, for the most part, Hollywood was squeaky clean. When Jack Lemmon and Tony Curtis made *Some Like it Hot*, the idea of men in drag was funny and acceptable—of course, they dressed that way in order to seduce women. Dustin Hoffman's *Tootsie* was legitimated by the fact that he was screamingly heterosexual, and once again, in pursuit of a female, Jessica Lange. Hoffman's character was never sexually compromised in the film, as there was never any boundary crossing. Lange's character's homophobia was revealed in her frightened reaction to Dorothy's (Hoffman) declaration of her/his love for her. Even though several men pursued Dorothy (one even proposed marriage), s/he was never in any sort of physical relationship with a male. Her spurned suitor remarked to him/her after the masquerade was revealed that "the only reason you're still alive is because I didn't kiss you." Consequently, the Dorothy character was rendered sexless. Similarly in *Victor/Victoria* and *Yentl*, the protagonist appears in drag, falls heterosexually in love and causes discomfort and fear on the part of the desired one, who believes the suitor-in-drag to be of the same sex. This uncomfortable disclosure is a secret joke between the audience and the suitor; heterosexual audiences are secure because we know the true gender—in the end it will all work out: man and woman will couple, heterosexism is reinscribed, it never really was threatened.

As we laughed through the variety shows of the 1960s, the image of Flip Wilson's Geraldine, in drag, charmed even the most macho of audiences—he was in drag, but he was always straight. Robin Williams's character, *Mrs. Doubtfire*, was also created in order to allow the male invisibly to insert himself into a female's life; he couldn't do it as a male, so he masqueraded as a woman to get closer to his estranged family. Each of these films was acceptable to even the youngest of audiences. The conquest of women through "cleaning up" drag became a popular medium for a leading man to circumvent circumstances and achieve his heterosexual goal.

Films in the 1980s and 1990s that touch on or deal directly with homosexuality are often sanitized in order to make them palatable to the moviegoing audience. For instance, *Philadelphia* was a film that dealt with a gay man with AIDS—a gay man, played by a straight man who was strangely asexual with his partner throughout the film. In a personal conversation with Ron Nyswaner, the screenwriter of *Philadelphia*, my suggestion that the film was depoliticized and sanitized was met with an angry defense of such practices. Indeed, the creator of *Philadelphia* told me that there was no political agenda within his script, he just wanted to "talk" about AIDS to the public. Heterosexual audiences were not alienated, because the film focused on the prejudices surrounding the illness; what gay men indeed *did* in bed was erased. In contrast, *Torch Song Trilogy* is about gay men in bed with gay men and is written by and stars a gay man. Men kiss and display sexual desire in the film, and consequently, the film has never been considered mainstream. These two films exemplify two main categories of films dealing, in some way, with queerness. I label the first *liberal*, as in viewed by the American public, palatable, considered for public awards, and comfortably discussed in the news media; and the second, well, I'll just call them *queer*, as in awkward to the American public, nonpalatable, *alternative*, and not discussed in the media. My contention in this chapter is that liberal movies presented to normalize queerdom and to create a comfort zone with heterosexuals serve to reify homophobia in tacit and dangerous ways. Because mainstream cinema has yet to produce a queer movie, this category remains, by and large, for films for and by gays and lesbians in an alternative genre.

As discussed in *The Celluloid Closet*, gay stock characters have been cast in plays and films for decades. Humor in the form of identifying the swishing, limp-wristed queer in films is easily won. Dressing in drag also elicits laughter from viewers, as there seems to be something innately funny about a man in women's clothing. Ed Wood's early film, *Glen or Glenda*, was a quasi-documentary about his own transvestitism. However, viewers were told more than once, being a transvestite did not mean that one was a homosexual. Wood's caution to the audience was obviously connected to his own homophobia and sexual confusion.

Many films of the past have dealt with queerness as an illness, something to be cured, something to hide. A liberal rejection of this tradition of the condemnation has emerged in films of the last decade, creating a false comfort zone among many progressive viewers. As I left the theater after watching *To Wong Fu, Thanks for Everything, Julie Newmar*, a gay male told me that he was celebrating the fact that so many straight and fraternity-type males in the audience were not offended. I argued that his comfort was illusionary, and that he should *still* not walk down frat row at night without an escort. These males were not legitimizing queerness, they were merely enjoying Flip Wilson turned into Wesley Snipes in an updated romp through dragdom. *To Wong Fu*, and *Priscilla, Queen of the Desert*, are two liberal films that reinscribe heterosexism and avoid the political. Sex is not topical in either film, that is, no one has it. In both films queers romp around in high heels looking for the "right" man—but no one has sex. Indeed, when a character in *To Wong Fu* does fall in love, holding hands is as far as they get. As queer as the dragqueens appear, they are depicted as sexless, libidoless, and there is no mention of what exactly it is that queers *actually do* sexually. Face it, queers fuck, just like heterosexuals do (well, maybe not *just like* heterosexuals). I understand, of course, that queerdom involves more than just having sex, but to deny the sexual element in homosexuality is problematic and insulting.

Sure, Wesley Snipes can go in drag. Was there ever an instant when we supposed that he could possibly swing over to males? Not in our lifetime. The straight audience's comfort with films like *To Wong Fu*, and *Priscilla*, is embedded in the fact that the viewer still sees the males as heterosexuals playing at being gay. To be fair, in *Priscilla*, there are indeed a couple of scenes that border on the transgressive. The queens' bus is vandalized with homophobic/AIDS slogans—their feelings are hurt; they are hassled in a bar—however, we are always aware as an audience that these are straight men playing gay—we know they don't *really do it.*

Indeed, I contend that when sex is explicitly discussed and engaged in (on, with, upon), the diversity romanticization of gayness by liberals is lost. Once the abstract ideal of queerness is made concrete, once gay men get physical and inscribe the body in queerness, acceptance disappears and homophobia is reinscribed. In the spirit of *Guess Who's Coming to Dinner?* liberal audiences proclaim that queerness is okay, just so it "isn't with *my* son or daughter." The liberal emphasis on diversity—all of us are different—is, on the surface, liberating. However, such a position is frightened by confrontation with the queer body. The liberal reading of gayness in films becomes dangerous to homosexual freedom and homosexual rights in the long run. When the penis comes out, all the warm and fuzzy liberal notions of acceptance retreat into a heterosexist cocoon.

To this point, the films discussed present homosexuality and drag in a humorous or sexless way. The last two decades have witnessed a new type of film, one that proclaims diversity and acceptance but reveals homophobia and disgust when issues of sexual diversity are confronted. *The Crying Game* was an independent film that many claimed shed a different, more positive light on same-sex love. In fact, *the big secret* was kept from friends and family so that *it* wouldn't be spoiled when one went to see the film. Viewers were caught up in a bittersweet tragedy cum love story; a man falls in love with a young hairstylist, an ex-lover of a man for whose death he feels responsible. The audience is enamored with the growing love affair, but when the action moves to the bedroom, and the stylist's clothes peel off to reveal a penis, the protagonist is repelled and runs to the bathroom to vomit. In the *Rocky Horror Picture Show*, young and innocent Brad believes he is having euphoric sex with his fiance. When he discovers that indeed, he is being orally titillated by a male drag queen, he jumps and runs out in horror. Both films proclaim a liberal text in that they are assumed to be crossing borders, moving beyond traditional boundaries; but when the ol' John Thomas comes out, the only *proper* reaction is to be reviled. In the same tradition, *M. Butterfly* takes it a step further; after 18 years of marriage to a man whom he believes is a woman (figure this), the character played by Jeremy Irons finds out that his wife is, indeed, a man. The only way out—suicide. Retreating to an early theme in cinema, justifiable suicide legitimates the inappropriate sexual activity. As in *The Children's Hour* in the 1950s, death is the proper solution to homosexual behavior.

More alarming are the newest wave of pro-gay films—*Jeffrey*, for example. A favorite of many queer activists, *Jeffrey* is written and produced by Paul Rudnick, a *known queer*. The film directly discusses sex (as in not being able to have any). Jeffrey is terrified of AIDS and decides to become celibate. The film opens with his narration and comment that "I love sex." However, due to the fears ushered in by the 1990s, he selects to "just cuddle" and not fall in love. Because "sex was never meant to be safe, or negotiated or fatal," Jeffrey chooses to live without a lover and without sex. His plan works until he falls in love with bulked-up Steve, the bartender. Marginally acting as his muse, Patrick "we know he is really straight" Stewart (from *Star Trek: The Next Generation* fame), as the character Sterling, tries to convince Jeffrey that love is all he needs. As an interior designer, Stewart's character flames, swishes, and flirts uncontrollably. As risky as this role appears for a straight actor, the character never kisses anyone on the lips, indeed, even his own lover is given only a couple of gratuitous pecks on the cheek. In *The Celluloid Closet,* Harvey Fierstein states that queers need "visibility at any cost." He endorses any and all depictions of queerness in the cinema, hoping that the exposure will eventually soften mainstream audiences to "gay images." I argue that this "any cost" exposure only serves to reinscribe homophobia by creating a pedagogy of heterosexism through the antiquated Hays Code. On the one hand, *Jeffrey* makes political claims about queerness, the recognition of AIDS, and men loving men. As in previous films, however, sex is implied but never explicit. One never really does know what one *does* when he is queer. Staying out of the bedroom becomes the theme of these liberal queer movies—say it, act it, just never *do* it. Hollywood films with queer content still adhere to the Hays Code:

- *open mouth kissing?* no way;
- *lustful embraces?* Only in your mind;
- *sexual perversion?* What perversion? This is a film about sexual preferences;
- *rape?* Only in prison movies, sometimes with minority men and rednecks ("squeal like a pig"), and *never* with the hero;
- *abortion?* Physically impossible;
- *prostitution and white slavery?* Yes, this is addressed, the end result usually being suicide or heterosexual conversion;
- *nudity?* Never penis-with-penis shots;
- *obscenity?* Sure, why not, well not *all* obscenity—you can call someone a cocksucker, just don't show anyone sucking cocks.

Probably the most revealing scene in *Jeffrey* is the first scene where Jeffrey and Steve have a loving kiss. Within a moment the scene dissolves into the audience focusing on two all-American hunks and their female dates eating popcorn. The males are totally grossed out, the girls think "it's cute." In this short scene, Rudnick's direction endorses the homophobic feelings one might expect in the audience. What is going on here? Why spoon feed and pander to the audience? Is this really coming out? This scene actually validates anticipated homophobia with a "that's ok, I understand that it is gross" signification.

Queer females seem to fare better in Hollywood depictions. Mainstream films bankrolled by large production companies tiptoe around the idea of woman-with-woman sex. What man—heterosexual man—is not turned on by the thought of more than one woman? Women in Hollywood's lesbianesque films are heterosexual turn-ons. The male audience is grateful to see private fantasies acted out, the female audience keeps quiet. Lesbianism (for heterosexual male consumption) is totally acceptable, and even has become a matter of media discussion. *Fried Green Tomatoes* never reveals a lesbian relationship—but come on! Sharon Stone turned both sexes on with her bisexual character in *Basic Instinct,* I don't believe anyone felt uncomfortable with his or her own sexuality as a result of Stone's performance. *Bound* is a film that both terrorizes and turns on as two women engage in a lesbian relationship. Thematically, these films come from the same root: it is evident that the women have had relationships with males and *being* a lesbian is not the point—*having sex with women is.* In *Chasing Amy,* the lesbian protagonist is converted as she becomes straight and conservative when told by a male suitor that she just needs a "deep dicking"; previous sexual liaisons are behind her, she confesses, repents, and becomes a moral, heterosexual woman. Films with women having explicit sex with women invert the themes we have explored in films about male queerness. At all costs, in a patriarchal society, dominant masculinity must be protected. The reinscription of patriarchy takes place whenever dominant masculinity is threatened. However, in female same-sex movies, there are no societal demands for women to protect a similar ideology. Consequently, in male–male movies, depiction and elongated explanations of gay lifestyles abound, with no evidence of sex. In female–female movies the opposite occurs: the emphasis is on the explicit sexual experience— rarely is there a need to explain or deepen the backgrounds of the women as gay/lesbian.

The Incredibly True Adventures of Two Girls in Love centers around two high-school girls, one straight and one gay, who fall in love. The ending of the film is not clear as to whether or not the lovers will stay together. Parents, friends, and family shout for them to cease their behavior, and the film ends with the two girls coming out of a hotel room to "face the music." Each of these films points out that at least *one* of the women wasn't *always* gay. *Ellen's* coming out in the spring of 1997 was heralded by many gay and lesbian groups as the final taboo coming of age to primetime television. The outing episode with Ellen Degeneres and entourage was accompanied by weeks of media coverage. Ellen introduced her real-life lover to the world, making sure that in every interview we were told and retold that before meeting Ellen, indeed, she (the lover) was straight. The softening of the blow of gayness is in the possibility that maybe this is just a phase. Ironically, the television network has been explicit in the promise that there will *never* be a scene with Ellen kissing another woman. While other television shows in primetime depict men and women humping in every possible way, Ellen is forbidden from a mere kiss. This is empowerment? Not quite. The question becomes: did the *Ellen* outing serve as yet another sanitation device for Hollywood's attempt to clean up queerdom?

Pedagogically as progressives we must engage in an analysis of the cultural curriculum, in this case, more critical readings of films with queer content. The sanitized notion of queerness within films does not serve either the heterosexual or homosexual community in a positive manner. Rather, it removes itself from questions of identity, community, and personal growth while neglecting recognition of the power of dominant masculinity/patriarchy. Current films romanticize queerness—queerness without sex—and exploit women fucking women who are not *really* lesbians. These antibacterial soap sprayed movies "film" over any conversation or outing in mainstream cinema. I believe as cultural consumers we can demand more in our viewing; we deserve multidimensional, thrilling, erotic, and intelligent portrayals of people that are unafraid of depicting the queer world. To take one step *out*, then two steps back, as in *Philadelphia, The Crying Game, M. Butterfly,* and the rest is not sufficient. Film as gay counterhegemonic cultural work must not apologize to homophobes for the practices of queerness. Indeed, homophobes should not tacitly dictate the operation of gay cinema. Harvey girlfriend, I love you, I worship you, and I disagree with you—visibility is not enough. Responsible, unsanitized, and self-conscious film making is.

FILMOGRAPHY

Adventures of Priscilla, Queen of the Desert, The, 1994
Basic Instinct
Bound
Chasing Amy, 1997
Children's Hour, The, 1961
Crying Game, The 1992
Fried Green Tomatoes, 1991
Glen or Glenda: Confessions of Ed Wood, 1953
Guess Who's Coming to Dinner, 1967
Incredibly True Adventures of Two Girls In Love, The 1996
Jeffrey, 1995
M. Butterfly, 1993
Philadelphia, 1993
Rocky Horror Picture Show
Some Like it Hot, 1959

The Celluloid Closet, 1995
To Wong Foo, Thanks for Everything, Julie Newmar, 1995
Tootsie, 1982
Torch Song Trilogy, 1988
Yentl, 1983

Chapter 9

Telling Tales of Surprise

Dennis Sumara
Brent Davis
York University

I'm a storyteller. I'll work to make you believe me. Throw in some real stuff, change a few details, add the certainty of outrage. I know the use of fiction in a world of hard truth, the way fiction can be a harder piece of truth. The story of what happened, or what did not happen but should have—that story can become a curtain drawn shut, a piece of insulation, a disguise, a razor, a tool that changes every time it is used and sometimes becomes something other than we intended.

The story becomes the thing needed.

—Dorothy Allison, 1996, p. 3

In her autobiographical fiction, *Two or Three Things I Know For Sure,* Dorothy Allison (1996) presents a textual performance of the way in which identity is, as Elspeth Probyn (1996) suggests, lived "on the surface." Although both Allison and Probyn acknowledge that identity is influenced by past experiences, they remind us that the remarkable thing about the human sense of self is that it constantly shifts—moving this way and that along with the fluid topographies of experience. And, although experience is always larger than expression and can never quite be captured by the words intended to describe it, for each of these writers, it must be interpreted. This rendering of experience is, of course, always an effort of fictionalizing where, through a process of what Probyn (1996) calls reconnaissance, the autobiographical moment is simultaneously an act of recognition and re-cognition.[1] It is these ongoing acts of narration and interpretation that constitute not only knowledge about oneself, but knowledge about other matters. As Allison (1996) suggests, "The story becomes the thing needed" (p. 3). As the place where memory and fantasy intertwine in strange ways, the story becomes the structure for a self that one continually struggles to know—a knowing that, of course, is never fully achieved.

As Foucault (1990) has explained, making sense of one's sexuality is understood as a method for discovering certain truths about oneself. Following his insistence that knowledge of self and knowledge of sexuality are inextricable, Sedgwick (1990) has shown that because sexuality has been expressive of both identity and knowledge it has become the centering force of the heterosexism—and of the generalized and pervasive homophobia that continues to exist. This homophobia is difficult to untangle, for as Britzman (1995) explains, "[E]very sexual identity is an unstable, shifting, and volatile construct, a contradictory and unfinalized *social relation*" (p. 68).

Understanding sexuality as a relational construct that functions to reinforce heteronormative and homophobic structures underpins the work of queer theory. As a form of cultural study, queer theory aims to take account of the polyvalent ways in which desire is culturally produced, experienced, and expressed. As Morton (1996) suggests, "Queer theory is seen as making an advance by opening up a new space for the subject of desire, a space in which sexuality becomes primary" (p. 11). Following Sedgwick, this means universalizing sexuality as an analytic category. As elaborated by Britzman (1995), this process begins by interrupting commonsense understandings of what constitutes "sex," "sexuality," "pleasure," "desire," and the relationships between these and human methods of learning about and enacting these differences.

Bridged to the work of curriculum theory, queer theory asks that the form of curriculum and the relations of pedagogy be appropriated as spaces to interpret the minutiae of differences among persons, not merely among categories of persons. "Queer" functions as a signifier that does not so much represent gay, lesbian, bisexual, and transgendered persons, but that exists as a collecting place for interpreting instances of curriculum/pedagogy that refuse what Halley (1993)[2] called the "heterosexual

---

[1]This idea, of course, is not new to curriculum theory. It was described by Pinar (1994) in his essay "The Method of *Currere*" and further developed in his and Grumet's (1976) book, *Toward a Poor Curriculum.*

[2]In her essay "The Construction of Heterosexuality," Halley (1993) explains the "heterosexual bribe" as the situation that occurs when the class "homosexual" becomes deviant by constructing it with reference to particular bodily acts—acts in which, presumably, not-homosexuals do not participate. Whereas homosexuals can be clearly defined by these bodily acts, the unruly class of "not-homosexuals," because they are only defined as those who exist outside this regulated category, cannot. This has particularly privileging conse-

bribe." In so doing, the possibilities of what might count as "knowledge" are broadened—not just knowledge about sexuality, but knowledge about how forms of desire are inextricable from processes commonly known as perception, cognition, and interpretation. Queer theory asks not that pedagogy become sexed, but that it excavate and interpret the way it already *is* sexed and, further, that it begin to interpret the ways in which it is explicitly *heterosexed.* As well, it asks that, rather than understanding not-heterosexual identities as those that can be defined with reference to a particular set of bodily acts and by aberrant and quirky lifestyles, that the continued construction of mythologies supporting that unruly class "heterosexual" be continually interrupted and re-narrated.

To enact a performance of this queer work we borrow from Foucault (1973, as cited in Probyn, 1996) the term *heterotopia.* He describes heterotopias as "disturbing places that make it impossible to name this *and* that, because they shatter or tangle common names" (p. xviii, as cited in Probyn, 1996, p. 7). A heterotopia is a *form*, a set of relations where things not usually associated with one another are juxtaposed, allowing language to become more elastic, more able to collect new interpretations and announce new possibilities. We suggest that heterotopias are critically hermeneutic spaces where "normal" is shown to be a construction and, further, where this construction is rendered available for interrogation. Our specific aim in this textual performance is to attempt some articulation of recent queer theories with curriculum theories by creating several heterotopic textual spaces. Through the use of examples from popular culture, from represented memories of our own experience, and from anecdotes from several research projects, we attempt to fashion some of the character of what we are beginning to understand as a queering of curriculum.

BAD MANNERS

As dog owners, we found a recent "Mother Goose and Grimm" (Peters, 1997) comic strip amusing. Presenting readers with an adult dog chastising a youth for inappropriate behavior when two adult canine guests arrive at the door, the caption read "Junior, where's your manners? Now go over and smell the Hendersons' butts!"

The most interesting aspect of this cartoon, of course, is the juxtaposition of smelling with human intentionality associated with forms of regulated sociality. Whereas for dogs, butt smelling is more intimately tied to com-

---

quences, for as Halley argues: "Both their epistemological privilege and their exemptions are contingent, however, on their continued silence about the heterogeneity and fabricatedness of their class—on their acceptance of what I have called the 'bribe' " (p. 97).

bined expressions of pleasure, identification, and communication, the anthropomorphic quality of the characterization of dogs in the cartoon expresses the human interdiction to regulate processes of identification. The imperative for Junior to engage in butt smelling revolves around the desire to exhibit a socially acceptable identity by engaging in appropriate social behavior. Linked to the idea that this way of social knowing renders covert the *erotic pleasure* of butt smelling, the desired performance of junior's identity announces the paradoxical ways in which knowledge of self and knowledge of sexuality work with and against one another.

How might the regulation of Junior's polymorphous sexuality and the relationship between this regulation of "sexuality" and of "knowing" contribute to curriculum theory? The most obvious interpretation is that, although we might imagine that Junior may wish to engage in butt-smelling behaviors with others, he is not much interested in doing so with the Hendersons. Rather than arguing that this lack of desire points to his disinterest in the Hendersons, it may, instead, have more to do with the social situation as it has been conditioned by experiences of the past. Perhaps, in previous butt-smelling events, Junior has had some unpleasant experience with the Hendersons. Or, perhaps it is not so much to the Hendersons that Junior objects but, rather, the structure of the experience. It may be imagined that there have been other instances where Junior has been directed to perform with unpleasant results. This rather thinly veiled psychoanalytic reading, where Junior enacts a repetition,[3] is intended to point to the ways that knowledge emerges from strange crannies and complex minglings of the expressed and the repressed.

At the same time, it is interesting to note how an act involving the touching of nose to butt (really, genitals) has, within this context, been reinterpreted from a sexualized act to a social greeting. As what Brecht (in Salvio, 1997) would call a "social geste," this ritual collects not only currently understood and approved notions of what constitutes polite behavior between adults and children but, at the same time, the other forms of knowing that circumscribe this act. Although Junior's parents are undoubtedly concerned that he will not engage in proper social behavior, they are, it could be said, not well aware that identical acts produce different social meanings and that in any act, however contextualized, these often dissonant and contradictory social meanings are, all-at-once, presented. And, one could further argue that it was Junior's *refusal* to engage in an approved act that represented his understanding of the heteroglossic quality of the social geste. The refusal, we could thus say, is not so much an ignorance of social manners but, rather, a greater awareness of the fullness

---

[3]See Pitt (1996, chap. 15, this volume) for a fuller explanation of this concept and its applications to pedagogy.

of the social gesture that was being required. If socialization is understood as a process of learning, and if learning means learning to *not* see as well as to see, then one could say that Junior had not yet learned to fully participate in the discarding function that is necessary to a schooled cognition (Davis & Sumara, 1997).

Simply put, we might argue that Junior's exhibition of "bad manners" was a refusal to engage in social contact, which, for him, is much more than a ritual of greeting. Like the handshake, the kiss on the cheek, the pat on the back, the embrace of welcome or departure that humans continually perform, the act of butt smelling is a deliberate physical contact that collapses, into that lived gesture, memories of the past and fantasies of the future. Like the knowing look that passes between two humans at a public gathering, a look that is much more than just an acknowledgment of presence, the ritualized gesture of greeting always captures more than it can contain. It is this supplement, this absent but always present meaning, that continues to seep into any social situation, often creating moments of tension, anxiety, paranoia, refusal, and arousal.

As a form, then, this ritualized act of greeting demonstrates the inextricability of desire and knowledge. One cannot perform a knowing gesture without investing oneself in expressions of desire. As Fuss (1995) suggests, practices of identification are always inseparable from processes of identity performance. Of course, this desire is always a relation, not an object. And so, in the continued interpretation of this social form, we might wonder about how adults become implicated in this ritualized greeting. One could imagine that the relation between Junior and the adult dogs is a pedagogical one and that the directive to participate in regulated social forms is a curriculum imperative. Rather than inquiring into whether or not this reproduction of a particular knowledge is of any value in this instance, it seems more interesting to wonder about adult (teacher, we might say) desire. What does this teacher want? How does this wanting, in some way, become both revealed and concealed within this curriculum form?

If curriculum is understood as being comprised of sets of relations, and if both identity and sexuality are also understood as relations that are inextricable from the production of knowledge, then it seems that curriculum forms are always tied to expressions of the sexuality–identity matrix. Further, if we concur with Butler's (1990) view that this matrix is always already heterosexualized, then the complex relations of identity–sexuality–curriculum must not only find ways to suppress the homosexual, they must necessarily suppress any form/knowledge that coexists with these sexualized forms. This means, as Sedgwick (1990) argues, that in thinking about the suppression of sexualities, we must engage in a meditation about the forms of knowledge that exist with them.

SURPRISING PARTIES

Although Junior's experience with the Hendersons most certainly will become, in some way, configured into his memories of his youth, it hardly seems correct to suggest that these will, in any simple and direct manner, create some later effect in his adult life. Rather, following Probyn (1996), we suggest that childhood is not a prototypical event for any identities, certainly not of identities understood to be queer. Although the developmental literatures in education are fond of explaining adulthood as an effect of childhood, the relation must be understood as much more complex.

This is especially impoi 'ant when considering the testimonial literature emerging from the biographical representations of gay, lesbian, bisexual, and transgendered identities. In these, the common tropes of *different* are collected together into childhood memories of "too smart, too sensitive, fondness for the wrong kind of clothing, the wrong kinds of playmates and games," and so on. Our experience working in communities with those who identify as gay, lesbian, bisexual, and transgendered has suggested to us that there really is no more common ground among the experience of queer adults' childhoods than any childhoods. Rather, like all experiences, those of childhood emerge from complex phenomenological structures. There are, as Sedgwick (1990) suggests, queer kids who do not become queer adults and kids who were not queer that do. Attempting to create an interpreted bridge between currently lived identities and memories of experience continues not only to pathologize queer identities but to support the belief that if one could control childhood experiences, one might be able to create more predictable and suitable identities. Of course, because this has been the explicit desire of most curriculum and pedagogy in North America, it is not surprising that "testimony" of the past, even the past of the socially rejected and stigmatized, continues to function as fuel for the normalizing curriculum machine.

Although we do not contest the importance of the coming-out literature and the work it accomplishes, we worry that it continues to participate in the construction of the identity of the homo as necessary other to the hetero (Halley, 1993). At the same time, we understand that this coming-out-of-the-closet work functions, in important ways, to unveil what Sedgwick (1990) called the "open secret"—that is, to demonstrate there *are* identities other than hetero that successfully exist and that contribute to the ongoing production of knowledge, and that these identities do not depend on particular bodily acts and particular forms of social organization for their existence. We wonder, however, about the continued evacuation of the homo closet in the absence of evacuation of the hetero closet. Whereas it is becoming increasingly clear that what constitutes "not-hetero" is immense and varied, there remains a generalized set of mythologies about that vast hetero closet and the unruly lines that articulate homo/hetero. What forms are available for interpreting and rearticulating these lines? We offer the following as two collecting locations for further interpretation of this question.

Several years ago, a heterosexually identified male colleague of ours insisted that we view the 1992 film, *The Crying Game*. Because we were curious about his urgency we complied. Soon after, we found ourselves in the middle of a discussion of the movie's complex plot that traces the experience of a transsexual hairdresser and her/his relationship with a heterosexual male. Although we found *many* aspects of the film fascinating, our colleague was most interested in one—an issue of identification. Precisely *when*, he wanted to know, during our viewing of the film were we aware that the main character was male and not female. "Immediately!" we responded. Although the performance of female gender identity was certainly accomplished, it seemed obvious to us that this was someone who was more accustomed to performing male than female. Our colleague told us that he had not realized the "secret" until the scene, later in the film, when the character Dil removes her/his clothing to reveal a penis. Most shocking for him was not the unveiling of the penis, but his inability to resolve his erotic feelings toward the "female" character with the new knowledge of this character's "true" identity. Rather shakily, he confessed, "I found that I continued to be attracted to this character." Now, how were we to respond to this confession of complications arising from the disclosing of what we thought was not a secret? And, how can we begin to account for his misrecognizing identity?

Our colleague's response is not as interesting as his explicit desire to confess this response to his gay colleagues. It is also interesting that this confession needed to occur only *after* we had viewed this particular film. Did he hope that we, too, had misrecognized and that we, too, might have been drawn into an erotic attraction—only in our case, the eroticization *confirmed* at the unveiling of the penis? Or, was this confession of continued attraction in the face of evidence of the penis a representation of the presence of other desires—shall we say, gay desires? Or, might we imagine that this disclosure of continued erotic fantasy constituted evidence of the complex way in which erotic, sexualized fantasies always exist *relationally*— that it is not so much the presence or the absence of *this* or *that* genitalia that matters in sexual desire but, rather, the way in which the relation is narratively constructed and interpreted? If we imagine that our colleague's continued erotic attraction emerges from this act of engagement with relations mediated by film, what might we suggest about what constitutes the boundaries between perceived and expressed knowledge and perceived and expressed sexuality? Could we begin to imagine, as Britzman (1996) suggests, that more polymorphous ways of identifying and being identified might become less of an "open secret" if these responses were more available for interpretation?

Our curiosity about the complexity of this confessional narrative prompted us to wonder about the myriad ways that sexual identities and identifications continue to evolve, depending on the specific relations and contextual and phenomenological details of experience. Linked to theories that understand identity to be co-emergent with the evolving social topography, we continued to puzzle over how we might, as researchers interested in this idea, interrupt our own notions of how the cognitive and the sexual are intertwined.

Following work that Sumara (1996) accomplished with reader-response research practices, we invited eight gay, lesbian, and transgendered teachers to respond to various texts of literature, one of which was an excerpt from Pat Califia's *Macho Sluts* called "The Surprise Party" (Califia, 1995). In this story, a young butch lesbian is abducted by three gay men uniformed as police officers. Over the course of the story she is forced to participate with the three men in various S/M sexual acts including oral, vaginal, and anal penetration, bondage, spanking and whipping, and humiliation. What is most interesting about this erotic tale is not so much the acts described as the way in which the gay men and lesbian woman experience sexuality and pleasure within this ritualized, performative structure. Although it appears that one man who controls and shapes this event is bisexual, the woman and the other two men are less decidedly so. Involved in this situation, however, their erotic identifications shift:

> Her own experience with straight sex had been as unsatisfying as Mike's and Joe's. But this act of penetration was firmly situated within a context of dominance and submission—the core of her eroticism. She had been brought to a point where there was nothing that she craved more. There could be no self-deception, no lies about not really wanting it. And these men were incredibly good at what they did. They liked fucking and being fucked, they knew how to do it, and they wanted her to like it. The element of mutual homosexuality made it seem more perverse, yet safe. (Califia, 1995, pp. 117–118)

In the discussion of our reading of "The Surprise Party," most unexpected and disconcerting to us was the experienced pleasure of our readerly involvement in this sexualized narrative. Dayna expressed our feelings most succinctly in her response:

> Although part of me was repulsed by the sex scenes, another part of me was totally aroused by them. Now I'm trying to understand whether I was aroused because there was a woman in the scene, whether I was aroused by

the idea of anal penetration by a man, or whether I was aroused by the S/M/bondage activities. I must say, I was caught off guard by these feelings and, since reading this, have had dreams and fantasies that seem contrary to ones that I want to have. I mean, how am I to continue to maintain my hard-won dyke identity when I dream about being fucked by a man?

In response to Dayna, Karen suggested that the fucking in the scene was not just being accomplished by any men, but by men who identified and were identified as gay. The pleasure of the sex act was, of course, not simply the pleasure of penetration, but penetration with knowledge of the identity of the penetrator: "I felt aroused by this scene too, but I think that I was because I experience gay men differently than straight men. I can imagine having sex with gay men but not with straight men."

Jim concurred with Karen, suggesting that, although he did not continue to have fantasies about sex with women, he believed that the arousal he experienced in the reading had to do with the structure of the sexualized act, rather than with the participants:

> Like the woman who describes her attraction to the situation more than the men, I think I found the passage intensely erotic because I am drawn to domination–submission scenes like that myself. Although I have never participated in them with women, I can imagine that I would, like her, experience them as pleasurable.

What do these responses suggest about the relationships between expressed and experienced identities, forms of sociality, and experiences of pleasure and desire? It is obvious that humans experience events of pleasure that are not necessarily understood as proper hetero- or homosexual conduct, however, the various technologies of regulation around gender and sexuality force open secret about what constitutes (sexual) pleasure. Although the closet is usually understood as the place where gay and lesbian sexualities simultaneously hide and make themselves comprehensible to themselves, following Sedgwick (1990) and Britzman (1996), we suggest that the closet's boundaries must be understood to include the polymorphous ways in which pleasure is produced. If sexuality is understood as the pleasure that is co-constructed from the various and overlapping technologies of self-formation and reformation, then the cultural mythologies around what constitutes the category of heterosexual must be called into question.

Whatever the category in which one chooses to place oneself or others, the problem becomes one of what constitutes sex or sexuality. Is sex to be confined to some act of (oral, vaginal, anal) penetration where some sort of orgasm is achieved? This narratives of what constitute the ultimate in sexual pleasure is, of course, not convincing to, we might say, our pet dog or, one might further venture to say, the human infant. Although this is not the place to enter into a discussion about whether or not children experience sexual pleasure, any adult caregiver can attest to the obvious delight that infants and young children have in sucking (nipples, fingers, toes, for example) and of manipulating the genitals. And, whereas babies are not prone to butt smelling (likely only because they are less ambulatory than puppies), these practices, certainly, for many of the human species, become popular later in life.

If, as Sedgwick (1990) and Fuss (1995) argue, sexuality is to be understood as one of the intertwining valences of what constitutes the experience and activity of identity and identification, there is a need to come to some decisions about what constitutes, for the human species at least, sexuality. As Foucault (1990) has shown, in the last 100 years or so, sexuality has been primarily associated with a particular kind of identification called sexual orientation—which, in turn, is complexly linked with same or opposite-sex attraction. Because sex, in this usage, is synonymous with the distinction made between male and female, it is understood as gender. But, of course, sex is also understood as that which is chromosomally or gonadally determined—or, as Epstein (1995) suggests, when evidence of unambiguous sexual genitalia are present. And so sex announces at the same time acts and bodies that complete these acts. Sexuality, although often collapsed with sex, is generally used to signify the larger experience of the way in which sex and one's identified sex collapse to form a particular way of expressing physical pleasure or, we might say, participation in an agreed-on set of sexualized event structures. For those who identify as heterosexual, sex is generally understood to be comprised of a relatively narrow selection of copulatory and/or oral experiences (penis–vagina, penis–mouth, vagina–mouth, mouth–mouth). For those who identify or who are identified as not-heterosexual, sex includes activities that are, remarkably, similar. Substitute "anal" for "vaginal" in male–male interactions and "vagina" for "penis" in female–female and the *imagined* picture is more or less complete.

What would happen if sex and sexuality were not understood as discrete acts enacted by particular identities but, rather, as sets of social relations that produce physical, emotional, and psychic pleasure? And, what if one's identification with one form of attraction or desire over another were understood to co-evolve with the constantly shifting relations that comprise all aspects of human subjectivity, including those experiences we have come to call sex?

Our male colleague's disrupting and surprising response to *The Crying Game* and the responses of certain members of our reading group to "The Surprise Party" point to the complex ways in which identities and sexualities are formed and reformed through ongoing acts of remembered and fantasized acts of relationality. Most important, these surprising responses interrupt the certainties about what might constitute a gay or lesbian identity. As Sedgwick (1990) suggests, "People are different from one another" (p. 22). Lives are not lived as stereotypes (Britzman, 1995) or as categories (Probyn, 1996). As was clear during the 2 years of meetings with our Queer Teachers Study Group, the particular identifications each of us made could not be confined to what might constitute a "proper" gay or lesbian identity. In fact, it seemed that, rather than finding convergence on the basis of our explicit queerness, we continued to locate points of radical difference among ourselves. Lived and experienced identities as reported in the group, particularly as these were disclosed in response to involvement with works of literature, suggested that Sedgwick (1990) is correct when she contends that:

> [T]he sister or brother, the best friend, the classmate, the parent, the child, the lover, the ex-: our families, loves and enmities alike, not to mention the strange relations of our work, play, and activism, prove that even people who share all or most of our own positionings along these crude axes may still be different enough from us, and from each other, to seem like all but different species. (p. 22)

Most surprising to us, then, was not so much that our erotic identifications revealed identities that interrupted our understanding of who we imagined ourselves to be but rather, that these identifications suggested that we needed to refuse to believe that we could use identifying signifiers such as gay, lesbian, and transgendered as if we knew precisely what they meant. Further, we needed to understand the complex ways in which cultural mythologies about sexuality and identity collected within these categorical signifiers and, most importantly, of the supplement that continued to exist, rather untidily, all around them. Although we would have liked to believe that gay and lesbian was something we were or were perfecting, in the end, we concurred with Sedgwick (1990) in understanding that we could not come to any agreement about what that really meant. Acknowledging the way in which identities and sexualities were complexly situated with/in remembered, lived, and fantasized experiences and expressions meant rejecting the minoritizing view that queer could become a signifier that captures the various identities of those who do not identify as heterosexual. Instead, it helped us to understand queer as a collecting signifier for the notion that, just as knowledge cannot be in control of itself, neither can experiences of sex and expressions of sexuality be in control of themselves.

What, we wondered, could these interpretations contribute to an understanding of schooled cognitions and identities?

STRANGE STIRRINGS

As part of a larger research project with a group of teachers from a small inner-city school, we participated in a 2-month teaching project with one teacher and her grade five/six class. This teaching unit was developed around readings and responses to Lois Lowry's (1993) novel, *The Giver*. Decidedly Orwellian, this novel presents the reader with a futuristic society where all historical memory is lost to the general population but is retained by one person, designated the "receiver of memories," whose task it is to use this knowledge, when necessary, to advise political leaders. The rest of the population exists in State-controlled and regulated family units comprised of two adults, one male and one female, and one or two adopted children. Reproduction is accomplished by birth mothers, and the biological origin of the children is not known by the parents. Sexual feelings, or "stirrings," are forbidden—and, when they arise in adolescent children, they are quickly extinguished with daily doses of medication. The onset of stirrings is detected by parents through the daily practice of "dream telling," which is a required activity by all members of each family unit. The principal character in the novel is Jonah, who, like all 12-year-olds in the community, has been assigned his life's work—in his case, the very honorable position as the new Receiver of Memories. In preparation for his new role, Jonah must meet with the current receiver—newly renamed the "Giver"—who, by laying his hands on Jonah's bare back, transmits, in installments, all historical cultural memories, including those such as memory of color, of pain, and of pleasure to which no other citizens have access.

In interesting ways this literary fiction shows the complex manners in which knowledge about things cannot be dissociated from knowledge about historical forms and knowledge about oneself. By way of illustration, as Jonah learns about the pain associated with war and the pleasure associated with seeing a color or riding a sleigh, he becomes aware that his identity is changing. As well, new knowledge about how "unacceptable" babies and how the very old are euthanized, casts the identity of his father—"nurturer of babies"—in a new light. Although access to knowledge is exciting for Jonah, it is also exceedingly painful because he is not only forced to reconsider what he knows, he is compelled to reinterpret past relations with his parents and other community members and to make new decisions about who he thinks he is. Additionally, because he has been directed to refuse the medication that controls his sexual feelings (his stirrings), he must now learn to understand the complex way in which desire and knowledge intertwine with experiences of identity.

Prior to reading the novel with the children, we participated in two reading group discussions: one with teachers from the school, the other with teachers from the school and a number of parents who had also read the book. The first discussion occurred as part of a planned research strategy to inquire into teachers' understandings of the function of the literary imagination in school settings; the second discussion emerged from the teachers' fears, voiced in the first discussion, that parents in this community would be offended if this particular novel were used as part of the elementary school curriculum. Whereas this concern provided the impetus for extending the invitation to parents, when we met with them, worries of possible censorship were quickly extinguished by a general fascination with the themes announced in *The Giver*. Although the teachers had anticipated that parents would be primarily concerned with whether the book was suitable for their children to read, it seemed that all present were rather insistent that it be read. As a form, they strongly believed that this piece of literature accomplished some necessary *work*—interestingly, the sort of work that they were not prepared to do—that is, to discuss and interpret what might constitute human sexuality and desire, and to examine the complex ways in which this is regulated.

As a heterotopia, then, the shared reading of this novel with teachers and parents of school-age children created an opportunity for us to consider, with them, important issues related to the surveillance and regulation of knowledge, of economic production, of sexuality, and of identity. It was these discussions, which asked adults to interrupt the transparency of their current lived experiences, that prompted their strong desire for their children to become involved. Most important, this literary form became a moving and adaptive one that continued to mediate and collect relations among adults in this community, among parents and children, among teachers and parents and children, and so on. Because it refused the suppression of the necessary relation between identity and sexuality, we suggest that this heterotopic form created a particularly interesting queer curriculum.

Most fascinating to us were the focus group discussions, conducted at the end of the project, involving several groups of the children, their teacher, and one of us (Sumara). Organized to create another heterotopic space for continued inquiry into the ongoing interpretations we and the children were making to our readings of *The Giver*, these discussions focused, most interestingly, on the way in which particular knowledge generated complex changes in one's experienced and expressed identity—and, further, in one's perceptions and interpretations of others' identities.

Most interesting, of course, was our discussion of the suppression of the stirrings. Referring to her own experience of learning about sexuality, Gina suggested that information had not come directly from her parents but, rather, through forms such as books and videos that they provided for her. For Gina, discussion of stirrings was an uncomfortable subject because, as she told us, "My family's really weird around that subject and now I think that I'm weird around it too." Although it was clear to Gina that knowledge about sexuality was, in some way, part of the expressed identities of her parents and of herself, this knowledge was always mediated by forms such as books and videos given to her by her parents in the absence of any discussion. Although one might imagine that this pedagogical short-coming might be overcome in school, our discussion showed that, like at home, knowledge about sexual feelings was also mediated by forms—in this case, curriculum artifacts such as the films shown in health class.

Margaret, on the other hand, although generally rather quiet and with-drawn in class during our work with *The Giver*, provided lengthy elabora-tions of her knowledge about matters related to sexuality during our focus group interview. This knowledge, it seemed, emerged, in part, from her family's habit of talking about books: "My mum, my brother, and I like to build up conversations around books. One of the things from this book we talked about was stirrings. We even told some of our stirrings. Talking about them helps us to learn more about each other." Margaret continued to reveal the complex way in which her knowing about her own and her parents' sexualities was related to her knowing about other matters—most specifically matters about relations among her peers at school. When Trent, during the same interview, indicated that he did not understand the sig-nificance of stirrings in his confession, "I don't have stirrings," Margaret responded by explaining, "Don't worry, you'll have them soon. Girls usually get them before boys. Most of the girls in our class have stirrings, but hardly any of the boys do. I'm just starting to have stirrings."

The most interesting question emerging from this frank disclosure of "just starting to have stirrings" is not so much the disclosure but rather, what we imagined was disclosed. What, for Margaret, constitutes a sexual stirring? What, for that matter constitutes a sexual stirring for anyone? It is clear that Margaret's comment emerges, in part, from schooled mytholo-gies about what constitutes adolescence and the awakening of sexual desire, but the question of what might constitute pre-adolescent stirrings is ob-scured. Trent's comment, "I don't have stirrings," is perhaps the most helpful here, for it exposes a general ignorance that, as Sedgwick (1990) suggests, necessarily exists alongside any expression of knowledge:

> Insofar as ignorance is ignorance *of* a knowledge—a knowledge that may itself, it goes without saying, be seen as either true or false under some other regime of truth—these ignorances, far from being pieces of the originary dark, are produced by and correspond to particular knowledges and circulate as part of particular regimes of truth. (p. 8)

What ignorance is presented when Margaret suggests that she has stirrings and Trent suggests that he doesn't have them? And, following Britzman's

(1996) argument that sexuality education must become more interested in what structures the production of knowledge about sexuality (not just in providing information about sex), we must wonder how curriculum could begin to insert itself into the tangled web of ignorance that currently exists in and around discourses about sexuality.

What was most fascinating to us about this matter-of-fact exchange of information about sexual feelings among these children was not so much that they were having it, but the cultural mythologies around what constituted a *sexual* feeling that was being reproduced in their tale. Although there was considerable evidence to suggest that their sexuality education had been, at best, sporadic and flimsy, it was clear that they had formed very definite opinions about what constituted a sexual feeling, about when this feeling might occur, about which sex achieved these feelings first, and about how these feelings were to manifest themselves. It may seem that it was the discussion in and around the stirrings that created the most interest for these readers, but it became clear that this was, for them, rather mundane when read alongside various other specific events associated with the deliberate suppression of historical and cultural memory.

When both adults (that is, parents and teachers) and young readers were pressed to describe what they imagined a stirring to be, or what kind of situation might create the experience of a stirring, predictable responses were given. Inevitably, stirrings were feelings that one had when in situations involving the opposite sex. Stirrings, it seemed, were always associated with feelings one imagines one might have when in the presence of a certain someone of the opposite sex, particularly if there was some promise of a specific sort of sexual activity. In other words, stirrings were explicitly associated with the very narrow band of sex activities described earlier in this chapter. When asked whether stirrings could be, say, the pleasure of chocolate, a good book, or a roller coaster ride, both children and adults, although considering the possibilities, insisted on demarcating stirrings as something that was contained within a specific narrative of (hetero)sex. Although passing mention was made by one of the parents that, of course "there are those who *do* have sexual feelings for the same sex," this was offered as an aberrant possibility.

Because neither the Giver of Memories nor Jonah (the new Receiver of Memories) are permitted to take the medication that suppresses sexual desire, the question of what they *do* with this desire emerged. Because biological reproduction occurred outside human acts of copulation, rendering it unnecessary for survival of the species, we wondered, with the children and the adults, how stirrings might weave their way through each character's lived experiences. Most of the conversation around this topic was rather mundane, emphasizing discourses of suppression and redirection. However, 11-year-old Gina's response was most interesting:

I think that stirrings means something different for Jonah and The Giver because they have memories of other things. . . . They can see other things like color. And they know things that other people don't know—like the stuff about the killing of old people and babies. So, I think that—I'm not sure why—that stirrings are different for them.

If, following Foucault (1990), we believe that knowledge about sexuality becomes the primary link to all other knowledges, all other forms of knowing, then it seems that Gina's intuition about different experiences of stirrings is profoundly correct. Learning to see differently, learning to see what is not previously noticed, does not merely add a layer of information to what is already known. Rather, as an act of re-cognition, the self that knows freshly understands itself differently and, as a consequence, cognizes the world differently. What might constitute a stirring for one who can see the color "red" might not for one who cannot.[4] And, of course, as Sedgwick (1990) and Britzman (1995) have suggested, people are different and experience sex differently. Most interesting for understanding what constitutes a queering of curriculum might be to read Gina's interpretation against the responses of Junior to the Hendersons, of our colleague to *The Crying Game*, and of our coresearchers to "The Surprise Party."

Junior's resistant response to the butt-smelling imperative, it was suggested, may have emerged from his understanding of the heteroglossic nature of any gesture and the complex ways in which any social gesture always performs more than it intends. The gesture, as an historically effected and culturally situated act, then, carries what Bakhtin (1981) calls, the "smells" of its past, the genealogy of its prior use. The process of acknowledging, through a ritualized act, the presence of the Hendersons— of identifying through a particular form of identification—then, is not merely a relational act that is lived out within the limitations of current perception and cognition. Rather, this act of identification necessarily participates in a complex hermeneutic interpretation of past, present, and projected understandings of what butt smelling means. Resistance to this act, it seems, is not merely resistance of what is readily available to Junior's perception and cognition; resistance, in part, occurs within the interpretive location that includes Junior's memories, cultural mythologies of what constitutes recognition and identification, and of the complex relation between a gesture that is merely polite and one that is part of an act of sex (however sex might be understood by Junior).

What does this suggest about our colleague's anxiety about continued sexual attraction to the character Dil and about our reading group's surprising erotic attractions to male–female sex? In each of these erotic re-

---

[4]See Oliver Sacks' (1995) essay "The Colorblind Painter" for an interesting discussion of the effects of altered sensorial abilities and its relation to "knowing" "identity" and "sexuality."

sponses it seems that identification and misidentification depended on knowledge of the particular relations that constituted "sex." If we could imagine that our male colleague located eroticism within relations of seduction and teasing, as played out by the hyperfeminized other (toward which heterosexualized males are socialized), it seems not at all surprising that his erotic attention would continue to be gathered by the persona created by Dil. This is particularly so because Dil, of course, did not only look like the sort of sexual partner to whom he would be attracted, but she/he performed the complex relations of gender identity in ways that refused (even with evidence of the penis) the possibility of male gender. Following Butler (1990, 1993), who suggests that gender is always a relational performance rather than an object to be apprehended and perfected, it seems that the heterosexualized male subject necessarily participates in a set of relations that, in their structural familiarity, produce erotic responses. This theorizing of the erotic as relational helps us understand the female character's enjoyment of the S/M/bondage scene in "The Surprise Party" who claimed ownership of her erotic enjoyment by suggesting that it was the existence of the *structure* of submission–domination that permitted the eroticism to surface and maintain itself. It is not so much, then, the act of sex—nor was it the particular genitalia of the participants—that mattered for erotic fulfillment; rather it was a particular set of structures and associations contained within a particular narrative structure that permitted eroticism. To put it crudely, satisfaction depends more on the complex relationship among fear, pain, submission, domination, and pleasure that structures the fulfillment of erotic desire than any particular physical, emotional, or psychic gesture or part of human anatomy.

Stirrings, then, as Gina brilliantly interpreted, are not objects, but relations that depend on particular forms of knowledge and interpretation. Given this understanding, we may question one of the most fundamental aspects of the plot of *The Giver*—the very possibility for sexual stirrings even to occur when historical and cultural memory is nonexistent. If the erotic emerges from the complex relations of memory, of presently lived experience, and of fantasy, could stirrings occur without memory?

These were some of the questions announced by the curriculum form created by our shared readings of "The Surprise Party" and of *The Giver*. Although the specifics, of course, differed in our conversations with our Queer Teachers Study Group and with the 10- and 11-year-old children, these commonplace locations for interpretation became, for us, a curriculum that was noticeably queer. Even though our originating intentions in these various forms of curriculum inquiry had been vague, our continued participation in and interpretation of these events helped us better understand what might constitute a queering of curriculum.

QUEER CURRICULUM

In 1967, at the Ohio State University Curriculum Theory Conference, James Macdonald presented a paper in which he suggested that "Curriculum theory should be committed . . . to human fullness in creation, direction, and use" (Pinar, Reynolds, Slattery, & Taubman, 1995, p. 181). For Macdonald, and for the reconceptualist curriculum theorists follow,[5] curriculum theory became an incitement to action. That is, curriculum theory became understood as an ethical imperative for politicized cultural work rather than as a discursive practice that only commentates from the sidelines. Although Macdonald's work predated the development of the field of "cultural studies," his words echo alongside more recent comments by cultural theorist Lawrence Grossberg (1995), who suggests that the most important work of cultural studies is to develop theory that opens up new possibilities, even if these possibilities begin in the realm of the imaginative. Additionally, Grossberg insists that work done in the name of cultural studies must be, in the end, optimistic. And, as Macdonald suggested of curriculum theory 30 years ago, cultural studies must primarily become concerned with sharing new knowledge with people who aim to do something with it. This means, of course, that both cultural studies and curriculum theory are interested in the pedagogical as a relationship and curriculum as a form within which to enact these interventions, these transformations of thinking and of cultural practice. Understood as such, curriculum theory is not subsumed within the larger category of cultural studies, but is a necessary valence to it.

This chapter has been developed around a general interest in issues of culture and curriculum, and has been specifically focused on trying to understand the developing relationship between queer and curriculum theories. Not surprisingly, queer theorists have suggested that, as a necessary participant in cultural studies, queer theories must do some difficult work. This is most aptly put by Michael Warner (1993) who insists that:

> For academics, being interested in queer theory is a way to mess up the desexualized spaces of the academy, exude some rut, reimagine the public from and for which intellectuals write, dress, and perform. Nervous over the prospect of a well-sanctioned and compartmentalized academic version of "lesbian and gay studies," people want to make theory queer, not just to have a theory about queers. (p. xxvi)

This is our understanding of the intersection of queer and curriculum theories. And, whereas "queer" has recently been used to collect studies

---

[5]See Pinar et al. (1995) for an historical survey of the reconceptualist curriculum movement.

of the relation among sexuality, perception, cognition, interpretation, and their attendant identities and practices, we suggest that there have been, for many years, curriculum theorists who have attended to these complex relations. These writers have not, in the past, identified themselves as "queer" theorists, but they most certainly have attempted to "make theory queer" and to "mess up the desexualized spaces of the academy."[6]

This chapter has not so much presented an outline of what queer curriculum theory might be, but a textual performance of how curriculum and pedagogy might begin to understand both the production of sexuality and the production of human perception, cognition, and interpretation as inextricably entwined valences of the ongoing surface structure that we commonly call human identity. What makes this performance queer is not so much that it deals specifically and explicitly with sex, but that, following the work of Britzman (1995, 1996), it attempts to perform this understanding of sex as a *relation* rather than as an *object*. This, of course, is an obvious evolution of the sort of curriculum theorizing work that Macdonald announced in 1967. As such, it is a necessary valence to cultural studies—and, we believe, an interesting contribution to queer theories. Although we acknowledge our debt to those disciplines that have so deliberately and tenaciously continued to develop queer theories, we strongly believe that the work of queer curriculum theory has much to contribute to that interdisciplinary work.

Because of our conviction that curriculum theory must, in some way, find words to describe itself so that it might be useful for those who aim to use it, we conclude by offering our preliminary understandings of what, for us, constitutes a queering of curriculum and pedagogy. It is important to state that we do not list these as principles or characteristics or requisites but, instead, as placeholders that, we hope, will continue to collect a deeper understanding of what it might mean to interrupt the heteronormative relations of curriculum. And, because we readily admit that these conceptual placeholders are, for us, tentative, we imagine that they might become useful beginning forms for continued exploration of how the spaces of pedagogy might become more attentive to the complex relations of sexualities and identities.

First, we suggest that queer curriculum attempts to come to some deeper understanding of the forms that curriculum might take so that sexuality is included not as an object of study but as a necessary valence of all knowing. The character of this was announced by Britzman (1995) when she asked the provocative question, "What might it mean for educators to explore the dynamics of sexual subordination and sexual pleasure in ways

---

[6]See, for example, Aswell Doll, 1995; Britzman, 1996; in press; Grumet, 1988; Pinar, 1994; and Sears, 1992.

that require the involvement of everyone?" (p. 68). We believe that the hermeneutic interpretive work accomplished by our Queer Teachers Study Group and the work done by teachers, parents, and elementary-age children around shared readings of *The Giver* perform some of this work. By attempting to interpret the complex relations among knowledge, desire, and identities (not just gay and lesbian identities), these commonplace locations for interpretation yielded complexified understandings of the ways in which knowledge–ignorance, hetero–homo, male–female are always articulated in and through one another. Further, as we hope that some of our interpretations have shown, the continued wondering about how ignorance is always already a valence of knowledge created situations where, as readers and teachers, we were able to create locations for the rearticulation of the lines of knowing and identity.

Second, we believe that instead of focusing on the elaboration and interpretation of gay, lesbian, bisexual, and transgendered identities, a queer curriculum wonders about the unruly heterosexual closet and seeks to render visible the always known but usually invisible desires and pleasures that circulate throughout it. Curriculum forms that do this work are not those that ask persons to identify identifications that are aberrant to what is understood to be proper heterosexual conduct. Rather, queer curriculum forms invite persons to participate in structures that create surprising (and often troubling) moments of contact and revelation. Like our colleague's response to *The Crying Game* and our attempts to interpret that response, a queer curriculum calls into question the very existence of heterosexuality as a stable category—and, in so doing, shows how very queer it can be.

Third, because a queer curriculum practice understands forms such as sexuality, identity, and cognition as relations rather than objects, and believes these to be entangled in and through one another, it tries to create situations where the complexity of these is made available for study. This means, of course, that rather than studying sexuality as a subset of, say, cognition, a queer curriculum understands that all knowing is sexualized and all sexuality is cognitive. Most aptly demonstrated in our reading group's erotic responses to the structure of domination–submission portrayed in Pat Califia's "The Surprise Party," this conception of queer curriculum suggests that erotic responses, rather than being understood as products of one's identity, must be more complexly caught up in one's manners of identification with forms and structures (rather than with body parts).

Fourth, queer curriculum practices are interested more in understanding and interpreting differences among persons than in understanding differences among categories of persons. So, although queer curriculum must continue to be interested in identities that do not identify themselves as heterosexual, it is more interested in wondering under what circumstances one might identify oneself as *this* or *that*. Whereas a queer curriculum continues to be concerned with the complex relations among past, present, and imagined experience, it rejects the notion that events during childhood are prototypical for events in adulthood. Instead, a queer curriculum is intrigued by how identities are topographically arranged and the remarkable ways they can become rearranged. As a move to the transformative, this understanding of the possibility for adaptation and rearticulation is vital to any curriculum that claims to be queer, for it rejects the notion that we must continue to be responsible to and for identities that we have long since rejected, forgotten, or abandoned.

Fifth, a queer curriculum is always interested in questions of desire, of pleasure, and of sexuality—and, most importantly, in wondering how we might continue to interrupt our understandings of what constitutes each of these and how they make themselves known. Linking our male colleague's responses to *The Crying Game* and our responses to "The Surprise Party" and to the signifier "queer," generally—and to an understanding of queer curriculum, specifically—means making the move to believing that sexualities, identities, and epistemologies are inextricable from one another; they are *relations*. When identity-and-identification is understood as a complex relation, it becomes less surprising that one would experience an unexpected erotic pleasure, for in this formulation sexual pleasure has less to do with the object of identification than with the way in which the identifications and identities are relationally involved. Brought to curriculum, this queer idea suggests that the forms known as curriculum become not so interested in reporting on existing knowledge but in inquiring into the ways in which knowledge becomes available, in the ways knowledge is structured, and in the complex manner identities are continually formed through curriculum identifications.

Finally, events where curriculum is queered are always heterotopic. As locations where unusual juxtapositions are made, these heterotopic spaces are meant to function as interruptions to the familiarity of normalized perception and cognition—and, as such, are intended to create possibilities for new understandings. As a form, the relations that might constitute a queer curriculum must strive to create collecting places for hermeneutic interpretation of the various technologies that function to reproduce heterosexual and not-heterosexual identities and, further, that it inquire into the complex ways in which knowledge becomes structured and made available within these heteronormative forms. A queer curriculum is interested in creating forms where the heterosexual matrix is rendered visible and available for interpretation. As an aesthetic form, the relations that comprise a queer curriculum function to expose the formulated as being in need of reformulation and to render the transparent opaque.

In the end, of course, the most important function of a queer curriculum is to remind us that knowledge is never in control of itself. As Dorothy

Allison's character Aunt Dot explains, "Lord, girl, there's only two or three things I know for sure.... Only two or three things.... Of course it's never the same things, and I'm never as sure as I'd like to be" (Allison, 1996, p. 5).

ACKNOWLEDGMENT

The research that supported the writing of this chapter was funded by The Social Sciences and Humanities Research Council of Canada (Grant #639252).

REFERENCES

Allison, D. (1996). *Two or three things I know for sure.* New York: Plume.

Aswell Doll, M. (1995). *To the lighthouse and back: Writings on teaching and living.* New York: Peter Lang.

Bakhtin, M. (1981). *The dialogic imagination: Four essays* (M. Holquist, ed., C. Emerson & M. Holquist, trans.). Austin: University of Texas Press.

Butler, J. (1990). *Gender trouble: Feminism and the subversion of identity.* New York: Routledge.

Butler, J. (1993). *Bodies that matter: On the discursive limits of "sex."* New York: Routledge.

Britzman, D. (1995). What is this thing called love? *Taboo, 1*(1), 65–93.

Britzman, D. (1996). On becoming a "little sex researcher": Some comments on a polymorphously perverse curriculum. *Journal of Curriculum Theorizing, 12*(2), 4–11.

Britzman, D. (in press). *Lost subjects, contested objects: Toward a psychoanalytic inquiry of learning.* Albany: SUNY Press.

Califia, P. (1995). The surprise party. In P. Califia & J. Fuller (Eds.), *Forbidden passages: Writings banned in Canada* (pp. 110–124). San Francisco: Cleis Press.

Davis, B., & Sumara, D. (1997). Cognition, complexity, and teacher education. *Harvard Educational Review, 67*(1), 105–125.

Epstein, J. (1995). *Altered conditions: Disease, medicine, and storytelling.* New York: Routledge.

Foucault, M. (1973). *The order of things.* New York: Vintage Books.

Foucault, M. (1990). *The history of sexuality: An introduction.* New York: Vintage.

Fuss, D. (1995). *Identification papers.* New York: Routledge.

Grossberg, L. (1995). Cultural studies: What's in a name (one more time). *Taboo, 1*(1), 1–37.

Grumet, M. (1988). *Bitter milk: Women and teaching.* Amherst: University of Massachusetts Press.

Halley, J. (1993). The construction of heterosexuality. In M. Warner (Ed.), *Fear of a queer planet: Queer politics and social theory* (pp. 82–102). Minneapolis: University of Minnesota Press.

Lowry, L. (1993). *The giver.* New York: Bantam Doubleday.

Morton, D. (Ed.). (1996). *The material queer: A LesBiGay cultural studies reader.* Boulder, CO: Westview Press.

Peters, M. (1997, January 13). Mother Goose and Grimm. In *The Vancouver Sun*, p. A-22.

Pinar, W. (1994). *Autobiography, politics and sexuality: Essays in curriculum theory 1972–1992.* New York: Peter Lang.

Pinar, W., Reynolds, W., Slattery, P., & Taubman, P. (1995). *Understanding curriculum.* New York: Peter Lang.

Pinar, W., & Grumet, M. (1976). *Toward a poor curriculum.* Dubuque, IA: Kendall/Hunt Publishing Company.

Pitt, A. (1996). Fantasizing women in the women's studies classroom: Toward a symptomatic reading of negation. *Journal of Curriculum Theorizing, 12*(4), 32–40.

Probyn, E. (1996). *Outside belongings.* New York: Routledge.

Sacks, O. (1995). *An anthropologist on mars.* Toronto: Alfred Knopf.

Salvio, P. (1997). On keying pedagogy as an interpretive event. In T. Carson & D. Sumara (Eds.), *Action research as a living practice* (pp. 247–261). New York: Peter Lang.

Sears, J. (Ed.). (1992). *Sexuality and the curriculum.* New York: Teachers College Press.

Sedgwick, E. (1990). *Epistemology of the closet.* Berkeley: University of California Press.

Sumara, D. (1996). *Private readings in public: Schooling the literary imagination.* New York: Peter Lang.

Warner, M. (Ed.). (1993). *Fear of a queer planet: Queer politics and social theory.* Minneapolis: University of Minnesota Press.

Chapter 10

Understanding Curriculum as Gender Text: Notes on Reproduction, Resistance, and Male–Male Relations

William F. Pinar
Louisiana State University

INTRODUCTION: THE REPRODUCTION OF FATHER

Reproduction theory, that is, the explanation of the context, structure, and experience of the curriculum by pointing to its reproductive function for the socio-politico-economic status quo, has now been surpassed. Its mechanicalness, its reduction of the Subject to passivity, its obfuscation of structural contradictions and of resistance, have been condemned in several recent essays (Apple, 1981; Giroux, 1981) and conferences (Wexler, 1982). With few exceptions, curriculum theorists on the left now call for examination of resistance, not only as an empirical reality to be documented and understood, but also as a call for political action.

I wish to situate reproduction and resistance theory oedipally. I do so not to reduce them to their oedipal status and functions. I offer this sketch in order to illumine feminist and gender issues that, in their current stages of formulation, are only cursorily acknowledged by reproduction and resistance theory. Although such courtesy is appreciated, it is insufficient. It denies the seriousness and scope of gender issues as it co-opts the anger and actions of those who live them. Further, I believe the broad political project of which resistance is a historical, theoretical moment, is finally sabotaged by reducing feminist and gender issues to their political and economic concomitants.

What is the oedipal status of reproduction theory, and of its offspring, resistance theory? In a word, I see them as the analyses of the heterosexual son as he observes how the authority of the Father is reproduced and can be resisted. The oedipal function of such theory is parallel to the action of the heterosexual son: the replacement, someday, of Father. Heterosexual sons become fathers, and fathers require sons, daughters, and wives, all metaphors for underclasses. Father is reproduced, regardless of the rhetoric of horizontal social relations (i.e., brotherhood and sisterhood). Educationally, resistance theory, née reproduction theory, appears confined to altering the content of curriculum but not its political consequences. The conversation of father may change but not his position at the dinner table. Schooling in this sense is the story of the sons' and daughters' initiation into the father's ways, and their consignment of the mother, sometimes with her complicity, to the status of unpaid or underpaid laborer and sexual slave. The family drama is the cultural-historical drama writ small and concretely.

Understanding curriculum and curriculum theory oedipally is not fortuitous. The feminist and gay movements[1] have brought to attention issues of gender origin, identity, and prejudice. In curriculum studies, rapid theoretical movement is evident (see Pinar, 1981). For instance, Madeleine R. Grumet (1988) traces the gender history of pedagogy in American common schools during the 19th and early 20th centuries. She concludes that the growing number of female teachers—"the feminization of teaching"—functioned to ensure "pedagogy for patriarchy" (pp. 165–184).

Grumet argues that male administrators enlisted the assistance of female teachers to induct the children into their ways, ways that conditioned the boys to become docile, efficient workers, and the girls to become willing and grateful housewives and full-time mothers. Feminist analysis attacks this complicity and passivity, and in so doing has helped initiate and name the struggle beyond them. In curriculum theory this struggle and its naming have just begun.[2] It is a struggle that will be sabotaged by men who refuse to examine their role in its origin and necessity. Feminist literature has examined this role from points of view that are hers; I wish to sketch it from his. Specifically I am interested in how male–male relations are implicated in male–female oppression. My focus is primarily, but not exclusively, male pre-oedipal, oedipal, and post-oedipal experience. Although

---

[1]Guy Hocquenghem (1978) suggests it is no accident that the two movements have been co-extensive: "Experience in Europe and the U.S.A. has shown that the women's movement and the gay movement have coincided. It is as if society could not bear to see in man what it demands to see in women, as if to dominate women and to repress homosexuality were one and the same thing" (p. 126). Misogyny and homosexual repression are of course related.

[2]The initial interest in sexism expressed itself in textual analyses, such as examination of textbooks, especially textbooks used in elementary schools, for sex stereotyping. In the past 5 years, feminism has had a more theoretical impact on the field. See, for instance, Grumet (1981) and Miller (1982).

this focus may make this chapter of minimal use to feminist struggle and theory, I hope it will be viewed as politically allied with them. However, men's analysis cannot be expected to coincide with women's, even if they originate with them.

I suspect that men cannot usefully appropriate feminist understanding and substitute it for their own. We cannot become "feminist men" for long or very deeply without denying our gender-specific life histories. As feminists have discovered for themselves, we must distance ourselves from those we learned to need and love and—as feminists have documented—violate. Such psychological distance from women is in the service of understanding our relations with them, not only from their point of view and certainly not from our taken-for-granted view. Whereas feminist understanding provokes an analogous process of our own, that process is undergone by ourselves. Further, I agree with some feminist separatists that women cannot fully support us without denying their oppression. If aware of that oppression, women have little goodwill to extend to us, at this historical juncture. Having relied on women, traditionally, for succor, we face a difficult, potentially dangerous task without them. We men do exhibit "stunted relational potential."[3] Intimacy with women threatens us, but less so than intimacy with other men. I am suggesting that in order to understand our oppression of women, we must work to understand each other. This work has begun in the culture at large, with men's groups of various but often superficial sorts. Our work with ourselves is well behind the work women have done with themselves. This analysis, I hope, can contribute to an acceleration of this necessary study of male–male relations.

PRE-OEDIPAL RELATIONS AND POST-OEDIPAL DISTORTIONS

To begin to understand male gender history, we can focus on two items that influence that history. One is the nature of the pre-oedipal relationship with the mother; the other is the inferential character of paternity. Both are described by Nancy Chodorow (1978) in her *The Reproduction of Mothering: Psychoanalysis and the Sociology of Gender*.[4] This is a carefully argued work that delineates the constellation of elements associated with the fact that it is women who mother. Chodorow outlines the implications of that seemingly natural fact for ego and gender differentiation. The book focuses

---

[3]This is a conclusion of a rather elaborate argument concerning the consequences of women being primary caretakers of infants by Nancy Chodorow (1978) in *The Reproduction of Mothering*.

[4]In this section, I amend Chodorow's thesis to suggest that the initial pre-oedipal identification with the (heterosexual) mother places the son in a homosexual position.

on the experience of women appropriately enough, and tends only to hint at the experience of men. I attempt to take that hint and suggest what male experience tends to be.

Let us begin with the second item, namely that paternity is necessarily inferred. The male seed is nameless and not easily identified. Even the physical appearance of the child cannot be relied on to verify the identity of the father. Jokes about the milkman illustrate the commonness of male concern arising from the ultimate ambiguity of paternity. Chodorow suggests that this fact stimulates an anxiety that males attempt to mask and control by specifying rather precisely kinship patterns. He becomes excessively interested in the lines of reproduction, and in most cultures insists on the use of his name to identify ownership of "his" children. The compensation appears to succeed. Fatherhood tends not to be the vague, inferred status that it is. Instead, it is the father who is the "cause" of children; the woman is said to only carry "his" baby. The woman becomes a kind of cocoon in which the father's creation incubates until ready for "delivery," surely not a woman's word for childbirth (Grumet, 1981).

Ambiguity of paternity is intolerable for men possibly because ambiguity of ego was renounced. This is an outcome of the oedipal crisis, and the second item of male gender history we notice. Ambiguity of ego refers to the relative sharpness of ego differentiation. Chodorow argues that during the early phases of the pre-oedipal period, both mother–daughter and mother–son relationships are undifferentiated. During pregnancy, the infant was literally a part of his or her mother, and during the early months the infant is totally reliant on her. During this period the infant has no defenses and internalizes without much modification the emotions, and in the case of breast feeding, the milk of the mother. The infant identifies with his mother; he is his mother. Only slowly, during moments of absence, does it begin to dawn on the infant that he or she is a separate being. Chodorow locates the beginning of individual ego differentiation during these moments. As soon as the process of ego differentiation begins, it begins to differ for boys and girls. The mother–daughter relationship remains less differentiated than the mother–son relationship. The mother knows that this daughter will also know pregnancy, parturition, possibly breast feeding. Because they are the same sex, and because it tends to be women who mother and men who do not, the mother projects sameness onto her daughter, permitting the elongation of their ego merging and intertwining.

The son elicits a different response. He will not know pregnancy; probably he will not share the same experience of feeding and caring for "his" infant. The son is different than she, and she projects "otherness," sometimes eroticized, onto him. As a result, the process of ego differentiation proceeds more quickly for him than for his sister. By the time he confronts and is confronted by his father over each other's relationship to the mother/wife, and over their relationship to each other, the boychild is separate enough to experience his mother as separate and as an object of desire. The otherness projected onto him by the mother makes more facile his compliance with his father's demand that he move further away from her and from "women's things," that he see as strange and not-male the domestic, female world, more credible the stigma of "sissy," and finally more complete his repression of his initial identification with her.

Chodorow underlines the matrisexual nature of the infant's experience. She concludes that this mother–infant relationship leaves the daughter in a homoerotic position vis-a-vis her mother, a position she must abandon during the oedipal crisis. The boy is in a heterosexual position, a position reinforced by his later identification with his father. This analysis is incomplete, however, as it ignores the primal layer of social experience that occurs before the process of ego differentiation has advanced sufficiently to permit the mother to be an other to be desired. The initial relationship to the mother, a relatively undifferentiated and undefended one from the infant's position, suggests that underneath the desire for the mother is incorporation, in the case of the heterosexual mother, of that mother's desire for the father. If this is so, and the relatively undifferentiated mother–infant relationship would suggest so, then the primal layer of sedimented memory is heterosexual (again in the case of heterosexual mothers) for the girl-child and homosexual for the boy-child. Only as both separate and distinguish themselves from her do they experience desire for her.

From this view, the male child's earliest pre-oedipal experience, the oedipal admonishment to put away childish things (i.e., mother and female-associated items and feelings) is also a call to suppress his desire for the father. Thus the oedipal resolution for the son involves not only heterosexual sublimation (i.e., postponement and redirection of his desire for the mother) but it involves homosexual repression as well (i.e., the denial of desire for his father). This repression is reinforced during subsequent social experience as males "police" themselves, ensuring that no action interpretable as homoerotic is expressed. Further, young boys tend to seize on the discovery of a feminized boy as an opportunity to locate, or more precisely, to dislocate and displace, their own repressed homosexuality. Heterosexual male relations, then, are complicated by homosexual repression; they become fragile, easily sabotaged, and conflictual. The result of contemporary male heterosexuality, because it requires repudiation of the initial identification with the mother, is misogyny, and because it involves repression of the internalized desire for the father, heterosexual warfare, literal and symbolic. With this observation, however, we have jumped ahead of our story.

We may surmise that the pre-oedipal period, with its vulnerability and increasing awareness of dependency, has terrifying moments for the infant.

For the daughter this terror is complemented by her submersion in the mother. For the daughter, the oedipal crisis permits further differentiation from the Other, but it is a struggle for ego identity that often lasts long into adulthood, so powerful is the mother–daughter symbiosis. Ego identity and differentiation, according to many psychotherapists, is a common, if not the most common, presenting symptom in women seeking psychotherapy (see Pinar & Johnson, 1980).

As noted, the symbiosis of the mother–son relation is briefer as the mother projects "otherness" onto him, creating a distance from her that makes the construction of a male identity possible. It is an identity that must be acquired through repressing his earliest identification with the mother, and through observation of his father's ways. Because the father's relative absence from the home makes him an idealized, nearly imaginary figure for both boys and girls, the son relies on the father's words as well for his picture of what it is that men do and do not do. As he becomes more male (i.e., aggressive, assertive, competitive), more identified with his father, he comes to feel his desire for his wife overlaying his nascent desire for his mother. We have reached the moments of oedipal conflict as the son's desire for the father has now been repressed, and sublimated into identification with him; he becomes now a rival for his wife. The father now moves to remove his son to a non-competitive position with him, transferring that competition onto his peers, symbolized into social activities of various kinds, such as school and sports. The father achieves this removal by logic and by force. Although not communicated succinctly or even verbally at all, he persuades the son that the son will be compensated for completing the repression of the now-attenuated identification with the mother, and for abandoning his desire for her. In return for his repudiation of the female in him, he can possess a female—a wife, a lover—later. In return for disowning the mother in him, the son as adult will obtain a wife (i.e., a woman reified and externalized) whose actions and presence in his life he can regulate according to custom and law. Such regulation is psychologically necessary for the male as her spontaneous movement would threaten evocation of Her inside; yet her presence in regulated ways satisfies his need for the woman he has denied internally.

If the son fails to accept the logic of latency, the father resorts to force. The careful father attempts to restrain the use of force as it inhibits the recently acquired and developing personality characteristics associated with being a man (i.e., competitiveness, etc.). Still, some force, some struggle, is necessary as it strengthens and hardens this imprinting. Excessive force may produce a defeated son, one who sees no point in resisting the father, or in identifying with him, in the latter case feeling betrayed by the father's oedipal treatment of him. The successfully endured oedipal crisis produces a son who delays his desire for the female and intensifies his identification with the male. Because both consequences involve mechanisms of denial and repression, the son produced is one with an overly determined ego, an ego with less access to emotion and to sedimented memory (i.e., unconscious process and content) than does the typical ego of the daughter. This overly determined ego results in stunted relational potential. Feelings of separateness and individuality can rather easily become feelings of loneliness and dissociation. To "stand up on one's own and be a man" comes at the cost of debilitating repressions. Post-oedipal intimacy, especially as an adult, with a woman, tends to stimulate his repressed pre-oedipal, undifferentiated intimacy and identification with the mother. Adult intimacy with another man threatens to renew his repressed desire for the father from the early pre-oedipal period and/or his less-repressed rage from "losing" the oedipal competition for the mother. Condemned then to an over-determined self, isolated from its own unconscious processes and content and capable of only attenuated forms of intimacy with others, the adult male in our time, in our culture, can tend to seek refuge and escape from his condition in work (careerism and the problem of the "workaholic") and pleasure (hedonism, including sexual promiscuity and drugs, including alcohol).

SEDUCTION, NOT RESISTANCE

The over-determination of the male ego makes the ambiguity of paternity intolerable. He compensates for its inferential character by claiming "first cause," the origin of creation. He further compensates with an excessive interest in kinship patterns (i.e., the lines of reproduction). In this sense the recent interest on the left in reproductive theories of curriculum are patriarchal in nature, although given the political status of the left in the United States, it is the nascent patriarchy of the aspiring son, not the mature and established patriarchy of the father. As the son, leftist curriculum theorists search for room for resistance, which at one conference was characterized as "non-reproductive" education (Anyon, 1981). It is oedipally significant that the inspiration for this move "beyond passive analysis" seems to have originated in Paul Willis' account of "the lads." It is the resistance of adolescent boys, of "boys being boys," a resistance the father understands as more-or-less normal, no final threat to his authority.

   The position of the reproduction theorist, and his most recent transmutation, the resistance theorist, can be likened to that of the son who observes the ways in which the father (the embodiment of power and ideology) reproduces his status. Young and powerless, the prepubescent son is awed if angered at the power of the Father, a power that seems to reproduce itself lawfully. Older, he sees the relative contingency of the

Father's position, and the possibility, indeed the duty, of resistance. Through "mobilization" and "struggle on all fronts" he can resist him. We need only examine the subsequent history of the son to observe the outcome of this struggle: the son rarely wins this battle; he ordinarily replaces the father by outliving him. The point is that the son does replace him; he occupies his position. Is it possible that resistance reproduces patriarchy?

I suggest an oedipal strategy that differs from the traditional one, in fact a strategy whose aim is dissolution of the oedipal complex, of the familial, social, and economic structures that accompany it. This strategy shares the interest in non-reproduction. It is a male who loses interest in his political status as first cause, as the locus and impetus of generation. He becomes a degenerate. He no longer wishes to resist him and thereby replace him. Now the son seeks to sleep with him. Such desire does not begin in love. Given the historical moment, it begins in the same fury as does resistance. But now the son turns on his father in a way the father is unprepared to co-opt. The son refuses circumcision, that index of the oedipal wound signifying male repudiation of the female and the father's consequent promise of the world for the son's complicity. Instead, the son stares at the father, saying: "I refuse your ritual of manhood and its denial of the woman in me and of the woman who gave life to me. My mother, the source of my life, from whose body I came, in whose care I have lived, my companion and lover, but through whose complicity with you is also my traitor, as she turned me over to you, I stand by her, remain a part of her, and refuse your contract. I refuse to exchange her for you, her world (the private, expressive, intimate, relational world) for yours (the public, abstract, codified, hierarchical world). I refuse your lie (that I can have her again when I'm big like you, in the form of a wife, trading my mother for sexual object and unpaid laborer), and your repudiation of me (now that I have relinquished her, now that I am your 'little man,' you dispense your affection, such as it is, in units designed to manipulate me to achieve the dreams you failed to realize), and I refuse to displace the pain from her loss and the fury at your deception onto all others female and male. I reject the whole oedipal contract, and in so doing retain my longing for you, a longing now laced with hatred. It is not your power I want now. It is you."

Phallocentrism is the embodied ideology of oedipally produced male sexuality. Screwing and getting screwed are what homosexual men do literally, and what heterosexual men do to each other symbolically; one form of sexuality is the shadow of the other. In their contemporary expressions, both tend to be socially distorted as they are dissociated fragments of a forgotten human whole. We men are at war with each other, on battlefields, in corporate meetings rooms, in lecture halls—all symbolizations and abstractions from the father wound and the mother repudiation. Homosexuality becomes the site of the politics of the concrete, of the body, the potential politics of authentic solidarity and mutual understanding. Let us confront each other, we the circumcised wounded ones, not on the battlefield as abstracted social roles and political pawns of the father, but in bed, as embodied, sexualized beings fighting to feel what we have forgotten, the longing underneath the hatred.

HETEROSEXUALITY AS POLITICAL INSTITUTION

Hocquenghem (1978) reminds us that the concept *homosexual* did not exist prior to the 19th century. The capacity and desire to sleep with a same-sexed person was presumed to exist to lesser or greater extent in everyone, hence the scope and intensity of efforts to prohibit the expression of such desire. During the latter part of the 19th century, a medicalization of the socially deviant began to occur. That is, medical terms became employed to describe the culturally marginal and the socially deviant. This medicalization of the social terrain served the political and economic interests of cultural homogeneity, which accompanied industrialization and bureaucratization. By assigning such labels as *homosexual,* which indicated illness, the medical and legal communities could identify, prosecute, and punish, under the guise of providing "helping services," those whose lives were viewed as intolerably outside the mainstream. Those who were observed (voyeurism, as Hocquenghem notes, accompanies law and medicine, themselves bureaucratic systematizations of desire) to sleep with same-sexed persons more often than not, and/or those who exhibited personality characteristics sufficiently incongruent with prototypical feminine and masculine ideals, could be classified as pathological. Hocquenghem traces this story of increasing medicalization, including the appearance of homosexuals during the 20th century, and documents that, contrary to popular belief, homosexuality is being increasingly suppressed, if more subtly.

The lie is that there is homosexual desire. Following Deleuze and Guattari (1977), Hocquenghem insists that there is only desire. The polymorphous perversity, as Freud would have it, of infancy, becomes codified into genital sexuality. The story of oedipus is in this regard the story of the production of "heterosexuals," and the eradication, however unsuccessful, of homosexuals. Adrienne Rich (1980) describes heterosexuality as "compulsory," and as such "needs to be recognized and studied as a political institution" (p. 637). Politically, it reinforces the position of the father and guarantees its reproduction. Contemporary forms of heterosexuality tend to be phallocentric. For the male, the phallus is the sign of his power as a man. Successfully socialized heterosexual women experience "penis envy" and desire its incorporation. Although the phallus is the occasion for a man's pride or shame, he does not sexualize it. It is as if that which a woman desires is unworthy to be desired by him. He scorns the homosexual's interest in fellatio and in anal intercourse. In a phallocentric culture, few homosexuals escape the fascination with the phallus; they concretize the heterosexual's fascination with its abstraction: power. Both groups reify their existence; both fail to see how the existence of each relies on the existence of the other.

Men's (and many women's) fascination with the traditional masculine ideal (i.e., the macho man) is not without some merit. This ideal is comprised of several admirable character traits, such as courage and strength. However, we must acknowledge that these qualities are the socially fortunate outcomes of oedipus; often as not the macho man utilizes his strength and courage to rob, rape, and kill. In both prototypes, these characteristics are not chosen but conditioned; they result from repressing the pre-oedipal identification with the mother and resisting semisuccessfully the authority of the father. His "manliness," that discernible way of being in his body, tends to come at the expense of being in his mind and heart. His maternal repression—the more macho he is the more complete the repression is—makes him clumsy interpersonally, primitive intellectually, and a Neanderthal emotionally.

For his more civilized variations, the physical is abstracted onto the social and intellectual. Boots and jeans are traded for three-piece suits (at least during the day), and his manliness is determined not by his muscle and phallus size, but by the size of his bank account, stock portfolio, and corporate position. He trades physical strength for acumen and shrewdness, and the macho man's narcissistic experience of himself as body is now mediated through the bodies of the women with whom he sleeps. These characterological prototypes are crude but common. Perhaps less common and less crude are academic variations, including one version we might call, not entirely for mischief's sake, the macho Marxist. His body and probably his bank account have been exchanged for a long list of publications, physical strength and corporate shrewdness for tough logic, witty asides, and a virtuoso knowledge of Marx, Gramsci, and Bourdieu. He vanquishes his oedipal foe not with his fists or by outpositioning him corporately, but via skillful argumentation and cogent denunciations of revisionist and obscurantist tendencies in his opponents' positions. The macho Marxist substitutes dialectical materialism for the crass kind, the terminal smile of the young executive "on the make" for the suffering frown and angry scorn of the wounded but resisting activist. The content of the personality and of the social relations that express and sustain it differs for each version of man. However, the structure of the personality and its social relations (competitiveness, aggressiveness, exhibitionism) does not. Each is interested in the phallus, his own and/or others; rather, each is interested in its abstracted social form: power. Each aggrandizes his own while diminishing his opponents; after the battle all tend to return to the nurse and lover for solace or celebration.

To attack patriarchy and fascism in their graduated and symbolic forms requires attacking one's own internalizations of them, however subtle their expression. We men are our fathers' sons; he resides within us, and his relation to his wife and to his children resides there as well. It is not only the Father we must resist, but our internalized relationship to Him. To be sure, working with one's relation to Her is useful and important. One can strive to become a feminist man. At some point, however, it is our repression of Her and identification with Him, with one's "compulsory heterosexuality," that must be unearthed and confronted. Political attitudes and actions are informed characterologically as well as systemically. In addition to a politics of the state, there is a politics of the individual, a hierarchy of internal object relations. If we are male and straight, it is likely we have repudiated the woman in us for the fabricated male we were and he pretended to be. In our renunciation of Her and identification with him we are committed to become Father ourselves, regardless of the political content of our rhetoric. And in becoming Father we will require wives and children, and the hierarchialization of power will be reproduced, however consciously denied or resisted. We might cease our longing to become the Father, and instead long for Him, seducing Him, bringing Him down to us, in bed, on the floor, no longer son–father, now lovers. In the act of love we might become brothers, and as brothers we might help Her to become our sister. De-oedipalization is pro-feminist, and during the present historical moment, homosexual. It represents the decodification of desire, the de-hierarchialization of power. It is the deterritorialization of the libido, the depossession of persons. In the discovery and expression of homosexual desire, we crack the dam of repression, psychological and political. What is leaked stains the social fabric, altering its composition even if it is reincorporated.

DIRTY WORK

Hocquenghem (1978) observes that "the law is clearly a system of desire, in which provocation and voyeurism have their own place" (p. 52). Systems of knowledge production and distribution, such as school curricula, are likewise systems, or in the present context, codifications of desire. The knowledge we choose for presentation to the young is in one sense like the parts of our bodies we allow them to see. Both the physical body and the body of knowledge are cathected objects, and decisions and policies regarding them follow from our own organization and repression of desire. This is not to ignore the so-called internal logic of the curriculum, those technical considerations which accompany its formulation and presentation. Nor is it to ignore its political, economic, and social functions. However, the present view does aspire to situate, although not reduce, these considerations and functions oedipally. Doing so reveals how curriculum reproduces compulsory heterosexuality and homosexual repression: the overdetermination of desire. Curriculum is the dictum of the Fathers, their conversation, rather pronouncements, to their children that seduce them to his reign, his power (phallus) at the center. And through the use of female teachers, as with mother's complicity in circumcision, the sons and daughters are delivered to Him. For sons, it is the circumcision ceremony in which they complete their repudiations of her, and accept the wound—the scarred penis, the over-determined ego—which demarcates their initiation into the tribe of heterosexual men.[5]

For most, the pre-oedipal experience is forgotten. It remains as "sedimentation," a primal memory of the nature of the world. One aspect of this memory is how the world is known. As Grumet has shown, the relatively undifferentiated relationship between mother and infant is inscribed epistemologically as subject–object reciprocity and mutual determinancy. The mother or the infant is the "other" or "object," but object boundaries are blurred. If the infant son could speak, his words might be: "She and I, we are one. My crying brings her comforting of me, sometimes her irritation with me, and my laughter brings her smile, her own laughter. No barrier insulates me from her love, sometimes from her anger, her joy, her impatience and fatigue. I taste these in her milk as I inhale them in the air, exuded as they are from her organs and her skin." The primal experience of the world is Mother, then gradually it moves to the bed on which he rests, the walls of the room, and so on, a slowly expanding world experienced through Her, changed through Her and through the infant. During the oedipal crisis, the groundwork for which has been laid by the mother's projection of "otherness" onto the son as well as the son's experience of her absences, the son dissociates himself from this viscous intermingling of self and other, subject and object. He denies mother so that she becomes the other, not me, as opposite. Father, the absent abstract one, identification with whom involves far less comingling than imitation of what I the infant observe, and remembrance of what He tells me to be, becomes the knowable other. I am to become like the other, depersonalized, desubjectivized, objectified. Father and I are separate, discrete, and it is possible to know what is He and that which is I. Rather than my subjectivity intermingled with objectivity in moments of continuous mutual constitution, subjectivity and objectivity are now divorced. My subjectivity becomes an

---

[5]Phyllis Chesler takes seriously the idea of the father wound, and at one point suggests that male heterosexual promiscuity may not represent a search for the mother, but rather for the father—a search, given the homosexual taboo, that is bound to fail. Misogyny is in this sense is related to the man's anger that she is not the man.

intrusion on my clear perception of what He is and what He tells me There Is. I understand that my emotions, fantasies, and so on, are "smudges on the mirror," to be kept cleaned off if I am to replicate without distorting the world "out there." In the oedipal experience is the gender foundation for a series of epistemological assumptions associated with 20th-century mainstream social science. These assumptions include claims of value and political neutrality, and the objective to discover, through increasingly refined methods of observation, quantification and analysis, the nature of human reality. Oedipally it is the heterosexual son attempting to comprehend his father, a world that is removed yet discoverable, as it is the world into which father disappears each morning, and from which he returns, with stories, each night. It is this primal oedipal experience of father as a discrete "other" to be known, and of the world as alien but discoverable and knowable, that has become elaborately symbolized in modern mainstream social science, and in the school curriculum.

The daughter's experience, as we have seen, is different. She retains a more-or-less undifferentiated relation to the mother; her sense of the world thereby remains more fluid than her brother's. Intuitively she understands that experience is flux, some of it beyond our words, much of it beyond our numbers. She understands that influencing one aspect of a situation alters all aspects, and that quantification tends to freeze situation as it stops flux, and fixes aspects of experience to one level of conceptualization. During the oedipal period, she complies with her father's desire for her, creating the distance from her mother necessary to feel her desire for her. Unlike her brother who must suppress identification with the mother, she maintains both that identification and desire for both parents. Thus a triangular relational configuration saturates her primal experience of the world. There is the relatively rigid, the demanding, the powerful and seductive: the father, world, objectivity. There is the relatively bending, the compliant, the intuitive: mother, self, subjectivity. Each influences the other; each contributes to the other's transformations, processes that she observes and perhaps reformulates. In this pre-oedipal and oedipal experience is the basis for a constructivist epistemology.[6]

For the son, a more linear view of events, their causes and effects, is compelling. In repudiating his early mother identification, he commits himself to contradicting his initial experience of Her and the world as relatively undifferentiated and mutually constitutive. This commitment expresses itself in his efforts to contradict the inferential character of paternity. Recall that in order to deny the ambiguity of his causal status in insemination, he posits himself as the cause, and the woman as the intervening variable, in the effect that is parturition. His compensation for his

---

[6]In this section, I have relied heavily on the argument Grumet develops in her essay "Conception, Contradiction, and Curriculum."

inferred status as father and for the loss of the feminine in his conscious ego knows few bounds as it extends into systems of kinship (his name replacing hers in marriage and becoming the children's is the familiar instance that hints at his general obsession with lines of reproduction), sexual slavery (including compulsory heterosexuality and homosexual repression), and epistemology.

In this latter domain he makes supreme systems of knowledge production in which knowledge of the objective world (a bifurcated, false concept in itself) is sought and systematized, and knowledge of subjective worlds, and their inter-relationships, is avoided or grudgingly accepted. We speak of "hard" research and "soft." Such gender values are expressed not only in the intellectual hierarchy within disciplines, but in the power structure of universities across disciplines. The highest salaries tend to go to the sciences, the lowest to arts. The apex of patriarchy is the age of science. Even the arts and humanities are masculinized as evidenced by the use of computer programs in historical research (which of course can be helpful but that become ideological as they become de rigueur) and formalistic prose in literary and aesthetic criticism.

Where are we historically in the process of masculinization? Its abstracted forms will lag behind—given their relative autonomy—specifically gender formation, and these indicate contradictory tendencies. For males, a subtle yet discernible demasculinization can be observed.[7] Its sign is an evidently increasingly male interest in the appearance of masculinity, implying its loss of substance. Specifically, traditional masculinity was unaware of its appearance. Beauty, and working to make oneself beautiful, were professions of the "lady," although this sex-role expectation varied across class and according to ethnicity. Men who were especially handsome, and certainly those men who spent time attempting to be, were somehow less masculine than those "rough and ready" types who knew women would love them for their prowess, for just being men, not for their moustaches, tight jeans, or clear skin. I believe that the interest in the signs of masculinity, including not only dress but cosmetics, small-bed trucks with over-

---

[7]A companion way to think about this process is the following. One consequence of the feminist movement has been a greater candor from heterosexual women regarding their sexual preferences and their appreciation of the male form (cf. *Playgirl* magazine). Many men, especially middle-class men, have become correspondingly more sensitive to their appearance, and groom themselves to amplify their sexual attractiveness to women. It is a short step to groom and appreciate one's body as it is attractive to women to appreciating one's body period. And it is a larger yet negotiable step to take from appreciating one's own body as an erotic object to appreciating other men's bodies as erotic objects. It would be an ironic outcome of that aspect of the feminist movement that has functioned to bring women's sexual preferences and voyeurism "out of the closet" if it initiated a process of male sexual appreciation for the male. In this scenario, feminism may produce male homosexuality on a scale not seen in the West since pre-Christian Greece and Rome.

sized wheels, the renewed interest in working out and in athletics generally signal the loss of a more traditional masculinity, a loss we can loosely attribute to changing market conditions (i.e., the increasing importance of "appearance" and "style" in successful corporate life), and to the feminist movement (including some women's explicit eroticization of the male body, for instance in publications like *Playgirl*). The emphasis on masculinity at the time of this writing represents a reactionary response to the feminist movement, as it attempts to reaffirm masculinity. But in its absorption in signs not substance men disclose their defeat. The delicate and changing balance between the opposite sexes is now clearly upset.

Although there is demasculinization, men have yet to recognize it. The reactionary response to feminism will probably pass, although not easily or quickly. The deep structural changes men must undergo to achieve equity with women come very slowly, partly because some women fear to press too hard, and mostly because most men are unwilling or unable to initiate or sustain such changes. Instead, they make surface alterations. Those middle-class men who apparently comply with their wives' and lovers' requests and demands for shared housework, parenting, and decision making are only complying, on the whole. The deep structure of sexism, the socially induced, oedipally produced desire to become the patriarch, is not changed. Resentment accrues in unknowing men and in possibly unsuspecting women. We can expect violent crimes against women to continue to escalate in the short term. We can expect abstracted masculine forms such as conceptual formalism to solidify and proliferate as compensatory developments to the disappearance of conventional masculinity.

Reinforcing this tendency is pressure on women who enter the work force (typically at unequal pay for equal work) to conform to male expectation and standards of conduct. Those few who have managed to enter the academic work force, for instance, are pressed to acquiesce to dominant research paradigms. Being a woman and an autobiographer or a phenomenologist is having two strikes against you in most curriculum departments. This conformity expectation often intersects with the developmental project of many women to extend and sharpen their ego differentiation from the mother. To achieve this distance, to contradict this symbiotic object relation, many women embrace the stark logic and conceptual neatness of mainstream academic work in most disciplines. It may be we men (men who refuse to participate in the reproduction of patriarchy, or at least attempt to refuse), joining with certain feminists (those who celebrate not contradict their matrisexuality) who might rediscover and reformulate hermeneutic research methods, methods that portray more fully, if more messily at first, the flux and multidimensionality of experience. Such an effort toward reconceptualization cannot occur intellectually only. It involves a de-oedipalization of the person, and with it, a de-oedipalization of the intellect. This intellect of he or she who remains in a relatively undifferentiated relation to the Mother is not the masculinized, calculating, instrumental intellectual, caricatured in modern literature by Joseph K. in Kafka's *The Trial*.[8] Instead it is the intellect that portrays the simultaneity of thought, feeling, and action, not of atomized individuals (those with overdetermined egos, characteristic of the modern professional male) but those still connected, comingling, capable of community. It is the intellect of Virginia Woolf.[9]

---

[8]Joseph K.'s rationality is an instrumental one. The questions he poses in attempting to comprehend his case begin "how," "who," and "what." "Who could these men be? What were they talking about? What authority could they represent?" (Kafka, 1968, p. 4). He asks such questions throughout the trial. Midway through the novel—he understands nothing more of his case, despite his questions, only that his position has somehow deteriorated—he continues his questioning: "And there were so many questions to put. To ask questions was surely the main thing. K. felt that he could draw up all the necessary questions himself " (p. 114). K. never critically examines this method, this mode of cognition; being led by his executioners he maintains that "the only thing for me to go on doing is to keep my intelligence calm and analytical to the end" (p. 225).

[9]A characteristic passage of Woolf 's (1955) which portrays the multidimensionality and simultaneity of experience is the following:

"Yes, of course, if it's fine tomorrow," said Mrs. Ramsay. "But you'll have to be up with the lark," she added.

To her son these words conveyed an extraordinary joy, as if it were settled, the expedition were bound to take place, and the wonder to which he had looked forward, for years and years it seemed, was, after a night's darkness and a day's sail, within touch. Since he belonged, even at the age of six, to that great clan which cannot keep this feeling separate from that, but must let future prospects, with their joys and sorrows, cloud what is actually at hand, since to such people even in earliest childhood any turn in the wheel of sensation has the power to crystalize and transfix the moment upon which its gloom or radiance rests, James Ramsay, sitting on the floor cutting out pictures from the illustrated catalogue of the Army and navy Stores, endowed the picture of a refrigerator, as his mother spoke, with heavenly bliss. It was fringed with joy. The wheelbarrow, the lawnmower, the sound of poplar trees, leaves whitening before rain, rooks cawing, brooms knocking, dresses rustling—all these were so colored and distinguished in his mind that he had already his private code, his secret language, though he appeared the image of stark and uncompromising severity, with his high forehead and his fierce blue eyes, impeccably candid and pure, frowning slightly at the sight of human frailty, so that his mother, watching him guide his scissors neatly round the refrigerator, imagined him all red and ermine on the bench or directing a stern and momentous enterprise in some crisis of public affairs.

"But," said his father, stopping in front of the drawing-room window, "it won't be fine."

Had there been an axe handy, or a poker, any weapon that would have gashed a hole in his father's breast and killed him, there and then, James would have seized it. (pp. 9–10)

Virginia Woolf's (1928/1955) literary accomplishment is, of course, beyond comment here. For curriculum theorists, her fiction holds considerable methodological as well as aesthetic interest, as it captures convincingly the immediacy and complexity of experience. Additionally, Woolf was an astute observer of gender politics, as this passage illustrates.

Similarly, in schools we cannot rely on all women to sabotage—even if conditions were favorable for attempting so—bureaucratization, standardization, and the bogus "individualization" of many classrooms. Grumet (1981/ 1988) notes:

> So the male educators invited women into the schools expecting to reclaim their mothers, and the women accepted the invitation and came so that they may identify with their fathers. Accordingly, female teachers complied with the rationalization and bureaucratization that pervaded the common schools as the industrial culture saturated the urban areas. Rather than emulate the continuous and extended relation of a mother and a maturing child that develops over time, they acquiesced to the graded schools, to working with one age group for one year at a time. Rather than demanding the extended relation that would bind them over time to individual children, they agreed to large group instruction where the power of the peer collective was at least as powerful as the mother bond. (p. 181)

Grumet locates this complicity with the father's agenda at the crossroads of male and female efforts to contradict their internalized object relations. The male attempts to recover the repressed other in him by arranging her presence about him, a presence he regulates as he controls—as administrator, schoolboard member, and textbook author and publisher—the curriculum. His political control intersects with her project to escape the symbiotic relation to the mother by gaining access to the public domain of the father. As Grumet concludes, pedagogy for patriarchy was achieved through the feminization of teaching.

The culture of the classroom is a patriarchal one as it is drained of the personal, the intimate, the psychological, as it is drenched in competitiveness, task-orientedness, and achievement. The overdetermined ego of the male (with gradations of the macho personality as a result) is celebrated in literature as it is required to adopt to the demands of those who serve it, those who do its dirty work—female teachers. She speaks in his absence, by his authority, and the tales of human life she tells the children ensure that the culture of the classroom is reproduced. Yes, there is resistance, as Willis has shown, autobiographers have always known and reproduction theorists have recently discovered. But it is the resistance of the oedipally produced son, a resistance that is tolerated because it can be co-opted. The son must not be squashed, only repressed. He must complete the estrangement from the feminine by amplifying the aggressive and angry. Of course, he must not "get out of hand." As Black radicals know, the gender of the enemy is male; it is "the man." Resisting pleases the father as it assures him the son wants what he has: power and position. His son's lust for the father has now been abstracted from the physical onto its political derivative. It is lust that will ultimately assure the complicity of the son in his father's regime, and his mother's domesticity and relative slavery.

Father's authority is communicated by his pretentious seriousness, his virility, his cold capacity to oppose and suppress the Other when he judges it necessary, to compete for scarce commodities (and to keep them scarce), by sons who serve as his policemen, his military, his bureaucrats, his rebels (who underline his importance as they keep him mobilized), and by women who praise his achievements, attend to his wounds, and do his dirty work.[10] This authority of the Father is corroded primarily by the son who refuses to obey or defy him, to be his cheerful clone or his frowning—with clenched fist—opponent. It is corroded by the woman who returns his lust with indifference. Authority is defined by the son who stares at him with a partly secret smile, and winks. The father's authority is demystified as it is returned from its abstracted form to its concrete presence, from the the body politic to the body. The son's eyes only momentarily meet his father's, but move quickly below them, wandering about his hips. The son who has not disclaimed his mother knows how she is humbled by his objectification of her, and now he uses this knowledge against him. The father is no longer authority; he is a piece of ass. The mother's gaze may solidify her husband's cockiness, his fascination with his power over her, his sense of himself as the Fuhrer. But the son's lascivious stare, which has embedded within it the rage of the oedipal struggle as well as the not-forgotten love of the wounded and wanting, mocks him as it transforms him into an object of desire, a plaything, and dissolves his seriousness into panic. If the son fellates him, acting out concretely what the complicit straight son performs symbolically, the father's power flows from his body into the son's. The blood-swollen phallus becomes limp in its orgasm, and the son knows what heterosexual women have always known: the father's power is transient; it can be consumed; in a moment it is gone. Now is limpness, weakness, sleep. If the father penetrates the son, the same dissolution of power occurs. However love is made, love is made. Father becomes lover. Even Freud (1953) knew that "the behavior towards men in general of a man who sees in other men potential love-objects must be different that that of a man who looks upon other men in the first instance as rivals in regard to women" (p. 232).

---

[10]Of course, this is hardly all that women do. Nor does this analysis disclose the ways in which women have used men's reliance on them to control them (men). In her chapter on "romantic love" in *The Second Sex*, Simone de Beauvoir (1974) details how the man's "for itself-ness," or the tendency toward isolation and independence, is the source for the women's interest in man and becomes what she attempts to control. If successful, the man loses that quality that drew her to him in the first place. Thus the woman is caught between being enslaved and being enslaving, with no exit.

"FROM BEHIND WE ARE ALL WOMEN"

Patriarchy is in one sense phallocentrism. The location of power in the male, and its hierarchical arrangement among men, requires the distillation of libido into the phallus: "The body gathers around the phallus like society around the chief" (Hocquenghem, 1978, p. 82). The phallus symbolizes power, which is organized vertically. This organization is a system of "jealously and competition," Hocquenghem (1978) writes. Of the phallus, he writes: "It is the detached, complete object which plays the same role in our society's sexuality as money does in the capitalist economic: the fetish, the true universal reference point for all activity. It is responsible for the allocation of both absence and presence: the little girl's penis-envy, the little boy's castration anxiety" (p. 81).

The phallus is a public organ. In locker rooms men compare its size. In parks they expose it, an act of exhibition, the aim of which is to frighten the female, and in so doing, reassure himself. It reminds the little girl of Daddy's power. Rape is her ultimate reminder, this forced entry into her private body and psyche. The phallus symbolizes power, and like power it is aggressive. It seek use. It seeks victims.

Whereas the phallus is social, the anus is private. It is hidden from public view by the buttocks, just as it is hidden from psychological view by its repression by the ego. This repression is necessary to the production of oedipalized individuals in competition with each other: "If phallic transcendence and the organization of society around the great signifier are to be possible, the anus must be privatized in individualized and oedipalized persons" (Hocquenghem, 1978, p. 82). Phallocentrism is inversely related to anal eroticism.

Freud associated the anal stage of sexual development with the formation of identity. Although Freud's theory is not a simple linear, maturational one, there is the suggestion that the anal stage must be lived through in order to achieve genital sexuality. Anal eroticism must be sublimated, or repressed, in order to reach phallocentrism. The "desiring function" of the anus is replaced by exclusively excremental one. The relegation of the anus to an exclusively excremental function bifurcates the private from the public, the subjective from the objective.

These bogus divisions accompany the formation of bifurcated persons whose internal lives are kept discreet from their public lives. Private psychological material is excreted at home in order that it not interfere with efficacious public performance. Hocquenghem (1978) notes:

> Every man possess a phallus which guarantees him a social role; every man has an anus which is truly his own, in the most secret depths of his own

person. The anus does not exist in a social relation, since it forms precisely the individual and therefore enables the division between society and the individual to be made. . . . Lavatories are the only places where one is alone behind locked doors. . . . The anus is overinvested individually because its investment is withdrawn socially. (p. 83)

One's private life is especially charged emotionally because it is withdrawn socially, because it is regarded as private. This withdrawal, the distillation of energy to the phallus (i.e., of conscious energy to the public domain) accompanies the particular vertical organizations of power characteristic of centralized states and corporate economies. The myth of the private individual keeps him or her politically weak and economically manipulable. Freud (1953) wrote, "The entire Oedipus complex is anal" (p. 101).

Surplus capital accumulation is made characterologically possible through anal repression; the joke, "he's a tight ass," is suggestive. In fact, the character structure of the capitalist is such that the anus, in effect, disappears. The private self, and the capacity to empathize and suspend ego boundaries, are repressed, buried under the mask, the persona, produced by social conditioning. In the present historical circumstances, the anus becomes more than itself; it symbolizes the body as well. Anal eroticism draws libido from its overinvestment in the phallus and diversifies it throughout the rest of the body, deterritorializing not only sexuality but power as well. The anus does not lend itself to comparison and competition, and from the anal point of view, what criteria could be employed to judge them? Sexuality is equalized as it is diversified, not only within the male sex, but between sexes. After all, as Hocquenghem (1978) notes, "from behind we are all women" (p. 87).

The overregulation of the anus accompanies the overdetermination of the male ego. The blocking of élan vital bodily mirrors the blocking of psychological life in the rigid male personality formation. Denying its undifferentiated relation to others, the individual male ego deludes itself into believing "what is mine is mine." Hocquenghem (1978) writes, "Control of the anus is the precondition for taking responsibility for property. The ability to 'hold back' or to evacuate the faeces is the moment of the constitution of the self. 'To forget oneself' is the most ridiculous and distressing kind of social accident there is, the ultimate outrage to the human person" (p. 85).

So it is when someone lets something personal slip during public conversation. Others are embarrassed or irritated that he has "forgotten himself." He has excreted the private in public. The reduction of the anus to self-regulation and excretion accompanies the commodification of self (see Wexler, 1981). Subjectivity becomes repressed, and its explication publicly thereby becomes one form of cultural sabotage. Autobiographical description, to the extent it escapes the commonsensical, becomes free associative and genuinely confessional, invites deregulation of others: "To reinvest the anus collectively and libidinally would involve a proportional weakening of the great phallic signifier, which dominates unconsciously both the small-scale hierarchies of the family and in the great social hierarchies. The least acceptable desiring operation (precisely because it is the most desublimating one) is that which is directed at the anus" (Hocquenghem, 1978, p. 89).

To refuse to maintain the schizoid distinction between public and private, and to excrete in public what commodification requires we save for our wives, lovers, or psychiatrists, soils the social fabric. The seriousness of the father at the dinner table, the taken-for-granted naturalization of social life, cannot be maintained by the jokes, wails, and confessions of the subjectively existing person. Subjectivity is suppressed intellectually across the academic disciplines as anal eroticism is repressed and organized around the male public organ. Father maintains his position by pretending phallic superiority, at least by persuading us that that is the name of the power game. He maintains his position by sitting "on his duff," hiding his private self from the scrutiny of others and perhaps from himself. He eradicates homosexuality because it threatens to bring his ass into public view. His reign depends on its absence.

Anal repression accompanies a certain order of character structure indicated by constant and relatively high tension as the organism is under (unconscious) surveillance and regulation. The erotization of the anus threatens this construction, and no doubt this knowledges makes anal intercourse one of the most dreaded punishments one man can inflict on other. The particular series of personality formations associated with macho men depends on the overdetermination of the ego as it has successfully suppressed the feminine in itself. Suppressed is not equivalent to gone, and the male regulates himself carefully in order to prevent its unwelcome surfacing. The masculine identity, based as it is on repression of the pre-oedipal identification with the mother and the construction of identification with a relatively absent father, is in fact fragile and easily threatened. The intensity and pervasiveness of homophobia among men suggests this constant need to "remember oneself." Homosexuality in this context becomes a call for a return to precommodified forms of experience and identity: "Homosexual desire is related in particular to the prepersonal state of desire. To this is linked the fear of loss of identity, as it is state of desire. . . . The direction manifestation of homosexual desire stands in contrast to the relations of identity, the necessary roles imposed by the Oedipus complex in order to ensure the reproduction of society" (Hocquenghem, 1978, p. 92).

The codification of desire according to Oedipus is the identification of individual self and social location. The biological interest in reproduction becomes culturally intertwined in the sociopolitical interest in reproducing his status. The resistance of the heterosexual son initially angers but eventually pleases the father as it assures him of the son's interest in the power the father claims. The resistance of the heterosexual son may result in the deposing of a particular father, but not in the deposing of the archetype—Father. The victorious son discovers that it is the father in himself he has resisted as he has resisted his father. Fathers are not deposed through resistance, only replaced. Vertical social relations continue. Fathers require children and wives as capitalists require workers. Brotherhood and sisterhood, concepts depicting horizontal social relationships, are not opposite-sexed relationships.

CONCLUSION: SCHOOLING AS CIRCUMCISION, CURRICULUM AS THE CODIFICATION OF DESIRE

From the viewpoint sketched here, schooling is a gender ceremony in which, as Grumet has suggested, female teachers transfer their children, particularly their sons, to the Father, to patriarchal conceptions of economic, social, and intellectual life. Circumcision demarcates manhood, the point after which the son is regarded as a member of the tribe of Patriarchs. The wounded phallus and the scar that remains are a cattle brand indicating ownership and gender identity.

The culture of the classroom is patriarchal. Circumcision occurs symbolically. The wound is psychic, political, and economic. The elements of the first category include hypertrophy of the fantasy life, loss of self to others, and internalization of the oppressor: the development of a false self-system (Pinar, 1975). Politically the sons are domesticated, conditioned to accept and participate in the "jealously-competition" system that sorts them according to class membership. As a gender ceremony of manhood, contemporary schooling compels heterosexuality as well, implicating it in the complex configuration which is suffering in the West. Homosexuality as it now exists is implicated as well. Many homosexuals, like most oppressed groups in initial stages of political-rights work, tend to believe what their enemies say about them. Thus many homosexuals tend to believe in some measure that they are indeed a "third sex," unique, "queer." They tend to believe in a substantive category called *homosexual*, not seeing that it is in the service of their oppression, and in the heterosexual's self-delusion regarding his own gender composition. Homosexuals are often embarrassed over the relative prominence of sadomasochistic sexuality in gay life, not realizing that they only act out concretely and privately what straight men do to each other abstractly in the public domain. In schools, as in homes and offices, men get women to do their dirty work.

Curriculum, like the oedipal complex, is a codification of desire, a symbolization of libido into codes that are patriarchal in nature and function as they contribute to bifurcated personality formations, suppressing what subjectivity remains from the pre-oedipal experience. Curriculum theorists and social theorists of education have correctly identified curriculum as the conversation of the father. Curriculum contributes to the reproduction of "civilization," but so does, finally, resistance to it. Resistance as a concept and as a call for political action is no doubt "beyond passive analysis." But it too is only a moment in dialectical understanding and action. Exposing its oedipal ties and functions suggests another moment coming, one in which we sons and fathers work to become brothers and lovers. It is a struggle fought not only on the streets and in classrooms, but in bed. On that "site," curriculum might become the de-hierarchicalization of power and, indeed, the celebration of desire.

REFERENCES

Anyon, J. (1981). Elementary schooling and distinctions of social class. *Interchange, 12*(2–3), 118–132.

Apple, M. (1981). Reproduction, contestation and curriculum: An essay in self-criticism. *Interchange, 12*(2–3), 27–46.

Chodorow, N. (1978). *The reproduction of mothering.* Berkeley: University of California Press.

de Beauvoir, S. (1974). *The second sex.* New York: Vintage Books.

Deleuze, G., & Guattari, F. (1977). *Anti-oedipus: Capitalism and schizophrenia.* New York: Viking.

Freud, S. (1953). Some neurotic mechanisms in jealousy, paranoia, and homosexuality. In *The complete psychological works of Sigmund Freud* (Vol. 18, p. 232). London: Hogarth Press & the Institute of Psycho-Analysis.

Giroux, H. (1981). Hegemony, resistance, and the paradox of educational reform. *Interchange, 12*(2–3), 3–26.

Grumet, M. (1981). Conception, contradiction, and curriculum. *Journal of Curriculum Theorizing, 3*(1), 287–298.

Grumet, M. (1988). Pedagogy for patriarchy: The feminization of teaching. In M. Grumet *Bitter Milk.* Amherst: University of Massachusetts Press. (Original work published 1981)

Hocquenghem, G. (1978). *Homosexual desire.* London: Allison & Busby.

Kafka, F. (1968). *The trial.* New York: Schocken.

Miller, J. L. (1982). Feminism and curriculum theory: The breaking of attachments. *The Journal of Curriculum Theorizing, 4*(2), 181–186.

Pinar, W. F. (1975). Sanity, madness and the school. In W. F. Pinar (Ed.), *Curriculum theorizing: The reconceptualists* (pp. 359–383). Berkeley, CA: McCutchan.

Pinar, W. (1981). Gender, sexuality and curriculum studies: The beginning of the debate. *McGill Journal of Education, 2*(3), 305–316.

Pinar, W. F., & Johnson, L. (1980). Aspects of gender analysis in recent feminist psychological thought and their implications for curriculum. *Journal of Education, 162*(4), 113–126.

Rich, A. (1980). Compulsory heterosexuality. *Signs, 5*(3), 389–417.

Wexler, P. (1981). Toward a critical social psychology. *Psychology & Social Theory, 1,* 52–68.

Wexler, P. (1982). Body and soul. *Journal of Curriculum Theorizing, 4*(2), 166–180.

Woolf, V. (1955). *To the lighthouse.* London: Hogarth. (Original work published 1928)

Chapter 11

From the Ridiculous to the Sublime: On Finding Oneself in Educational Research

Suzanne de Castell
Simon Fraser University

Mary Bryson
University of British Columbia

What would we make of a school-based research study in which all of our informants were heterosexual? This should be an easy question to answer, given that practically all educational research finds exactly this. Now, speaking hypothetically for a moment, what of a study in which all of the informants were lesbians? What might we say? That this must be a very unique situation? That the researchers are being led astray by their own desires? That they are being duped, like Margaret Mead in Samoa? Or . . . what indeed *would* we say in such a case?

As lesbians who read their fair share of research studies, we have often been troubled by the absence or invisibility of lesbian students, teachers, administrators, and, indeed, researchers in educational research accounts. But it has seemed rather impolite to mention this and, when we have dared nonetheless to raise this question of other people's research, we have been made all too clearly aware of its impropriety. Either there were not lesbian or gay subjects in the study, we are told, or they chose not to disclose, or they were not asked to because their 'lifestyle' was not relevant to or significant for this particular study. Asking whether such a perception of irrelevance, or whether the failure to find any lesbian subjects, might itself be a function of the (actual or enacted) heterosexuality of the researcher has proven to operate less as a question than as an affront.

But here we are, halfway through our 3-year research project, with a very odd discovery of, you might say, "finding ourselves" in our research, and wondering what it means and what to do about it. This volume of essays, specifically focused as it is on the significance of queer theory for education, seems one of the few places we can ask these questions and have any chance of their being taken seriously as genuine, sincere, and significant questions.

So let's try this again, shall we?

Imagine you were researching impediments to gender-equity in non-traditional fields—say technology, computer studies, and applied sciences. And imagine that in the course of your research, it quite quickly became obvious that, of the few women working in these sites, the great majority appeared to be lesbian. Now imagine *reporting* your research at a major educational research conference: What would you say? What *could* you say?

First, there is the obvious question of ethics, because virtually none of these people is "out" at work, and, especially when the worksite is a viciously heteronormative public school, it would be unethical and damaging to report this finding. Yet in terms of significance, such a finding would surely be of considerable interest and importance. Wouldn't it? And yet you couldn't report it, could you?

What does it mean to participate, as we do, in an American Educational Research Association Lesbian and Gay Research Group and to accept this as true? Let me ask this question another way: Are we who are involved in such a research group doing so in order to participate in the ghettoization and containment of gay and lesbian youth and their teachers, or are we involved in such a group in order to work toward the transformation of the whole field of educational research, so that it creates a genuine place for gay and lesbian subjects?

We come at this question partly out of a recent conference experience, when one of us (de Castell) was asked to respond to a number of papers concerned with the educational difficulties faced by minority-group adolescents. Stressed in the reply written for that session was the remarkable absence of any mention of sexuality, *except in papers specifically concerned with gay and lesbian youth*, and it was noted that being, for instance, both Black and gay, both Iranian and lesbian, would surely compound the difficulties faced by the students studied as much or more than the many other factors that did receive explicit recognition. This was not a point received gladly, either by the presenters, or by the audience. Indeed there was, it was all too evident, significant hostility, even expressions of outrage, seemingly at the perceived inappropriateness of such an observation. We were and remain puzzled by such a reaction, and the perhaps unrecognized and certainly unacknowledged heterosexism it conveyed to us, and we have since wondered retrospectively about the many research reports we've read over the years that have provided often extensively detailed profiles of student subjects in a diverse range of studies, and never once mentioned that any of these students were gay or lesbian, let alone bisexual or transgendered, except of course if this specific named group was the focus of the study. It seemed to matter greatly whether students were rich or poor, low or high achievers, of average or above-average intelligence, lived in the city or the country, had a part-time job or not, and a host of other considerations. But it did not seem to matter to the researchers whose work we've read whether the students in question were gay or straight, which is odd, considering how enormously such a thing appears to matter to gay, lesbian, and transgendered youth themselves, who are so greatly at risk not only of suicide, but of violence, self-destructive behaviors, dropping out of school, and so on—and on.

It's certainly worth asking, given the dialogical character of so much current educational research, whether researchers who are not themselves gay or lesbian are just not privy to this kind of information about their subjects—they don't have the "radar" so they don't see it and the students and teachers, wisely I suppose, don't volunteer the information, and so the troublesome question is never "in evidence." It is worth asking this because maybe this absence is not insignificant. Maybe it matters *enormously* to what is discovered who is doing the research, from what identity position—and this is certainly not something we hear much about at educational research conferences. Perhaps it is something that is only apparent to people who cannot actually go into a school and do research in person, because, being openly and visibly lesbian, access to the school would be refused right then and there—and we say this from experience (Bryson & de Castell, 1996). But whether apparent to most people or not, it surely matters (doesn't it?) that only heterosexual or faux-heterosexual people are usually welcome to do school-based educational research? I mean it surely matters if these same heterosexual people are either unable or unwilling to see or to report the presence of gay and lesbian subjects in their research population. And it surely matters a whole lot more if the area being researched is gender equity in non-traditional subjects, and if the vast majority of people found actually working in these non-traditional fields are gay or lesbian. The school's deep investment in the business of providing youth a strongly reinforced socialization into the dominant heteronormative order, to the extent that this concern shapes perceptions and invisibilities, is an investment that constrains what can be said and what must be silenced, and so it may also, of course, shape the responses of female students to opportunities for learning in gender anomalous subjects. Hence its central importance to equity-oriented research. Is our queer discovery, we wonder (immodestly!), precisely what has been missing in previous attempts to explain the extreme underrepresentation of girls in technology and applied sciences? So are we then denying ourselves the means to identify a critical factor in explaining how gender inequity happens, simply because we are expected to accept without a fight the heteronormative order of the public school? How then can we find out why girls are so greatly underrepresented if we are prohibited from making an observation that seems quite important, indeed quite remarkable, about the women who do succeed in those fields?

We are interested in this question of forbidden identities—both of the researcher and researched—and in the question of forbidden knowledges, knowledges specifically about the salience of sexuality to participation in non-traditional subjects and fields. We are interested in the question of how we shall ever find out what we need to know if we may not report what we think we see, and what this means for the compromised state of our professional knowledge if we must leave entire fields of inquiry out of account. We return again and again to Pierre Bourdieu's (1977, p. 189) remarks in *Outline of a Theory of Practice* that "for every profession, there exists an effect of censorship, questions which may not be asked"—to which I add identities that must not be acknowledged, observations that cannot be reported. Must we then accept and sanction incomplete and deceptive research because the homophobic environment of school sites and work-places puts certain knowledges and certain identities out of sight and out of mind? Must we consent to this suppression of information as a kind of epistemological tax paid to heteronormatively regulated research? And then must we accept the prohibition, one I think was at the heart of that recent conference experience, on even mentioning this fact?

But if we decide we cannot be silent on this matter, how on earth can we speak about it, at whose peril, and at what cost?

As a way to engage these questions, we have elected this trope of *imagining* as a way to introduce what we believe to be an enormously important, massively overlooked problem about the salience of sexuality to educational research. We use imagining as a discursive prosthetic device for gesturing at the unspeakable.

Because we cannot report what in fact we think we have been seeing and hearing over the last 2 years of work—the number of people in computing and applied sciences who are lesbians (and how can we ask them if we are right about this?), the fact (if it is a fact . . . and anyway what would it mean to try to find this out?) that when a male teacher agrees to participate in gender equity work, invariably it turns out that he is a gay man—how can we report the ways we have observed male students physically and verbally assault young women who venture into those subject fields, and specifically that they make female students' sexuality a target for male violence, violence that girls can only avoid by staying away or by performing a masculine gender identity, whether that means a full-blown "deviant" sexuality or simply the repudiation of femininity but not hetero-sexuality tout court—and in either case paying the price of being labeled a "lessie." We cannot speak, can we, about the behavior of heterosexual male teachers toward female students who venture into non-traditional fields, whether that be by flirting, patronizing, or outright undermining, a too-often explicitly sexualized discouragement, or about their behavior toward female teachers who dare to embark on even the most modest species of gender equity work, which seems to warrant from their male colleagues the label of "ball-breakers" at best, "man-hating dyke" at worst— and, of course, the all-too-typical identification of researchers concerned with gender equity as "raving" and "card-carrying" feminists?

So the best we can do is ask you to imagine that all this is true, and to take seriously the question of how we might, as researchers, speak about this if it were.

Having begun with sheer speculation, let us conclude with a manifesto:

NOTES TOWARD A QUEER RESEARCHER'S MANIFESTO:

1. **I will not** sacrifice the chance to learn about how homophobia works in schools simply to be permitted to work in them.

2. **I will not** tell lies about what I see and what I do not see in my school-based research, simply to get that research published.

3. **I will not** accept other researchers' silence about the presence of queer youth and queer teachers in their studies no matter how uncomfortable such questions are for them or for me; on the contrary, I will insist on asking about them whenever the existence of queer participants in the research population is not mentioned.

4. **I will not** try to pass as straight in my research work, whether in the field or in the write-up of my research.

5. **I will not** encourage queer youth or queer teachers I encounter to pass as straight; in fact, I will seek out queer youth and queer teachers and do everything in my power neither to "out" them nor in any other way to place them in jeopardy, no matter how engagingly exotic might be the research I could then produce.

6. **I will not** engage in any educational intervention designed to promote heteronormativity in schools; on the contrary, any interventions in which I participate will be designed expressly to encourage and nurture difference. In short, I will try to make "queer education" possible.

7. **And I will** persist until queer research, that is, research explicitly by and for queer subjects, becomes a reality in this profession.

Alright then—Can you sign on? What will it mean for the future of your research if you do? What does it mean for the condition of your research if you cannot?

REFERENCES

Bourdieu, P. (1977). *Outline of a theory of practice.* Cambridge, England: Cambridge University Press.

Bryson, M., & de Castell, S. (1996). Learning to make a difference: Gender, new technologies, and in/equity. *Mind, Culture and Activity, 2*(1), 3–21.

Chapter 12

Carnal Knowledge: *Re-Searching* (through) the Sexual Body

Kenn Gardner Honeychurch
University of British Columbia

Sexual bodies are a hot preoccupation in contemporary thought.[1] The critical literature is arrayed, often colorfully, with interest in tongues, tattoos, rectums, and masturbating girls (Edelman, 1994; Grosz & Probyn, 1995; Sedgwick, 1993). Sex and knowledge, as Sedgwick (1990) suggests, have become conceptually inseparable from one another so that "knowledge means in the first place sexual knowledge; ignorance, sexual ignorance; and epistemological pressure of any sort seems a force increasingly saturated with sexual impulsion" (p. 73). Sex has become, as Foucault has argued, the forum where our truth as human subjects is decided (see Kritzman, 1988). However, as theory lends a more curious and amiable face to the erotic, there is, at the same time, more caution around the possible implications of corporeal sexuality in the activities of social research—the sites where bodies actually come together to construct or test knowledge. The theoretical subjects may indeed be sexualized, but the bodies that incarnate these epistemologies may not.

While the idea of the sexually neutral researcher might well be considered optimal in the tomes of methodology, in the performances of these

---

[1]Sexuality is here constituted as organized and expressed around body sensations and pleasures—concerned, not only with desire and behavior, but also with individual identity. Sexuality then, refuses containment and spills over into the whole of lived experience where, as Merleau-Ponty (1962) notes, it becomes impossible to separate actions or motivations that are sexual from those that are not.

imperfect behaviors joined together to be called social research, the body and sex may not always, easily, or reasonably, be disregarded. Further, although admitting that anthropological research always needs bodies and that these bodies are sensing and sexualized, the precise consequences and limits of the *matter* in question are, to be sure, nothing if not imprecise. As an example, in my recent research with adult gay male artists, the first day of interviews with one new subject became the unanticipated occasion in which to become immersed in the dilemmas and perimeters of the corporeal in social scientific inquiry. As a gay, White, male artist/re-searcher, I was on a hunt for *material* that drew on the experiences of other gay artists. It was a long-standing interest to which I could assign no particular origin. However, because the opening of this *story*[2] has to be found somehow, my walk through the cold gray September morning, along the unlovely wall toward Hastings, seems as opportune a place and time as any. As my boots hit the cement, I could hear the plump rattle of a tambourine that accompanied the melodies of an elderly Black woman with salvation in her throat—silvery promises of deliverance when the body's work on earth was done. Farther ahead, exhaled from the grated end of a mottled building, pungent grains of dust left me covering my face and clipping my breath. I hurried by, shifting my briefcase, heavy with inklings, raising my arm to shoulder level, flexing my elbow, loosening a tightness brought on by an early morning at the weight bench that oth-erwise had defined a desirable coherence in the muscles of my chest. Past the clouds of stifling exhaust, a slight mist left the air damp and I now breathed in deeply to calm the sense of anxiety that seemed tethered to any first encounter. I rounded the corner fashioned by a stiff iron gate, opened the glass door, climbed three narrow but formidably long flights of stairs and, again taut and breathless, arrived at a new threshold.

In the midst of unfamiliar territory already rife with sensual pleasure and urgency, standing on the top landing, damp from the trace of rain, exertion, and the uneasiness of soft knocking, I waited for the door to open. Up to this moment, although I had given substantial thought to the theoretical speculations on which the research was predicated, I had given little consideration to the bodies that would carry them out. As a gay man, my interest in the gay male body might appear to be obvious. However, although gender and sexual orientation were factors in the selection of the research subject(s), I had otherwise looked over even imagining the bodies that might be looked over. The oversight was particularly odd given an expansive interest in the body and sexuality in cultural and political

---

[2]I use the word *story* to speak of ethnographic projects in a way that acknowledges that fieldwork makes possible an inevitably partial narrative—a persuasive *fiction*. See Strathern (1987).

terms, and an active long-term commitment to my own body's (physical) *definition.* Although I had immersed myself in varying accounts of (homo)sexualities, and long recognized the personal consequences of a corporeal dedication within a gay sub-culture, I had until now considered my body's physicalities as eccentric to my performance as researcher. In simply wending my way to the site of inquiry, it was a profound and unquiet sense of my body and the kinesthetic that revealed my role as physically conscious and engaged participant rather than corporeally detached but intellectually interested onlooker. Poised on the verge of this first interview, I felt tangible and wondered about this curious disparity.

For the purposes of this portion of the discussion, I have limited my *attention(s)* to one particular subject—Gayle Ryon, the artist whose studio I understood to be just beyond the door at the top of the last breathtaking flight of stairs. Prior to reaching this location at this hour, there were only five particulars that I knew about him: he met the criteria of the non-probability selection procedure; he had agreed to participate in the inquiry; and further, he was, reportedly, "bright," a "skillful painter," and a "beautiful man." The first two pragmatic pieces of information had been personally established by telephone; the last three enticements were the views of a heterosexual female art writer who had recommended him for the research. The door opened, hinges creaked, and the veracity of the woman's final observation was confirmed. Beauty is demanding and this man was a knockout. After brief introductions and the short, tense motions of a first handshake, Gayle and I walked the full length of the building to the windowed front of his spacious studio, returning to the soft complaining echo of the tambourine now not far beyond the glass—the bright side of trouble.

The movement of physical bodies in space and time had already disrupted the anticipated, so, as it was differently commanding, the more static body of art leaning against the walls became peremptory. Prior to beginning the first body-to-body interview, I edged toward the still-sticky surface of the wet-into-wet blended gradations of the various lights of painted flesh. The first canvas offered an unfinished nude portrayal of the artist who, in oils, as well as in the regimes of his life, courts the viewer, constructing and presenting himself as an object of sexual desire. There is an unerring and palpable interest both in how he looked and how he looked—that is, in how he viewed, and appeared to, others. There was no doubt that this body was in charge—an embodiment of Foucault's (in Gordon, 1980) claim that mastery of the body is acquired only as a consequence of an investment of power in the body, a "glorification of the body beautiful" (p. 56). On the floor were tempting, color nude photographs, on which the paintings were based. A further study of the naked artist and a second nude male, one from the front, one from behind, a double portion where neither side is the winner, stood slanted against the opposite wall—sensuous strokes of thought in varying shades of ochre and English red.

It was Nietzche who suggested that "aesthetic experience had more in common with sexual ecstasy . . . than it did with the quiet individualistic contemplation of a work of art in a spirit of disinterested, rational inquiry" (in Turner, 1991, p. 12). Here in the studio, at the beginning of the inquiry, the vast and seductive pleasures of looking were simply undeniable. Although it didn't last for the duration, as I stared into the canvas, it was hard, at first, to see what was directly in front of my eyes. I was looking, but wasn't registering anything. In facing a perhaps excessive pleasure of research, my gaze was focused, but my thoughts wandered independently of my eyes as if they were at cross-purposes. My eyes already persuaded, I blinked to connect my thinking to my looking. I glanced over at Gayle and thought how much I had learned about his body in a very short time, which concomitantly, had reinforced what I already knew about mine. Five minutes into the first contact, I faced a contradiction: the dispassionate expectations of the conventions of research and a corporeally registered and integrated experience of the aesthetic and the sexual. My own body's visceral knowledge was confirmed to the bone—at least for the danceable moment. I was looking intently but was also aware of my mind's shifting—aware of being surrounded by a physical presence—a clothed body, standing beside me, the same body—naked and so tenaciously represented—both in front and to my rear. I was seeing and thinking double. Surrounded by the power of bodies, I was looking and thinking, and thinking about thinking, imagining this moment—that is, the writing, inevitably wondering if, or at which juncture, censorship might be most propitious.

After seating ourselves at a long, hand-constructed table, the first formal, recorded interview began. With fluent lips and a brave tongue, Gayle provided interview data that was substantial and provocative. Perhaps predictably however, despite the seductive constituents, the conversation concluded without any mention of the body and sexuality outside of abstract terms of the topic of inquiry. Clad in the demand for the body's denunciation, I spoke not a word about it, and that omission created a paradox: an insistence on considering and affirming the homosexual body and desire as topic, exploring their manifestations in an abstract sense but concomitantly denying them in the flesh. By thinking the idea of the body, I submerged any desire to address the body in action. It was an uneasy but apparently necessary effort to think all around homoeroticism, yet steadfastly maintain a disembodied a(void)ance at its center.

Nonetheless, given the early engagement of the body in my investigation, how, I felt forced to now wonder, might the sexualized corporeal be accounted for in the research, and inscribed in the resultant texts in ways that reproduced the circumstances in which the other was encountered if, as Wittgenstein (1977) suggests, it is not possible to write anything "that is more truthful than you yourself are" (p. 33)? Although not suggesting that inquiry must necessarily be a painstaking accounting of the body's every breath and shudder, two further examples from the present project expose more of the body's seductive possibilities. In addition to the series of interviews, I was interested in what visual art could contribute to knowledge: four different paintings were selected as sources of research data. Although recognizing the limitations of attempting to *sight* the visual through the mechanisms of written language, one particular painting, entitled *Pos.i.tive*, makes the referential odor of the sexualized body inescapable. Photographically representational in its rendering, the painting's complexities are embedded in the synthesis of a range of the artist's diverse interests and experiences, relevant to this work. The painting invites speculation, not only into its subject, but also compels in its privileging of the sexualized young, muscular, adult male body and the simultaneous admission that below the seductiveness of the surface, the body, its desires yanked from unencumbered coition, holds the risks of contagion. Painted in San Francisco, the artist is portrayed with his hands and wrists tied and pulled slightly to his right over his head. His pants and underwear are at his ankles. With dropped eyes, he gazes hypnotically down at his own body—across his belly toward his tumid penis sheathed in a condom. Attention firmly cemented, it is a narcissistic revelation where the *truth* is located in his body before it is exposed in his mind. Although there is discomfort in looking so low, in doing so, the viewer must also reckon with the figure's relentless focus on his own sexuality—to share, or reject, to ponder, but never to elude. In viewing the canvas on exhibition, my eyes wonder over the bound upstretched arms and my own body's implication in this particular body's constraint. My gaze wanders down to the chest, following the lighter areas across nipples up into the other armpit before going down to his abdomen, through the bracelet of pubic hair to the tip of his penis, moving over to his legs, dropping to his knees, his shorts, and then back up over his body into the corners of the space where flesh nears the margins of background color and offers a way out.

Although inclined to preterition, a commitment to including all informing episodes, however awkward, makes sidestepping irreconcilable with a set of methodological intentions determined to refuse the body's concealment. In addition to the scheduled interviews, the activities of inquiry seeped beyond the borders of its original design. As an example, Halloween night fell shortly after the scheduled interviews had been concluded but long before the data collection and analysis had been completed. By chance, Gayle and I, both in costume, and without prior knowledge, attended the same extravaganza. Although our costume choices may both be considered drag, they were otherwise disparate. For the first time, the researcher, and two gay, male friends, chose, not to dress as women, but to dress in women's clothes. Maintaining my short-cropped dark mustache and beard, with extravagant red fingernails and lips, shoulder length blond wig, a black dress slit up the leg, I was, to understate, in my 40's and six-foot-four-inches in heels, unseemly and profligate. Conversely, Gayle and his late 20's companions, highly sexualized embodied vestiges of Anthony Burgess' penetrating work, wore bowler hats and were shirtless, suspenders draping seductively over legs and buttocks clad in white "very tight tights with the old jelly mold, as we called it, fitting on the crotch underneath the tights, this being to protect and also a sort of design you could viddy clear enough in a certain light" (Burgess, 1962, pp. 5–6). Damp from dancing and spotting the apparition in black lace, Gayle moved across the floor to exchange a few smiling words with the discomforted researcher who, knowing the future in the instant, would have preferred to have evaporated into his pumps.

THE SEXUAL BODY IN THEORY

As the unimagined prospects of an infatuating subject had now become more than prospects, I could not reasonably continue to avoid attending to the body and speculating about its consequences. Initially, however, in any decision to explore the body's possibilities, it is recognized that the first outcome might be the inevitable risk of offense. A conundrum is thereby created. The risk of transgression becomes more likely as relationships between researchers and subjects become intimate beyond standard methodological conventions. By adhering to research customs that most often suppress the body and, in particular, any sense of desire or erotic inclination contained in this intimacy, the risk of offense is minimized, whereas the likelihood of dissemblance is increased. The active concealment of the corporeal, that is, damages the sufficiency of results through the violation of a different research convention—that the results are veracious.

Further, whereas the possibilities of sex and the body may become more charged when those possibilities are faced outside of theory, any endeavor to *express* those actualities also cannot escape the challenge of its troublesome terms. As noted, any accounting of the movements of and between sensual/sexual bodies in the texts of social research may be seen as nothing more than an unwarranted and obscene commotion. Any text of the Academy that expresses sexuality through erotic words and phrases may be deemed tense and unacceptable. Alternately, if considering, or cruising, the body as a sensual site of agency, and allowing for at least a peek at the possibilities of desire in social research, are deemed permissible, any ensuing discussion is still not without its kinks. To be more precise, although the intercourse of much academic writing is unlived and abstract—to be blunt, bland and just not sexy at all—there is, in contradistinction, the perhaps ineliminable perception of impertinence on one other count. While any medical guide might consider the body's distresses from (a)bdominal wounds to (z)inc poisoning, in endeavoring to think through the body and trying, however momentarily, to pin it down, there are also its *complications*. As illustration, I have drawn from many diverse disciplinary initiatives in anthropology, sociology, art history, neuropsychology, and philosophy as examples. I have touched the various, overlapping, inexact, and sometimes colliding landings of feminist, modernist, poststructuralist, and queer perspectives, all of which intersect at a site of re-complication—education. It is, afterall, at the critical places of pedagogy where bodies of the learner, the teacher, and knowledge come together.

Accordingly, the complexity of the body's issues and the tissue of numerous voices in the labyrinth of contemporary discourses makes lucidity—that is, absolute plain-speaking—not only arduous but improbable if the intricacies of the contemporary body's circumstances are to be revealed. It is not that I, or others so inclined, prefer to muddle for muddle's sake or are unremittingly enchanted with immodesty in language or style. It is rather that I do not presume to know what the body is, nor do I assume all its languages to be *straight*. In writing against what might be considered a commonsense understanding of the body, occasional excesses, or potential and deliberate confusions in syntax serve not only to speak of, but to perform the inevitable perplexity that emerges from any simultaneous attempt to entertain such a contradictory subject, to sustain the voices of a profusion of others, and, to speak in one's own tongue. In the juggling of the options, once-over clarity is at risk. It is hoped, however, that any intentional immoderation may extend conceptions of the body in productive ways by making it harder, not easier, for readers and writers to make (monovocal) sense of it all. Perhaps little about the body, if not quandaries, seems assured.

However, when the uncertainties of bodies are so embraced, not everyone gets satisfied. Critics of many persuasions patrol the various jargons of the body like enemy territory. The policing of the language of analysis, both inside and outside the Academy, becomes an originary site of (dis)pleasure. As an example, a writer for the *New York Native*, a newspaper by and for the gay community, notes: "the current crop of gay and lesbian 'queer theorists' puts both their ivory-towered forbears and contemporaries to shame when it comes to sheer, ignorant, gobbeldygook [*sic*]" (Edelman, 1994, p. xviii). The pretension however, is more likely to be located elsewhere—in the *fiction* that there is such a thing as a common language that can be unquestionably adopted to speak of universally available facts regarding the many points of view of the slippery body. The trouble with the truth is that it is often not: writing about the body and desire reflectively, that is, in a way that mirrors the complications of the lived-body, becomes, as Edelman suggests about queer theory, the necessary interruption to a perception of the self-evidence of language that is otherwise conceived as an unproblematic tool through which the dominant cultural logic displays its presence to itself. Perhaps little is unadulterated anymore—or pure pleasure.

SEXUALITY IN FIELD RESEARCH: GETTING MARRIED, EMBROIDERING FANTASIES, OR GETTING LAID

Although gender, ethnicity, age, and social class have been noted as factors that may impact the collection of data and are therefore deemed to be ingredients that must become a planned aspect of inquiry, the possibilities of the sexualized body and desire have received scant attention in the literature.[3] Consequently, whereas the neutered researcher is nothing more than an impersonation, social inquiry continues to be most often practiced against a set of admonitions that insists on a stance of erotic non-interference. Sexual detachment is upheld because, as Newton (1993) suggests, "the distanced neutral observer . . . is at the opposite pole from the sexually aroused (repelled? ambivalent?) fieldworker" (p. 4). However, although mention of sexuality is infrequent, the embodied intrigues fieldwork have not escaped notice entirely. Geertz (1988), as an example, notes that ethnographies "tend to look at least as much like romances as they do like lab reports" (p. 8). Ball (1990) suggests that ethnographic inquiry is more similar to going on a blind date than it is to going to work. In response to such suppositions, Newton (1993) poses a likely question: is this " 'romance of anthropology' only a matter of speaking?" (p. 3).

In the discipline of education, two polar examples reflect the opposing contest between, on the one side, purported and idealized sexual neutrality and, on the other, the potential for the sexualization of the experiences

---

[3]See Ball, 1990. For a consideration of gender in research, see Eichler (1988). Notably, when gender is discussed as an issue, it most often refers to women's experience, as men have been tardy in our consideration of ourselves as gendered beings. Ethnicity also sets particular limits and poses problems. See Hammersley and Atkinson (1995). For a research inquiry which includes the issue of social class, see Roman (1993). Since writing this chapter originally, two valuable additions to the discussion of sexuality and/or lesbian and gay identity and fieldwork have been identified. See Kulick and Willson (1995), and Lewin and Leap (1996).

of adult ethnographers.[4] In the first inquiry, Norris Johnson, a presumably heterosexual male researcher who interviewed female teachers in a small American town, recognized the evidence of gender and sexuality, but kept his distance. In the early interactions, Johnson (1986) notes, the women sought to determine if he was going to recognize their professional status or if he would "*act like a man* and exhibit sexually inappropriate behavior" (p. 168, emphasis added). In what would appear to be a reasonable response to the concerns of the research subjects, Johnson reports that he refrained from prolonged periods of eye contact, sitting close during interviews, perusing their physical forms, catching their attention as they crossed their legs, or complimenting them on their clothing and hairstyles. Although exhibiting considerable verbal and nonverbal restraint and abiding by the prescribed (non-sexualized) conventions of inquiry, Johnson (1986) admits: "I remember feeling a bit frustrated by the need for such *posturing* for several of the teachers were attractive and I would have enjoyed flirting with them" (p. 168, emphasis added).

At the other side, perhaps the most notorious incident that relates sexuality to research in education is both the most riveting, and the one I am most hesitant to retell because the vast prerogatives of heterosexism will lay blame upon blame. Homosexuals have a contemptible name—constituted at the mercy of those who hold in contempt. Further, with the now popularly understood correlation of homosexuality with AIDS—its *fruits* are seen as ripe with death. As an example, art educator Edmund Feldman (1993), however unintentionally, scatters homosexuality and murder in the same hand when he claims that the homosexuality of Leonardo and Michelangelo were no more important than the fact that Benvenuto Cellini shot and killed a man in 1527. In the minds of some readers, made narrow with dismay, homosexuality remains a grave and often deadly pleasure. As a result of such continuing and unhappy conflations, even for the most informed reader, research accounts that place homosexuals in proximity to behavior deemed deviant, immoral, murderous, or simply irresponsible, raises ire and most often closes down, rather than opens up, thinking about matters of sexual variance. It is not, I would add, that

---

[4]In educational *theory*, although the terms may mean differently between authors, the role(s) of the body, the sensual, the erotic, and eros have been of some sustained interest. Grumet (1988) suggests that "the repudiation of the body was a blight that fell upon the curriculum" (p. 53). Pinar (1994) acknowledges that the erotic in curriculums may be repressed and forgotten but it is not gone. Alston (1991) calls for a renewed understanding of the relationship between education and eros where students are "invited to encounter eros for themselves, for their own development and purposes" (p. 386). Sears (1992) notes that sexuality is no longer an easily hidden aspect of the curriculum. I am significantly indebted to all of these authors for their insights around sexuality and/or eros and education. It is also imperative to reiterate that the present discussion is concerned with the relationship of adult researchers who are engaged with other adult participants.

homosexuals are *never* near these human possibilities; it is that they are rarely constituted outside of them.

With these cautions noted, and in the hope that moving forward may happen by stepping backwards once more into the ruins, the brave account of Harry Wolcott affirms that social research, like living, is the labor of blood of ordinary bodies. Wolcott details his relationship with "Brad" (a pseudonym)—a young man with whom he was physically involved and with whom he undertook a social research investigation. Wolcott (1990) emphatically notes that "our mutual involvement preceded the life history project and in a sense opened the way for another dimension in our relationship and dialogue" (p. 139). Regardless of timing, Wolcott's candid account underlines the possibility that "the ways humans become involved with each other—physically and emotionally—far exceed the prescriptions our various societies endeavor to so diligently impose" (pp. 138–139). The by-now-familiar catastrophe was devastating—a chronicle of appalling maliciousness. After some time, Brad returned to the home of Wolcott and his partner, and, during a maniacal attack, the house and the entire collection of two lives were burned to the ground.

Although sex is sometimes sorry, whether Wolcott's decision to become physically and professionally involved with this man was a gross ethical misjudgment or not is not for me alone to decide. What Wolcott does do however, is boldly bring the most-often silenced question(s) around living sex and the body in inquiry out into the open for discussion. As readers, we become voyeurs and are able to consider our own embodied research experiences in the safety of the, perhaps extreme, reflection provided by Wolcott's account. Perhaps, for many, the first inclination might be to reject the total inquiry and abhor Wolcott's behavior as a serious ethical transgression, but, alternatively, caution might prove to be more sagacious. To use a Wittgensteinian approach, it might indeed be more reasonable to examine the claim about which we have otherwise been quite certain, that is, sexual bodies have no place in the registers of inquiry because they are either unmanageable or inappropriate, and therefore, extraneous to its outcomes. As Wittgenstein proposes, doubting necessarily comes after, and presupposes belief in, something else. It is an examination of this first belief that might instead facilitate a revelation of the body's aptitudes.[5]

Although there might be many issues around Wolcott's account that deserve examination, two deserve brief mention. First, on initial consideration, a reader might hold that Wolcott's behavior is a violation of a power relationship between what has been viewed historically as an always

---

[5]I have utilized Wittgenstein's approach to doubting and certainty. See Wittgenstein (1974).

more powerful researcher and an always less empowered subject. On the other side, a more careful reflection on Wolcott's account might cast doubt on such a belief. In other words, the ways that age, gender, sexual orientation, and social class are mutually configured in Wolcott's research are complex and contradictory. As Foucault (1990) has argued, where there is desire, the "power relation is already present" (p. 81). In a culture that tends to venerate youth, hesitation seems prudent in any conjecture that declares Wolcott's behavior a clear violation of privilege in ways in which the middle-aged researcher is the one who always, or even occasionally held the *greater* power. Second, a reader might use the outcome of Wolcott's story as *proof* of the unmanageability of sex and the body. Rather, in considering the long anguish of Wolcott's narrative, reservation is urged against a constitution of the (homo)sexual relationship of the researcher and subject as the sole, or even contributing provocation for the ravage. Although thought may move so that it comes to hate that which it used to love, it was not just passion that caused alarm, nor lust that turned the house to ashes.

Outside of the discipline of education, a number of other diverse accounts flesh out a range of the sexual body's possibilities in social inquiry. Researchers have noted that: being heterosexually married reduces the risks of violating cultural sexual values (Fluehr-Lobban & Lobban, 1986); efforts are made to neutralize the researcher's sexual presence (Angrosino, 1986); and, prevarications are constructed to preserve the sexual image of the researcher (Whitehead, 1986). In some cases, methodological adaptations have been required because the sexuality of the *subject(s)* was seen as interfering with the researcher's ability to concentrate, to ask questions in an intelligible manner, and sometimes, even to remember them. As an example, presumably heterosexual researchers Skipper and McCaghy (1972) describe a research subject in mesmerizing detail:

> The respondent was a striking woman. She was tall and slender, with a pretty face, long graceful legs, a slim waist, and hips which swayed provocatively in her natural walk. While her bust was well developed, it was not so prominent as to seem disproportional from the rest of her body. In addition to her natural qualities, her manner of interaction oozed "femaleness." (p. 239)

In order to save the inquiry, Skipper and McCaghy sought solutions that they believed were necessary to the very survival of the investigation. In response, the researchers conducted the balance of the interviews in tandem in order to support each other (presumably against the irresistible power of female sexuality), and completed the data collection in more public settings where the research subjects would be limited in their potential for seductiveness.[6] By making these adaptations, Skipper and Mc-Caghy (1972) report that the project became no more difficult than that which might be experienced in "interviewing any young and attractive females" (p. 241).

Despite prohibitions to the contrary—and although actual frequencies are impossible to determine—researchers, in the practice of other disciplines, have similarly moved their bodies into the more intimate spaces experienced by Wolcott. Sexual fantasies, that is, and other physically sexual interactions involving researchers and the subjects of research are not totally outside of explicit documentation. In a posthumously published diary, Bronislaw Malinowski (1967), as an example, admits to indulging in impure thoughts in the field. Peggy Golde (1970) acknowledges that her concerns about detachment and objectivity "didn't prevent me from embroidering some fantasies of my own in those occasional cases when I found a man attractive" (p. 85). While Malinowski and Golde were weaving fantasies, Paul Rabinow (1977) was getting laid—joking and boasting to members of his group and to his readers of his sexual vigor in a liaison with a Moroccan woman. Although less revealing, researcher Walter Williams (1986), in his study of the berdache among American Indians, acknowledges that "several masculine Lakota men made sexual advances to me" (p. 93).

It is also in the spaces of ambiguity that the possibilities of desire have been revealed. Although noting that personal propriety restrained a full accounting of his affective bond with a research subject, Kenneth Read (1965) acknowledges that he had difficulty in thinking of the subjects of his investigation "simply as objects of clinical concern, as the repositories of needed information" (p. 251; see also Read, 1980, 1986). In taking leave at the end of his first field visit, the anthropologist turned to his subject Makis for the last time and comments that his arms responded to the pressure of the Black man's body, and, in doing so, accepted all that had transpired in the past 2 years. Ignoring his own cautions about revealing too much, Read (1986) reminisces about Makis:

Sometimes (I) expected him to appear silently in my room, emerging with a marvelous physical solidity into the circle of light cast by my lamp, all the planes of his chest, his face, his abdomen and thighs chiseled from black and shining marble, his lips lifted upward . . . his eyes holding mine with

---

[6]I would argue, to the contrary, that it was not the *subject's* sexuality that was problematic, but rather, it was the *researcher's* sexuality *in relation to* the subject's sexuality that required the methodological adaptations. Contrary to the researcher's suggestion that *all* men would probably have reacted the same way, as a gay man, I, for one, would not have been the least bit sexually distracted in these circumstances.

the implications of at least a partial understanding neither of us could express in words. (p. 75)[7]

Apologetically, Read (1986) continues: "I had not been able to meet his expectations, but I hoped he had found in me something else, that he felt it now in the pressure of my hands, the only gift I have, the only one I need to receive" (p. 253).

Esther Newton, a researcher who names herself as lesbian, more veraciously addresses romance and sexuality in field research—telling the wishes of sex in inquiry to an end that is not often told. Admitting her eroticized draw to one of her research subjects, Newton courageously dares to say the unsayable. Although acknowledging that she did not set out looking for sexual adventure in the field, Newton (1993) boldly outlines a relationship where, in a "pattern of flirtation and teasing," she and one of her female subjects entertained "the idea of making love." Although the subject's "physical pain and chronic illness precluded sex," their daily visits, during which research data was collected, were "affectionate and full of erotic byplay" (p. 13).

THE *MATTER* OF BODIES IN CONDUCTING SOCIAL INQUIRY

In an examination of a number of diverse research experiences, it is apparent that if we, as social scientists, are to fully admit the verities of our investigations, the sensual, sometimes hot, pleasures of the body may not easily, or always, be extricated from the cool demands of inquiry. I have referred to a small and diverse range of accounts where the sexual body has, at least in some ways, been admitted. However, it is clear that the matter of these bodies does not matter the same. First, all bodies are differently and multiply inflected by the peculiarities of class, age, gender, race, and sexuality and therefore, are partial and limited perspectives from which the world is contemplated. As Arthur Frank (1989) notes, "acting sexy . . . and having possibilities all depend on the body, but these can be enacted differently in different bodies" (p. 143). Second, as diverse bodies are assigned meaning in the culture(s) of inquiry, the visibility of the body

---

[7]I am startled and aroused by the homoerotic quality of this and Read's other accounts of his love for his subject. Newton (1993) shares this perception and notes that Read's attraction "is, or borders on, homoerotic desire" (p. 9). In contrast, an anonymous reader who had previously used the same copy of Read's text had, in the margins, written, following the last line quoted, "i.e. the common bond of humanity." To this reader, Read's comments had no evident homoerotic element and I am again reminded of the partiality and limitedness of each of our perspectives and the necessity for *admitting* to the locatedness of knowledge.

has most often been inversely related to its privilege: high privilege–low visibility. With respect to gender, as an example, women have often borne the corporeal for men who, outside of sports and war, have laid the body *on* the female. In cultures of the West, the slack academic gown and loosely cut collar-to-cuff clothing worn by men in educational, religious, commercial, and political institutions are (ill)fitting visual reminders that it is the male head that is the cardinal site of theoretical knowledge. Still further, as gender has been constructed as a distinguishing factor in the experience of the body, so too has sexuality. As an example, heterosexual male desire has been embedded in the structure of discourse itself so that heterosexual men, or closeted homosexual men, have been able to abstract themselves from their bodies and to make universal generalizations that point away from desire as specific and informative to all undertakings.[8] By not making an issue of their own sexuality in research practice, heterosexual men, as Newton (1993) suggests, make heterosexuality and male gender the "cultural givens, the unmarked categories" (p. 4).

In those cases where the sexual body has been admitted, both (male) gender and (hetero)sexuality offer a quieting, relative protection. As an instance, whereas Rabinow (1977) acknowledges that thoughts of a "romantic setting and a possible sexual encounter of my own combined to whet my appetite" (p. 63), his sexual liaison is seen as a conquest—a cause for boasting of sexual prowess in which the woman involved is dismissed as wanton. Even further, under these presumably heterosexual circumstances, the event comes as no surprise because of the assumption that *everybody* gets laid in the field.[9] Alternately, Harry Wolcott and Esther Newton have shared recountings of homosexual desire as it was connected to their respective inquiries. Whereas Wolcott and Rabinow *admit* sexual interactions with research subjects, Newton's amour stops short.[10] Although

---

[8] Although this essay opened with an argument for the recognition of the interimplications of sex and knowledge, Pierre Bourdieu (1977), allowing that theory as a human activity or practice is embodied, contends alternately, that it is naive "to reduce to their strictly sexual dimension the countless acts of diffuse inculcation through which the body and the world tend to be set in order" (p. 92). What Bourdieu's argument appears to contain, however, is the presumption to a monovocal and transcendent perspective that contains a disavowal of the potential for varying sexual perspectives to infuse *differently* and radically alter each aspect of the socially informed body that Bourdieu so aptly describes.

[9] In articulating that the same men who appeared to be opposed to sexual involvements in the field also belittled his laments about the difficulties in maintaining that position, Whitehead (1986) suggests that the acceptance of (hetero)sexual relationships may make them appear as a non-problem because of a belief that "everybody gets laid in the field" (p. 232).

[10] The outcome, for Newton, personally and professionally, had she acted and reported on her sexual inclinations can only be speculated. What she intrepidly reports, however, is that it was the subject's health condition rather than a prefigured commitment to sexual abstention that determined their behavioral outcomes.

Newton notes that her fieldwork was fraught with sexual *dangers*, those pitfalls, apparently incidental to Rabinow, became brutally manifest in Wolcott's case. The differences between the consistent bliss, heralded ribaldry, or cruel wrongs of Newton's, Rabinow's, and Wolcott's respective accounts, however, speaks not only to a difference in outcome, but also to the differing valence afforded diverse permutations of these sexed bodies. In naming their desires, Wolcott, Newton, and now myself, have been stamped with a visibility that is inversely related to our privilege as sexual beings. It is a well-known phenomenon. As bodies are assignated as queer, that is, as I refer to it here, as other than heterosexual, they serve, to varying degrees, as sites of alarm for the conflation of sex and knowledge in theory and practice. Again, the diversity of these *particular* queer bodies is pertinent. Although there may be other factors of note regarding age, gender, and race, with respect to sexuality, Newton, Wolcott, and I all report homosexual interest and gain high visibility in the act of doing so. However, our desires are variantly constituted in contemporary culture. To illustrate, all accounts are detailed in journals or texts aimed primarily at academic audiences. Research suggests that, whereas women in these communities are more inclined to be less homophobic than men, women and men are more likely to feel considerably more distressed over male homosexuality than over lesbianism (see Clift, 1988; D'Augelli & Rose, 1990). Although the differences between admitting and acting on sexual desire are clear, as audiences assign properness to certain sexual bodies and acts and indecency to others, without discretion, as examples, Newton's, and perhaps for reasons to be discussed, my own, account may remain delicate transgressions; Rabinow's—no transgression at all; Wolcott's—an unmitigated corruption.

THE EVIDENT BODY: THE BODY AS EVIDENCE

Having noted a wide range of diverse engagements of the sexualized corporeal, in the pursuit of reason, it appears that the body may not reasonably be overridden. If the body is ineluctably evident, what then of the body's evidence in the testing, affirmation, or construction of knowledge? How might a recognition of the body contribute to understanding? How might the body and desire be put to work in the productive service of inquiry? To that end, the balance of this chapter briefly considers the role of the senses, the possible impact of the erotic on motivation, rapport, candor, and perception, and finally suggests that a questioning of the possibility or appropriateness of corporeal exclusion allows for a wider range of differently imagined, and lived, (sexual) bodies in the pursuit of knowledge.

Sense and Sensibility

In social research, the senses operate to create a unity of experience through the integration of that which is seen, touched, heard, tasted, and smelled. A researcher may not secure the sum of sensations and add them to the findings of the inquiry, but, as the way the body attends, and, the means of its excitation, the body's senses contribute, not only to its sensuality, but to its sensibility. In other words, it is through the senses that our bodies make sense of experience. However, although inevitably seeking knowledge in bodies, social researchers have often remained insensitive to the impact of the senses that are the origins of experience by which we come to know the milieu(s) around us. Indeed, the body's responses have been devalued and scientific orientations have shifted "the centre of gravity of experience, so that we have unlearned how to see, hear, and generally speaking, feel, in order to deduce, from our bodily organization and the world as the physicist conceives it, what we are to see, hear, and feel" (Merleau-Ponty, 1962, p. 229).

Alternatively, inquirers might productively remain open to a recognition of what *all* the senses might contribute to knowing. Further, as the senses are both biomaterially and socially informed, particular investigations might be impacted by a specific researcher's sensual strengths and shortcomings. As an example, given the senses of hearing, taste, smell, and sight, it is both the biology of researcher and the cultural context that might alter the sensory experience. As illustration, the body's sense of smell has been among the most ignored, perhaps out of bourgeoisie embarrassment, but also because of its association with receptivity and femininity. The senses of taste and hearing are also constructed as more passive. To speculate in terms of social research, given that the latter is constituted as a nonactive sense, although I am not given to universalizing statements based on gender, it might be hypothesized that male investigators would not be particularly good listeners (see Duroche, 1990). At the same time, it might be anticipated that (many) male researchers would privilege sight as a consequence of its traditional associations with distance, cognition, and abstraction. Consistently, Eisner (1991) presents the notion that sight is the privileged sense: it is the "shorthand way of referring to all the senses and the qualities to which they are sensitive" (p. 68). To push that possibility further, if male researchers, as a group, are inclined to be remarkable observers but ineffective listeners, it might be reasonable to suggest that particular methodological adaptations would be, not only advantageous, but obligatory in order to account for a particular researcher's sensual strengths, limitations, and inhibitions that might, if left unchecked, restrict the kind and range, and therefore, the trustworthiness, of the data collected.

Other senses might also have much to contribute to knowledge if only we could find ways to let them. In social inquiry, sight, as noted, has been a preferred sense perhaps because it is sight that distances the researcher from her or his body. Alternatively, it is the sense of touch that draws the experience of the body nearer: there is a built-in reversibility as we are touched when we touch the body of another. Although touch has been taboo in inquiry, the sense of touch could, alternatively, be of particular interest because the skin, in the form of sensations and excitations, potentially contributes to understanding through its registration of nonverbal messages. Didier Anzieu (1989) suggests that the skin of the body, the boundary between inside and outside, or what he has termed the *Skin Ego*, is a principle means of communicating with others. In arguing for three underlying bases of human thought: the cerebral cortex, the skin, and sexual union, Anzieu suggests that thought may be as "much an affair of the skin as of the brain" (p. 9). However, since the skin is also considered a center of seduction, restrictions against touching, in research as well as in the broader culture, are seen as necessary guards against over-excitation. Whatever there is that might be learned by doing so, touching the other in inquiry is prohibited. Such caution is grounded in a cultural fear that touching each other's bodies is an intimate act that may result in arousal and could lead to havoc as individuals become incapable of acting in the best interests of themselves or others. It is a paradox that we are permitted to touch those that we know well, but in the pursuit of social knowledge, although we may touch objects in the research, we are ill-advised to touch those we are trying to get to know better.

The Implications of Eros

It has been demonstrated that inquiry may bring together participants who desire, not only knowledge, but each other. Whether we approve or not, sex is sometimes a factor in social inquiry. Sexual relations between research participants are already occurring. In most instances, these sexual engagements have been considered slips to be denied or meaningless *affairs* to be ignored and separated from the *truth*. As with the extended possibilities of the senses, there remains considerable resistance to any different consideration of the possible contribution(s) of desire in the everyday(s) of social research. Alternatively, because sexuality is unlikely to be totally absent from inquiry between adults, as with the senses, it might be more productive to actively ask after the specifics of desire where sex and knowledge are experientially, and not just conceptually, linked.[11]

---

[11]To date, it seems that any such puzzling over the body's potential irrepressibility and the sometimes inevitable conflations of sex and knowledge *in action* has remained only scantily addressed because the lived body's questions are most often considered either too disruptive to ask outside of theory, or the asking precludes a genuine openness to a range of answers. In the event of the first, the silence around sexuality in research is taken as evidence of its unspeakability, ineluctable disruptive impact, or its irrelevance. In the case of the latter, in the midst of much uncertainty, the inquirer, novice or seasoned, is forced to make individual choices constrained both by a lack of information and by an actual lack of choice.

Although a more complete discussion is warranted, and although there might be many consequences, three seem especially relevant here: motivation, rapport and its connection to candor, and perception. First, interactions in the research environment are undertaken through a particular feeling or mood that could include sexual desire. It is, afterall, the experience of emotion that inaugurates our motor projects and propels us toward desired goals (Leder, 1990). Further, it is eros or libido that breathes life into the world, gives meaning to external stimuli, and influences the use that each subject makes of the body (Merleau-Ponty, 1962). As such, eros, as a source of human motivation, may not only influence the researcher's ideas for research, but may invigorate and fuel the entire body-to-body inquiry process as participants anticipate the undertaking and commit greater amounts of time and energy than they might otherwise consider. In my research with other gay artists, as an instance, eros was central to the initiatory processes, and was, at least in part, responsible for sustaining engagement and productivity. Most aptly, desire acted as mobilizer, that is, desire went to work on behalf of knowledge and the research experience proceeded, not only at higher throttle, but was, in the end, taken somewhere different than it otherwise might have been.

Second, as a motivating life-force, the possibilities of strong erotic feelings may influence rapport, and therefore, candor. Although liking a research subject may not be a prerequisite to understanding, the limits of liking and disliking—of an optimally efficacious relationship—are ambiguous. Researchers, as an example, are warned of the dangers of over-rapport whereby the subject's view may be taken without question. Inquirers are further cautioned to note that whereas positive rapport may be the key to completing good interviews, it is only some rapport that produces maximum validity.[12] As eros may influence rapport, what ultimately is the relationship of desire to candor or to *truth?* Among the possibilities, participants who feel attracted to one another may speak more, or less, honestly than they might otherwise. Erotic attractions, as an example, may enhance truth-telling—where each wants to know everything there is to know about the other. Desire may also distort as a consequence of a romanticized halo effect where a researcher imputes more to a subject—practicing a generosity in interpretation that may otherwise be lacking. On the other hand, subjects who wish to impress one another may be less candid about aspects of their experience and understanding that may influence the other person's impressions negatively. Finally, uneven desire between participants

---

[12]Despite such cautions, however, the degree of rapport cannot be dislocated from the particularities of the circumstances. As an example, high levels of rapport may not only be more possible, but more likely, perhaps unavoidable, between similarly sited and socially marginalized research participants. See Honeychurch (1996).

may injure both rapport and candor and generate a negativity toward all aspects of the project that otherwise might be absent.

Third, because emotion is rooted in the visceral, strong emotions such as sexual desire may also, perhaps most importantly, influence perception. Sensation and emotion are not attributed as one to the object and the other to the subject. Rather, the social world is presented to the sensing subject whose perceptions are qualified, at least in part, as a consequence of his or her emotional response to what is being presented. Initially, for the researcher, strong emotion such as desire may serve as a source of perceptual information about herself or himself. Affect, that is, may be a means of storing and retrieving antecedent conditions about the inquirer (Kaplan, 1991). In research, as well as in other aspects of life, emotional experience "serves as feedback from the appraisal system, signifying or confirming that a situation is personally significant" (Clore & Parrott, 1991, p. 109).

Sexual interest may also alter perception in ways that may stimulate a more thorough knowledge about the targeted subject(s)—surely the purpose of research. As Grosz (1994) argues, "the sexual object is not perceived like any other perceptual object. The desexualized object does not beckon or entice the subject with its secret recesses as does the sexual object, inducing greater intimacy" (p. 109).[13] The shift in perceptions that occurs around a sexualized subject may not be merely imagined; rather, altered experiences might have a physiological basis. As an instance, emotions, including sexual attraction, alter bodily processes such as breathing rates, stomach secretions, body temperature, heart rate, and the like. As visceral responses most often cannot simply be willed away, perceptions are shaped by the body's corporeal adaptations. Heightened conditions of arousal and accompanying physiological responses may intensify levels of attention to all stimuli in the research milieu. Sexual desire in inquiry, that is, might enhance attention. Further, desire might also influence perceptual responses to such other aspects of the research process as data analysis. In other words, research suggests that positive mood impacts cognitive processes by influencing thinking in broader, more flexible, and more integrated ways (Isen, 1987). Consequently, the results of inquiry may be differently considered because higher creativity and less-inhibited analytic processing strategies have been associated with elated mood.

Ultimately, social research comes down to the experiences of bodies. Through pointing to sex and the body, I have endeavored to argue for a

---

[13]In allowing that the body of the other may be viewed as sexual object, and that much derogating objectification occurs, sexual objectification is *necessarily* neither brash nor disrespectful: it is rather, the very condition on which our human sexual reciprocality is predicated. In other words, in the objectification of the other, there is a recognition that the other might be sexual object for me, and I, as subject, may also be sexual object for the other.

more conscious inclusion of the corporeal, for a recognition of a fuller range of the body's sensual capacities, and for a recognition of how some inquiries are impacted by the presence of specific desires. As such, bodies, in all their sensing and sexual capacities, become central rather than marginal, not only to the theoretical connections of sex and knowledge with which this essay opened, but to the day-to-days of social research wherein those knowledges are constructed and tested. Accordingly, sensual bodies become allies in—not aliens to—understanding. Such an admission of sex and bodies allows for altered knowledges and a recognition that an entire range of the body's answers might fall outside of the pervasive and powerful shadow of an exclusive masculinist and heterocentric perspective. Perhaps most importantly, by acknowledging all of the body's sensing and erotic potentialities, by allowing for the senses and flagging the hot as well as the cool spots of the sometimes private amity of inquiry, in asking after the body, accountability is demanded in ways which may be ultimately productive.[14]

Before concluding, I have a final confession to make. It is an admission to which I have already alluded. Although I have written to recommend less restrictive views of sensual and sexualized bodies in research, I have not been slouching toward what could be seen as a scorching revelation, which this particular absorption with the body was intended to justify. In my research, there were no bawdy performances. Simply put, there is nothing to redress. Whereas my interest is in the constituting role of the corporeal, and although I endeavored to account for a wide range of sensual stimulation and recognized the ways in which eros had imbued the entire project with a quality it otherwise would have lacked, I otherwise very carefully adhered to the research protocols as they are most often practiced. In doing so, I joined a long tradition of inquirers who have reinforced them. Nonetheless, this coming to knowledge was nothing if not passionate work.

COMINGS AND GOINGS

During the last interview, it began to pour rain, and as the final recorded conversation concluded, I breathed in deeply and exhaled a melancholy linked to endings—a disharmony not far from the blues. The studio had

---

[14]Asking about the body challenges the assertions of Western culture's general sex-negativity, which conceives of sexuality as a dangerous and destructive force meant only to be contained. Asking about the body and desire in research challenges unequal relationships between individuals and groups that differentially empower one over the other. Asking about the body challenges the prerogatives of certain bodies to authorize particular bodies and sexual experiences and to delegitimate others.

been a luscious research site and I lingered for a moment and eased one last sensual indulgence from it. Gayle and I shook hands as in the beginning and the final flights, the strain made easy in descent, led me back through the glass door and the iron gate to the silent, puddled streets. By the time I reached the tambourine player's corner—empty but for an old crate— mute but for plaintive memory, I listened, motionless in the downpour. Protected by the broad, flat awning, I closed my eyes and paused to re- connect with this morning's remembered pleasures—the bodies of re- search, bodies of knowledge, and a full-bodied voice, now impossible to separate from the inquiry, singing about the body's run on earth—"from the cradle to the grave." At this moment, somewhere in the complications of the middle, a drop of rain ran down my face. There was no particular bliss in this immediate solitude, and yet there was exhilaration at the same time—the pleasure of past memories and future images, restless visions of analysis and writing, other bodies, other places, other times.

The end of this part of the story, imprecise as its origin, is to be found on the street where it began. There was the body in the beginning and now again, there is the body at the end. In the chronicle of those bodies, however, in the uncertainty of beginnings, the fluidity of endings, and the weave of the mysterious intricacies in between, the conclusions remain irresolute. Although much about the sensual/sexual body has been specu- lated, it is evident that the body's answers are multiple and shifting—much is yet to be detected or invented. In finding ways of thinking through the matter of bodies, and believing that all bodies matter, there is little definite, save that, and perhaps the tenuous routes of the body's discoveries. None- theless, there is pleasure to be found in continuing inquiries whose strange destinies do not know their ends until arriving there. In the meantime, the body's significance can perhaps best be imagined by conjuring a world in which sensuality plays no part—a human drama in which sensing and sexual bodies are absent. The immense disappointment of such a conjec- ture speaks to the irrepressible itch of the body, of the connections of pleasure, desire, and knowledge that this project has only begun to scratch.

REFERENCES

Angrosino, M. (1986). Son and lover: The anthropologist as non-threatening male. In T. Whitehead & M. E. Conaway (Eds.), *Self, sex, and gender in cross-cultural fieldwork* (pp. 64–83). Chicago: University of Illinois Press.

Alston, K. (1991). Teaching philosophy and eros: Love as a relation to truth. *Educational Theory, 41*(4), 385–395.

Anzieu, D. (1989). *The skin ego.* New Haven, CT: Yale University Press.

Ball, S. (1990). Self-doubt and soft data: Social and technical trajectories in ethnographic fieldwork. *International Journal of Qualitative Studies in Education, 3*(2), 157–171.

Bourdieu, P. (1977). *Outline of a theory of practice.* Cambridge, England: Cambridge University Press.

Burgess, A. (1962). *A clockwork orange.* Middlesex, England: Penguin Books.

Clift, S. (1988). Lesbian and gay issues in education: A study of the attitudes of first year students in a college of higher education. *British Educational Research Journal, 14*(1), 31–50.

Clore, G., & Parrott, G. (1991). Moods and their vicissitudes: Thought and feelings as information. In J. Forgas (Ed.), *Emotion and social judgments* (pp. 107–123). Oxford, England: Pergamon Press.

D'Augelli, A., & Rose, M. (1990). Homophobia in a university community: Attitudes and experiences of heterosexual freshmen. *Journal of College Student Development, 31*(6), 484–491.

Duroche, L. (1990). Male perception as social construct. In J. Hearn & D. Morgan (Eds.), *Men, masculinities, and social theory* (pp. 170–185). London: Univin Hyman.

Edelman, L. (1994). *Homographesis.* New York: Routledge.

Eichler, M. (1988). *Non-sexist research methods.* New York: Routledge.

Eisner, E. (1991). *The enlightened eye: Qualitative inquiry and the enhancement of educational practice.* New York: Macmillan.

Feldman, E. (1993, September). Best advice and counsel to art teachers. *Art Education,* 58–59.

Fluehr-Lobban, C., & Lobban, R. (1986). Families, gender and methodology in the Sudan. In T. Whitehead & M. E. Conaway (Eds.), *Self, sex, and gender in cross-cultural fieldwork* (pp. 182–195). Chicago: University of Illinois Press.

Foucault, M. (1990). *The history of sexuality.* New York: Vintage Books.

Frank, A. (1989). Bringing bodies back in: A decade review. *Differentia, 3–4,* 131–162.

Geertz, C. (1988). *Works and lives: The anthropologist as author.* Stanford, CA: Stanford University Press.

Gold, P. (1970). Odyssey of encounter. In P. Golde (Ed.), *Women in the field: Anthropological experiences* (pp. 67–93). Chicago: Aldine.

Gordon, C. (Ed.). (1980). *Power/knowledge: Selected interviews and other writings 1972–1977 by Michel Foucault.* New York: Pantheon Books.

Grosz, E. (1994). *Volatile bodies: Towards a corporeal feminism.* Bloomington: Indiana University Press.

Grosz, E., & Probyn, E. (Eds.). (1995). *Sexy bodies: The strange carnalities of feminism.* New York: Routledge.

Grumet, M. (1988). *Bitter milk: Women and teaching.* Amherst: University of Massachusetts Press.

Hammersley, M., & Atkinson, P. (1995). *Ethnography: Principles in practice.* New York: Routledge.

Honeychurch, K. (1996). Researching dissident subjectivities: Queering the grounds of theory and practice. *Harvard Educational Review, 66*(2), 339–355.

Isen, A. (1987). Positive affect, cognitive processes and social behavior. In L. Berkowitz (Ed.), *Advances in experimental social psychology* (Vol. 20, pp. 203–253). New York: Academic Press.

Johnson, N. (1986). Ethnographic research and rites of incorporation: A sex and gender-based comparison. In T. Whitehead & M. E. Conaway (Eds.), *Self, sex, and gender in cross-cultural fieldwork* (pp. 164–181). Chicago: University of Illinois Press.

Kaplan, M. (1991). The joint effects of cognition and affect on social judgment. In J. Forgas (Ed.), *Emotion and social judgments* (pp. 73–82). Oxford, England: Pergamon Press.

Kritzman, L. (Ed.). (1988). *Michel Foucault: Politics, philosophy, culture.* New York: Routledge.

Kulick, D., & Willson, M. (Eds.). (1995). *Taboo: Sex, identity and erotic subjectivity in anthropological fieldwork.* New York: Routledge.

Leder, D. (1990). *The absent body.* Chicago: The University of Chicago Press.

Lewin, E., & Leap, W. (Eds.). (1996). *Out in the field: Reflections of lesbian and gay anthropologists.* Chicago: University of Illinois Press.

Malinowski, B. (1967). *A diary in the strictest sense of the term.* New York: Harcourt, Brace & World.

Merleau-Ponty, M. (1962). *Phenomenology of perception.* New York: Routledge & Kegan Paul.

Newton, E. (1993). My best informant's dress: The erotic equation in fieldwork. *Cultural Anthropology, 8*(1), 3–23.

Pinar, W. (1994). *Autobiography, politics and sexuality: Essays in curriculum theory, 1972–1992.* New York: Peter Lang.

Rabinow, P. (1977). *Reflections on fieldwork in Morocco.* Berkeley: University of California Press.

Read, K. (1965). *The high valley.* New York: Charles Scribner's Sons.

Read, K. (1980). *Other voices: The style of a male homosexual tavern.* Novato, CA: Chandler & Sharp.

Read, K. (1986). *Return to the high valley.* Berkeley: University of California Press.

Roman, L. (1993). Double exposure: The politics of feminist materialist ethnography. *Educational Theory, 43*(3), 279–308.

Sears, J. (1992). *Sexuality and the curriculum: The politics and practices of sexuality education.* New York: Teachers College Press.

Sedgwick, E. (1990). *Epistemology of the closet.* Berkeley: University of California Press.

Sedgwick, E. (1993). *Tendencies.* Durham, NC: Duke University Press.

Skipper, J., & McCaghy, C. (1972). Respondents' intrusion upon the situation: The problem of interviewing subjects with special qualities. *The Sociological Quarterly, 13,* 237–243.

Strathern, M. (1987). Out of context: The persuasive fictions of anthropology. *Current Anthropology, 28*(3), 251–281.

Turner, B. (1991). Recent developments in the theory of the body. In M. Featherstone, M. Hepworth, & B. Turner (Eds.), *The body: Social processes and cultural theory* (pp. 1–35). London: Sage.

Whitehead, T. (1986). Breakdown, resolution, and coherences: The fieldwork experiences of a big, brown, pretty-talking Man. In T. Whitehead & M. E. Conaway (Eds.), *Self, sex, and gender in cross-cultural fieldwork* (pp. 213–239). Chicago: University of Illinois Press.

Williams, W. (1986). *The spirit and the flesh.* Boston: Beacon Press.

Wittgenstein, L. (1974). *On certainty.* Oxford, England: Basil Blackwell.

Wittgenstein, L. (1977). *Culture and value.* Oxford, England: Basil Blackwell.

Wolcott, H. (1990). On seeking—and rejecting—validity in qualitative research. In E. Eisner & A. Peshkin (Eds.), *Qualitative inquiry in education: The continuing debate* (pp. 121–152). New York: Teachers College Press.

Chapter 13

Unresting the Curriculum:
Queer Projects, Queer Imaginings

Marla Morris
Louisiana State University

> *Ida woke up. After a while she got up. Then she stood up. Then she ate something. After that she sat down. That was Ida. . . . In a little while there were more of them there who sat down and stood up and leaned. Then they came in and went out. This made it useful to them and to Ida.*
>
> —Stein (1972, p. 55)

That was Ida. That was Gertrude Stein's *Ida*. When I first read *Ida*, I was riding a Greyhound bus destined for New York City. Ida also, in one part of the novel, journeys to New York—that's the way Ida was. "Oh dear she often said oh dear isn't it queer" (Stein, 1972, p. 141). Yes it certainly was queer, whatever it was was certainly queer. Gertrude Stein captures seemingly innocuous moments in Ida's life and queers them: Stein insists that the familiar be made strange. If Gertrude Stein were to queer the curriculum, she would insist that the curriculum, like Ida's life, become strange.

Strangeness is one way to describe the word *queer*. Queer theorists struggle to define queer not without difficulty. Let us dwell on these difficulties for a moment. Enter queer theorist Alexander Doty. Doty (1993) seems to fly around in circles:

> I want to construct "queer" as something other than "lesbian," "gay," or "bisexual"; but I can't say that "lesbian," "gay," or "bisexual" aren't also "queer." I would like to maintain the integrity of "lesbian," "gay," and "bisexual" as concepts that have specific historical, cultural, and personal mean-

ings; but I would also like "lesbian," "gay," and "bisexual" culture, history, theory, and politics to have some bearing on the articulation of queerness. (p. xvii)

On one level, I understand what Doty is attempting to say: We must in some way move beyond rigid categories of gay/lesbian/bisexual because they tend to lock people into fixed prescriptions for living. But at the same time these categories are important to maintain for political and historical reasons. Where does that leave us? Back at the airport flying around. Back to square one asking the question, What is queer? Queer suggests a self-naming that stands outside the dominant cultural codes; queer opposes sex-policing, gender-policing, heteronormativity, and assimilationist politics. Jeffrey Weeks (1995) suggests that queers may include "radical self-defined lesbians and gays ... sadomasochists, fetishists, bisexuals, gender-benders, radical heterosexuals" (p. 113). To this list I would add transgendered peoples, either transsexuals or cross-dressers, hermaphrodites, and eunuchs.

According to Doty, Judith Butler and Sue-Ellen Case suggest that queer is "beyond gender"; queerness is an "attitude" that moves beyond the debate over male–female, homo–hetero (Doty, 1993, p. xv). But what exactly is "beyond gender"? Mustn't we first examine the problematics of gender if we are to move beyond it? And if queerness is an attitude how can one determine who has this attitude and what this attitude is? Doesn't having an attitude imply a certain vagueness?

Queer, if defined as an attitude, becomes so broad as to be rendered meaningless; if defined as only concerning gender problematics is too narrow; if defined as subsuming differences within it (by lumping together marginal peoples who have different social and political histories) becomes dangerous because it obliterates the situatedness of individuals. A further problem is the very category of queer. Does this category simply instantiate yet another binary: queer–not queer? Can we ever really dissolve binary thinking altogether and would this non-binary strategy even be useful? Does queer simply provoke hatred from non-radical homosexuals, bisexuals, and transgendered peoples? Does queer provoke hatred from non-radical heterosexuals? The questions are endlessly problematic. However, in spite of these and other problems, queer theory has much to offer and may change the tide of history.

Missing from most of the discussions on queer theory is what I would term a queer sensibility or queer aesthetic (with the exception of Mary Doll's chapter "Queering the Gaze" in this collection). A queer sensibility concerns the reception and reading of a text (a text may include art, music, literature). The text is a site of interpretation. Thus there is nothing inherently queer about a text, even if one may read a text queerly. As Alan Block (1995) points out, reading constructs the reader as well as the text. Reading creates the reader; reading queerly creates a queer reader. For me, a queer reading of a text uncovers the possibility of the text's radical political potential. More specifically, my queer reading of a certain piece of music, say, may lead me to believe that that particular piece of music, in some way, radically challenges the status quo by introducing new genres or new styles. However, queer readings should not reduce art, music, and literature to politics, although art forms may be read through political lenses.

A queer aesthetic or queer sensibility adds to the discussion on queerness, because most queer theorists center the conversation on identity/politics. My defintion of queerness, then, contains three ingredients: (a) Queerness as a subject position digresses from normalized, rigid identities that adhere to the sex = gender paradigm; (b) Queerness as a politic challenges the status quo, does not simply tolerate it, and does not stand for assimilation into the mainstream; (c) Queerness as an aesthetic or sensibility reads and interprets texts (art, music, literature) as potentially politically radical. A radical politic moves to the left, challenging norms.

Queer debates, I must add, do not necessarily have to include all three ingredients. It is possible, I think, to talk about a queer sensibility, for example, without engaging in a discussion of the sex = gender paradigm. However, my chapter touches on all three elements and their curricular implications. My ultimate project is queering the curriculum.

Much writing on queer theory tends to focus on the problem of identity (Butler, 1990; Doty, 1993; Weeks, 1991). Carrying out Foucault's (1980) work, queer theorists attempt to examine oppressive categories such as sex–gender by discovering how these categories came to be constructed and how certain individuals have been produced by them. Once these categories have been de-coded, queer identites may begin to emerge. Queer identites overturn the liberal humanist project that pretends that straights/lesbians and gays/transgendered peoples are all really alike at bottom. The liberal humanist project pretends that there is some abiding structure that stands under all human beings in spite of any differences. Queer identites move toward what I term foundationless dis-similarities. There are no abiding structures holding us together as if we were one big, happy family: we are not alike, we are not the same, we are not one.

Those who buy into the sex = gender paradigm assume that there is a foundational abiding structure to which all humans must adhere. If you are of the biological sex male, your gender must be masculine. Masculine behavior must fulfill certain prescriptions concerning dress, gestures, attitudes. If you are of the biological sex female, your gender must be feminine. Likewise, feminine behavior must fulfill certain prescriptions concerning dress, gestures, attitudes. The diagnostic statistical manual used by psychiatrists, social workers, and psychologists (APA, 1994) states that those people who do not fit the sex = gender paradigm suffer from "gender identity disorder" (pp. 246–247). If a person feels uncomfortable with her or his sex or gender, she or he suffers from this "disorder." If a child insists on playing games "inappropriate" to her sex, she also suffers from this disorder. The notion of an identity "disorder" presupposes that there is a right, proper, correct, true identity. However, is there a true identity? Of course not. Furthermore, many point out that the sex = gender paradigm is at least problematic if not, at most, totally flawed (Butler, 1990; Foucault, 1980; Herdt, 1994; Martin, 1992; Phelan, 1994). Gender is socially constructed, politically controlled, and discursively instituted by religious, medical, psychological, and scientific communities (Foucault, 1980). As Martin (1992) warns: "We are constantly threatened with erasure from discursive fields where the naturalization of sexual and gender norms works to obliterate actual pluralities" (pp. 94–95). There is nothing natural about human beings: we are socially constructed, produced by language, television, family albums. As Spence (1995) points out, we must redo our family albums. Spence points out that our narratives have already been planned out by our parents through how they choose to represent us through the beloved family album.

There is nothing natural about the family album, about sex or gender, about our lives generally. The invention of the sex = gender paradigm serves to oppress, control, and reduce people to two types: male and female. These two types are only supposed to act in two ways: the masculine way or the feminine way. But I contend that there are probably thousands, millions, trillions of genders. Herdt (1994) contends that not only are there more than two genders, but there are more than two sexes (hermaphrodites make up a third sex). If marginalized peoples are not to become obliterated by forced assimilation into the norm, tearing down the walls of the sex = gender prison becomes necessary. As Garber (1992) suggests, we need to create a "category crisis" (p. 16).

Serene Nanda's study of "Hijras" in India demands this category crisis, demands a rethinking of the actual fluidity of sex and gender. Hijras are a group of peoples who live in India as devotees (followers) of the goddess Buhuchara Mata. These devotees initiate sacred rituals during births of males and marriages. Hijras also serve as prostitutes with men. It may be difficult for westerners, and even some easterners, to associate priesthood with prostitution, but in this particular sect of Indian culture, priests as prostitutes do exist. Moreover, these priests/prostitutes are "intersexed and eunuchs . . . they are neither male nor female, man or woman. At a more esoteric level, the hijras are also man plus woman, or erotic and sacred female men" (Nanda, 1994, p. 373). Basically there are three types of Hijras: females who do not menstruate, males who are born as hermaphrodites and emasculated, or males who are not born as hermaphrodites and are emasculated. As Doll (1995) points out, images such as these "move us out of the center of normality. We find ourselves in a different space where the unfamiliar beckons us because it resists labels" (p. 129). Hijras do indeed resist labels, resist the sex = gender paradigm, and in fact confuse these categories completely.

I surveyed college texts on Indian religions and culture and found that all of them omitted any reference to Hijras (Berry, 1971; Hopfe, 1994; Kitagawa, 1989; Kramer, 1986; Matthews, 1995; Nielson, 1993; Nigosian, 1990; Sharma, 1987; Tyler, 1973). The conspicuous absence of Hijras from these college texts perpetuates heteronormativity and the sex = gender prison. College texts must be queered by introducing teachers and students to groups like the Hijras. It is by queering texts that curricularists may begin to tear down the walls of the sex = gender paradigm. Queering the curriculum demands paradigm shifts.

I would say that Hijras, because they have no interest, or no concept really of this western paradigm of sex = gender, inhabit a queer space. A queer space opens the possibilites for transformation and change. Becoming queer is just that—a constant becoming, a constant transformation. As Phelan contends, identities are "works in progress [not] . . . museum pieces" (p. 41). The ontological pronouncement "I am queer" bespeaks this museum quality, for it seems fixed, eternal, unchangeable. Rather, I become queer in relation to my desires, fantasies, readings, reactings, writings, experiences. A queer identity is a chameleon-like refusal to be caged into any prescribed category or role.

This refusal to be normalized is, most fundamentally, a political move. Identities are necessarily political. At this juncture, I examine three possible political stances queers might appropriate: transgressive, resistant, and what I term digressive. One who embraces a transgressive politic assumes that she or he can completely transgress, or completely transcend, history and culture in a new and radical way by appropriating a new queer identity. As I, for instance, take up the identity queer, I can, in perhaps an epiphanal moment or series of moments, move completely beyond my oppressors, the prison guards of the sex = gender paradigm. However, as Foucault (1980) has shown, we have been produced by so many intersecting discursive and nondiscursive practices that it is simply naive to think we can step outside culture and history to create identites anew. Even if I am able to create myself somewhat, I will always remain, to some extent, trapped by my culture.

A more realistic politic, then, takes into account the ways in which we have been produced. Resistance politics does just this. According to Philip Auslander (1992), Fredric Jameson and Hal Foster suggest that resistance politics positions "the subject within the dominant discourses . . . offering strategies of counterhegemonic resistance by exposing . . . cultural control . . . emphasizing the traces of nonhegemonic discourse without claiming to transcend its terms" (p. 24). Jameson and Foster are right in saying that it is impossible to transcend completely the given cultural forms we've inherited. We are embedded, at both conscious and unconscious levels, in our own cultural codes. Resistance is a way to refuse these codes without admitting to radically departing from them, because we are produced by them. Auslander (1992) points out that neither Jameson nor Foster, however, "takes into account . . . the issue of audience" (p. 29) in his analysis. Neither Jameson nor Foster considers how others will react, read, respond to my actions, whether I consider my actions resistant or transgressive. Auslander is suggesting that both theorists assume that my audience will receive my performance well. My audience will read my performance the same way, my way. This was the very mistake Martin Luther made as he translated the bible into German: He simply thought that all Germans would read the bible just as he did; Luther thought everyone would agree with his interpretations. Luther would roll in his grave if he knew just how Protestantism split because everybody did not read the bible the same way.

It seems that both resistance and transgressive politics point toward some place over the rainbow, toward a set of golden arches, toward heaven, nirvana, utopia. But there is no guarantee that resistant or transgressive politics will yield anything at all. And even if these moves do produce results, we cannot be sure how others will be affected. As Simone de Beauvoir (1948) reminds us, all actions are necessarily aporetic. My so-called resistant or transgressive actions may simultaneously benefit some and harm others. Every action has ambiguous results.

I contend that a different form of politics is needed that takes into account the reception and reading of our performances. This path might be termed digressive. A digressive politics, like resistance politics, must examine the cultural codes and discursive strategies located within the dominant culture and attempt to illuminate how we have been produced by these codes. Unlike resistance politics, digressive politics is not utopian. A digressive politic is one that might embrace a certain cynicism about what it is, realistically, I am able to accomplish. To digress from dominant cultural codes is to move away from mainstream discourses. This digression does not guarantee anything; it does not guarantee my success or failure. This digression does not necessarily change either micropolitical land-scapes or macropolitical horizons, although certainly these are some of my goals. I cannot be sure, either, how others will be affected by my digressions; I cannot be sure how others will read my performances. If anything, digressive moves admit an ambiguous dystopian effect, a more sober approach to queer politics.

Queer performances may include queer readings or queer sensibilites. Queerness as a sensibility interprets texts as potentially politically radical. I would like to read queerly some minimalist and grotesque texts to illustrate my point. Mark Rothko's paintings, I would say, are minimalist. Sometimes he uses two or three colors in simple geometrical shapes; other times he uses just one color. At the Rothko Chapel in Houston, Texas, displayed all around the interior are huge dark-blue canvasses. This is not, by the way, an art museum (a place for dead things) but a sacred space for living art. Some walk into the Rothko Chapel and say, Is that all there is? Where's the art? This, I would term an antiqueer reading. An antiqueer reading might interpret these huge blue canvasses as stupid, for anybody can take a can of blue paint and splash it on canvasses. Many feel that if art does not in some way imitate nature, it simply is not art, it is garbage. Rothko's paintings imitate nothing; nothing is on the canvasses except blue.

My reading of Rothko's work is what I term queer. On entering the Chapel for the first time I was struck by the awesomeness of these huge blue canvasses. I felt the power of the sacred in the face of this blue nothingness. There is no attempt on the part of Rothko to imitate nature, to "get a likeness," to align himself with "normal" artists. To me, Rothko moves against, digresses from mainstream painting by re-presenting nothing on huge blue spaces.

Like Rothko, Philip Glass's music re-presents a form of minimalism. The first time I heard Philip Glass was at the Aspen Music Festival during the summer of 1980. Sixteen years ago I would venture to say that Glass was still relatively unknown. The performance I heard was during the afternoon in a wide open outdoor tent. I recall a lot of empty seats (imagine that today!). Because it was light in the tent I could see nearly everyone around me. What I remember so vividly is the reaction of the audience to Glass's performance. About 5 minutes into these sort of Debussy-ish scales and repetitious triads, the audience began to show signs of discontent, contempt, restlessness, and downright indignation. I turned to my friend, as I recall, and said to her: "This guy must be a joke." Finally, when Glass finished, hardly anyone clapped.

Although there were other minimalists around during the late 1970s, like John Adams and Steve Reich, none became largely respected until around 1986 or even later still. The problem was that minimalism didn't fit into any acceptable genre. "New music," as it is called in the so-called "classical" world, had been dominated, for the most part, by serialists after the tradition of Berg and Schoenberg. God forbid a composer dare to write tonal music. And tonal music was just what the minimalists were writing. My initial reaction to Glass's music was certainly an antiqueer reaction. At the time, like most of the others in the audience (who, by the way, were probably trained classical musicians like myself, because Aspen is a place where mostly trained musicians study during the summer), I couldn't understand what on earth Glass what up to. In retrospect, I must say that Glass and other minimalsts who are less well known have changed the music scene forever. Minimalist forms have finally overturned atonal serial music, although serial music is still around.

Like minimalist forms of art and music, the grotesque writings of François Rabelais (1459–1553) may also be read queerly as radically challenging the status quo. Rabelais lived during the early years of the Protestant Reformation. Rabelais' novels *Pantagruel* (1532) and *Gargantua* (1534) caused a terrific scandal. The Paris Faculty of Theology condemned his writings and as Michel Jeannert (1995) points out, Rabelais spent most of his life in hiding. Many in the church found Rabelais distasteful if not blasphemous. Even a postmodern reader, such as myself, may find *Pantagruel* shocking. Rabelais mixes humor with seriousness, high theology with grotesqueness. *Pantagruel* and *Gargantua* are epic in proportion and weighty in wit. To say the least, scholars seem baffled by these strange works.

There seem to be two general schools of thought concerning Rabelais' work. One camp suggests that Rabelais' writings simply mirror the thoughts of Erasmus and the Christian humanists (Coleman, 1971; Duval, 1991; Frame, 1977b; Screech, 1979). Erasmus and the Christian humanists were generally critical of the Roman Church because of its ever-growing corruption. Like other reformers, the Christian humanists wanted a less pompous, less arrogant church. Thus, scholars who defend Rabelais' piety in spite of his criticism of the church tend to align him with the Christian humanists. I would say that this interpretation is rather blind and perhaps reflects the piety of the scholars who interpret Rabelais rather than Rabelais himself.

Other scholars, taking a more radical position, suggest that Rabelais was completely irreverent, completely irreligious, and wanted to overturn church authority altogether (Berrong, 1986; Febvre, 1982; Lefrank, cited in Duval, 1991; Morris, 1994). Bakhtin (1994), for example, contends that Rabelais meant, through his writings, to oppose completely the "official" medieval ecclesiastical culture. I would have to align myself with Bakhtin and this camp of scholars after reading *Pantagruel*. In fact, I call this interpretation of Rabelais a queer one because I think Rabelais (Frame, 1977a) digresses from the norm of official church doctrine and challenges, in a radical way through grotesque strategies, his culture. To illustrate my point, some highlights from *Pantagruel* are in order.

Generally speaking, *Pantagruel* mocks biblical stories. Pantagruel, the character, represents some sort of Adam or Christlike figure who must save his race from destruction. The story of Pantagruel begins when Cain slays Abel. The race born of this blood suffered "a terrible swelling of the body" (Rabelais, 1977, p. 138). Already, the reader is jolted by this reference to the biblical Cain and Abel with the slight twist of "swelling" bodies. Clearly, this is not the Genesis account. Some males "swelled in the member that is called nature's plowman, so that theirs was wonderfully long, big, stout, plump, verdant, and lusty in the good old style, so that they would use it as a belt, winding it five or six times around them" (p. 138). I can only imagine the faces of the Paris Faculty of Theology as they read this passage. However, the males who suffered this sort of swelling vanished. A second lineage of persons was born also of the blood of Cain and Abel and from this line Pantagruel was born. Pantagruel's was a race of giants.

Gargantua, Pantagruel's father, and Babedee, Pantagruel's mother, gave birth to a miraculous child. "And seeing in a spirit of prophecy that one day he would be the dominator of the thirsties . . . there issued from his belly sixty eight salt vendors . . . nine dromedaries laden with hams and smoked ox tongues" (p. 142). Pantagruel was "dominator of the thirsties" because he was born on the very day the earth broke out into a sweat and created the sea. Pantagruel means all (Panta) thirsty (Gruel). This description of creation is a radical digression from Genesis 1:1–2:4a where God, a transcendent and all-powerful being simply says "Let there be light . . . Let the waters under the sky be gathered together" and the sun and sea were born. The sweating earth, for Rabelais, does not need a creator God; it simply creates its own sea. The church would have seen this as blasphemy.

When Pantagruel grows up he visits the Library of Saint Victor where he browses through titles of "great" theological treatises: "The Donkey Prickery of the Abbots," "Tartaretus, Demudo Cacarel: Craparetus, or The Method of Shitting," "The Rap-Trap of the Theologians," "The Handcuffs of Piety" (pp. 155–157). It becomes evident to me that by page 155 in the text, Rabelais doesn't merely criticize the church. These grotesque illustrations suggest that Rabelais attempts to overthrow so-called sacred dogma by throwing the dogma to the dogs.

One of the most shocking illustrations of Rabelais' utter contempt for Christianity in general is his parody of the resurrection of Lazarus (John 11:1–12:12). In chapter 30 of *Pantagruel*, a character named Panurge raises Epistemon, who apparently was decapitated, from the dead. Panurge "cleaned off the neck with good white wine, and sprinkled on it some quack dungpowder . . . he took fifteen or sixteen stiches . . . so that it [Epistemon's head] should not fall off again. . . . Epistemon began to breathe, then to open his eyes, then yawn, then sneeze, then let out a big household fart" (Rabelais, Frame, 1977a, p. 231). Clearly, this scene mocks the sacredness of Lazarus's resurrection. A farting Lazarus is simply not part of John's gospel.

Rabelais seems to be stuck on lower bodily functions and may be mocking the high christology of the church; Rabelais may be mocking the transcendent nature of God, who seems so aloof that the earth can sweat out the sea by itself; Rabelais is certainly mocking the pretentiousness of theologians, as they need methods on everything including shitting.

I contend that both grotesque and minimalist art forms may spark queer readings and queer reactions. For me, Philip Glass, Mark Rothko, and François Rabelais engage in a digressive politic that challenges radically established norms, shifting fields of discourse.

Shifting fields of discourse should be a prime concern for curriculum theorists. Curriculum itself is a shifting domain whereby students, teachers, and texts react and act depending on what is being said or not said in the classroom. In fact, Pinar (Pinar, Reynolds, Slattery, & Taubman, 1995) points out that curriculum is "an extraordinary complicated conversation" (p. 848). And this complicated conversation is made up of a continual series of moments shifting from epiphanal to dull, from exciting to boring. In the dull and boring moments of classroom life, shifting fields of discourse becomes necessary: the familiar must become strange, queer. These strange moments, as Dennis Sumara (1996) reminds us, depend on the complex relationships among teachers, students, and texts. These relationships must be queered, must be made strange.

Like Sumara, James Macdonald (1995) contends that "the moral question of how to relate to others or how to best live together is clearly a critical part of curriculum" (p. 137). I would like to illustrate two possible ways of living together in the classroom. Both ways are initiated by the curriculum worker. First, enter the antiqueer curriculum worker. The antiqueer curriculum worker does not live queerly because she or he (a) does not digress from "normal" or "official" discourse; (b) does not challenge the status quo by reading texts queerly (uncovering potentially radical politics), or by queering texts (pointing out silences or absences of marginalized peoples like the Hijras and adding them to the text); (c) separates gender, race, class, and politics from curriculum; (d) sees herself or himself as a dispenser of facts and students as receptors of knowledge; (e) views curriculum as a set of methods or procedures. This antiqueer curriculum worker may produce students not unlike Pink Floyd's students in *The Wall*, whereby students are pushed through a meat grinder (the schoolhouse) only to become worms (fascists).

Unlike the antiqueer curriculum worker, the queer curriculum worker lives queerly because she or he (a) digresses from mainstream "official" discourse; (b) challenges the status quo by queerly reading texts (uncovering potentially radical politics), or queering texts (points out silences or absences of marginalized groups like the Hijras and adds them to the text); (c) understands that curriculum is gendered, political, historical, racial, classed, and aesthetic; (d) sees herself or himself as a co-learner with students. This queer curriculum worker may produce students not unlike the proteges of the Bauhaus Movement in pre-World War II Germany who exploded, so to speak, the art world by radically digressing from previously accepted genres. And as Ron Padgham has pointed out, the Reconceptualist Movement forefronted by William Pinar similarly exploded the field of education by radically altering the ways educators think about curriculum (Pinar et al., 1995).

The queer curriculum worker, if anything, might trouble curriculum, troubling the very relationships of the day-to-day lived experience of school life. A queer project unrests curriculum. Curriculum as a queer text makes strange gender, politics, identities, and aesthetics. Imagine unresting the curriculum. Curriculum as a queer text turns the everyday of school life inside out, upside down, backwards. Isn't it strange that most of us do not choose to sit home and rest like Gertrude Stein's Ida. But even in her resting, she was unresting the notion of resting as we might unrest the curriculum.

> Once in a great while Ida got up suddenly. When she did well it was sudden, and when she went away not far away but she left. That happened once in a way. She was sitting just sitting, they said if you look out of the window you see the sun. Oh yes said Ida and they said, do you like sunshine or rain and Ida said she liked it best. She was sitting of course and she was resting and she liked it best. (Stein, 1972, p. 142)

REFERENCES

The American Psychological Association. (1994). *Diagnostic criteria for DSM-IV desk reference.* Washington DC: Author.

Auslander, P. (1992). *Presence and resistance: Postmodern and cultural politics in contemporary American performance.* Ann Arbor: The University of Michigan Press.

Berrong, R. M. (1986). *Rabelais and Bakhtin: Popular culture in Gargantua and Pantagruel.* Lincoln: The University of Nebraska Press.

Berry, T. (1971). *Religions of India: Hinduism, yoga, buddhism.* Beverly Hills, CA: Benziger Bruce.

Block, A. (1995). *Occupied reading: Critical foundations for an ecological theory.* New York: Garland.

Butler, J. (1990). *Gender trouble: Feminism and the subversion of identity.* New York: Routledge.

Coleman, D. (1971). *Rabelais: A critical study in prose fiction.* Cambridge, England: Cambridge University Press.

de Beauvoir, S. (1948). *The ethics of ambiguity* (B. Frechtman, Trans.). Secaucus, NJ: The Citadel Press.

Doll, M. (1995). *To the lighthouse and back: Writings on teaching and living.* New York: Peter Lang.

Doty, A. (1993). *Making things perfectly queer: Interpreting mass culture.* Minneapolis: The University of Minnesota Press.

Duval, E. (1991). *The design of Rabelais's Pantagruel.* New Haven, CT: Yale University Press.

Febvre, L. (1982). *The problem of unbelief in the sixteenth century: The religion of Rabelais* (B. Gottlieb, Trans.). Cambridge, MA: Harvard University Press.

Foucault, M. (1980). *The history of sexuality volume 1: An introduction* (R. Hurley, Trans.). New York: Vintage. (Original work published 1978)

Frame, D. (Trans.). (1977a). *The complete works of Francois Rabelais.* Berkeley: The University of California Press.

Frame, D. (1977b). *Francois Rabelais: A study.* New York: Harcourt Brace Jovanovich.

Garber, M. (1992). *Vested interests: Cross-dressing and cultural anxiety.* New York: Routledge.

Herdt, G. (1994). *Third sex, third gender: Beyond sexual dimorphism in culture and history.* New York: Zone Books.

The holy bible. (1989). New revised standard version. Iowa Falls, IA: World Bible Publishers.

Hopfe, L. (1994). *Religions of the world* (6th ed.). New York: Macmillan.

Jeannert, M. (1995). Signs gone wild: The dismantling of allegory. In J. C. Carron (Ed.), *Francois Rabelais: Critical assessments* (pp. 57–70). Baltimore: The Johns Hopkins University Press.

Kitagawa, J. (1989). *The religious traditions of Asia: Religion, history, and culture. Readings from the encyclopedia of religion.* New York: Macmillan.

Kramer, K. (1986). *World scriptures: An introduction to comparative religions.* Mahwah, NJ: Paulist Press.

Macdonald, J. B. (1995). *Theory as a prayerful act: The collected essays of James B. Macdonald.* New York: Peter Lang.

Martin, B. (1992). Sexual practice and changing lesbian identities. In M. Barret & A. Phillips (Eds.), *Destabilizing theory: Contemporary feminist debates* (pp. 93–119). Stanford, CA: Stanford University Press.

Matthews, W. (1995). *World religions* (2nd ed.). New York: West Publishing Company.

Morris, P. (Ed.). (1994). *The Bakhtin reader: Selected writings of Bakhtin, Medvedev, Voloshinov.* New York: Edward Arnold/Hodder Headline Group.

Nanda, S. (1994). Hijras: An alternative sex and gender role in India. In G. Herdt (Ed.), *Third sex, third gender: Beyond sexual dimorphism in culture and history* (pp. 373–417). New York: Zone Books.

Nielson, N. (1993). *Religions of the world* (3rd ed.). New York: St. Martin's Press.

Nigosian, S. A. (1990). *World faiths.* New York: St. Martin's Press.

Phelan, S. (1994). *Postmodern lesbian politics.* Minneapolis: The University of Minnesota Press.

Pinar, W., Reynolds, W., Slattery, P., & Taubman, P. (1995). *Understanding curriculum.* New York: Peter Lang.

Screech, M. A. (1979). *Rabelais.* Ithaca, NY: Cornell University Press.

Sharma, A. (1987). *Women in world religions.* Albany: SUNY Press.

Spence, J. (1995). *Cultural sniping: The art of transgression.* New York: Routledge.

Stein, G. (1972). *Ida.* New York: Vintage. (Original work published 1941)

Sumara, D. (1996). *Private readings in public: Schooling the literary imagination.* New York: Peter Lang.

Tyler, S. A. (1973). *India: An anthropological perspective.* Prospect Heights, IL: Waveland Press.

Weeks, J. (1991). *Against nature: Essays on history, sexuality, and identity.* London: Rivers Oram Press.

Weeks, J. (1995). *Invented moralities: Sexual values in an age of uncertainty.* New York: Columbia University Press.

Chapter 14

Queering the Gaze

Mary Aswell Doll
Our Lady of Holy Cross College, New Orleans, LA

> *When you make eyes in the place of an eye . . .*
> *then you shall enter the Kingdom.*
> —Guillaumont, Puech, Quispel, Till, & Abd Al Masih (1959, pp. 17–18)

This chapter is not about homosexuals (gays) nor about perception (gaze). It is not about identity (I) nor about projection (eye). It is about all of these sounding together; it is about the lowest form of humor, the pun. Why is it that when someone puns, people groan—a sound that mixes moan with growl, pleasure with pain? When the pun is uttered, it is as if a door in the mind clicks, and two nouns that have nothing in common come together instantly (I would say, marvelously). What lurks on the other side of the mind, normally closed against marvels, presents a punful surprise in a single word, amplifying possibility—tumbling into redundancy and reverberation. As I work through this chapter, I ask that the pun be remembered as a kind of *opus contra naturam*, a work *against* "nature," a move into lower forms. There in the depths and kinks of language, perhaps we can re-cognize what the "normal" mind views as "natural."

Such a process of undermining the natural is the special province of artists, writers, poets, and dramatists. If artists were normal, they would be CEOs or airplane pilots. But writers write from another side of experience, I try to explain to my business, nursing, and education students. My mostly third-generation students have clear ideas about what is normal and natural, taught to them by the church. After the third week they start asking me if they can read something upbeat, nice (normal), for a change. Invariably the question is posed: Why are writers neurotic (not normal)? Once a student whispered to me about Alice Walker's *The Color Purple*, "Dr. Doll, this book is nasty." With a shock of recognition I realized that, as an English teacher, I have a special duty. I must work against the dulling tendency to make nice. I must teach the nonnormal, be the nonnormal.

Remarking on the expectation of our students toward us as teachers, William F. Pinar (1994) encourages us to resist their demands for normalcy. He writes, "Understood from a social psychoanalytic perspective, we teachers are conceived by others, by the expectations and fantasies of our students and the demands of . . . policy makers, and politicians, to all of whom we are sometimes the 'other' " (p. 247). We are, he adds, "formed" by them. If, as I sincerely believe, the task of teaching is to authenticate experience, then it becomes absolutely necessary to keep birthing ourselves, not to allow others to birth or conceive us. Further, it becomes our sacred duty to midwife the texts we teach in such a way that student-readers can confront their own unexamined identities. As Jeffrey Weeks (1995) puts it: "Self-identity, at the heart of which is sexual identity, is not something that is given. . . . it is something that has to be worked on, invented, and reinvented in accord with the changing rhythms, demands, opportunities and closures of a complex world" (p. 90).

The ancient alchemists had no less a project in mind when they performed their alchemical experiments on base lead. In working· on it, so Carl Jung wrote in his three volumes *Psychology and Alchemy, Alchemical Studies,* and *Mysterium Coniunctionis,* they were really reinventing themselves. Reading, then, becomes not simply a matter of discovering themes and symbols but of visiting other worlds in the expectation of discovering selves within.

I find myself in a paradoxical position as an English teacher interested in queering the gaze. On the one hand, I teach literature, which introduces complexity. On the other hand, I teach writing, which emphasizes clarity. But these are not opposites at all. It is essential that one be clear in discussing complexities by clearly distinguishing the particulars that make them complex. Similarly, one must be clear in stating what one is not discussing—negations not needing to be contraries. Negations, rather, may move a discussion from a horizontal plane of opposition into a vertical plane of difference, where another rubric or zone or world exists. These clarifications are essential when working with terms that have been straightened out along the horizon of oppositional thinking.

Such is the precise point theorists, queer and otherwise, have made about the dangers of oversimplifying such "reals" as Truth, Nature, History, Gender, Identity. Thomas Moore (1983), in a piece written before his now-famous *Care of the Soul,* remarked that the danger of ideology is its "tendency to unify and codify, to find in them a source of truth and guidance rather than imagining" (p. 29). Conceptualizing without a sensitivity to depth and reverberation stalls ideas, literalizes them. Moore's mentor, the post-Jungian theorist James Hillman (1975), wrote in his groundbreaking book *Re-Visioning Psychology*: "We are no longer single beings in the image of a single God, but always constituted by multiple parts" (p. 24). For Hillman, as for Jung, the multiple parts that constitute our being must be separately honored, each given its due. In her lively work with myth, Patricia Berry (1982) calls gender a "dogma," the purpose of which is to assume a straight identity, either this or that: straight male, straight female, straight androgyne. Gender's singleness, "the monotheism of gender, gender as the epitome of unity and identity" (p. 45), is the problem of dogma, she insists. More recently, Weeks (1995) called identity-fixing "inadequate blocks to the flux . . . and range of possible ways of being" (p. 89).

Certainly, these blocks to being are mirrored everywhere in our culture of individualism, where to "be an individual" has an insidious hidden message: Don't change. As Katie Canon (1995) among others has pointed out, the institutions of culture depend on social control, particularly any church institution that appeals to the Bible as Truth source. Even less edifaced institutions, like the American Psychiatric Association, have a rockribbed agenda. Speaking as a member of that group, Berry (1982) observes about their procedures: "It doesn't matter which way one is straight, just so all kinks are made smooth, just so the person has been identified completely and unambiguously" (p. 47). Hollywood particularly panders to gendered-viewing. The blockbuster release of *The Rock*—with male heroes that defy death, car chases, bombs, FBI agents, poison gas, and prom queen girlfriend—busted no blocks of perception about maleness, solidifying the fantasy that men, muscle, and murder define the penis.

So, what strategies can emerge from this rubble to counter overly unified perceptions about human identity? How can we queer the gaze? I propose four ways, any one of which could serve as a means of going beneath the norm in an *opus contra naturam* that verticalizes the horizon of simples. These are the way of shock, the way of the joke, the way of myth, and the way of the perverse.

THE WAY OF SHOCK

In discussing shock as a way of queering the gaze of straight (mere) perception I am not referring to the shock-jock-Howard-Stern syndrome. Shock is effective not because it is cruel or hateful but because it grabs attention. But to what is attention turning its gaze? For shock jocks, the grab is at the expense of someone or some nonnormal group and arises out of a mean-spirited instinct to reify the norm and instill superiority. This sort of shock is totally literalistic. The shock to which I refer for queering the gaze is attacking in a non-phallic way but is confrontational nonetheless. I propose Frida Kahlo's Latin American art as example.

Kahlo's self-portraits are unsettling, fascinating, vivid, strange, beautifully grotesque. They feature bushy eyebrows that meet above eyes that stare back at the spectator with an expression somewhere between contempt and humor. In "The Broken Column," perhaps her most confrontational self-portrait, we see her upper naked torso punctuated by nails. She paints down the center of her body a broken spinal column, while her hands at her sides hold what could be a shroud. Of this crucifixion figure of herself she is reported to have said: "Look very, very, closely at my eyes. What do you see in them? My eyes are twinkling. The pupils are doves of peace. That is my little joke on pain and suffering, and your pity," (Richmond, 1994, p. 20). It is as if, knowing the long tradition of The Male Gaze in art, whereby male artists painted nude females for male inspection, she throws that tradition back on itself. Look at me! she seems to taunt. I will not be made into what you think you see!

Her numerous portraits of herself with small monkeys are further instances of Frida Kahlo's insouciance. Her signature piece is of her slightly turned face and long neck encircled by a simian arm or two. The juxtaposition of her eyes, often glacial and impassive, with the black-button eyes of monkeys seems to place her in another, more vegetable world, unreachable by our demands or needs. And then there are the paintings of female organs, etched as an aggression against the bourgeois notion of art as adornment; for who would want a still life of a bleeding uterus? Like Georgia O'Keeffe's vulvic and phallic flowers, Frida Kahlo's depiction of nature is overtly, almost embarrassingly, genital. Hers is truly a transgressive aesthetic designed to shock.

THE WAY OF THE JOKE

Less confrontational than shock as a way of questioning the norm is the joke. "The joke is the mystery, the absence. It is the game that must be played in the forming of relationships," writes Dennis Sumara (1996, p. 65). "What new game can we invent?" teases Foucault (Weeks, 1995, p. 100). Hide and seek, losing and finding, teasing, punning: These playful strategies open up possibility for thinking not Who am I, but Who do I want to become. Identity is make believe, let's play dress up; it is joshing with arbitrary assumptions. The joke is on us. This is serious business.

In my work with literary criticism, no postmodern writer does the joke better than Tom Stoppard. Born in Czechoslovakia but living in Singapore and India before settling in England, Stoppard wittingly describes himself as a "bounced Czech." His plays, the most famous of which is *Rosencrantz and Guildenstern Are Dead* (1967) are elegantly crafted travesties (the title of a 1975 play) that elevate the pun and the joke to stage dimensions. Stoppard utilizes humor, wit, and the joke as a dramatic strategy to dislocate the spectator. As I put it:

> Any attempt to name, point, place, picture or record any event as any kind of fact or certain thing is completely ironic—irony his chosen mode since it places the point beside the point. Stoppard presents serious issues—like war, death, love, art, deceit, and treachery—with a light touch. His intention is to divest us of certainty, which he sees as an arrogant attitude inherited from the postures of logical positivism and classical science. (Doll, 1993, pp. 117–118)

Stoppard's jokes with perception and identity make him, in my view, a superb example of art's ability to undermine spectatorship. His motifs include doubletiming, coincidence, and doublecrossing; his characters consist of twins, of different characters with the same name, of spies and counterspies; his language employs punning, repetition, paradox, slogan, undercutting; his genres include burlesque, vaudeville, melodrama, the thriller. His games include bridge, monopoly, cricket, dice, ping pong, tennis, dominoes, billiards, croquet, charades, and questions. When the name of the game is war, he shows us that words like *freedom* and *patriotism* kill. And—perhaps his trademark—Stoppard adapts and freely translates (plagiarizes) the works of others, all as part of his postmodern preference to doublecode. Whereas some critics see Stoppard's borrowings as merely derivative, that assessment misses Stoppard's thoroughgoing postmodern commitment to seeing "reality" as but the sheerest cover of another lurking order.

Typical of Stoppard is his taking an abstract idea, like The Spectator Theory of Knowledge, and literalizing it. He does this in *The Real Inspector Hound* (1993), which plays seriously with the idea of seeing as knowing. Stoppard's stage directions are part of the joke: "The first thing is that the audience appear to be confronted by their own reflection in a huge mirror. Impossible" (p. 2396). The audience cannot slip into the anonymous gaze of spectatorship because it looks at itself looking at itself while looking at the play. Similarly, and punningly, the play is also about an audience—two drama critics—reviewing a production. The play within the play concerns a drawing-room murder. There is a storm, a house party, an intruder, a murder. A cozy order is disrupted. The statement, "I could kill you for this, Simon Gascoyne," seems to be a clue to the murderer but is repeated by every suspect, making conclusion impossible for Inspector Hound, whose Sherlock Holmesian attempts at deductive reasoning predictably fail. The only clue, a particle of information in the repeated sentence, loops and repeats, thickening and embedding layers of complexity, so that the observed problem cannot be gotten at by traditional channels of thinking. Stoppard takes his joke farther when one of the critics becomes lured onto the stage (within the stage), takes the place of the Inspector, then gets murdered. The spectator, thus, is killed; long live the death of the spectator!

Stoppard employs a play-within-a play format in visual puns, where seeing becomes a replicating manifold. His 1968 *Enter a Free Man* mirrors Arthur Miller's *Death of a Salesman* as well as Robert Bolt's *The Flowering Cherry*. *Travesties* translates Oscar Wilde's *The Importance of Being Earnest*. *Rosencrantz and Guildenstern Are Dead* is an obvious reference to Shakespeare, whose *Hamlet* scenes are inserted full blown into the text. And so on. The joke behind all of these staged mysteries is the question of perception. If classical theater, like classical science, depended on a stable order, Stoppardian theater, like chaos theory, depends on dynamic orders. Perception shifts, disequilibrium ensues, and the part–whole relationship of observer to thing observed—once considered fixed—erupts. Does a Stoppard audience know it is looking at itself looking at itself? Does it feel the remove from the center? If so, the audience would come to know it is looking at an illusion. Then perhaps the individuals in the audience would begin to question whether seens can ever be knowns, knowns ever truths, truths ever reals. Such jockeying with disillusionment is Stoppard's very profound way of using the joke to question the idea of the *pure spectator*. He insists on unsettling an audience's expectations of what it is to be an audience; that is, to play the spectator role. Concerning *Travesties*, for instance, he gave this cheeky statement: "We'll have this rollicking first act and they'll all come back from their gin-and-tonics thinking 'isn't this fun? What a lot of lovely jokes.' And they'll sit down, and this pretty girl will start talking about the theory of Marxism and the theory of capitalism and the theory of value" (Marowitz, 1989, pp. 47, 50).

It is no wonder that Stoppard gravitated toward Dada art as yet another way of exposing the sophistry within every rational situation. The duty of the artist, one of his characters says, is "to jeer and howl and belch" (Stoppard, 1972, p. 37) at cause and effect logic. In his *After Magritte* (1971), Stoppard models his play on René Magritte's visual representation of a thing labeled as not that thing. As Foucault (1982) commented, Magritte's painting "aspires playfully to efface the oldest oppositions of our alphabetical civilization: to show and to name; to shape and to say; to reproduce and to articulate; to imitate and to signify; to look and to read" (p. 21). Art's role is not to name, signify, shape, or show. It is to be insouciant. Just as Foucault's writing about Magritte is a cornucopia of wordplays, wisecracks, and slapstick repetitions, so too are Stoppard's plays. And just as Magritte names his paintings wrongly in order to focus attention on the act of naming, so does Stoppard present representations wrongly so as to queer our gaze.

Writing about the lunatic world of Stoppard's theater (several of his characters are named Moon) has enabled me to live a little more with illusion; that is, to see the illusory quality of things. Sometimes, the result is hilarious. A few years ago I ran across an article in the paper about a museum guard in Florida. He observed through the window a gray-haired woman seated in a chair, not breathing. Immediately, he called the fire department, which rushed to the rescue—to discover an art exhibit of woman in a chair. The newspaper lead was, "Art imitates death" ("Statue Brings Rescue to Standstill," 1991, p. 2).

THE WAY OF MYTH

What I have suggested in the previous discussion of shock and joke are ways to think about seeing other than with the mind's eye. Seeing with the mind has turned identities of people into labels that the mind can understand, or realities of being into medical categories that empirical science can examine. I premise my objection to conceptualized seeing on a very old enterprise: an *opus contra naturam*. To go against nature, to work against "natural" tendency, is to see with imagination's eye. Myth works with images primarily; I propose it as a third way to queer the gaze of perception.

Myths have what I have called a replicating manifold. They are stories that are told again and again in culture after culture with ever so slight variations on the telling. This is a maddening quality, confusing a mind engaged in figuring "out" the story line. But that is the point. Myths are tellings on a different plane, not "out" but "down." Myths' vertical dimension present figures, images. *These* are the story; the line is in the *figure*. The significance of myth for queer theory is myth's insistence on seeing, not general identities, but specific images. Forms that appear human are also divine, animal, vegetable, even mineral. Constant transformations occur. What potentiality lies there for reconceptualizing the term *human being!* For there, in multiple interactions—hidden from surface viewing— lie the invisibles.

Mythologically speaking, the world of the invisibles is Hades, whose Greek name means "the invisibility-giving" (Berry, 1982, p. 31). Hades, as a place, lies under the surface, beneath the visible world—the underworld. Hades is also the underworld king, whose other name Pluto means wealth-giver, riches (Hillman, 1975, p. 205). Ironically, that which our Christian culture calls Hell is imagined very differently and nonjudgmentally in myth. Indeed, Christarians (dogma Christians) so resist imagining anything positive coming from the under regions that they are damned to live their faith without imagination.

The myth of Persephone draws me into this discussion because of her image as an innocent. The myth tells of the virgin daughter of the earth goddess Demeter who, one day out with the girls picking flowers in the bright sunlight is, suddenly, forced into the underworld. The sudden event is a rape. So distraught by the rape of her daughter is Demeter that she causes a drought to devastate the earth's bounty while she searches for clues to Persephone's whereabouts. Finally, with the help of Hecate, Demeter is reunited with Persephone—but only for part of the year; the rest of the year Persephone must spend with Hades. Before the rape, Persephone is all innocence and all her mother's child. Myth suggests that something in this exclusive all-ness must be darkened, complicated. The rape, myth implies, is necessary. It is also, importantly, a metaphor, as Hillman (1975) explains: "Hades' rape of the innocent soul is a central necessity for psychic change. We experience its shock and joy whenever an event is taken suddenly out of human life and its natural state and into a deeper and more imaginally 'unreal' reality" (p. 208).

Four Persephone motifs—the virgin, the rape, Hades, natural change—resonate with what I am trying to express about queer theory. Christarians, spectators, policymakers, institutions, and keepers of the norm are like Persephone before her underworld experience: innocent. I do not feel sorry for Persephone. Rather, I am fascinated by her story partly because it is the tale of the invisible daughter (my story) and partly because it cautions against single vision. In most worship of the mother grain goddess, Persephone was not named, called instead the Kore, meaning the secret, hidden "ineffable maiden." What she represents is beyond literalism, a move into depth. Because of her underground connection, Persephone is a psychopomp, a guide into seeing what the gaze, with its pure focus, wills not to see.

It is significant for a discussion about complicating perception that I focus on Persephone, the hidden one of a same-sex twosome. Two-ness opens gender fixing into a more-than-one possibility. Clearly, male heroes have often been portrayed as a duo: David and Jonathan, Castor and Pollux, Achilles and Patroclus, Huck Finn and Jim, Crusoe and Friday, Falstaff and Prince Hal, Lear and the Fool, Harlequin and Pierrot, Tambo and Bones, Don Quixote and Sancho Panza are among a host of examples. Popular culture, too, complicates male pairing from the heroic Batman and Robin to the antiheroic Beavis and Butthead, as Marla Morris (1997) points out. Typical of this doppelgänger (double) construct is the unevenness of the two. One is usually stronger or more socially prominent or smarter in the head or older; the function of the other is to correct an imbalance so as to provide a whole. But for Persephone–Demeter, a different dynamic pertains, because the tension between them depends on hiddenness, not visible presence. What requires correction in this female pairing (one of only a few in Western culture) is the need for both to see beneath surfaces. Conversely, what sustains the relationship is the mystery of absence.

The Eleusinian mystery rites were enacted in ancient Greece to enable initiates to go below, metaphorically. Theirs was the way of the wrong direction, a *via negativa*, a counterclockwise move into the sinister realm of "left." Initiates prepared themselves for a Demeter-like search for their own lost souls by imitating the actions of the grain goddess over 9 days. Like her, they fasted, dressed in long robes, sat on stones. At the climax of the mysteries a day-long procession wound its way dancing and singing from Athens through the pass of Daphni onto the Eleusinian Plain, circling around, until at evening they arrived at the temple of Demeter. There a grief dance was performed by moving to the left—so as to counter Demeter's upperworldy sense (Doll, 1994). The point is emphasized by Berry (1975): "Demeter consciousness tends to live life in a natural, clockwise direction; whereas, to connect to her daughter she must begin to live in a contra-naturam, counter-clockwise manner as well" (pp. 197–198).

The urgings of these mystery enactments is toward Hades, the place where unseen presences dwell. In that place, which the Greeks named and dignified as a kingdom, another consciousness exists. This consciousness puts to death all literalisms, all normalizing tendencies, all exclusions, all illusions. Pluto, called Dis, rules over that place where illusions disappear into disillusion. "Disillusionment," Miller (1995) says, "removes the illusions" (p. 81). Persephone's tie to her mother is through such a death of illusions. Demeter's tie to her daughter, then, is through the rebirth of imagination.

One does not have to go to Greece to discover the wisdom of the Demeter–Persephone myth. Traveling in one's head one feels reason's resistance to the tale. That is why, I suggest, the rape motif is central to Persephone's story: Persephone, like one's resistant ego, does not will her descent; it must be forced on her. Yet she is the chosen one because she is too innocent, too pure, the other invisible half of her mother's ego determination to rule the natural world. Such virginal consciousness of both mother and daughter must be sullied if one is to open oneself to a world beyond reason. Myth, as a way to queer the gaze of normalized perception, shows us a richness of identities and attitudes if only we dare die a bit in our heads.

THE WAY OF THE PERVERSE

Perverse as an adjective is described by Webster (1989) without any reference to pathology. "Perverse: 1. willfully determined or disposed to go counter to what is expected or desired; contrary. . . . 3. wayward; cantankerous. . . . 5.

turned away from what is right, good, or proper; wicked. **Syn.** . . . see willful." To be perverse, accordingly, can mean to follow a left (non right) path, a way not of the will. Similarly, to pervert is "1. to turn away from the right course"—again, which can mean to turn toward the left course, the one left over. By a fourth meaning, to pervert becomes associated with leaving the church: "4. to bring over to a religious belief regarded as false or wrong" and by an eighth meaning the verb to pervert becomes associated not just with sin but with a worse sin, abnormality: "8. *Pathol.* to change to what is unnatural or abnormal," which leads to the noun: "10. one who practices sexual perversion" and the pathologized noun: "11. *Pathol.* one affected with perversion" (p. 1076). As language becomes more and more fixed into nouns, people turn into diseases and actions become sins. The church and the medical community take over meaning.

My final example of queering the fixed gaze of normalcy involves Samuel Beckett's perverse work, which takes us deep into the unfamiliar. His titles suggest this intention: *All Strange Away, The Lost Ones, The Unnamable.* Beckett's perversity is such that both language and vision are obfuscated to the point that words are no longer adequate to express sights, and sights cannot be denoted by words. In his prose piece *ill seen ill said* (1981), Beckett's place of action is "beyond the unknown" (p. 9), so as to close "for good this filthy eye of the flesh" (p. 30). There, one must open a different eye willing to disbelieve what it sees. The situation involves such minimalist props as a window, a door, a cabin, a woman, some sheep, some stones, a man, a coffer, and "the twelve." Drama (as our "filthy eyes" see it) is introduced when the woman hacks up a sheet of paper or examines a scrapbook, but any suggestion of pathos is undercut by her settling down to eat "slop." Periodically, the woman leaves the cabin to venture to the stone pasture. But as the text warns with repeated references to eyes, pupils, and irises, no amount of careful viewing can ever capture either meaning or motive. The reader cannot figure out any clear sequence of events, because what one sees is recorded by a camera's eye that can only catch small screens ("figments"), which are then explained by way of an outdated language. The result is unsettling, funny, weird, trenchant. It is also Beckett's profound statement about perception; namely, that all seeing is translation through multiple screens—none of which is capable of capturing "it," both eye and mind being "equal liars" (Beckett, 1981, p. 40).

With my mythic spectacles, I see Beckett writing the Persephone–Demeter myth from an underground perspective, "the entire surface under grass" (Beckett, 1981, p. 10). But, despite references to betrayal, rape, and ritualized pacing such as Demeter's, I am forced to withhold any claim to explanation. After all, there are also references to the Christian theme of betrayal, with "the twelve," mention of lambs and a reference to cows unshepherded. There is throughout an intention to baffle the mind of the eye with archaic language, odd juxtapositions, and incomplete thoughts: "Less. Ah the sweet one word. Less. It is less. The same but less. Whencesoever the glare. True that the light. See now how words too. A few drops mishaphazard. Then strangury" (Beckett, 1981, p. 52). The only conclusion we can draw is inconclusive. Beckett leaves us lost in the land of art, which, according to one definition, "wrenches us away from ourselves" (Highwater, 1994, p. 13).

To be wrenched (raped) away from ourselves, finally, is to leave our ego claims behind. It is to open to a far-flung imagination, an exotic otherness, a vaster vision that expresses a freedom from limits. This move *contra-naturam* requires a preceding dying to "correct" speech and "right" behavior. I have selected four ways of accomplishing such a task: the way of shock, the way of the joke, the way of myth, and the way of the perverse. Perhaps these left-turn alternatives can offer paths wherein to confront the gaze of the homophobe. At the very least, perhaps these deviations from the straight and narrow can bring into question any notion of one, fixed, single gender identity, in the deeper knowing that the I is capable of many densities.

REFERENCES

Beckett, S. (1981). *ill seen ill said.* New York: Grove.

Berry, P. (1975). The rape of Demeter/Persephone and neurosis. *Spring: An Annual of Archetypal Psychology,* 186–198.

Berry, P. (1982). *Echo's subtle body: Contributions to an archetypal psychology.* Dallas, TX: Spring.

Cannon, K. (1995). *Katie's canon.* New York: Continuum.

Doll, M. (1994). Ghosts of themselves: The Demeter women in Beckett. In E. T. Hayes (Ed.), *Images of Persephone: Feminist readings in western literature* (pp. 121–135). Miami: University Press of Florida.

Doll, M. (1993). Stoppard's theatre of unknowing. In J. Acheson (Ed.), *British and Irish drama since 1960* (pp. 117–129). New York: St. Martin's Press.

Foucault, M. (1982). *This is not a pipe* (J. Harkness, Trans. and Ed.). Los Angeles: University of California Press.

Guillaumont, A., Puech, H.-C., Quispel, G., Till, W., & Abd Al Masih, Y. (1959). *The gospel according to Thomas.* New York: Harper.

Highwater, J. (1994). *The language of vision: Meditations on myth and metaphor.* New York: Grove.

Hillman, J. (1975). *Re-visioning psychology.* New York: Harper.

Marowitz, C. (1989, April 2). With the words of Tom Stoppard. *Los Angeles Times,* pp. 47, 50.

Miller, D. (1995). The death of the clown: A loss of wits in the postmodern movement. *Spring: A Journal of Archetype and Culture, 58,* 69–81.

Moore, T. (1983). *Rituals of the imagination.* Dallas, TX: The Pegasus Foundation.

Morris, M. (1997). Ezekiel's prophetic call: Toward a queer pedagogy. *Taboo: Journal of Culture and Education,* 153–166.

Pinar, W. F. (1994). *Autobiography, politics, and sexuality: Essays in curriculum theory, 1972–1992.* New York: Peter Lang.

Richmond, R. (1994). *Frida Kahlo in Mexico.* San Francisco: Pomegranate Art Books.

"Statue Brings Rescue to Standstill" (1991, January 4). *The Times-Picayune*, p. 2.

Stoppard, T. (1972). *Jumpers*. London: Faber.

Stoppard, T. (1993). *The real Inspector Hound*. In M. H. Abrams (Ed.), *The Norton anthology of English literature*. (Vol. 2, 6th ed., pp. 2395–2421). New York: Norton. (Original work published 1968)

Sumara, D. (1996). *Private readings in public schooling: The literary imagination*. New York: Peter Lang.

Webster's encyclopedic unabridged dictionary of the English language. (1989). New York: Random.

Weeks, J. (1995). *Invented moralities: Sexual values in an age of uncertainty*. New York: Columbia University Press.

Chapter 15

Fantasizing Women in the Women's Studies Classroom: Toward a Symptomatic Reading of Negation

Alice J. Pitt
York University

"Lesbians are not women." So concludes Monique Wittig (1980) in "The Straight Mind," an essay that reached English-speaking audiences in 1978. This terse sentence is amplified in a footnote that reads, "No more is any woman who is not in a relation of personal dependency with a man" (p. 111). Along with Wittig's "One Is Not Born a Woman" (1981), this essay identifies the heterosexual contract and its systems of thought and economic relations as the productive and reproductive *center* of all relations of subordination and domination, not only those that exist between men and women. Wittig's argument focuses on the material effects of language. It reconfigures a question that has been and continues to be central to feminist theoretical debate. For Wittig, to ask "What is woman?" is already to remain within the conceptual confines of heterosexual imperatives. To continue to speak of "woman" or even "women" will not effect the political, economic, or ideological transformations envisioned by feminism precisely because these concepts are irredeemably saturated by, even as they saturate, what she calls "the straight mind."

Although Wittig is quite adamant that, by virtue of their social practices, lesbians neither love nor are women, her little footnote of "no more" refuses ontological claims as the basis for resistance against oppression. For Wittig, *lesbian* must be thought of as a political category strategically poised potentially to include any woman "who is not in a relation of personal dependency with a man." This, of course, leads to different definitional problems: What is a lesbian? Can there be heterosexual relations that refuse the terms of the heterosexual contract? Does a woman's desire to alter her conditions of dependency qualify her to identify herself with the political category of lesbian?

From the perspective of much contemporary feminist theorizing, the resonance of these questions seems tied to the ethos and preoccupations of the "radical feminisms" of the late 1970s. Although it has become commonplace to work the categories "women" and "men" as political, historical, and social identities complicated by race, class, and sex, Wittig's dream of a world without women seems odd, if not downright chauvinistic. This is particularly the case in Women's Studies where female students' capacity to recognize themselves as women within the terms of the course is a significant measure both of the course's success and of students' success in the course. But even in Women's Studies classrooms where ongoing pedagogical attempts to challenge commonsense notions of what it means to be a woman, the figure of the lesbian continues to be a disturbing, perhaps even uncanny, presence.[1]

Freud's (1919) notion of the uncanny (*die unheimlich*) signals something that is familiar, but strangely so. He describes the uncanny as a particular quality of feeling provoked when an event or image unsettles a foundational certainty and returns the individual momentarily to the vulnerability of individual or collective infancy. In his words, "an uncanny experience occurs either when infantile complexes which have been repressed are once more revived by some impression, or when primitive beliefs which have been surmounted seem once more to be confirmed" (p. 249). The notion of the uncanny disrupts the dream of learning as a developmental progression through the fantasy of what Madeleine Grumet (1989) has termed "the beautiful curriculum." It also draws attention to the work of fantasy in individuals' attempts to figure out how knowledge, staged as curriculum, might be relevant to them. In Women's Studies classrooms, this process depends centrally on the extent to which students perceive that their feminist teachers and the texts that represent women from femi-

---

[1]The status of the lesbian may be equally, though differently, problematic in the emerging field of Gay and Lesbian Studies. As Judith Butler (1994; see also Martin, 1994; Walters, 1996) has pointed out, the emerging field of lesbian and gay studies may owe political and theoretical allegiance to feminist theory, but there has been a tendency to define this field as offering theories of sexuality in contradistinction to feminist studies, which offers theories of gender. Butler worries about how the definitional demands of institutionality work against the productivity of holding questions and issues of gender and sexuality in tension with each other. Her concern, in my view, is a valid one, and perhaps my questions about conflicts within Women's Studies that stick to the figure of the lesbian can be viewed as a different form of this new concern. Wittig was one of several theorists, including Adrienne Rich, to place the social construction of sexuality as a problem of and for gender identity on the feminist agenda. Both appear, as do many other feminist theorists, in the pages of *The Lesbian and Gay Studies Reader* (Abelove, Barale, & Halperin, 1993).

nist perspectives tell the truth about their own lives and senses of self. At the level of the everyday, one may not think very much about the categories of men, women, and children, even as one has no (apparent) difficulty in locating oneself within these categories. However, in Women's Studies classes, these positions are viewed as social constructions that are organized by larger social relations of power. In these classes, sociological notions of positionality in relation to women's civil rights and struggles for equality are offered to provide women with new ways to interpret their experiences and struggle for better futures. Just beginning to be explored (Felman, 1993; Finke, 1993; Gallop, 1995) is the question of how these new interpretations are lived at the level of the psyche where difference refers, not to social differences between individuals, but to differences within individuals. The pedagogical problem, I argue, is that much of the work of making a relation to knowledge takes place in the unconscious where fantasmatic ideals anchor the sense of the self as cohesive and coherent (Phelan, 1993; Silverman, 1996). This is the psychic work of identification, and its processes may be implicated in, but not subsumed by, social relations of domination and subordination.

Indeed, a recurring theme in recent educational research that investigates student learning about social difference is the persistence of a gap between the transformatory hopes articulated within pedagogical strategies and curricular scores and their apparent effects on students (Bogdan, 1994; Britzman, 1992; Ellsworth, 1989; Ladson-Billings, 1996; Lather, 1991). This theme takes shape in two directions identifying, on the one hand, some learners' refusals to understand the perspectives of *other* socially marginalized identities as having anything to do with them. On the other hand, several researchers have become concerned when counterhegemonic knowledge may be perceived as telling the truth, but the immediate effects of this new knowledge seem more debilitating than transformatory. What these two kinds of observations share is a concern with what knowledge does to people. They suggest that theorizing curriculum and pedagogy might benefit from understanding learning as a psychic event that involves the realms of both conscious and unconscious operations.

This chapter considers what such understanding entails by exploring disturbances to one woman's imagined relation to femininity. What is at stake in this story, however, is not so much our capacity to "read" the psychic difficulties individuals experience in their encounters with knowledge, an issue I explore in greater detail later. The kind of study I am proposing may help critical educators to re-examine our own assumptions and expectations about what we imagine students are up to when they speak (or not) and write (or not) in our classrooms. I develop this general claim by focusing on the specific context of an introductory Women's Studies course. When we consider psychic dimensions of learning in relation to some persistent dilemmas within feminist education, new questions emerge about the curious relationships among the (re)presentation of identities as curriculum, teachers' investments in the curriculum, and the nature of the work of learning. These dilemmas have to do with the organization of feminist curriculum within an epistemological framework that, on the one hand, privileges gender as its primary analytical category and, on the other hand, collapses the meaning of categories of social difference with and within North American feminism's own anxious history of exclusions and marginalizations.

I begin with a sketch of Wittig's polemic because the conclusion ("Lesbians are not women") of her theoretical argument works against the habit within much North American feminist education to include lesbians in the category of women. Within the dominant narrative, lesbians share gender identity with heterosexual women, and lesbians are oppressed both as women and as lesbians. What this narrative cannot admit is that gender identity may always be lived in very complicated ways in relation to normative (heterosexual) femininity. Wittig can be read as implying that normative femininity is a precarious construct that must be continually (re)enforced and that sometimes fails. Her essay can be taken as a comment on identity formation as that which can exceed such normativity.[2] Put somewhat differently, we could say that, for Wittig, the lesbian is a character in a theoretical work of fiction that holds new possibilities for how feminists might imagine and alter their social and psychic landscapes. In a more broadly conceived gesture, we could say that all representations present characters in theoretical works of fiction, and we might be surprised at the range of uses—at the level of fantasy—a reader may make of a character.

Notes on Methodology

Using excerpts from one woman's story of her participation in an introductory Women's Studies course (Pitt, 1995), I examine the relationship she articulates between her self-understandings as a woman and the relevant subject positions—woman, feminist, lesbian—articulated by the course curriculum. I focus on the ways in which this relationship can be seen as relying on, even as it is bothered by, the place within the course of the figure of the lesbian. The reading I offer of this student's response to lesbianism begins with two assumptions. The first assumption concerns

---

[2]It should be pointed out that Wittig, who, in this same essay, refuses psychoanalytic theory in general and the category of the unconscious in particular, may hold the view that her work (fictional and theoretical) is to elaborate aspects of women's social imaginary that already exist and to make these representations more widely available as a political project. But the "use" of representation can neither be guaranteed in advance nor permanently fixed to the goals of its historical moment of production (Simon, 1992).

what it means to bring individuals' narratives into our research stories. Just as "the lesbian" is a character in Wittig's theoretical fiction, the "real" student, who describes her encounter with feminist knowledge, is also a character in her own story. This is so, in part, because, as Linda Brodkey (1987) insists, narratives about experience must not be collapsed with experience itself. When it comes to interpreting narratives told to us in the context of research, the insights of poststructuralism meet the insights of psychoanalytic theory to compound the impossible dream of representation. As Roy Schafer (1983), a psychoanalyst who theorizes narration itself as experience, argues, "We are forever telling stories about ourselves. In telling these stories to others we may . . . be said to perform straightforward narrative actions. In saying that we tell them to ourselves, however, we are enclosing one story within another. . . . On this view, the self is a telling" (p. 218).

If the stories we tell to others are also stories we tell to ourselves, we might ask how these stories enhance our image of our identity as cohesive and coherent. By asking this question of the stories told as stories about classroom experiences, we can become curious about the stories as having to do with the encounter between how one represents the self to the self (and others) and how classroom experiences organize and disorganize these self-representations. Thus, I read this student's narrative for the struggles it reveals between commonsense understandings of what it means to be a woman and feminist understandings. I further argue that her response to lesbianism can be read as symptomatic of a conflict inherent in much feminist education. The conflict turns on the theoretical and pedagogical difficulties of retaining "women" as a unified political category while simultaneously dispersing the category to include feminist discourses' historically excluded "others." When we say that students who refuse to recognize themselves in relation to these new terms *resist* our pedagogical efforts, we may be foreclosing opportunities to gain insight into the work of theorizing identity that these students, however problematically, undertake. One of the purposes of this chapter is to consider what it means to interpret the work of resistance on the part of learners as the work of identification. Towards the end of the chapter I return to the conflict just named and the questions it provokes for theorizing pedagogy and curriculum.

My interpretive strategy of reading a student's engagement with a particular curricular staging of feminist knowledge as symptomatic of a conflict embedded within the staging itself can be compared with Gallop's (1992) method of "symptomatic reading" in *Around 1981: Academic Feminist Literary Theory*. She describes "symptomatic reading" as coming "out of psychoanalytic method by way of deconstruction" (p. 7) and she distinguishes her approach from that of new criticism:

> Where new critical close reading embraces the text in order to more fully
> and deeply understand its excellences, "symptomatic reading" squeezes the
> text tight to force it to reveal its perversities. New criticism is appreciative,
> even worshipful; symptomatic reading tends to be demystifying, even aggres-
> sive. (p. 7)

Perhaps acts of demystification are necessarily aggressive insofar as they
uncover something preferably left alone, something that, in psychoanalytic
terms, is repressed from conscious apprehension. Like Gallop, I am interested in what psychoanalytic theory offers to our understanding of the
dynamics embedded within social and political events. I bring this interest
to my study of classroom events—the organization and selection of knowledge as curriculum and the attachments and refusals enacted in pedagogical encounters. Gallop's method of symptomatic reading is useful because
it asks all of us to consider our implication in an intellectual and political
history that has been formative to what and how we teach and, more
importantly, what and how we learn.

For Gallop, the feminist critical anthologies used in Women's Studies
"are good places to witness the dynamics of collectivity." She proposes
reading anthologies as a whole, but what she attends to may be unfamiliar
to feminist readers whose epistemological attachments are structured by
humanistic notions of identity and experience. She offers the following
description of her goals:

> The necessary assumption . . . is that we are all inevitably symptomatic, we
> are all subjects and thus speak from within a field of conflict. It is not my
> goal to unveil the inadequacies of any individual. Reading an anthology as
> a whole is a method for getting at "symptoms" which recur across various
> authors. Rather than pointing to some individual's blind spots, these might
> indicate conflicts inhering in a collective situation. I am interested in the
> marks produced in the discourse of knowledge by a subject, not by an
> individual but by a collective subject, the academic feminist critic. (p. 7)

The period Gallop addresses in her study (1972–1982) also produced important writing, including several anthologies (Bowles & Klein, 1983; Bunch
& Pollack, 1983; Culley & Portuges, 1985), about feminist classrooms and
pedagogical practices. Rather than "squeeze" these texts, I want to bring
the notion of symptomatic reading to bear on a set of relations that are
performed in the feminist classroom. We might think of the text of pedagogy as the story of a collective situation that brings together not only
actors (teachers, students, and texts) but also dynamics (investments, interpretations, desires) that are historically situated and conflicted in very
particular and complex ways. Reading such a text as a whole means that
we attend not only to the curriculum and what it includes or leaves out.

Nor does the kind of reading Gallop proposes lend insight into the supposed relations between our pedagogical efforts and the student's success or failure. Moving backward and forward, the stakes of a symptomatic reading consider the tensions between two sites of interpretation to reveal the structures of their investment. One site concerns teachers' responses to students' engagement with the curriculum; a second site concerns students' claims about their engagement. Gallop's notion of symptomatic reading is useful because it distinguishes between texts, including the text of research data, and the individuals who produce these texts.[3] That is, by arguing that we are all symptomatic, Gallop insists that we attend to the ways in which we speak though the conflicts and contradictions inherent in a time and place even as these conflicts speak us. Gallop's symptomatic readings of the essays produced by people she considers to be her peers and colleagues are different from my symptomatic reading of one student's story and the curriculum she engages, in that the former take up the terms of a debate about how a field of knowledge production is to be defined. My own readings, however, insert a different sense of time into the equation. This is the messy time of learning where the histories of students meet the histories of teachers. Two central questions inform this chapter. One question asks what we can learn about our own (collective) pedagogical assumptions, intellectual histories, and investments when we study our students' stories of engagement. The second question asks what these stories of engagement can teach us about the detours of learning. I turn now to my version of one student's engagement with feminist knowledge.

STORIES OF REPRESENTATION: WHERE THE FICTIONAL SELF MEETS ITS FICTIONAL OTHER

Lynne Hunt, a White woman in her late 30s, volunteered to participate in my study of student engagement in an introductory Women's Studies course (Pitt, 1995). At the time of the course, she was in the process of making a life for herself that did not center around her responsibilities as a wife and mother. However, the changes in her life were not ones she had engineered. She was responding to the significance of structural changes brought on by the acrimonious breakup of her marriage due, to some extent, to her attempts within the marriage to exceed her roles as wife and mother. She recognized that her story was a familiar one to feminists. Still, she left the course unconvinced that feminism served her needs.

---

[3]In other words, although this strategy of interpretation uses psychoanalytic categories, it is not the same as the psychoanalytic dialogue. Where the analyst offers interpretations that the analysand uses to enlarge, elaborate, and evaluate her own history, my interpretations are useful to readers interested in their practices of theorizing curriculum and pedagogy.

Lynne was uncomfortable with what she perceived to be a demand of the class that she both tell her story and listen to the stories of others. This constitutes one set of refusals on Lynne's part to recognize herself within the sites of identification that were offered by the course. More pertinent to my concerns here, however, is Lynne's refusal to recognize lesbians as women and to consider discussions about lesbian sexuality as a relevant topic for a Women's Studies course. At first glance, her response seems to resonate with Bonnie Zimmerman's (1985) claim that "heterosexuals often have difficulty accepting that a lesbian, especially a role-playing 'butch,' is in fact a woman" (p. 203). This American feminist critic "knows" that lesbians are women just as Wittig "knows" they are not. But what, in fact, does Lynne know, and why, in my engagements with Lynne, did the topic of lesbianism dominate our discussions about the course?

According to Lynne, silence fell over the class when one instructor declared her lesbian identity and when she then asked students to consider what lack of mainstream representation meant for her day-to-day life and for the class's capacity to know about lesbians. For Lynne, the group's silence confirmed her view that lesbianism was an issue that did not belong in Women's Studies. But before considering Lynne's (mis)understanding of this event, what did the teacher want? This is the first turn of the teacher's implication in a structure of desire that overdetermines how students' responses can be read.

When representation is presumed to do the pedagogical work of affirming minority identities and persuading others of the intolerable conditions of their everyday life, two narrow sites of identification are offered. One site of identification this teacher offered was addressed to students who are lesbians. But this desire to be a role model may not work, for there are significant differences between lesbians. The other site of identification is addressed to students who do not recognize themselves as lesbians. There, two positions are offered that are complicitous. Students can either agree or disagree that the lesbian, as a woman, is doubly oppressed, first as a woman and second as a "sexual deviant." If they disagree, their response is still complicitous because it occupies (negatively) one of the positions implied in the structure of the demand. It may be complicitous in a second way as well, and this has to do with the ways in which these (negative) responses affirm the teacher's assumptions about students as homophobic.

Lynne's response complicates the two positions offered that require her to either accept or refuse to accept the view that patriarchal social systems place a double burden of oppression on lesbians. As we shall see, her response to the introduction of "lesbianism as an issue" and to the teacher's offering of herself as "a representative lesbian" is quite curious because Lynne agrees that lesbians should be granted civil rights. But she refuses to understand this political struggle as relevant to Women's Studies. For

Lynne, lesbian oppression is not a "women's issue." Her refusal, akin to the structure of disavowal, where one simultaneously recognizes and ignores a traumatic perception, is central to structuring her understanding of the course and of feminism. What is surprising (and instructive) about Lynne's story is that the meanings she attaches to the figure of the lesbian, which she returns to the real lesbian teacher, bother her sense of herself as in control of her identity. This desire for self-control is already complicated by what Lynne believes to be the pedagogical demand that lies at the center of the course: the demand to identify with women as victims of oppression. Is it possible to understand Lynne's refusal to identify as a victim as continuous with her refusal to identify lesbians as women? If these two refusals are continuous, how does this alter or complicate an interpretation of her response as blatantly homophobic? Let us take a closer look at her response.

Lynne denies the importance of a discussion of lesbianism to feminism and expresses dismay at the time devoted to it (one class of 12) when topics that seem more important, such as the plight of Native Canadian women, received what she perceived to be insufficient attention. A conscientious student, Lynne will not even read the assigned material on lesbians. She describes lesbianism as a gay-rights issue that has little relevance to Women's Studies and suggests that lesbians have seized opportunistically on Women's Studies because of a shared femaleness. During an interview she said,

> women who choose that lifestyle have as much right, I suppose, to say, "well, I'm a lesbian and therefore I'm entitled to be accepted by society. I shouldn't have to sort of hide my lifestyle because I choose this or feel persecution because I've chosen this lifestyle."
>
> ... [T]his makes this issue viable, but it's not viable if it's "well, here's an opportunity to bring women and their issues to the surface, and while we're at it, why not get a cause going for lesbianism and therefore if we can get, you know, women to support us on so many issues maybe they'll support us on this too."

The foregoing quote is a contradictory moment in a much longer passage where Lynne describes lesbianism as not relevant to Women's Studies and implies that lesbians are not women. However, Lynne also recognizes that it is on the basis of "femaleness" that lesbians stake a claim to Women's Studies space. But the quote identifies three identificatory positions: women, lesbians, and Lynne. Thus she must recast lesbianism as a personal choice that is neither relevant nor important to women's struggles against oppression. Lynne asserts a strong minoritizing view (Sedgwick, 1990) of sexuality: Lesbians are defined by their object choice and are only relevant to a minor population and have nothing to do with her. Hence, for Lynne, lesbians are irrelevant.

But at the same time as Lynne is refusing to know lesbians or know about lesbians, she does engage the issue; in fact, it becomes the most elaborated topic for us. Her written and verbal engagement with the issue contradicts her stated refusal to know and, following Foucault (1980), can be interpreted as an erotic incitement to discourse on the taboos of sexuality. Foucault describes this as the "speaker's benefit." He writes, "If sex is repressed, that is condemned to prohibition, then the mere fact that one is speaking about it has the appearance of a deliberate transgression" (p. 6). But this is no simple transgression as it plays itself out through the barriers of repression. Foucault is referring not only to one's own confessional talk about sexuality but to an entire culture's fascination with it. This is even more complex within Women's Studies. There, minoritizing understandings about sexuality—that sexuality originates in the self—clash with feminist attempts to address the colonization of women's sexuality by men and the exclusion and marginalization of lesbians within feminist discourse.

For Lynne, lesbianism exceeds the bounds of what she will identify as a women's issue—lesbians are oppressed because they are lesbians, not because they are women. At the same time, her preoccupation with a very minor part of the course is an indication of the significance that it holds for her. The lesbian, whether she is figured in terms of woman identification or in terms of a refusal of (identification against) normative femininity, may suggest to Lynne the precariousness of her own ability to present herself as a woman, already presumed heterosexual, to assert itself as natural and originary. The problem is that Lynne understands her identity as always already there, and what she cannot tolerate is the idea, central to psychoanalytic theories of the subject, of the subject who is not in mastery of herself. As is seen later, the figure of the lesbian destabilizes Lynne's belief in her identity, and it does so in two different ways. The first has to do with the similarities between Lynne's identificatory position and that which she attributes to lesbians. The second has to do with the collapse among woman identification, feminism, and lesbian feminism. This is what Katie King (1994) is signaling in her argument that lesbianism came to function as "feminism's magical sign" during the late 1960s and early 1970s, and it organizes the second turn in much of feminist education's structure of desire.

King (1994) argues that the familiar axiom "feminism is the theory, lesbianism is the practice," was deployed in "a historical context in which lesbianism and feminism are not automatically assumed to be necessarily overlapping categories, and in which the phrase is being newly evolved in the women's movement to privilege lesbianism" (p. 125). Apparently, however, in her 1970 talk to the New York chapter of Daughters of Bilitis, Ti Grace Atkinson, to whom the axiom is attributed, emphasized that lesbians and feminists were different groups, the first requiring civil rights for a small minority and the second naming the grounds for political revolution. Atkinson argued against their political agendas being collapsed when she said, "Feminism is a theory; but lesbianism is a practice" (King, 1994, p. 125).

The difference is significant but not because of the separation presumed between theory and practice. Rather, the misquoted but popularized version, instead of allowing a more universalizing discourse of sexuality that could hold on to the tensions *between* sexual desires and practices and political identifications, emerged from and re-installed a minoritizing view. That is, in the terms of Sedgwick's (1990) definition of the homosexual–heterosexual divide, the question of lesbianism for feminism might have become "an issue of continuing, determinative importance in the lives of people across the spectrum of sexualities" (p. 1).

Wittig's argument, referred to at the beginning of this essay, provides one way of exploring this terrain; Adrienne Rich's (1980) famous essay, "Compulsory heterosexuality and lesbian existence" provides another. However, as the concept of gender developed into the analytic category that could encompass heterosexual women and lesbians in a common struggle against misogyny, what has emerged is a dual claim that is overly reductive of the positions of both Wittig and Rich: all women could be lesbians, and all lesbians could be women. According to King (1994), this poses a new set of problems:

> Identifying with lesbianism falsely implies that one knows all about heterosexism and homophobia magically through identity or association. The "experience" of lesbianism is offered as salvation from the individual practice of heterosexism and homophobia as the source of intuitive institutional and structural understanding of them. The power of lesbianism as a privileged signifier makes analysis of heterosexism and homophobia difficult, since it obscures the need for counter-intuitive challenges to ideology. (p. 136)

Following King's insights, one could say that Lynne's refusal to identify lesbians as relevant to herself breaks the central assumption that visibility ensures representation. Visibility does something for Lynne other than what the teacher ostensibly desires. Indeed, Lynne is preoccupied with the figure of lesbian, and one might venture to view her refusal as acting much like the "no" in the psychoanalytic dialogue. For Freud (1925), the utterance of a "no" almost always turns out to be a "yes." The criticisms he experienced for this resonate with one of the central problems of critical and feminist pedagogical practice. That is, how are we to interpret resistance to knowledge that goes against the grain of common sense if we don't want to get stuck in the rut of "false consciousness" where the teacher holds the power of superior knowledge? Freud's understanding of negation can help us here.

He argues that the contents of the unconscious, repressed knowledge of the pre-oedipal, are not, strictly speaking, available to consciousness although they "speak" in condensed and distorted forms in dreams, slips of the tongue, and so forth. But negation provides another route from the unconscious to consciousness. Freud (1925) argues that "the content of a repressed image or idea can make its way into consciousness, on the condition that it is negated. Negation is a way of taking cognizance of what is repressed, indeed it is already a lifting of the repression, though not, of course, an acceptance of what is repressed" (p. 236).

Through this process of negation, a kind of intellectual engagement with what is repressed is achieved, but, at the same time, what is essential to the repression remains preserved, still out of reach in the unconscious. This, after all, is Freud's famous dictum: the return of the repressed. I interpret this to mean that an idea that is negated is associated with repressed content and that, although the negation of an idea permits an airing of the repressed content, the grammatical removal of the negation does not in itself result in an expression of the content of the repressed idea. This is, in fact, not unlike how Lynne understands the function of personal experience in the feminist classroom: the stories are told, but their narration achieves nothing. We will not be further ahead, then, if we merely hear Lynne's statement that lesbianism does not belong on the syllabus as a masked assertion that it is central, or that knowledge designed to contest negative stereotypes will change her mind. We have to understand that the denial stands for, but is not equal to, something that she cannot allow to become registered in consciousness. Essentially, Lynne's refusal of the lesbian may serve as a decoy to her own attempt to maintain and assert a semblance of her identity as cohesive and coherent. The lesbian became a substitute for acknowledging her own contradictory struggles, already provoked, at least in part, by her belief that feminism demanded that she see herself as a victim. Thus one might say that the reason Lynne views the lesbian as beside the point is because the point itself is unbearable.

What lies at the center of my interpretation of how the figure of the lesbian threatens to destabilize Lynne's identity is the contradictory, yet familiar, image of the lesbian as both a man hater and a man imitator. The first image shores up Lynne's assertion that feminism has trouble separating itself from man hating, and the second recalls her own investments in positive identifications with men. She tells two stories about the lesbian instructor as proof that lesbians must be seen outside the project of feminism. In the following interview excerpt, antimale bias slides onto the lesbian instructor:

And while in the term papers one cannot be biased against men, there can't be sort of anti-male content in the term papers, in the open discussions there was very much that content in it, and the issue of lesbianism, especially because of (the instructor's) being a lesbian, she was very much anti-male.

This description is part of a story about a classroom incident in which one woman's male partner arrived to view a film about women and pornography. The class had previously voted that this would be permitted, but this was at a time when the other instructor was present. The instructor on this occasion told the young man that the class would have to vote on whether or not he would be permitted to stay. Lynne interpreted this action as unfairly and aggressively singling him out and embarrassing her and the other members of the class:

I rather thought that singled him out and isn't this what women are trying to change?

. . . and we all had to vote and she took an—I thought was aggressive in her manner. It wasn't even a matter of—it wasn't even directed towards him, it was directed towards the rest of us. . . .

There were quite a few women there who weren't shy about speaking up, so I don't think is was a matter of her having to rescue us or anything like that, and actually, most of us felt embarrassed because she had put him in such a position.

In this story, Lynne associates the lesbian teacher with antimale attitude that she suggests permeates the course. However, this is the only specific incident she refers to, and, in her retelling of it, she makes the lesbian responsible for antimale bias even as she separates her from what she perceives to be the proper role of feminism.

In the second story, Lynne associates present-day lesbians with the butches and femmes she observed in her childhood, which she spent in an area of Toronto known even then for its gay population. Her memories focused on the women whose "imitation" of masculinity was articulated through their attire, their voices, their use of "coarse" language, and their mannerisms. As a child she was fascinated by the strangeness of these women, who, along with prostitutes and their clients, made for exotic street scenes, the explanations for which Lynne relied on an older sister-in-law.

When she carries these images forward into the classroom where lesbianism has been accorded a place alongside what she considers to be more important and relevant issues, she translates the appearance of the 1950s butch (apprehended from a distance) into a new form of tyranny over women. The instructor had told students that they could drop their assignments off at her home (not mentioned by Lynne is the fact that this arrangement allowed students more time with their assignments). However, she warned them that they should not come after a certain hour in the evening because her partner would get upset. Lynne concludes from this that women who seek female partners fail in their bid for equality and only repeat the tyranny of heterosexual relationships, a tyranny with which Lynne has first-hand experience. Elsewhere she writes:

> While I do not advocate anti-lesbian rights, I am not willing to join causes to endorse lesbianism as a way of life for myself or my daughters. The bottom line for my lack of clarity on this issue of controversy is that the very reasons lesbians exist is because some women have chosen to become pro-female, but in some cases as a retaliation against males. Ironically, even one of the female role adopts the traditional male behaviour, the same behaviour most heterosexual women are committed to eliminating.

In this jumble of contradictory statements, Lynne seems to imply that opportunities to learn about lesbians are little more than thinly veiled recruitment efforts. Although lesbians "have chosen to become pro-female," their efforts fail precisely because one partner assumes the male role of oppressor. Lynne understands lesbian relationships in terms that refuse their difference, choosing instead to reinscribe them as a bad imitation of heterosexuality and, as such, they become anti-feminist as well.

There is, however, a caveat in Lynne's refusal: she acknowledges that gay men and lesbians do need to struggle for social equality. Still, she sums up her position in relation to the matter with this statement: "I try to be balanced in my thinking and I have to say that I would prefer not to know lesbians." But how might knowing lesbians make Lynne lose her balance? I take a closer look at what Lynne is refusing later in the chapter. As we do so, we might want to be mindful that "balancing acts" are already implicated within Women's Studies. These might be characterized as three dimensions of ambivalence that are provoked by Women's Studies but that cannot be resolved there. The first has to do with what one does with the difficult knowledge of women's oppression, male dominance, and the different ways in which these are lived. The second has to do with the awareness that Women's Studies is something of an island, in relation to both the university and the larger social world. Finally, there is the question of what Women's Studies does with the social knowledge that lesbians are suspect just about everywhere but in Women's Studies.

Although these ambivalences may constitute the conditions of learning within Women's Studies, they are also pushed aside when Women's Studies relies on a theory of knowledge that assumes that counterhegemonic representations transform learners unproblematically. Unaccounted for in this theory of knowledge, which only *appears* to bypass these ambivalences, is the question of how one psychically attaches to new knowledge. Ambivalence, however, returns in encounters with new knowledge because there is something uncanny about knowledge itself. That is, knowledge promises but never quite delivers the truth about the self. In the Women's Studies classroom, the promise that cannot be delivered concerns the truth about gender identity. As we return to Lynne's claim ("I try to be balanced in my thinking and I have to say that I would prefer not to know lesbians"), we take a closer look at a psychic drama that is shut out of pedagogical considerations of what knowledge about gender means to individuals. At first glance it may appear that the contours of this drama are particular to Lynne. It is, after all, her narrative that I have centered in my discussion. What I am suggesting, however, is that Lynne's story expresses the impossibility of occupying unambivalently a gendered identity, and that this impossibility is a condition of identity in our culture. Whereas it is the figure of the lesbian that returns Lynne to this uncanny apprehension, it may be her story that returns Women's Studies to its own uncanny knowledge summed up famously by Denise Riley (1988) when she asks, am I that name?

THE UNCANNY RETURN OF THE AMBIVALENCE OF GENDER

As we have seen, within the terms offered by the course and, indeed, within the now-familiar educational attempts to reduce homophobia in the classroom, Lynne's refusal to see the relevance of lesbian sexuality for feminist struggles can only be read as the familiar homophobic response of a heterosexual woman. This reading functions within the demand that those who occupy the socially dominant positions (heterosexual women) develop the capacity to tolerate and accept lesbian difference. This demand, however inadvertently, may collapse gender identity with sex and sexuality (see Cornell, 1992). Now, given that the concept of gender is useful for feminist discourses precisely because many believe that it separates sexual difference from biological difference (de Lauretis, 1987), this is a serious problem. What I am suggesting is that replacing sexual difference with gender difference as an analytical tool for "referring to the exclusively social origins of the subjective identities of men and women" (Scott, 1986, p. 1056) continues the tradition of relying on the categorization of sexed bodies into two. Left unexamined is the logic of heterosexual imperatives that demands a stable separation between masculinity and femininity. Lynne's story muddles this equation and reveals the psychic work of fashioning a sex/gender identity, work that remains concealed within contexts that conceptualize gender and sexuality as stable and as originating within the self. Here I am referring to the curriculum.

The stories Lynne tells about lesbians hold three clues about the psychic dilemmas that she may be attempting to work through via the figure of lesbian. By excluding lesbians from the category of women, Lynne displaces her own ambivalence about membership in that category. This is the first clue, and it echoes Wittig's insistence that women who are not in a relation of dependence on a man require a new conceptual category. By insisting that lesbians hate men, Lynne maintains her own belief that she can wander between the generalities of critique of male oppression of women and the specificities of her own experiences (which she acknowledges as the effects of male domination) without risking outrage at men. In other words, the difficult emotional labor required to maintain a boundary between an attack on sexism and an attack on men is attenuated when lesbians are represented as man haters. This is the second clue. And, finally, by attributing to lesbians some of what she considers to be male sexist behavior, Lynne's idealization of a positive identification with men remains uncontaminated. That is, and paradoxically so, it is lesbians who are the real men! Taken together, these clues serve her representation of herself as a heterosexual woman.

These clues require the logic of psychic negation. This is so because, in order to examine and in a sense work through the repetitions required for such a story to cohere, Lynne would have to "self-destruct."[4] What I mean by this is that the identificatory processes that work ongoingly to secure identity also expose identity as always and already threatened by its own failure to assert itself as natural and originary. But the fantasmatic structure of identity that is secured, however provisionally, by the processes of assuming a sexed position bears, as well, an identificatory relation to its own disavowed imperatives. Judith Butler (1993) argues that "Sexuality is as much motivated by the fantasy of retrieving prohibited objects as by the desire to remain protected from the threat of punishment such a retrieval might bring on" (p. 100). The normalized positions of the masculine and feminine are configured by the regulatory demands of heterosexual desire and identity. Butler suggests that, whatever other complexities are involved in the ongoing process of performing identity, identification with a sexed position is a double identification. Entailed here is not only the identification with the phantasmatic ideal of the position (which requires identification with the same-sex parent and an identification of the

---

[4]In one of her journal entries, Lynne describes her desire to recognize herself in images of women that exceed normative ideals of femininity. She considers this to be necessary to the work of healing in the aftermath of her divorce, an event that has separated her physically and emotionally from her children, but she worries that she will "self-destruct" in the process. When Women's Studies relies on knowledge to transform learners, it may not sufficiently take into account the difficult knowledge women already hold about their condition as female in a sexist society.

opposite-sex parent as an object choice). What is also entailed is identification with the position's constitutive limit. In the case of the feminine position, according to Butler, this limit is the figure of the castrator, the figure of excessive phallicism who symbolizes *for* the masculine position the threat of castration.

This framework conceptualizes sexual positions as relations, not self-reliant units, and it can help us to better understand Lynne's response to feminism. What is at stake for her is any disruption to the ways in which she has already negotiated her identity as a woman who loves men. This position does not approximate or idealize "ideal femininity" but rather it is one that approximates identification with the masculine position. It is a position that is invested in both "being"—functioning as the guarantor that the male is not castrated—and "having" the phallus—refusing her status as castrated. What Lynne must disavow is that a position that approximates "having" the phallus cannot be so easily reconciled with the feminine position of "being" it.

Not only is this position prohibited within the symbolic order of patriarchy, but, for different reasons, it seems to be prohibited within feminist discourses as well. Biddy Martin (1994) describes this as "feminists' injunctions to identify with and as women, over and against masculinity" (p. 105). Butler (1993) speculates that the abjected figure of the feminine position's constitutive other is symbolically represented by the "phallicized dyke." But in a more broadly conceived gesture, she also argues that the "hierarchized and differential specular relation" between the masculine and the feminine "is itself established through the exclusion and abjection of a domain of relations in which all the wrong identifications are pursued; men wishing to 'be' the phallus for other men; women wishing to 'have' the phallus for other women; women wishing to 'be' the phallus for other women" (p. 103).

Lynne's contradictory positionings of the figure of the lesbian and the meanings she attaches to this figure represent the repudiated forms of both of her significant identifications. That is, through her abjection of the lesbian, Lynne repudiates both her status as castrated and her prohibited wish to "have" the phallus.

PEDAGOGICAL IMPLICATIONS

When lesbianism is treated as a category of social difference among women, gender identity is reduced to a fact of biology, and heterosexuality is re-aligned with gender identity. When feminist pedagogy assumes that women's political mobilization emerges on the basis of a collective gender identity, it cannot account for or address the different and complicated ways in which women make their gender identity. Finally, when lesbianism is offered as the only sexual position available to women who wish to refuse male control over their bodies, how women negotiate their heterosexuality is left unexplored. A symptomatic reading of the text of Lynne's response to the inclusion of lesbianism as a "topic" for an introductory Women's Studies course reveals the traces of particularity inherent in the psychic work of making identity in relation to the prohibitions and imperatives of the impossibility of the "feminine" position. It comes as no surprise that such work, which for the most part is performed at the level of the unconscious, becomes visible precisely at a moment of profound vulnerability.

It is, however, when we consider the relationship between Lynne's response and the identificatory positions she has been offered that symptomatic reading becomes a valuable analytic tool for curriculum theory. Lynne's contradictory response to the lesbian, which denies the lesbian's claim to the category of women and to the category of feminists, can be read as a response to the contradictory positions that the lesbian occupies within the curriculum of Women's Studies. One position situates the lesbian as feminism's magical sign; a second position situates the lesbian within feminism's history of privileging the experiences and interests of White, middle-class, heterosexual women.

Figured as feminism's magical sign, the lesbian appears to offer women new identificatory positions that refuse "ideal femininity." However, to return to Wittig's (1980) sly conclusion, we are reminded that this work to create new identificatory positions cannot be reduced to one category (lesbians) in relation to its own constitutive limit category (women). Let us read her statement as a grammatical whole: "Lesbians are not women, no more is any woman who is not in a relation of personal dependency with a man" (pp. 110–111). Wittig insists on examining the material effects of conceptual categories as well as economic relations of power. The lesbian she offers can be seen as a kind of battle cry that wanders between risking and refusing what King refers to as the trap of seeing lesbianism as feminism's magical sign.[5] By asking us to consider identity as a relation to both conceptual categories and practices, Wittig poses the question of what it means to make and claim positions as identity. This, it seems to me, could be a question of ongoing interest for feminist education. Ironically, given Wittig's antipathy to psychoanalytic theories, her assertion that lesbians are not women can be read against Jacques Lacan's famous assertion, *La femme n'existe pas.* Just as "woman" exists as an ideal category to which women must make a relation, "lesbian" can also be recognized as a category

---

[5]King's designation of lesbianism as feminism's magical sign is reminiscent of Donald Winnicott's understanding of "magical thinking" (see Phillips, 1988). For this psychoanalyst, the baby believes that she produces the mother (or a feed) merely by wishing it, thus assuring herself of her omnipotence at a time when knowledge of her profound dependency would be overwhelming.

of identity that is "ideal" to the political demands of feminism, at least as Wittig understands them at the time of writing. Lynne's story requires us to pay close attention to the complicated ways in which individuals make and remake their identities in relation to the fictions of ideal categories of identity, including those offered by feminist discourses.

Lynne's story also demonstrates that the two categories of the tolerant and the tolerated imagined within an ideology of representational visibility are insufficient to make sense of how representation works at the level of identificatory processes. Lynne refuses lesbian difference, but her staging of this refusal is not organized by a concern for or even an interest in feminism's history of exclusions. Rather, her refusal is staged as a more personal and intimate dynamic of warding off a perceived threat to her identity.[6] What she resists when she resists lesbian difference is the failure of her identity as a woman to secure an image of itself as natural, cohesive, and originating in the self. This, as Wittig implies, is the risk and possibility of feminism, but Lynne has had little opportunity or even need to explore such an idea.

A symptomatic reading of students' engagement with feminist knowledge within Women's Studies helps us to examine what is at stake in the curricular selections and sequencing and in the pedagogical imperatives that operate there. Such a reading invites interpretations that reveal the anxieties and contradictions inherent in the pedagogical positions assumed by the course and that allow us to exceed these positions. In this case, a symptomatic reading asks to consider the limits of the sociological push to connect representation, with its emphasis on voice, experience, and visibility. Using the strategies of symptomatic reading, we begin to see the need to understand the role of fantasy in the work that individuals do to render their identities as coherent and as relevant to learning. This is so whether we are students or teachers.

These strategies, as I have developed them here, may, however, be untranslatable to the day-to-day of classroom life. There are several reasons for this. One reason concerns the inevitable delay between the emergence of a set of curricular and pedagogical imperatives and our capacity to perceive the "conflicts inhering in a collective situation" (Gallop, 1992, p. 7). A second reason concerns the qualities of research into classroom dynamics. The content of the research story I discuss in this essay was not available to the instructors of the course. This may be so because, as Constance Penley (1989) notes, "the student can always sense the hidden demands of the teacher or parent. The student . . . is almost clairvoyant

---

[6]This does not mean, of course, that Lynne's response is unimplicated in the repetition of heterosexual women's anxieties about lesbianism. The problem concerns the pedagogical assumption that knowledge about this history is all students need to disentangle themselves.

when it comes to understanding the desire of the Other and how best narcissistically to mirror what the Other desires" (p. 169).

The problem is that it is difficult to learn the features of our hidden demands from our students if, for instance, we believe we know in advance the meaning of their silences or the purpose of their strategies of refusing the topics we have organized for discussion. Unfortunately, such beliefs privilege a theory of knowledge over a theory of learning. The theory of learning I am advocating here requires that we become curious about "symptoms" of engagement in our work with students. As we do so, we may be able to conceive of the work of pedagogy as the work of creating conditions of learning where everyone is invited to study the structure of her response to the representations we offer. Such an invitation might begin with the study of the fantasmatic ideals embedded within these representations. In this exploration, an essay such as Wittig's "The straight mind" might be examined, not because it *represents* lesbians or problematizes normalization of heterosexuality. Such an essay might be engaged for the interesting ways it allows us to think about representations of gender and sexual identities as sites of identification where our fantasmatic ideals might be called into question, assessed, and perhaps even reconfigured.

ACKNOWLEDGMENTS

The author acknowledges the helpful readings provided by *JCT*'s editors and reviewers as well as those of Bronwen Low and Joanna Williams of York University.

REFERENCES

Abelove, H., Barale, M. A., & Halperin, D. (Eds.). (1993). *The lesbian and gay reader*. New York & London: Routledge.

Bogdan, D. (1994). When is a singing school (not) a chorus? The emancipatory agenda in feminist pedagogy and literature education. In L. Stone (Ed.), *The education feminist reader* (pp. 336–349). New York: Routledge.

Bowles, G., & Klein, R. (Eds.). (1983). *Theories of women's studies*. New York: Routledge.

Britzman, D. (1992). Structures of feeling in curriculum and teaching. *Theory Into Practice, 31*(3), 252–258.

Brodkey, L. (1987). *Academic writing as social practice*. Philadelphia: Temple University Press.

Bunch, C., & Pollack, S. (Eds.). (1983). *Learning our way: Essays in feminist education*. Trumansberg, NY: The Crossing Press.

Butler, J. (1993). *Bodies that matter: On the discursive limits of sex*. New York: Routledge.

Butler, J. (1994). Against proper objects. *differences: A Journal of Feminist Cultural Studies, 6*(3&4), 1–26.

Cornell, D. (1992). Gender, sex, and equivalent rights. In J. Butler & J. W. Scott (Eds.), *Feminists theorize the political* (pp. 280–296). New York: Routledge.

Culley, M., & Portuges, C. (Eds.). (1985). *Gendered subjects: The dynamics of feminist teaching*. Boston: Routledge & Kegan Paul.

de Lauretis, T. (1987). *Technologies of gender: Essays on theory, film and fiction.* Bloomington: Indiana University Press.

Ellsworth, E. (1989). Why doesn't this feel empowering? Working through the repressive myths of critical pedagogy. *Harvard Educational Review, 59*(3), 297–324.

Felman, S. (1993). *What does a woman want: Reading and sexual difference.* Baltimore: John Hopkins University Press.

Finke, L. (1993). Knowledge as bait: Feminism, voice, and the pedagogical unconscious. *College English, 55,* 7–27.

Foucault, M. (1980). *The history of sexuality, volume one: An introduction* (R. Hurley, Trans.). New York: Vintage.

Freud, S. (1919). The uncanny. In J. Strachey (Ed. & Trans.), *The standard edition of the complete psychological works of Sigmund Freud Vol. XVII.* London: The Hogarth Press & The Institute of Psycho-Analysis.

Freud, S. (1925). Negation. In J. Strachey (Ed. & Trans.), *The standard edition of the complete psychological works of Sigmund Freud Vol. XIX.* London: The Hogarth Press & The Institute of Psycho-Analysis.

Gallop, J. (1992). *Around 1981: Academic feminist literary theory.* New York: Routledge.

Gallop, J. (1995). *Pedagogy: The question of impersonation.* Bloomington: Indiana University Press.

Grumet, M. (1989). The beauty full curriculum. *Educational Theory, 39*(3), 225–230.

King, K. (1994). Lesbianism as feminism's magical sign: Contests for meaning and U.S. women's movements, 1968–1972. In K. King, *Theory in its feminist travels: Conversations in U.S. women's movements.* Bloomington: Indiana University Press.

Ladson-Billings, G. (1996). Silences as weapons: Challenges of a Black professor teaching White students. *Theory Into Practice, 35*(2), 79–85.

Lather, P. (1991). *Getting smart: Feminist research and pedagogy with/in the postmodern.* New York: Routledge.

Martin, B. (1994). Sexualities without genders and other queer utopias. *Critical Crossings, 24*(2–3), 104–121.

Penley, C. (1989). Teaching in your sleep: Feminism and psychoanalysis. In *The future of an illusion: Film, feminism, and psychoanalysis.* Minneapolis: University of Minnesota Press.

Phelan, P. (1993). *Unmarked: The politics of performance.* New York: Routledge.

Phillips, A. (1988). *Winnicott.* Cambridge, MA: Harvard University Press.

Pitt, A. J. (1995). *Subjects in tension: Engaged resistance in the feminist classroom.* Unpublished doctoral dissertation, University of Toronto.

Rich, A. (1980). Compulsory heterosexuality and lesbian existence. *Signs, 5,* 631–660.

Riley, D. (1988). *Am I that name? Feminism and the category of 'women' in history.* Minneapolis: University of Minnesota Press.

Schafer, R. (1983). *The analytic attitude.* New York: Basic Books.

Scott, J. (1986). Gender: A useful category of historical analysis. *American Historical Review, 91,* 1053–1075.

Silverman, K. (1996). *The threshold of the visible world.* New York: Routledge.

Simon, R. (1992). *Teaching against the grain: Texts for a pedagogy of possibility.* New York: Bergin & Garvey.

Sedgwick, E. K. (1990). *Epistemology of the closet.* Berkeley: University of California Press.

Walters, S. D. (1996). From here to queer: Radical feminism, postmodernism, and the lesbian menace (or, Why can't a woman be more like a fag?). *Signs, 21*(4), 831–869.

Wittig, M. (1980). The straight mind. *Feminist Issues, 1*(1), 105–111.

Wittig, M. (1981). One is not born a woman. *Feminist Issues, 1,* 47–54.

Zimmerman, B. (1985). What has never been: An overview of lesbian feminist literary criticism. In E. Showalter (Ed.), *The new feminist criticism: Essays on women, literature and theory* (pp. 200–224). New York: Pantheon Press.

Chapter 16

On Some Psychical Consequences of AIDS Education

Deborah P. Britzman
York University

In my explorations of the psychical consequences of learning, I have been wondering about pedagogy's capacity to address the ego (Britzman, 1998). This project renders as curious pedagogy's current preoccupation with making the proper curriculum that can somehow prop up the coherence of knowledge and its subjects. The detour, psychoanalytic indirection really, moves from a pedagogy preoccupied by knowledge to one that attempts a dialogue with psychical dynamics of learning, with the failure of knowledge and then a move toward what Jacqueline Rose (1993) terms, an "ethics of failure" (p. 36), or attempts to do less harm in social, ontological, and an epistemological breakdown.[1] In this chapter, I suggest the relevancy of new conceptualizations in AIDS education. For even as we attempt to offer less damaging information and ready ourselves to rethink current representations of the virus, its global trajectory, medical interventions, at-risk bodily practices, and community campaigns, we also

---

[1]The argument Rose makes for an ethics of failure emerges from her meditation on the question, "Why war?" Rose argues that war is the limit of absolute knowledge, a time when cause and effect collapse, and when projection and reality cannot be separated. If war signifies the failure of knowledge, the violent attempt to reunify knowledge through war only makes the matter worse. At the end of this essay, Rose (1993) posits the following: "Knowledge will be possible only if we are willing to suspend the final purpose and ends of knowledge in advance" (p. 37). This view works against the entire enterprise of education and its founding insistence on the lineal relation between teaching and learning. Much of this present chapter argues against this developmental view of teaching.

know those appeals to a rational, cohesive, and unitary subject in the name of toleration, role models, and the affirmation of and reliance on identity return the damage. Whereas those who do attempt to assist students in a creative and ethical engagement with AIDS already know the difficulties in terms of subject, object, and conceptual reformulations demanded and in terms of institutional and legal prohibitions against frank discussion and uncensored texts, the *little* difficulty addressed in this chapter concerns what it might mean for a pedagogy to attempt to address the ego's work of making reparation in learning and unlearning.

But why the preoccupation with the ego? What is the ego that it should be the destination of a pedagogical address? From the writing of Sigmund Freud (1968e), and then, those who follow after, we learn that the ego is first of all a bodily ego, a "frontier-creature" (p. 56) whose work is perception, hallucination, and reality testing. We learn as well that the ego attempts to synthesize that which cannot be resolved, namely the strange relations between psychical dynamics and social demands. Here, we have the most intimate expression of the failure of knowledge. Furthermore, we learn that precisely because of its desire to synthesize and the impossibility of fleeing from itself when things, inevitably, do not work out, the ego, as that great seat of anxiety, has special methods called defense mechanisms that are put to work in order for the ego to live through its interminable dilemmas. But then Freud complicates the picture even more in his portrayal of the ego as tragic. The ego's defense mechanisms are formed at a time when the ego is just emerging, too young really to understand that in its lonely attempts to defend itself, to differentiate itself from its own anxieties, it will set in motion the very dilemmas it desires to flee. Perhaps this is why in his defense of lay analysis, Freud called the ego "feeble." In a rather condensed discussion of the flawed ego, Freud (1968c) suggests that the very work of the ego can cause it to fall ill:

> The point at which the illness makes its breach is an unexpected one, though no one acquainted with general pathology will be surprised to find a confirmation of the principle that it is precisely the most important developments and differentiations that carry in them the seeds of illness, the failure of function. (p. 202)[2]

The work of the ego places the ego at risk. But Freud also argued something more, and here is where education might pay attention. Al-

---

[2]Georges Canguilhem's (1991) discussion of the concepts (and hence point of view) of illness and health makes this very point. Says Canguilhem: "The problem of the existence of perfect health is analogous. As if perfect health were not a normative concept . . . Strictly speaking a norm does not exist, it plays its role, which is to devalue existence by allowing its correction. To say that perfect health does not exist is simply saying that the concept of health is not one of an existence, but of a norm whose function and value is to be brought into contact with existence in order to stimulate modification" (p. 77).

though he acknowledges the ego's loyalty to the world, a loyalty that tends to spin the ego against the "it" or the "id" of itself, and that tends toward the wish for an absolute knowledge and unification, Freud supposed that the forces at work within the ego also push the ego to change the world, as opposed to adapting to and complying with its demands. Although education also has this same constitutional ambivalence in its attempt to distinguish between change and adaptation, a more intimate movement tends to be ignored. This is a movement of libidinality that Melanie Klein (1994) calls, "the desire to make reparation." Throughout this chapter I invoke the fragile potential of the ego to make reparation and discuss why pedagogy must attempt an address to this other learning.

A series of sentences, phrases, and little footnotes serve as a guide. From there, I move to the thought of a method of implication. I conclude with a brief description of what pedagogy might then consider because it has considered the vicissitudes of instinct and of the social. I leave it up to the reader to name the pedagogy at stake.

First the sentences: for Sigmund Freud, Ladies and Gentleman I can offer you no consolation; for Anna Freud, We should not expect so much of each other. Whereas Sigmund Freud promises nothing, Anna Freud considers the promise to be too harsh, for the expectation is always anxious. They are both addressing the ego as that great seat of anxiety that must console itself and as that great possibility for a movement toward risking its own history of libidinality. In this dreamy history, knowledge will always be fragile, subject to reversal, displacement, substitution, and condensation. The ego is a precipitate of its own libidinal history, its capacity to touch and be touched. This libidinal history, although never fully present or even acknowledged, nonetheless exerts great force. Yet if the ego is an effect of love, if the ego is to be affected by its own love, Freud (1968d) goes on to suggest another potential, a queer relation that may be of interest to a certain pedagogy: "Where id was, there ego shall be" (p. 80). Suppose, then, that pedagogy could attend to the time of delay noted by the two Freuds. For something like this to be attempted, pedagogy would have to address what Erik Erikson (1968), in his discussion of classroom life calls "a communality of egos" (p. 221) and then incite something in excess of what Hans Sachs (1947) in his consideration of literature calls, "a community of daydreams" (p. 281).[3]

---

[3]Erikson's (1968) notion of a communality of egos reminds educators of the complex circulation of influence and resistance in the classroom. But it is also a way to consider Freud's insistence that social processes and psychical processes are indistinguishable. Hans Sachs (1947) is also concerned with influence, but the influence of literature on psychical freedom. Thus a community of daydreams is not a community made from identity but from the capacity to imagine the poetic creations of the unconscious. This leads Sachs to advocate for the work of the daydream to come closer to the work of art, to renounce the wish for heroism and rescue, and live without ulterior motives in order to meet the unconscious.

If pedagogy can reside in the fault lines of these sentences—promising nothing, not expecting so much—it might begin again with another sentence of delay, the time that inaugurates Sarah Schulman's (1990) novel, *People in Trouble:* "It was the beginning of the end of the world but not everyone noticed right away" (p. 1). We know in the field of education, not everyone notices right away. And if one attempted to write the history of AIDS in educational discourse, by which I mean if one could study the contemporary responses to the pandemic known as AIDS in that place where the masses of people in North America are legally mandated to go, namely compulsory education, one would have to begin by writing stories of the woeful disregard toward the events known as AIDS and notice how even such tiny and intimate objects like condoms and safer sex pamphlets can contribute to a school district's hysteria, to the cruelness of social policy, to the passion for prohibitions.[4] We might also notice the silence of teacher education. These add up to a story of obscurantism, the withholding of knowledge, a confining of what Driscilla Cornell (1995) terms "the imaginary domain," or, the right to imagine something otherwise. This disregard, a disavowal really, would be, in Shoshana Felman's (1987) terms, a story of ignorance, a story of startling, rigid, coherence rooted in the desire to ignore. But even this desire would also be a story of stunning implication, entangled in what Jonathan Silin (1995) argues as that which might "radically call into question the pleasures and dangers of teaching" (p. 56). The pleasure and the danger have to do not just with how knowledge is used but the very poesies of its in-betweeness, namely the social relations of cultural experience, play, and creative work where Winnicott (1986) locates the potential space, the question of freedom.

If pedagogy can ready itself to question such a radical call—a call that would ask for an account of its pleasures and dangers—it must also admit to its tally: the symptoms of not noticing right away. For in education, the story of AIDS would resemble a symptom-formation, a defence against noticing. In Freud's (1968c) words: "The symptom-formation scores a triumph if it succeeds in combining the prohibition with satisfactions so that what was originally a defensive command, or prohibition acquires the significance of a satisfaction as well; and in order to achieve this end it will often make use of the most ingenious associative paths" (p. 112). One such path in education is made from its obsessive worry about invoking controversy as a defense against its own incapacity to acknowledge the fragility of its meanings. The controversy is one of the having to speak to the symptom formation and its deep investment in ignorance, in not noticing right away. All this is to say

---

[4]The pathetic history of condom distribution in schools and clean needle distribution campaigns in clinics in North America are key examples of what Cindy Patton (1996) calls "the national pedagogy." One can also bring into this discussion Jesse Helms' social policy of refusing funding for safer-sex campaigns that address gay and lesbian subjects.

that education gains satisfaction in the story of its woeful disregard. This strange turn is what Freud (1968c) in another essay, called "resistance" or, "the gain from illness" (p. 223) or, the holding on of being ill in the name of innocence. Much later, Christopher Bollas (1992) would call this work, "the violence of innocence" (p. 165).[5]

And yet, this story of woeful disregard may not explain why Bill Haver (1996) writes, "Not even education can save us now" (p. 23). The sentence is not just a warning about educational myth and its passionate identification with the rescue fantasy, with the idealization of the good object, and then, with having to split the ego so that what becomes unthinkable is what Melanie Klein (1994) calls the "making of reparation" (p. 313). Perhaps Haver's warning marks the limits of a certain education. However, even the marking of the limit is not the same as experiencing it. Again, Schulman (1990) writes, "It was the beginning of the end of the world but not everyone noticed right away" (p. 1).

What then is it to notice? And, why is not noticing so common? We can turn to a different sort of warning offered by analyst Alice Balint (1954): "Education begins at an age at which it is too early for us to be able to count on understanding" (p. 119). Balint's concern is not with the bringing up of culture, the *bildungsroman* of the educational romance. Nor can this observation be consoled through the progress of chronology and its promise of maturity. The story of regression should bother our attempts at cure. The strange time of learning Balint marks is curious; *too early* and *too late, belated.* If education cannot count on understanding—after all, learning is only a movement toward what is not yet understood or perhaps even tolerated—then on what can pedagogy count? It must count on the question of not understanding, of misrecognition, and only from these flaws may come a possibility, perhaps a desire, to make reparation. Before leaving these fragments of delay, let us consider why a theory of delay in the strange time of learning is of some psychical consequence.

Balint posits the ego's work of perception as contributing to its own circumscription. She calls this first flawed attempts at learning *identificatory thought.* Balint defines this way of thinking as the ego's attempt to make a relation to the world while still desiring both to console its own impossible status as omnipotent and to ward off its fear of annihilation. But the very attempt is flawed because identificatory thought is so closely linked to the ego's primary narcissism and hence does not mean to distinguish or tolerate difference. In Balint's (1954) words, "identificatory thinking is em-

---

[5]In a short section titled, "Never Mind," Bollas (1992) situates the violence of innocence as the refusal of relationality. "Clearly it is a form of denial, but one in which we observe not the subject's denial of external perception, but the subject's denial of the other's perception" (p. 180). We might venture to speculate that two relations are being denied: the self's otherness and the other's otherness.

ployed for the purpose of avoiding what is unpleasurable and obtaining what is pleasurable, and it aims at transforming a strange and consequently frightening external world into one that is familiar and enjoyable" (p. 93). Identificatory thought is a symptom of the ego's capacity to hallucinate. And, for Balint, identificatory thought is a strategy of resistance, not yet love. In Balint's terms, the lover must tolerate the vicissitudes of the loved object and find pleasure in the unfamiliar.

Those of us who attempt to center AIDS in the curriculum know that many students may well center their own resistance to learning from AIDS, and may wish for the teacher's removal when such a topic is introduced. Indeed, identificatory thinking may well be a defense against the unpleasure of confronting AIDS and a symptom of the ego's conservation investment in a life without consequence. And yet, the common and typically cruel statements that accompany the refusal to learn, the dismissal of the learning, and the desire to ignore may not easily map onto literal and conscious meanings, nor even invoke any insight into the latent content of resistance. Resistance is not transparent; its very qualities refuse its own unveiling. Freud (1968b) suggests resistance will show up in two ways: "as critical objection and through allusive approximations . . . more remote from the actual idea" (p. 41).[6] Because resistance is carried within so many interminable disguises and essentially repeats the logic of dream-work through condensation, distortion, reversal of content, and so on, even resistance, itself a symptom formation, requires interpretation as opposed to the centering of the educator's moral judgment. The problem becomes even greater, for if the resistance is interpreted well by an outsider, it is still the author of the resistance who must become willing to risk her or his own satisfaction made from not learning. Furthermore, appeals to rationality are of no help because the defenses at work are built on anxiety and ignorance or the refusal to implicate oneself in what one may already know. Again, this is also why education occurs at a time when it is too early for us to count on *anyone's* understanding, including, of course, the educator. Thus, the pedagogical address must take a detour through the structures of repression.

Because the desire to make reparation begins with a working through of aggression, pedagogy may need to attend to the question of the ego's capacity to repress. Repression is one of the ego's special methods of defense, a means "to struggle against painful or unendurable ideas or affects" (A. Freud, 1995, p. 42). There are two ego defense strategies that are central, I think, when considering why a pedagogy of AIDS is so fragile:

---

[6]Resistance is one of the most difficult concepts in psychoanalysis, because the term implicates thinking itself as one of its primary methods. The problem, then, is not that a better idea can somehow transcend psychical wounds. This may be why Lyotard (1991) argues that thinking is a form of suffering.

the mechanism of "undoing what has been done" and "isolation." Freud calls "undoing" a negative magic because it is not just the consequence that must be ignored. The event itself is "blown away." A person decides an event did not happen. Isolation is the second defense where, although the event is acknowledged, the individual decides it will not matter: "the event is deprived of its affect, and its associative connections are suppressed or interrupted so that it remains as though isolated and is not reproduced in the ordinary process of thought" (Freud, 1968a, p. 120).[7] One does not have to go very far to suggest that isolation and undoing may be the chief structure of a certain educational design, a certain formulation of disciplinary knowledge, a certain structure of authority in academic legitimation.[8] More locally, these defense mechanisms render pedagogy, from whatever side, inconsolable. This is partly because undoing and isolation refuses any obligation to implicate oneself in what one might notice. At the same time, even a well-meaning pedagogy cannot predict how or when its address is felt as a threat or as too much. But there is another sense of the inconsolability of pedagogy and it has to do with the question of its own unconscious dynamics and therefore how pedagogy is constituted from its own flaws. Here, pedagogy is inconsolable because it cannot be in mastery of itself and like the ego subjects itself—in ways it does not notice—to its own unpedagogical anxieties and defenses.

Curiously, the mechanisms of undoing and isolation are oddly intellectual in structure in that they require a flawed cognition and a certain contained logic that are oriented toward the view that knowledge and bodies are capable of securing their own boundaries. We first learn about these two methods in Freud's essay, "Inhibitions, Symptoms, and Anxiety." There, Freud makes a rather startling observation. He says that at a root in these defenses called "undoing" and "isolating" is an archaic taboo against touching. We are, of course, back to the question of AIDS and the ego's tragic defense against being touched by AIDS. In Freud's (1968a) words,

> If we ask ourselves why the avoidance of touching, contact, or contagion should play such a large part in this neurosis and should become the subject-matter of complicated systems, the answer is that touching and physical contact are the immediate aim of the aggressive as well as the loving object-cathexes. Eros desires contact. (p. 122)

---

[7]Alice Balint (1954) seems to take these defenses as central to her concept, *identificatory thinking*.

[8]Bill Reading's (1996) study of the university raises the stakes of an inconsolable pedagogy and the need for the social bond to be rethought without alibis such as grand narratives of emancipation or melancholy longings for a lost wholeness. In Reading's words: "The sheer fact of obligation to others is something that exceeds subjective consciousness, which is why we never get free of our obligations to others, which is why nobody is a *model* citizen (the citizen who would not have any bond to anyone else in the community because he or she would stand for the community as a whole)" (p. 186).

There are two sorts of touching engaged in Freud's view. One is aggressive touching, a paradox of hatred really: a touch that is made in order not to be touched, a touch that aggravates, wounds through destruction. The other touch is loving, for this touch is without condition, cannot guarantee, only desires. The loving touch is vulnerable to loss; these touches are what risk the ego. The aggressive touch is already one of loss, but a loss it does not know. Both destructive touching and loving touching, in Melanie Klein's terms, must be engaged, for if the subject does not come to notice her own capacity to do harm—including her capacity to do conceptual violence—then there can be no desire to make reparation.

We can begin to see that AIDS education makes difficult demands on the ego, demands that ask the ego to let go of its defenses, be touched by that which puts it in danger, obligate itself to change its conceptual and affective work, attempt to acknowledge a thought in excess of itself. This potential space is where thinking might move toward an ethical relation, and engage its potential to become contaminated, wounded by thought. In this philosophical move, one that refuses the boundaries of certitude, of properness, indeed of conceptual prophylaxis, the ego may meet its own interminable demands, notably the demand for love.

So far, we have been considering questions of disavowal, withdrawal, with the ambivalence of touching, being touched, and the capacity to be touched. We have suggested that these intimate dynamics are repeated at the level of the social and epistemological. These internal and external dynamics are central to the question of AIDS, to what Bill Haver (1996) calls the question of "the erotic, the global, and the historicity of the social." At the same time, this refusal to secure the boundaries of AIDS does not mean that the other side of disavowal—or undoing and isolation—is the finding of the lost object of the correct knowledge and then possessing the security of understanding. What renders AIDS inconsolable and hence what renders any pedagogical undertaking insufficient is that when it comes to the subject of AIDS, we do not know the subject of AIDS. What we have yet to learn from AIDS is a lesson in the failure of the calculations of knowledge.[9] In Haver's words:

[9]For a discussion of the failure of the calculations of knowledge in the pandemic, see Delany's (1994) novella, "The Tale of Plagues and Carnivals, or: Some Informal Remarks Toward the Modular Calculus, Part Five." The novella was published three times, and each succeeding edition carried a new appendix and postscript. The first postscript, however, summarizes its own symptomology: "The Tale of Plagues and Carnivals is, of course, a work of imagination; and to the extent it is a document, largely what it documents is *misinformation, rumour and wholly untested guesses* at play through a limited social section of New York City during 1982 and 1983, mostly before the 23 April 1984 announcement of the discovery of a virus . . . as the overwhelmingly probably cause of AIDS" (p. 361). The novella, then, becomes not just an ethical meditation on an ethical problem, of whether the reader distinguishes between the study and the stories of misconceptions. The unit of analysis, if such a reduction

What is called AIDS poses an essential threat not only to our commonplace assumptions about the capacity to manage or control the pandemic, but also to our equally commonplace assumptions about the nature of the world, the social, the economic, and the political—and *thereby* to the assumption that it is possible to posit the world as an object of knowing. (p. xviii)

If there is to be a pedagogy that can address the circuitous work of a social breakdown, the ego's capacity to destroy, and the interminable and fragile work of making reparation, then the symptoms of knowledge that come to be known as AIDS must become the subject of AIDS. The pedagogy might begin in the way Tony Kushner's (1984) play *Angels in America: Part Two: Perestroika* begins, with a question that can tolerate its own unaswerability. Says Alekssi Antedilluvianovich Prelapsarianov:

The Great Question before us is: Are we doomed? The Great Question before us is: Will the Past release us? The Great Question before us is: Can we Change? In Time? . . . And *Theory?* How are we to proceed without *Theory?* (p. 13)

But shall we rethink these symptoms again, this time with a methodological note offered in Samuel Delany's (1988) short meditation on an event and its narrative reconstruction in his own education? The strategy of making method from fiction is a central one in psychoanalytic writing. de Certeau (1993) explains this shift in terms of conceptual shorthand: "fiction as being a knowledge jeopardized and wounded by its otherness (the affect, etc.) . . . In the analytic field, this discourse is effective because it is 'touched' or wounded by the affect" (p. 27). Precisely because fiction has no authority—in that it is not in mastery of its meaning, but voices the ambivalences of its flaws—fiction has the capacity to touch itself and then be wounded. And although, traditionally, educational studies have a history of legitimating themselves through the authority of social science, this turn to literature as a model for both pedagogy and social theory is one that may be capable of imagining the vicissitudes of love and hate in learning.[10] Still, the making of this sort of method is not bound by the rules of application, but rather, following the detours fiction offers, the only rule is that of implication, a willingness to be touched without the consolation of prior knowledge or even an understanding of its effects.

We return to the ninth grade, Delany's first day in the prestigious Bronx High School of Science. Well actually, Delany comes to narrate this event

---

can be made, in constituting this AIDS novella, is the self/other in all of its various transient guises. What is followed is the course of an event and its alternation by otherness.

[10]See, for example, Young-Bruehl's (1996) study of the failure of social science to theorize prejudices and her turn to the literature of Robert Musil.

in three conjectures of time: the ethnographic, or the place of detail; the reflective, or the consideration of significance and its anxieties; and the uncanny, or the force of secrets, where affect and idea might touch and in that erotic connection begin the work of reparation. The time is wounded, out of joint.[11] And yet the time affects something surprising, what Sue Golding (1993) calls "a 'route' a mapping, an impossible geography—impossible because *it exists and does not exist exactly at the same time*" (p. 166).

The first telling is filled with the romance of the ethnographic: A 15-year-old Delany enters the classroom for that first day, peruses his new classmates, complies with the teacher's request that the students' rearrange themselves through alphabetizing their seating order, and then he listens to the teacher's request that classmates nominate someone for student government. A boy named Chuck nominates Delany, and Delany wins the election. In this ethnographic telling, perhaps too good to be true, too easy to tell, everything happens well: his peers acclaim him, he meets a new friend, and his teacher seems friendly.

In the second telling of the story, these details return as difference, as anxiety. Writes Delany (1988), "what strikes me is how quickly the written narrative closes out—puts it outside of language" (p. 25). There resides an older story buried and preserved by the ethnographic present. What our 15-year-old Delany notices that first day and cannot bear to leave alone is the beautiful hand of Chuck. It is through noticing the beauty of Chuck's hand that Delany begins to fall in love. In this second telling, what is told is the body of Chuck: his height, the color of his shirt, the fall of his hair, the tone of his skin, the way he sighs. In the momentary chaos of the students finding their seats, our narrator loses sight of Chuck and in this loss, feels the loneliness of that first day. And then there is a panic: had I only imagined Chuck? If I see him again will I see the same Chuck I first saw? But through the coincidence of alphabetical seating, Delany finds himself in a seat to the left of Chuck. And then their hands can finally touch; the surprise comes in the form of a handshake. The touching of the hands leaves behind a trace. Yes, it is that same Chuck who nominates Delany. And so the moves of anxiety, that strange dialogue Delany sets up between the id and the ego, momentarily rest like a community of daydreams, until the next troubling of the telling.

There is always more to the story. That excess makes our third sense of time, the uncanny, what both tells have not yet noticed. Still, the uncanny can only be examined in bits and pieces, too late really, for whereas its persistent force depends on it being buried, its return is never complete.

---

[11]Derrida (1994) calls this out of joint time, "learning to live," a learning to live with ghosts. The principle is *"non-contemporaneity with itself of the living present* . . . this respect for justice concerning those who *are not there"* (p. xix). This sort of learning, perhaps the work of mourning, is what AIDS education must also invoke.

This, after, all is the complex of repression. In commenting on the second retelling and in the refinding of the lost quota of affect that returns, Delany maintains that his first story—the ethnographic one—does not explain the second try at retelling. Readers are offered an interminable question, "Why speak of what's uncomfortable to speak of?" (Delany, 1988, p. 29). Delany might be worried about how his story can be understood, how his imagined readers may lend their own continuities, their own identificatory thinking, and then shatter his fragile obligation. Delany may be worried about the reader's capacity to undo what has already been done, and to isolate the affect from its idea. In this curious architecture, where the imagined boundaries of the inside and the outside refuse to be known, Delany (1988) tests his narrative experiment with the following paradox:

> If it *is* the split—the space between two columns (one resplendent and lucid with the writings of legitimacy, the other dark and hollow with the voices of the illegitimate)—that constitutes the subject, it is only after the Romantic inflation of the private into the subjective that such a split can even be located. (pp. 29–30)

That space that signifies the split between falling in love and recounting that first day as if there was no fall means there can be no making of reparation. The discomfort is the symptom of that split between the aggression of social rejection over the form of love and an Eros that must risk contact.

"Why speak of the uncomfortable?" Part of the answer, for Delany's (1988) method, is to locate "the where" of the discomfort and, of course, the split:

> What damages might [this other story] do to women, children, the temperamentally more refined, the socially ignorant, the less well-educated, those with a barely controlled tendency toward the perverse . . . ? Since publishing it in most cases explains nothing or nothing of the public narrative, why not let it remain privy, personal, privileged—outside of language? (p. 29)

Samuel Delany cannot keep outside of language what is inside himself. One boy falls in love with another boy. The authority says, "Keep this love to yourself and therefore renounce it. Surrender your desires for the sake of the social. Identify with the aggressor. Undo, isolate, don't touch." We are back to the ethnographic story of AIDS in education, a story that contains the logic of repression, a certain burial and preservation, a story that explains nothing, designed not to notice. Delany's three senses of time are a working through, a desire not to "blow away" the event but to live in its affective force and to tolerate its interminable obligations, to tolerate touching and being touched.

What might pedagogy learn from Delany's retelling and from the other sentences considered? We will promise nothing and not expect too much. I sketch three moves in relation to a pedagogy of AIDS that attempts the work of reparation, for this belated work begins with the recognition that something can be destroyed, that education can inflict harm, strengthen the superego's prohibitions, turn these prohibitions into satisfaction, isolate the ego from the id. Again, because we are considering some psychical consequences of learning and unlearning, the three moves are not being taken as progressions. Indeed, if we are to sketch an impossible geography, our efforts might imitate the work of a kaleidoscope: with each turn, a variation of perspective, accidents, coincident.

In a pedagogy that attempts to address the question of AIDS, the first move must reside in ethnographic stories of AIDS, noticing the contradictory details of syndrome, of the HIV virus, of the woeful disregard of the event, of ACT UP, of the language of AIDS. The historicity of terminology must be accounted, from its beginning around 1976 as a discourse of "gay-related immune deficiency" to the four H-groups (Homosexuals, Hemophiliacs, Haitians, Heroin users) and on to what Paula Treichler (1988) has called "the epidemic of signification." The ethnographic are the stories of discourses and the constitution of bodies of knowledge and knowledge of bodies. But also, this history should be situated in a larger study of illness and then the study of how societies across time go about distinguishing the healthy from the ill, the guilty from the innocent, the general public from the risk group. The ethnographic stories must consider cacophonous perspectives and arguments between and within communities. To defy the impulse to think that representation is the answer, the ethnographic must examine its own wounds: fiction, music, dance, film, journalism. The ethnographic move is curricular, necessary, and insufficient, demanding much in the way of engagement from teachers. As it turns out, the ethnographic cannot divide itself from its own anxiously uncanny.

So, the ethnographic must be returned to, disrupted with a second move, a reflective narrative addressed to the ego's anxieties and defenses and to the strange time of delay. The significance at stake has to do with the work of perception, hallucination, and reality testing. The ego will be warned that it is being interfered with, that it should try to notice when it stops noticing, that it should confront its fears before its fears diminish its capacity to respond. This is an exploration of how the work of not noticing, although seemingly strengthening the ego's mechanisms of defense, actually aggravates forces of aggression and militates against being touched, the desire to make reparation. The pedagogy that must address the ego resides in the fault lines of resistance: where meaning breaks down, becomes fragile, loses its object, defies certitude, becomes ambivalent. There must be an address to the ego where the ego is asked to risk its history of libidinality, enlarge itself really, and attempt something generous, like a debt one cannot repay but must nevertheless acknowledge. The complex of symptoms that constitute the subject's responses to AIDS will be explored. We can bring in the spectres of life once lived and consider the interminable, the work of mourning.

In all of this, one more movement must be incited. We are referring to the uncanny, where the force of the return of the repressed can bother the ego's work of consolation. The force of the uncanny, that place of secrets, fragments, really, must be traced in order for Eros to be centered, in order for the bodily ego, that frontier creature, to risk the vulnerabilities of love. Our topic moves to safer-sex practices, to the difficulties of these practices, to the vicissitudes of sexualities and to what sexualities notice. This third move refuses the taboo against touching, against becoming touched and touching AIDS. And perhaps, in this third move, the ego can begin to place AIDS in its own every day, in the ordinary process of thought. Still, as with any learning, the pedagogy that attempts to approach its own inconsolability, its own uncanny, is not in charge of itself but lingers in the fault lines of its own hesitations, its belatedness.

We can now return to Freud's curious calculations of the ego's potential. "Where id was there ego shall be." The sentence is offered as a beginning to a psychoanalytic cure, a potential space that refuses transcendence, perfection, and immunity from being touched. The ego may fall in love so as not to fall ill. But in falling in love, the ego makes itself ill—vulnerable really—to the wishes and obligations of others, to the question and insistence of loss, and to the failure of knowledge. The story of love is the story of learning to love, of tolerating the question and the vicissitudes of desire. The ego shall become as generous as the id. This returns us to the question of ethicality and the ego's interest in making reparation. For education, it is something like the capacity to be touched by its own flaws. This is the learning that can tolerate its own failure of knowledge, which can tolerate the detours of not understanding.

The pedagogy that offers no consolation, that cannot help education save itself, is the pedagogy that forces itself to explore the vicissitudes of love and the fragile work of making reparation. These are certainly the obligations AIDS poses, and, too, the obligation posed by any learning. We can call this pedagogy "whatever" and still make of it some psychical consequence. We must wonder "where id was and where ego shall be." The pedagogy allows a community of egos to approach a community of daydreams, and then craft that work of in-betweenness, a potential space, an impossible geography, a question of freedom. But then, the question is no longer "Why speak of the unspeakable" but instead, "What is reparation in this learning?"

REFERENCES

Balint, A. (1954). *The early years of life: A psychoanalytic study.* New York: Basic Books.

Bollas, C. (1992). *Becoming a character: Psychoanalysis and self experience.* New York: Hill & Wang.

Britzman, D. P. (1998). *Lost subjects, contested objects: Toward a psychoanalytic inquiry of learning.* Albany: SUNY Press.

Canguilhem, G. (1991). *The normal and the pathological* (C. Fawcett, Trans.). New York: Zone Books.

Cornell, D. (1995). *The imaginary domain: Abortion, pornography and sexual harassment.* New York: Routledge.

de Certeau, M. (1993). *Heterologies: Discourse on the other* (B. Massumi, Trans.). Minneapolis: University of Minnesota Press.

Delany, S. (1988). *The motion of light in water: Sex and science fiction in the East Village, 1957–1965.* New York: William Morrow.

Delany, S. (1994). *Flight from Neveryon.* Hanover, NH: Wesleyan University Press.

Derrida, J. (1994). *Spectres of Marx: The state of the debt, the work of mourning, and the new international* (P. Kamuf, Trans.). New York: Routledge.

Erikson, E. (1968). *Identity: Youth and crisis.* New York: W. W. Norton.

Felman, S. (1987). *Jacques Lacan and the adventure of insight: Psychoanalysis in contemporary culture.* Cambridge, MA: Harvard University Press.

Freud, A. (1995). *The ego and the mechanisms of defence, revised edition: The writings of Anna Freud, volume II.* Madison, WI: International University Press. (Original work published 1936)

Freud, S. (1968a). "Inhibitions, Symptoms, and Anxiety (1926 [1925])." In J. Strachey, A. Freud, A. Strachey, & A. Thompson (Eds.), *The standard edition of the complete psychological works of Sigmund Freud, vol. XX, 1925–1926.* London: Hogarth Press.

Freud, S. (1968b). "An Autobiographic Study (1925 [1924])." Vol. XX pp. 7–76.

Freud, S. (1968c). "The Question of Lay Analysis: Conversations with an Impartial Person (1926)." Vol. XX, pp. 179–258.

Freud, S. (1968d). "New Introductory Lectures (1933 [1932])." Vol. XXII, pp. 3–184.

Freud, S. (1968e). "The Ego and the Id. (1923)." Vol. XIX, 1923–1925, pp. 3–66.

Golding, S. (1993). Sexual manners. *Public, 8,* 161–168.

Haver, W. (1996). *The body of this death: Historicity and sociality in the time of AIDS.* Stanford, CA: Stanford University Press.

Klein, M. (1994). *Love, guilt and reparation and other works, 1921–1945.* London: Virago.

Kushner, T. (1994). *Angels in America: A gay fantasia on national themes, part two: Perestroika.* New York: Theatre Communications.

Lyotard, J.-F. (1991). *The inhuman: Reflections on time* (G. Bennington & R. Bowlby, Trans.). Stanford, CA: Stanford University Press.

Patton, C. (1996). *Fatal advice: How safe-sex education went wrong.* Durham, NC: Duke University Press.

Readings, B. (1996). *The university in ruins.* Cambridge, MA: Harvard University Press.

Rose, J. (1993). *Why war?: Psychoanalysis, politics, and the return to Melanie Klein.* London: Blackwell.

Sachs, H. (1947). Community of daydreams. In S. Lorand (Ed.), *Yearbook of psychoanalysis, vol. I, 1945* (pp. 281–302). New York: International University Press.

Schulman, S. (1990). *People in trouble.* New York: Dutton.

Silin, J. (1995). *Sex, death and the education of children: Our passion for ignorance in the age of AIDS.* New York: Teachers College Press.

Treichler, P. (1988). AIDS, homophobia, and biomedical discourse: An epidemic of signification. In D. Crimp (Ed.), *AIDS: Cultural analysis, cultural criticism* (pp. 31–70). Cambridge, MA: MIT Press.

Winnicott, D. (1986). *Home is where we start from: Essays by a psychoanalyst.* New York: W. W. Norton.

Young-Bruehl, E. (1996). *The anatomy of prejudices.* Cambridge, MA: Harvard University Press.

Chapter 17

We "Were Already Ticking and Didn't Even Know" [It]: Early AIDS Works

Roger Platizky
Austin College

> . . . *it is how and what one remembers that defines much of AIDS literature . . . and film.*
>
> —Clum (1993, p. 208)

With 20 million people already infected worldwide with HIV, it would be an act of sublime denial not to realize that AIDS has already deeply entrenched itself into our world's history and consciousness as well as its bloodstream. As difficult as it might now be to remember, there was a time before AIDS, a pre-history that made its presence felt like a gradually darkening sky before an eclipse. This premonitory mood, a time of increasing anxiety and epistemological uncertainty, can be detected in many early works about AIDS, especially those written by middle-class gay men who were among the first stigmatized (yet vocal) minorities to be ambushed by this disease. Frequently in these early works of witnessing, testimony, survival, and loss, there is a boundary drawn between the "Before" and "After," an imaginary line that divides the pre-history of AIDS from the point of no return. Especially within gay literature and film, the "Before" stage is often remembered with longing that comes close to being prelapsarian, whereas the "After" stage is an inconclusive journey—part heroic quest, part death march—because there is still no known cure for those afflicted with the disease. We find this pattern illustrated, and occasionally challenged, in many early works about AIDS and, perhaps, most notably in the influential works *And the Band Played On* (by Randy Shilts, 1988),

Borrowed Time (by Paul Monette, 1988), *The Normal Heart* (by Larry Kramer, 1985), and *Longtime Companion* (written by Craig Lucas; directed by Norman Rene, 1990).

A key distinction between the "Before" and "After" stages of AIDS is emphasized in these early works on the disease. In *And the Band Played On*, Randy Shilts (1988), who chronicles the impact of AIDS from its inception to the creation of the Quilt, writes with the gift of tragic hindsight, "Before and after. The epidemic would cleave lives in two. . . . Before meant innocence and excess, idealism and hubris. More than anything, this was the time before death" (p. 12). In the elegiac AIDS novel *Borrowed Time*, Paul Monette (1988) designates the post-diagnosis stage of AIDS as the time he and his lover, Roger Horowitz, "began to live on the moon" (p. 2), the "before" stage having been a very secure time of living with protective economic status on the earth before "time itself began to seem a minefield, the year ahead wired with booby traps" (p. 17). As the death toll mounts, Paul and Rog have trouble sometimes even remembering the time before the siege: "my friends in LA can hardly recall what it felt like any longer, the time before the sickness" (p. 2). This sentiment is echoed both in Harvey Fierstein's (1987) play *Safe Sex*—"We can never be as before 'Now' will always define us" (p. 58)—and in Susan Sontag's (1986) short story "The Way We Live Now"—"everybody is worried about everybody now . . . , that seems to be the way we live, the way we live now" (p. 5). In *Longtime Companion*, the Fire-Island survivor, Willy, summarizes the calamity between the Before and After: "Seems inconceivable doesn't it? that there was ever a time before all this when we didn't wake up everyday wondering who's sick now, who else is gone."

Although there were premonitory rumblings before the cataclysm struck, few were heeded: the "tip of the iceberg" remained barely visible because, as Monette (1988) contends, just about everybody—from the media and the government to the medical field and the individuals first infected—were practicing enough denial "to power Chernobyl" (p. 64). Denial, of course, was aided not only by political conservatism and homophobia, but also by the insidious nature of the disease itself. According to Andrew Holleran in his introduction to *The Normal Heart*, AIDS arrived at the ball, like Poe's red death, wearing a mask. In the beginning of *And the Band Played On*, Shilts (1988) personifies AIDS—a not-yet-named or recognized disease—even more stealthily:

> To be sure, Death was already elbowing its way through the crowds on that sunny morning, like a rude tourist angling for the lead spot in the [Gay Pride] parade. It was still an invisible presence, though, palpable only to twenty, or perhaps thirty, gay men who were suffering from a vague malaise. This handful ensured that the future and the past met on that single day. (p. 12)

Like Shilts, Monette and Holleran describe human blindness to the onset of AIDS as a product of tragically ironic fate. Comparing the sudden volatility of AIDS to a time bomb, Monette (1988) writes, "A lot of us were already ticking and didn't even know" (p. 5). Alluding to the epistemological confusion that attended the first stages of the Holocaust, he adds, "The disappearing had begun" (p. 19). Holleran, in his collection of essays, *Ground Zero* (1988), compares the onset of AIDS to nuclear fallout in an unsuspecting city: "The bomb fell without anyone's knowing the bomb had fallen" (p. 22). Perhaps ironically, or even prophetically, Holleran had foreshadowed this "nuclear" nightmare in his pre-AIDS novel, *Dancer From the Dance* (1978) when he described the Lower West Side as a wasteland where the "whores, the bums, the pimps . . . , the pieces of garbage blowing in the wind, the metallic tops of garbage cans all stood out in the surreal, radioactive glare of the atom bomb" (p. 147). Even more presciently, Holleran's protagonist, Malone, says before he disappears in an apocalyptic fire at the Everard Baths, "Imagine a pleasure in which the moment of satisfaction is simultaneous with the moment of destruction: to kiss is to poison."

Holleran's friend and contemporary, Larry Kramer (1978), had, of course, sounded the alarm against sexual excesses even earlier in the gay community when he had his protagonist, Fred Lemish, proclaim in the controversial novel *Faggots*, "It all needs to change . . . before you fuck yourself to death." As arguably erotophobic as he has been accused of being, Kramer, more than the other writers of early AIDS literature, holds individuals accountable for their fates, even though external forces—homophobia, denial, political genocide—are also heatedly blamed. Even so, the first pages of Kramer's *The Normal Heart* are filled with rhetorical signs of the epistemological confusion that AIDS caused before it was known in any other way than by its deadly effects. Panicked phrases like "I know something's wrong"; "They're inside me"; "Dr. Brookner, what's happening?"; "I don't know. . . . Not even any good clues yet"; "What is going on in your bodies?" show that denial was just one of the problems ushered in by this new, misunderstood, and terrifying plague. Thus, if infected people—educated, literate, and sensitive—were slow in reading the handwriting on the wall, maybe that was because the writing, initially, was as cryptically encoded as the HIV virus itself.

Two other shared ways that many early AIDS works differentiate the "Before" from the "After" stages of the crisis are by contrasting the impact that AIDS has had on formerly healthy—even beautiful—bodies and by associating the "Before" period with nearly prelapsarian nostalgia. Two vivid examples of this first kind of differentiation are found in Shilts's accounts of what Gaetan Dugas ("Patient Zero") and Simon Guzman come to represent as a result of AIDS. About the former, Shilts (1988) writes: "At one time, Gaetan had been what every man wanted from gay life; by the time he died, he had become what every man feared" (p. 439). In describing the latter, Shilts's contrasts a "Before" picture of Simon Guzman looking tanned, smooth, taut, and muscular to an "After" portrait: "Simon Guzman's body now, however, was barely more than a skeleton with sallow, lesion-covered skin sagging loosely, and tubes coursing in every conceivable orifice and vein" (p. 121). In his early short story "Slim" (in which AIDS is never named but consistently implied), Adam Mars-Jones (1986) has his stricken character describe his own "Before" and "After" stages in socio-economic terms: ". . . to understand what was happening to me perhaps I should think of having fifty years added to my age, or suddenly having Third World expectations instead of First" (p. 21). Not unexpectedly, we find this particular kind of "Before" and "After" pattern also in recent works about AIDS. For example in Edmund White's (1995) collection of short stories *Skinned Alive*, the narrator of "Running on Empty" describes Luke as having "been a brilliant student. Now . . . his brain was usually fuzzy—becoming like overcooked minestrone during the toxoplasmosis crisis" (p. 32). In Holleran's (1996) recent novel, *The Beauty of Men*, the formerly handsome friend Sutcliffe is unrecognizably "wasted, gaunt, skinny as a stick"; and in his best-selling novel *Like People in History*, Felice Picano (1995) describes the last stages of AIDS in Matt, a once-vibrant friend: "I held him by the shoulder, the skin burning, the fleshless joint almost pure anatomy" (p. 480). Those of us who are still witnessing the progressive stages of AIDS deterioration in people we know and love are no strangers to these kinds of transformations. We find similar examples of deterioration in *Borrowed Time* as Roger Horowitz—once a much-in-de-mand, brilliant lawyer—becomes jobless, blind, and completely incapaci-tated, and in *Longtime Companion* as David's lover Sean changes from a talented telescript writer to a dying man dribbling in diapers.

Because these "After" stages are so often associated with loss, deterio-ration, and despair, especially in early works on AIDS, it is small wonder that in the majority of AIDS works, particularly those written by gay men, the past or "Before" stage is frequently associated with idealism, bordering on fantasy, for a golden world lost. D. S. Lawson (1992), who finds this pattern in many early AIDS works, and most particularly in the play *As Is*, explains the phenomenon this way:

> Certainly this wistful remembrance of the past is meant to convey a positive gay image—a time when the gay men . . . were happy and more or less carefree. One is left hoping that somehow, miraculously, this world could return. (p. 148)

John M. Clum supports this position but argues, further, that this pattern is what distinguishes AIDS narratives written by gay and non-gay authors.

Whereas non-gay authors generally focus on the family of the PWA, gay writers emphasize "the characters' changed relationship to their past sexual activity" (p. 207). He adds insightfully that in "AIDS literature, one cry of anguish comes from the 'Stonewall generation,' who once thought they had found paradise and lost it through AIDS." Clum supports his conclusion in numerous ways, one of his best examples being the last scene of *Longtime Companion*. He interprets Willy's dream on the beach to be one not only of a "world without AIDS . . . of recapturing the past, of bringing his beloved friends back to life," but also a dream of restoring the "carnival [life] of the Fire Island summers" (p. 218). In fact, the lyrics of the music that is playing while Willy fantasizes support this claim:

> Do you remember when the world was like a carnival openin' up?
> If I could have one day with you the way it used to be
> All the things I should have said would pour outta me. . . .

This kind of search for an Edenic past is also poignantly captured in *Borrowed Time* (Monette, 1988) when Roger is "looking out toward the garden, though by then he could scarcely see the light. He cried out softly, in an agonized voice, 'What happened to our happy life?' " (p. 352). With similar nostalgia, he and Paul also remember the days when their eventful calendars were full of exciting prospects and not empty except for torturous doctor's visits; when their enviable Saturday nights were shared vicariously by their parents, not alone in rented hospital rooms; when their Fourth of July parties were spent overlooking "the Hatch Shell where the Boston Pops held forth to a half million people"—before all the sparkles of those fireworks vanished into the dark night forever. In contrast, Elizabeth Cox (1990), in her heterosexual AIDS journal, *Thanksgiving*, associates the past with something fallen. Although she considers her husband Keith Avedon's AIDS diagnosis as the end of her old life—"the life I had lived, no longer existed—and never would again" (p. 34)—she also avoids thinking about her husband's past—"In my effort to accept AIDS I created a taboo of my husband's past" (p. 24) because Keith had been involved in gay relationships.

Although the majority of the gay writers of this period hold an antithetical point of view about the past (particularly the sexually liberated past), Larry Kramer is one major gay author of the period who refuses to view the past so romantically. In *The Normal Heart*, Kramer's (1985) spokesman, Ned Weeks, accuses the gay leaders of the liberation movement of having "been the death of us." Although this viewpoint is challenged, and somewhat mitigated, by the liberationist Mickey, who reminds Ned "how important it was for us to love without hiding, without guilt" (p. 103), the only paradisical image in the play is the ironic one of the 2-million-dollar home Ned's lawyer brother, Ben, plans to build: a utopian mansion on "some land in Greenwhich, by a little river, completely protected by trees" (p. 43)—as if this Arcadia could keep death out. For Ned, hope does not come from remembering the sexual liberation of the "Before" stage, and it does not come from building utopian fortresses in suburbia, but rather from looking back further into the past, before Stonewall, and reclaiming cultural heroes like Socrates, Michelangelo, Leonardo da Vinci, Dag Hammarskjöld, and Alan Turing, who had to hide their gay sexuality from a persecutory world without giving up the gifts they still chose to share with humanity.

Kramer's play also ends with some uncharacteristic hope about the "After" stage of AIDS, as he tells his deceased lover Felix about a gay and lesbian dance, attended by 600 "smart, exceptional men and women" on the Yale campus across from the "tiny freshman room where I wanted to kill myself because I thought I was the only gay man in the world" (p. 123). Because Kramer had not been diagnosed with AIDS at the time he wrote this early play, that may explain why some of the hope of the "After" stage in *The Normal Heart* is not replicated in the ending of his more recent play *The Destiny of Me* (1993), written after Kramer's AIDS diagnosis. In this more recent play, Ned Weeks asks, "What do you do when you're dying from a disease you need not be dying from?" (p. 17) and concludes, alluding to his roles both in GMHC and ACT UP, "I failed them. I wanted to be Moses but I could only be Cassandra" (p. 87). At the end of the play, Ned, having yanked his transfusion tubes out of his arms and smashed six bags of blood against the hospital walls, plaintively concedes after this orgy of rage, "I want to stay a little longer" (p. 122).

As we all "stay a little longer" with this disease, where will prophecy and representation take us next? At present, the "After" stage of AIDS is, by necessity, inconclusive because there is still no cure, though the new protease inhibitors and combination therapies seem promising enough to make HIV a chronic instead of an always-fatal disease. New hope is also offered by world AIDS conferences and other global, national, and grass-roots efforts to contain and combat this disease. Nevertheless, it will likely take years before most of the non-industrialized world will be able to afford any of the newly proclaimed, but very expensive, treatments to fight AIDS. By correspondence, it would not be surprising to find signs of guarded optimism in contemporary works about AIDS. Already in plays like *Jeffrey* and *Angels in America*, we find more evidence, respectively, of humor and spirituality as AIDS becomes less foregrounded in works of art and more a part of the fuller tapestry of life's experiences. Although gallows humor and spirituality have been present in AIDS works from the onset of the disease (for instance, in *And the Band Played On* and in *Longtime Companion*), the humor and spirituality today more than in the past might be considered what Linda and Michael Hutchon (1996) have termed new "countermy-thologies" in AIDS works or, more precisely, ways to "wrest from the domi-nant culture the wholly negative if not annihilative representation of HIV infection and AIDS to instruct in its stead a discourse of empowerment, meaning, and possibility" (p. 222). We find a revisionist example of another kind of this countermythology in Peter Cashorali's (1995) *Fairy Tales: Tra-ditional Stories Retold for Gay Men* in which the postmodern answer to Rum-pelstiltskin's new riddle to a gay man instead of a maiden—"Why are you HIV positive?"—receives the correct reply, "It's just something that was there—a terrible one, but just a virus" (pp. 50–52). A similar kind of empowerment and healing can also be located in the testimonies—both spiritual and secular—from long-term survivors, AIDS activists, and celeb-rities: from Michael Callen and Mary Fisher to Greg Louganis and Magic Johnson. Although future works about AIDS will continue to witness, warn, and commemorate those who have already been impacted by this disease, the shapes those works take, the voices invoked, and the details emphasized are likely to be richly variable. Among the many different groups now affected worldwide by this disease—people of different races, genders, ages, classes, religions, and ideologies—the narrative responses to AIDS in future years will be as mutable as the virus—and the treatments used to combat it—may become. As John Clum wisely reminds us, the way we remember is as important as what we remember. In fact, in responses to AIDS, "re-membering [does] become a central act." And who among the witnesses to AIDS, past, present, and future—prophets of hope, doom, and irreso-lution—would not agree with Willy of *Longtime Companion* when, looking back upon the high and low tides of his memories, he affirms, "I just want to be there if they ever find a cure" and with Holleran (1988) when he writes in *Ground Zero*, "We want there to be a whistle, or siren, that signals 'All Clear' " (p. 48)?

REFERENCES

Cashorali, P. (1995). *Fairy tales: Traditional stories retold for gay men.* San Francisco: Harper.
Clum, J. M. (1993). "And once I had it all": AIDS narratives and memories of an American dream. In T. Murphy & S. Poirier (Eds.), *Writing AIDS: Gay literature, language, and analysis* (p. 208). New York: Columbia University Press.
Cox, E. (1990). *Thanksgiving: An AIDS journal.* New York: Harper & Row.
Fierstein, H. (1987). *Safe sex.* New York: Atheneum.
Holleran, A. (1986). *Dancer from the dance.* New York: Plume. (Original work published 1978)
Holleran, A. (1988). *Ground zero: Essays.* New York: William Morrow.
Holleran, A. (1996). *The beauty of men: A novel.* New York: William Morrow.
Hutchon, L., & Hutchon, M. (1996). *Opera: Desire disease death.* Lincoln: University of Nebraska Press.
Kramer, L. (1978). *Faggots.* New York: Random House.

Kramer, L. (1985). *The normal heart.* New York: NAL.

Kramer, L. (1993). *The destiny of me.* New York: Plume.

Lawson, D. S. (1992). Rage and remembrance: The AIDS plays. In E. S. Nelson (Ed.), *AIDS: The literary response* (p. 148). New York: Twayne.

Lucas, C. (1990). *Longtime companion* (N. Rene, director). American Playhouse for PBS.

Mars-Jones, A. (1986). Slim. In S. O. Warner (Ed.), *The way we write now: Short stories from the AIDS crisis.* New York: Citadel Press.

Monette, P. (1988). *Borrowed time.* New York: Avon.

Picano, F. (1995). *Like people in history.* New York: Viking.

Shilts, R. (1988). *And the band played on.* New York: Penguin.

Sontag, S. (1986). The way we live now. In S. O. Warner (Ed.), *The way we write now: Short stories from the AIDS crisis.* New York: Citadel Press.

White, E. (1995). *Skinned alive.* New York: Alfred A. Knopf.

Four Poems
by
Roger Platizky

Coming Out

When I was invisible from Me
The face in the mirror smiled back
In recognition of a son's face, for a child's choice.

When I became visible to Me
The face in the mirror stared back
Like a stranger through a darkened window.

When I became visible to Me but invisible to the World
The face in the mirror knew me but paled
Afraid it would never be held or smiled at again.

When I became visible to Me and the World,
The face in many men's eyes
Looked back
And I, the son of the father,
No longer stared alone at my own reflection.

Denied Too Long

The boys scouts are always prepared
To reject him
If they can find him
In their pup-tents
Behind their crackling fires.
The military will allow them
To march across the windy desert,
Get sprayed with napalm and agent orange
So long as their purple hearts
Don't bleed into pink triangles and red ribbons
As they march single file in the long veterans' parade.
The police force enjoy Cagney and Lacy
But only on television—
After all, the law **is** the law.
His art and her art
Are not art
So say the men at the helm of our culture
Who hold out insurance premiums
Like wild cards in a marked deck—
As if AZT and HIV were not part
of their alphabet

(This, too, is the law).
But we
Who have been burned and flogged,
Gassed and incinerated,
Stoned and pilloried
But we
Who have been excommunicated and blackmailed,
Despised and rejected,
Called sinful, insane,
Unnatural and abnormal
Yes, we
Who have been fired and shunned
Stigmatized and silenced
Even in this land of spacious skies and specious lies,
Reject the unutterable chants
The unkind, unholy political slants
That deny a whole people
The way a blind astronomer
Misses a firmament of dazzling stars
Ever growing in number
Symphonic like the sky.

Unforgotten
(for my friend Kirk)

Hospice. He is looking at
The gold leaves on the memorial wall,
And I can almost tell, looking
Behind his back,
Behind his long, flowing hair
That he is staring, staring
At his own name and wondering
Who will notice, years from now,
Who will notice and remember him
Before KS scarred his lovely skin
Before shingles made track marks down his back
That bore so many other people's struggles.

I cannot tell him that
I am watching him with the same waitful eyes
That turn from channel to channel
As I try to escape from Bosnia and Waco,
Try to escape from my own
Small, expanding circle of pain.

But not for you with the Loreal hair,
Not for you with the X-rated smile and GQ spirit,

Oh, not for you with the eyes like crystals
That were made to dance and never deserved to break
But like bronze flashing out in gold memory,
Blazing off the wall of so much loss,
Like a million banners at the Pride march
Resisting, then gusting through the wind
Like your flowing bright hair
Forcing our eyes to stare
And remember who you were and will always be.

David's Poem

Around the AIDS quilt
in Ft. Worth, Texas,
A perimeter of bright white cloth
Narrowly separates
The living from the dead.
For two years, David,
We tried to keep you away from that frightening edge
With AZT and DDI,
With Donna's kalaches and Charlotte's hugs
With Judy's stuffed animals and Trudy's stained glass
With Martha's cute cards and Gene's gentle shaves
With Jerry's strong shoulders and Kenneth's rejoinders
With new squeak toys for Prissy
And enough cartons of high-tar cigarettes
To scare away even the Marlboro Man.

As your limp worsened
And your breath and body grew thinner and thinner,
The red ribbon in your black hat began to glow,
And we tired to lure you to stay
With promises of future cures
And food drives and fund raisers
With fishing trips and service awards
With visits from your family
And presents for your final Christmas.
We even let you paint Glen's orderly white walls
In Pepto-Bismol pink,
Circus colors
To scare away the nightmares
And fill the sky with angels.

But despite all our best efforts,
You still eluded us, David,
Stared down at all those names
In gold and green, in denim and velvet

And at all those tributes in crepe and crayon
And at all the friends you had lost and lost and lost
Until on a day of blinding Texas sun,
You found your own name spelled out in red roses
While we stared back at the eclipse in silence.

Chapter 18

Of Mad Men Who Practice Invention to the Brink of Intelligibility

William Haver
Binghamton University

> *. . . I practice invention to the brink of intelligibility . . .*
> —Timothy Hasler, in Samuel R. Delany (1994a), *The Mad Man*

For a very long time now, we—teachers and those who think about teaching—have come perilously close to a consensus. Almost unanimously, we have very nearly agreed that the pedagogical enterprise is about the production of subjects. True, we disagree, sometimes quite vehemently, about the nature of that subjectivity—about whether it is the actualization in beings of a possibility immanent in being itself or is historically embodied; about whether it is the expression of a natural ontology or a coming-to-culture as a separation from nature; or about whether subjectivity is constituted and maintained in a relation to an abstract, disembodied reason or is the sensible manifestation of an identity. And we by no means agree on the goals or effects of pedagogical practice—whether pedagogy is about the production of good citizens loyal to a transcendent community to the point of self sacrifice, or about the cultivation of a critical, thorny, irascible intelligence; whether the point is to precipitate among our students the recognition of a certain self (mathematician, physicist, historian, teacher, African American, woman, man, lesbian, gay, "human being," for example) in the specularity of our wisdom and mastery, or whether as intellectual heros in the making they are to disavow such identifications. And we incessantly worry a certain disagreement over the techniques of pedagogical practices—whether we should take upon ourselves the mastery of the Father who judges and disciplines his and/or her students according to their distance from the True and the Good, or be good Mothers who nurture our broods into feeling good about themselves. Yet, not so much in spite of, but in and by means of our very real disagreements, we incessantly confirm our agreement, stultifying if not fatal for any thought of the queer, that pedagogy is the work of *Bildung*, a coming to subjectivity as jubilant and relieved self-recognition. Born to stupidity, our students need us, we are almost agreed.

Such a near agreement on the nature of the pedagogical enterprise can be sustained, however, only according to the protocols of a prior agreement that there exists an essential relation between the pedagogical and the philosophical, as well as the institutions that sustain both. Maurice Blanchot (1993) has argued that philosophy has long been "a form of teaching," and that, at least since Kant (which is to say, in our "modernity"), the philosopher has been, not simply by virtue of institutional contingency, a professor; thought, and philosophy as thought thinking to think the thought of thinking, has been necessarily bound to the cultural work of *Bildung*. Conversely, pedagogy—however inarticulate it most often has been on the matter—has always, at least since Kant, been committed to philosophy as the aspiration to explain the world, to "speculate the elements" and elaborate the "systems of the world," to make sense, and to transmit the sense that it makes, and in that transmission to bring the stupid to subjectivity, however construed. At least ideally, thought might master that of which it thinks, thought might master that which provokes thought; a subjectivity rescued from stupidity would be that enlightened mastery of Enlightenment itself, divorced from its object, almost.

Almost. Historically of course, and even within the "history of philosophy," there have been any number of exceptions to this agreement on pedagogy as a coming-to-"philosophical"-subjectivity. Most germane to our present concerns with queer thought and education, however, is the fact that this agreement, as well as the agreements that maintain it, cannot be sustained against the existential insistence of the social, of which queer studies, queer politics, queer thought, and our queer lives are multiple articulations. What I am calling the existential insistence of the social—that which profoundly interrupts the scene of an agreement—has two principal foci in the current situation. The existential insistence of the social (a phrase which it is the entire purpose of this essay to elaborate) comes to us first of all as that infinite loss we call the AIDS pandemic. The social insists first of all as that untranscendable interruption that is the death of friends, lovers, and strangers; the insistence of the social emerges first of all as utter abjection, absolute extremity (see Haver, 1996). Yet at the same time, the social insists as the affirmation of another extremity, the extremity of pleasure, and in the affirmation of the impossibility of dissociating pleasure from abjection. As a matter of existential exigency, the pandemic has taught us the impossibility of any securely discrete conjugation of abject mortality and pleasure. Nowhere is this more apparent—or more vehemently disavowed—than in the various discourses on safer-sex education and in the abysmal failure of safer-sex education with its assumption that reason necessarily leads to "good action" and the further assumption that it is only duty, not pleasure, that risks extremity to think the sociality that is at stake in a pandemic that is, after all, strictly contemporaneous (not accidentally) with the emergence of queer theory, queer politics, and queer culture in the Anglophone world (see Hart, 1996; Odets, 1995, 1996; Patton, 1997; Wickham, 1997). Here the social insists as that primordial contamination that *is* our (queer) being-in-common.

If the existential insistence of the social makes itself felt as an irrecusable encounter with extremity, with the extremity of suffering and the extremity of pleasure, it is also, and not coincidentally, articulated as an infinite proliferation of difference, of identities and identifications, as a certain impossibility of containment, that is to say. The social insists as the endless proliferation of subjects, subject positions, cultural identities and identifications, that always and essentially exceed the capacity of any polity, liberal or otherwise, to adjudicate those differences that political philosophy assumes, at least in principle, to be finite: it is the very proliferation of subjectivities that makes it impossible to say what (least of all who) a political subject is. This is a point made very succinctly by Samuel R. Delany (1994b) when, having suggested that cities grow because people go there first of all to find sex (well, didn't you?), and that therefore it would be plausible to find cities to be "among the oldest of human institutions, rather than among the youngest," he speculates that "Sodom and Babel are our two archetypal cities, both destroyed by God (read: a mystified market collapse), both more likely mirror images, if not intimate explanations, one for the other" (p. 135). Here is a thought of sociality as a primordial conjunction of the erotic with an originary heteroglossia, the thought of an originary erotic contamination (of which the subject is simply one among multiple articulations, the "pseudopodia of sexuality," as Foucault says) conjugated with—and perhaps as—a proliferation of languages, differences ("cultural" and otherwise) so excessive that its differences cannot, can never be, never could have been, translated into a metalanguage, a philosophy, such as would simultaneously express and erase their differences. Here, then, is a thought of an erotic, heteroclite, queer sociality that cannot be mastered by thought (for the concept of this sociality is simply a concept of that which is irreducible to its concept).

So, queer thought, queer politics, perhaps even a queer pedagogy, emerges in a double relation: to the existential exigencies of the AIDS pandemic, and to the (excessive) proliferations of the social that necessarily figures for the thought as its supplement. In other words, in a double relation to extremity. At stake in both relations, and in and as their conjunction, is the erotic—an erotic relation to the extremity of pleasure, certainly, but also (and this is the difficult part) an erotic relation (strictly speaking, a relation of non-relation) to the extremity of abjection, to death. Here, it is precisely the erotic relation/non-relation that makes any consummation of thought, any final reunion of thought with itself in the concept, an impossibility; queer theory is queer only to the extent that it sustains an erotic relation/non-relation to the extremity that interrupts it: queer theory is queer precisely in its incompleteness. That queer theory might overcome that interruption, or resolve its essential incompleteness, that it might transcend the erotic, that thought might close in upon itself in the forgetting or occlusion of that of which it speaks, is a danger of which we have recently been warned by Bill Readings (1996) who writes that "A queer theory that canonizes a generalized idea of sexuality as and object of academic study is nothing more than the opening of sexuality to academic administration" (p. 211). It is a point underscored with particular reference to the AIDS pandemic by Simon Watney (1995) at the fifth annual Lesbian and Gay Studies Conference, and with particular reference to the erotic by Samuel R. Delany (1995) in his keynote address to the same conference. What if, Delany seems to ask, queer theory (or "lesbian and gay studies") were not so much about feeling good about oneself as about feeling good? And in *The Mad Man* (1994a), at once the *Bildungsroman* of a coming-to-philosophical-subjectivity (a pedagogy, therefore) and the unworking of that subjectivity, it is an erotic relation of non-relation to heteroclite, queer, sociality *in extremis* that interrupts the philosophico-pedagogical reunion of thought with itself in the concept.

    The Mad Man (Delany, 1994a), a "novel" according to the subtitle (and Bakhtin would not disagree), can be read as a congeries of multiple intersecting, but by no means coterminous, frequently contradictory, narratives.[1] We might, for example, identify a detective story (who killed Timothy Hasler?: David Franitz, as narrator-protagonist-detective John Mawr discovers), or a sentimentally satisfying love story (for John Mawr and Leaky Sowps live happily ever after). Both narratives obey the classical structures of their respective genres, above all in that both achieve narrative closure. But there is another narrative in *The Mad Man*, that of a philosophical *Bildungsroman*, the story of a coming-to-philosophical-subjectivity, of a becoming-a-philosopher, a narrative that inscribes a philosophico-pedagogi-

---

[1] It might almost go without saying that I am not interested here in reading *The Mad Man* from within a culture of aesthetic appreciation. Indeed, such a reading would be confounded by the anti-aesthetic of the novel itself. Rather, I am trying to be attentive to the text as a "philosophical novel," a *provocation* of certain irremediable questions.

cal trajectory. This is a story of the work of education, but also and at the same time, a story of the unworking of philosophical subjectivity, culture, and of philosophico-pedagogical desire. Insofar as it is at all points the story both of the work and unworking of philosophical subjectivity, insofar as it both does and does not achieve philosophical closure (for John Mawr both becomes and can never possibly become a "philosopher"), it sustains the question of the philosophical as the only philosophical question. It is only in a certain ultimate extremity, in Heraclitean *ekpyrosis*, in the all-consuming fire of an absolutely undifferentiated pure difference (at the very limit of thought, therefore), that the multiple narratives of the detective story, the love story, and the making and unmaking of a philosopher (in fact, of two philosophers: Timothy Hasler and John Mawr) coincide absolutely. And it is this extremity, which is not only a historical event, a philosophical crisis, or a narrative climax, that both unworks and sustains the aspiration to philosophical subjectivity; perhaps, indeed, the only possible coming-to-philosophical-culture here is sustained in and as its necessary incompletion.

Let us first of all rehearse, retrace, the trajectory of *The Mad Man* as *Bildungsroman*. Narrator, protagonist, and philosopher-to-be, John Mawr is the queer son of a middle-class African-American family from Staten Island. Something of an intellectual prodigy, and certainly sexually precocious, Mawr excels in elementary school, skipping "a couple" grades; he enters high school at 12, college at 16, and graduate school at 20. As an undergraduate at Enoch State College, Mawr encounters the Hegel of the *Philosophy of History* and the *Phenomenology*, and is inspired to undertake graduate work at Stilford University on the west coast in order to undertake the systematic philosophical articulation of the "Systems of the World." At this point, then, Mawr aspires to philosophy as metaphysics (indeed, later he will be woken from a dream by the words of Marlowe's *Doctor Faustus*, "Metaphysics, thou has ravished me!"); Mawr enters on philosophy in search of a thinking adequate to that which is its provocation (the "world" as totality), hoping to reunite thought with itself in the concept. But the first lesson he learns in the courses of his professionalization is that contemporary academic philosophy is structured around the resolute rejection not only of metaphysics, but of the question of the metaphysical altogether; professional academic philosophy constitutes itself *as* that rejection. What constitutes a putatively antimetaphysical philosophy these days, a chastened John Mawr gradually learns from guide and mentor Irving Mossman, is a logic of the appropriate, a logic of the propriety of the proper, a logic of discrimination, of non-contamination, and its philosophico-pedagogical work is the labor of category maintenance, above all the maintenance of the categories of the appropriate and the proper as the proper and appropriate categories of thought: any thought of the indiscriminate, of fuzzy logic, or of an indeterminate pointing is not, properly speaking, philosophical.

Thus, a proper coming to full philosophical subjectivity transpires within an appropriate temporality; Mossman himself is chastised by his chair for "premature" publication, and it is simply in waiting that he will accede to the accomplished subjectivity of a full professorship. Mawr, already of course an intellectual and sexual prodigy (thus partaking of the monstrosity of excess), is never punctual in fulfilling the narrative of his philosophical career; always too soon or too late, like Hasler before him, Mawr is never in the right place at the right time. His encounter with philosophy proper is always in this respect a missed encounter.

A time and place for everything, and thus everything in its proper time and place might be Mossman's reading of the Kantian *a priori*, for he is dedicated to category maintenance. He will not countenance the possibility that Foucault died of AIDS, for example, because "philosophers just don't carry on the way you apparently have to in order to get it" (Delany, 1994a, p. 109). So too, Mossman categorizes a triptych of photos on his desk of himself, Mawr, and Hasler as "the Jew, the Oriental, and the black boy" (p. 10), only to revise his categories when he learns that Hasler and Mawr are both gay, and reclassifies the two photos as those of two queers and a Jew. What matters in all of these discriminations—between public and private, AIDS and philosophy, ethnicities and sexualities, for example—is not as much the content or existential valence of these differences, but the possibility and necessity of categorization altogether, because it is only in sustaining these discriminations that one can sustain the possibility of discriminating between reason and madness, between what counts as philosophy and metaphysics. This is a logic not of difference but of non-contamination. And it is to this philosophical culture that Mossman is charged with bringing Mawr.

Irving Mossman, teacher (or, less politely, philosopher-cop), professionally sensitive to the possibility that the appropriate time for "Hasler studies" has arrived, "suggests" to Mawr that he write his dissertation on the published formal philosophical essays of Timothy Hasler, Korean American, former student of Mossman's at Stilford, an acknowledged, albeit eccentric, genius who until his inappropriately premature death (and, above all, before he completes his own dissertation—a matter of infinite, finally eternal, delay), had worked largely within, but also at the very limit of, the Anglo-American tradition of analytic language philosophy (only one respect in which Hasler bears a more than casual resemblance to Wittgenstein). Mawr, disabused of his Hegelian aspirations, had already been thinking of his coming-to-philosophical-subjectivity in terms of a series of tentative identifications with (queer, male) philosophers—Wittgenstein, Plato, Foucault—and falls in with Mossman's suggestion. Mawr will, at last, become a "real philosopher" in identifying with, and as, the formal philosophical texts of a posthumously certified but nonetheless authentic—real—philosopher. And this identification is to be achieved in a rigorous working-through that is also a repetition of the accredited texts of Hasler philosophy. But if this is to be Mawr's passage to philosophical culture, it is also the limit of his project, for Mossman, who knows a bandwagon by the footnotes it leaves behind it in professional journals, is to write the authoritative Hasler biography. Mawr's philosophical *Einbildung*, then, depends as much on this division of labor, this separation of the "work" from the "life," this non-contamination of one by the other, as it does on working through the officially sanctioned "philosophical" *oeuvre*: philosophy is what it is only insofar as it maintains itself in a prophylactic separation from that to which it is presumptively attentive. Thought can recognize itself in its jubilant specularity only on the condition that it withdraws from that which is its provocation into a certain reserve. Mawr's own life, up to a certain point, had likewise been negotiated according to the protocols of just such a separation, and it is precisely the unbearable tension of maintaining that separation that will trouble the philosophico-pedagogical narrative throughout *The Mad Man*. This tension will not be resolved, for Mawr both does and does not become a "philosopher"; thought neither achieves the perfection of its reason, nor does it simply become one with its objects. But the boundary of this separation, the limit of the logos, is at all points indeterminate.

The identification through repetition that is to be Mawr's passage to philosophy is at the same time the unworking of the work of philosophico-pedagogical culture, precisely because it comes dangerously close to being an absolute identification; in becoming *like* Timothy Hasler, John Mawr (almost) *becomes* Timothy Hasler, and this precisely in exceeding the limits of what counts as philosophy. In the division of labor between Mawr and his mentor that is to consecrate the emerging field of "Hasler studies," Mossman is to account for the extra-philosophical life. (Here we should be careful and note that it is completely unimportant whether one assumes the life, the context, explains the work, the text, or vice versa; what matters is that the discrimination between private life and public work, context and text, philosophy and the extra-philosophical, is made at all; what matters is that it is the "philosopher" who determines the philosophical proper precisely in the rejection that constitutes the extra-philosophical context as such, and thereby lays claim to philosophical mastery over the extra-philosophical.) Although Mossman claims to be unperturbed by the virtually simultaneous discovery that both Hasler and Mawr are gay, he begins to distance himself from the project when he finds evidence of Hasler's "sexual experiments" (foot fetishism, public sex); Mossman will excuse himself from the project on the basis of a certain non-empathy with, non-understanding of, Hasler's sexual life, a certain incommensurability between the philosophical and the extra-philosophical; finally, Mossman will literally remove himself from the picture. (Here, of course, Mossman has company, as any reader of certain biographies of Wittgenstein or Foucault will recognize.)

If Mossman can only maintain the integrity of what counts for him as philosophy through a certain disavowal (*Verleugnung*), Mawr will at the very same time identify with, and repeat the trajectory of, a Timothy Hasler who Mossman disavows. This identification never accomplishes an identity, Mawr never becomes Hasler; this repetition not only enacts similitude but difference. Mawr will explicitly identify with Hasler to be sure; indeed, even though Hasler was a foot fetishist and Mawr is into water sports, Mawr will eroticize Leaky Sowps's feet and entertain the possibility of an empathy with Hasler's desire. But Mawr will also repeatedly emphasize the differences between them, in their respective objects of desire, for example, but above all as a matter of historical difference: Hasler belonged to a world before AIDS, Mawr to a world in large part defined by AIDS. Yet it is precisely as Mawr abandons his work on Hasler (thus abandoning his dissertation and his philosophico-pedagogical Bildung), that he begins to write a text called *The Mad Man*, the very text Hasler left unfinished at his death. Thus it is not merely that this repetition is the repetition of an identification/disidentification, but that identification occurs precisely as that disidentification; the more Mawr distances himself from Hasler, the more nearly does he become Hasler, and this precisely in the essential incompletion of the philosophical project of coming to subjectivity: his subjectivity *is* that incompletion. In *The Mad Man* (by Hasler? Mawr? Delany?: where is the author here?), what unworks the work of philosophico-pedagogical Bildung, the identification that undoes the work of disidentification that is philosophy, the repetition that is no longer the repetition of a simple identity, is first of all a relation—a relation of non-relation, rather—to extremity: an extreme relation to temporality and death, to destitution and the abjection of heteroclite sociality, to pleasure.

In the first, and perhaps in the last instance, it is a relation (a relation of non-relation) to the extremity of temporality, an extreme relation to death. True, the emergence of AIDS means that there is an untraversible historical distance between Hasler and Mawr, but both exist in an immediate relation to their own finitude, the incompletion of their philosophical subjectivities (and the interruption of their dissertations). Hasler was afflicted throughout his life by severe hypochondria, always convinced in body if not in mind that he was on the verge of death; for Hasler, the race was already run, he was always proleptically his own corpse; he obtained relief from, a forgetting of, his immanent and imminent death only with occasional medical reassurances and in the pleasures of sex and philosophy. "But finally, ultimately," Mawr notes, "Timothy Hasler was his own shocking death" (Delany, 1994a, p. 12). Hasler is stabbed to death at The Pit, a hustler's bar, quite by accident; he dies in the place of his lover, Mad Man Mike Kerns; he dies gratuitously and in an absolute contingency, but he dies for love. Hasler's death, a *Liebestod*, is that very impossibility of subjectivity's coming to terms that is his subjectivity: his death is his identity. So too Joey, a friend and sometime lover of Mawr's, will die quite by accident in place of another, at the same bar, in the same way, and for the same reasons, many years later. And John Mawr, cocksucker extraordinaire, will figure himself in relation to the fatality of AIDS: "I do not have AIDS, I am surprised that I don't" (p. 7), the novel begins. And throughout, Mawr sustains this surprise that he is not dying of AIDS. Indeed, for three years Mawr "assumed my death was only months away" (p. 244); just as Hasler was in part his conviction that he was about to die, so too Mawr either assumes he is about to die, or *is* the surprise that he is neither dead nor dying: in both cases, "live" is thought as the surprise of not being dead. But whereas Hasler carries that existential surprise, the surprise of existing at all, to his grave (and thus becomes his ownmost death), Mawr's trajectory leads elsewhere. In the course of a long letter to Mossman's wife (who will later affirm her own lesbianism) detailing his relation to the pandemic and his sexual adventures, Mawr writes that

> When I entered the Variety Photoplays Theater [in search of casual sex], doubtless, like half the men there, I was terrified of AIDS. As I walked around the theater, doing what I did, like most of the men there, I thought about AIDS constantly and intently and obsessively. [So far, this is a straightforward and undifferentiated repetition of Hasler's being-for-death.] But when I left . . . I no longer had any fear of the disease.
> At all. (Delany, 1994a, p. 172)

Seemingly, AIDS imposes upon us all, but most obviously upon urban, "sexually active" gay men, Hasler's destiny; just as Hasler only became Timothy Hasler in his death, so too we are who we are only in the abjection of the gay man's teleological being-for-death. But if it is in an acceptance and embrace of his own finitude in the Liebestod of The Pit that Hasler finds his being and consummates philosophy, it is in another extreme relation, a relation of sovereignty, that Mawr undoes the work of philosophy and of repetition, for "it is the realization that one is gambling, and gambling on one's own—rather than seeking some possible certain knowledge, some knowable belief in how intelligent or in how idiotic the chances are—that obliterates the terror" (Delany, 1994a, p. 176). Thus Mawr's course takes him "farther and farther away from Tim": "What I must live with—and quite possibly die with—is a certain sense of its risk, knowing my 'sense' of both are absolutely without experimental foundation; and, somehow because of it, . . . I can now live without any basic terror or basic hope" (p. 177)—"Though you may think me mad" (p. 178). Mawr's relation to the extremity of AIDS is sovereign precisely because it is the unjustifiable affirmation of the erotic, without the guarantee or support of what counts as knowledge (of the risk factor in blow jobs, water sports, scat): this is madness, the outside that unworks the work of philosophy, and, insofar as it is without a future ("without any basic terror or basic hope"), unworks any philosophico-pedagogical narrative: sovereignty is an unmediated (hence impossible) (non-)relation to extremity. And *The Mad Man* is very much an affirmation of *that* "madness" (see also Delany, 1993). And perhaps the sovereignty of this affirmation of the erotic as the supplement of philosophy as the erotic.

For Timothy Hasler, the relation to death is a passage through abjection to transcendence as Liebestod and as philosophy; for John Mawr, the relation is a passage in abjection to a sovereignty that is the affirmation of non-transcendence. Mawr repeats Hasler, but queers the itinerary. Yet in both cases, it is a matter of an extreme relation to destitution and the abjection of heteroclite sociality, to the being-in-common of singularities in their abjection. Here, we would probably do well to remember that "the social" is in fact heteroclite and irregular declension or conjugation of our being-in-common; thus, there is nothing one can say of the social altogether, except that it belongs to that which it is impossible to characterize in general. One therefore cannot take any particular description or articulation of sociality to be a synechdoche for the whole, because that sociality is the very non-accomplishment of the totality, the very impossibility of totalization. But this does not mean that it is impossible to say anything at all. So let us say, however tentatively and however incoherently, but also, I think, necessarily, that what is at stake here is an erotic relation of non-relation, that extreme relation that is sovereignty, to destitution (homelessness), to an economy of pleasures and love rather than a psychic economy of desire and possession, and thus an erotic relation of contamination to all that philosophy must refuse in order to become what it presumptively is; it is Mawr's repetition of Hasler's extreme relation to destitution, to an economy of pleasures, and to contamination that the philosophico-pedagogical projects meets its limit. Mawr is too good a student.

"*The Mad Man* is not a book about the homeless of New York—or, indeed, of the country" (p. xiv). This is undoubtedly true in the sense that it cannot be taken to be an adequate interpretation, account of, or explanation for homelessness. But what is at stake in this disclaimer is not merely the interpretative insufficiency of a sociology that has, unaccountably, not quite gotten around to exhibiting its conceptual mastery of the phenomenon. Consider, for example, the episode that Tony, a homeless man, relates to Mawr about Dirty John, another homeless man, who was given leftover noodles mixed with broken glass by a restaurant on the upper west side; Mawr's sole reflection, addressed to the reader, is this: "A history of homelessness on the Upper West Side for the last decade. How would you go about researching it?" (Delany, 1994a, p. 315) Which suggests that there is something here that essentially escapes its concept; it is no accident that we have never produced a history of the *Lumpenproletariat*. Thus, an entire "population" of "bums, hoboes, and winos," or "the marginal, the dispossessed, the underclass," increasingly is defined in terms of their exteriority, their non-relation, to the property, genealogical propriety, and domesticity of the *domus* as the conceptual and practical foundation of social structure altogether. "Homelessness" in this respect names the limit of its concept. Yet it is no "mere" metaphor. The term "homelessness" here points toward all that which most nearly approaches absolute abjection in any society such as "ours" entirely organized according to a logic of production. It hardly matters here whether that logic of production sustains a capitalist or socialist economy; or whether that economy is symbolic, industrial, or virtual; or whether the society governed by the protocols of production ultimately does no more than reproduce itself. In all cases, "homelessness" designates pure luxury (all time is "free," time is not transmuted into labor value), but also the suffering and destitution is pure poverty. "Homelessness" designates both pure excess, a nothing-but surplus value, and exchange unfettered by value (or by what is called "the market") and a nothing-but use value (if you can't eat it or fuck it, piss on it); "homelessness" thus designates what any logic of production must expel as sheer surplus, as superfluity, or as waste, as sheer abjection, as shit, but in any case as that madness which is, as Foucault says, the absence of work. Thus, the homeless do not enter an economy of labor, they produce no value and thus cannot even call philosophy "home"). "Homelessness" designates the outside not only of philosophical culture, but of the cultural altogether; the economies, etiquettes, and protocols of the homeless, no less rigorous than those which obey the logic of production, are nevertheless entirely other than the latter.[2]

Consider, for example, the recollection by the man who calls himself, aptly enough, Piece o' Shit, of an interview with one of his doctors in the "crazy hospital" (where he has been admitted for excessive masturbation in public): "I got this one real old doctor, and I asked him if he would suck it for me. He asked me why. And I told him, 'Cause it *feels* good, motherfucker!' " (p. 257) Here we have the difference between a symbolic economy of desire and a materialist economy of pleasures: the point for

---

[2]Although not a discussion of "homelessness," Delany insists on the rigorous etiquette of similarly disavowed practices of "public sex," for example in *The Motion of Light in Water* (pp. 205–206).

Piece o' Shit is not to feel good about himself, but to feel good; this insistence wrecks every economy of interpretation, for feeling good produced no meaning. Or consider the game whose rules are articulated by Mad Man Mike Kerns (Hasler's lover, he who survived by accident and who is thus in his very existence pure excess, for he outlives his narrative term by virtue of an incalculable sacrifice): men can own, buy, and sell each other for sex, even for love, but the price is beyond barter, beyond value. *Prix fixe* one cent, no more, not less. A penny, the shit of the U.S. economy, can buy nothing—except a man: a penny, but not for your thoughts. The homeless, shit of the economies of production and of value, exist both in pure luxury (for their time is inalienable) and in the destitution of pure use value; the economy of this sociality is therefore one of pleasures than of desire. But this economy of pleasures and love is not a simple alternative to the economy of production and desire; rather, it exists—happens—in the interstices of the dominant "mode of production," as the surplus, excess, or supplement of the economies of production and desire; the economy of pleasures is not outside of, does not transcend, the suffering of their abjection. Nevertheless, Mad Man Mike's economy of pleasures is indiscriminate in the sense that everyone is worth precisely; shit (a penny). Money is no longer the signifier of wealty, but of an existential poverty, of the shit that money as such *is*. It is thus an economy of anonymity, of an infinite substitutability; readers of Sade will recognize this economy, for it is one of indiscriminate and infinite permutation and combination. This is therefore an economy of pure exchange, an economy unhinged from any essential connection to the intersubjective recognitions of a bankrupt humanism that made shit of them in the first place. As an infinite permutation and combination, as pure exchange, the economy of pleasures is one of banality, boredom, infinite repetition, and substitution. Hegel, the inspiration of John Mawr's "systems of the world," would call it a "bad infinity, without teleological necessity." The sociality of homelessness, as articulated in the Mad Man's (and *The Mad Man's*) game, is that of a society of masters, the masters of the perverse. All this belongs to what philosophy must refuse in order to become itself; but all this belongs to what seduces Hasler and Mawr in turn, and unworks the work of the philosophico-pedagogical culture.

In any case, of course, the economy of pleasures—a queer economy—is intolerable anathema to anyone who conflates the logic of production with what is called the world. Although the mutually incomprehensible economies of pleasures and production continually confront each other, often violently, throughout *The Mad Man* (indeed, the homeless have to live the violence of that confrontation, as Mawr's first encounter with Piece o' Shit demonstrates), it is at the Pit that the confrontation most dramatically articulates a *différend* (after Lyotard [1988]: a difference so profound there is no possible common ground on which that difference might be adjudicated); it is at the Pit that the *différend*, as the articulation of sociality altogether, is most forcefully, most violently, rendered visible. The Pit is a hustler's bar, consecrated to the economy of desire and production; its trade is in the exchange value of beauty: a large endowment, periodically and consistently invested, brings a large return; your beautiful face, your big dick, is your venture capital. Into the Pit, years apart, walk Mad Man Mike and Joey, both of fabulous endowments, both of spectacular sexual prowess, offering pleasure for a penny, neither more nor less. And this is intolerable, of course, to the bar's hustlers, for it threatens to unwork the entire economy, the entire culture, the rationality itself of the Pit. Both are attacked. Hasler takes the hit for Mad Man Mike, hence his Liebestod, his eschatological transcendence; Joey dies in the (non-positive) sovereign affirmation of the finitude of pleasure and death. I will return to this.

The economy of perverse pleasures, an economy not excluding the existentiality of the homeless in their destitute abjection, is for both Hasler and Mawr a lure that interrupts the punctuality of the philosophical-pedagogical narrative; this draws them away from their properly philosophical pursuits. The economy of perverse pleasures is thus the surplus, the supplement, or excess of the subjectivity that is presumptively the telos, the object, of their desire. When John Mawr moves to New York from Stilford to write his dissertation on Hasler, he rents an apartment directly over the one Hasler occupied when, years before, he had left Stilford for New York to write his own dissertation; Mawr interrupts work on his dissertation to head for Riverside Park in search of an erotic relation to the economy of perverse pleasures (that is, to suck cock and drink piss), thus repeating the seduction that captivated Hasler (who was looking for dirty bare feet to suck). But the economy of perverse pleasures is not merely excessive or exorbitant with respect to the philosophico-pedagogical, an excessive economy; it is also—oxymoronically, for excess is precisely what exceeds the economic altogether—an economy *of* excess. Everything in the economy of perverse pleasures is excessive, "larger than life," and it is precisely this excessiveness (rather than merely *what* is represented here) that makes of *The Mad Man* a "pornotopic fantasy." The dimensions of this pornotopic fantasy are mythic, perhaps even cosmic; those who participate are epic heros of sexual fortitude and performance. The pornographic belongs to the monstrous, as the Proem makes clear. Dicks are enormous, most often tumescent, certainly far beyond any experience of a biological male; yoni are excessively long; men come repeatedly, incessantly, and by the quart rather than the tablespoon; and perverse sex becomes, rather than a functional avocation, the universe itself; the erotic becomes the whole. The pornotopic fantasy is one of abjection of pissing on and being pissed on, in rimming and eating shit, in sweat, dirt, and semen—and in talking about it, in the erotics of ("dirty") language, including the language of domination and submission.[3] The economy of (these) perverse pleasures is an economy of excess not merely as an economy of the outside but as transgression. What belongs to the secrecy and propriety of what is called the self—semen, piss, shit, for example—and which one appropriately disposes of "in private," is externalized; conversely, what, particularly under the regime of safer sex pedagogy, is held to be necessarily and forever external is literally incorporated, internalized, in the innermost recesses of the clean and proper body. The inside becomes the outside, the outside the inside, and in that perverse semiosis, the self loses the structural integrity of the clean and proper, becoming a certain undecidable betweeness. Here, erotic sociality is not so much a relation between bodies as it is the fact of existential embodiment itself, what Cindy Patton (1997) calls the ob-scene. The body is not yet an object in fantasy with which one can identify or disavow, but the very happening, the place, of sociality; the body is not a "thing" but an "event," the event of its material thingness. This is the body that matters.

In other words, the "body" is the fact of a primordial contamination, a transgression more original than the law (logos) that is transgressed. It is not a matter of an undifferentiated primal fusion of self and other, but of the primordial alterities of the self. John Mawr does not become Timothy Hasler (or, for that matter, Leaky Sowps). And, of course, it is this contamination that what counts as philosophy must disavow in order to be "itself":

What made me look up was the sound of water—I turned to see lamplight over Crazy Joey's pimpled back, it's hard little muscles defined under them. In just his pants, he was urinating against the lower bookshelf. "What the fuck do you think you're—!"

"Takin' a piss, what does it—!"

"Cut it out, man! Those are my fuckin' books—!"

"Hey, I'm sorry! I was just—" not stopping, Joey turned from the bookshelf, mule dick still hosing from his fist its glittering yellow—"takin' a leak, man."

"Well, do it in the bathroom," Joey said. "Mad Man Mike and me, we don't do that."

. . .

"Joey—you have to have some limits when you're doing stuff like this."

"Yeah?" Joey said. "Oh. I didn't understand. I'm sorry—about the books. You read those, don't you?"

I took another breath and looked around me, then shook my head. . . .

"Didn't Mad Man Mike tell you about that—limits I mean?"

---

[3]There is a persistent thematics here, as elsewhere in Delany's work, of race and power; it is a subtle and complex relation, requiring an extended discussion, which I attempt in a longer version of this chapter (Haver, forthcoming).

Joey's eyes had an unhappy, questioning look. "No," he said. (Delany, 1994a, pp. 458–459)

Here, the erotic, as the primordial contamination of "self" and "other" in the material body, is that which interrupts any aspiration for thought's reunion with itself in the concept; that contamination that is the erotic, the ultimate impossibility of a secure, well-demarcated separation, is what constitutes subjectivity as essential incompletion; in other words, erotic contamination is the permanent interruption of the pedagogical project of coming to philosophical culture.

Now it happens that there is, in *The Mad Man*, a term for this interruption: *ekpyrosis*, a term from Heraclitus (who as a "pre-socratic" has long been regarded as essentially prephilosophical) signifying conflagration or apocalypse:

EKPYROSIS

That's what Hasler had written just before he and the Mad Man had gone down to the Pit. Written it, indeed, three times. [In shit, once on a window, twice on the walls.] Had that remarkable philosopher been explaining the meaning of that all-consuming, all-cleansing Heraclitean fire to Mad Man Mike sometime earlier that day—that fire which is itself the Heraclitean notion of change and flux raised to such a level beyond love or rage that nothing can escape it, that no man's or woman's flow can quench it? (Delany, 1994a, p. 480)

For Timothy Hasler, ekpyrosis becomes his death, his defeat, fate, or destiny, at the Pit; all that survives of Hasler is his writing, including his notes toward *The Mad Man*. For Crazy Joey, ekpyrosis (construed as his death at the Pit, the violent revenge of a logic of prodution on his economy of pleasures) is the moment of his sovereignty, the non-posititve affirmation of his material existentiality, the remainderless destruction of the *destrudo*. It is precisely in his destruction that Joey is forever undefeated. But for John Mawr, the extremity of ekpyrosis is traumatic, in some sense a missed encounter that is nevertheless an encounter; ekpyrosis is the ultimate impossibility of ever becoming nothing but a "philosopher." As one who is always already something more, something essentially other, than a "philosopher," Mawr's subjectivity resides in its essential incompletion, its irrecusable unaccomplishment. Hasler's relation to extremity is one of identity (and therefore not a "relation" at all): Hasler is his death. Mawr's relation to extremity is necessarily a relation of non-relation, the traumatic non-relation of the missed encounter, the non-relation of interruption.

It is to this relation of non-relation to extremity, to this interruption, that we must bring those whom we call our students. But we have hardly begun to think what a pedagogy *in extremis*, a queer pedagogy, might be. Perhaps, as Deborah Britzman (1995; see Haver, in press) once suggested to me, *The Mad Man* is unteachable; but perhaps that resistance to philosophy, that unteachability, the incompletion of subjectivity, is not itself without relation to what a queer pedagogy might be.

ACKNOWLEDGMENTS

This chapter was written while a member of the School of Social Science at the Institute for Advanced Study in Princeton, New Jersey, with financial support from the National Endowment for the Humanities and a sabbatical leave from Binghamton University. I am grateful to the Institute for its hospitality.

REFERENCES

Blanchot, M. (1993). *The infinite conversation* (S. Hanson, Trans.). Minneapolis: University of Minnesota Press.
Britzman, D. P. (1995). Is there a queer pedagogy? Or, stop reading straight. *Educational Theory, 45*(2), 151–165.
Delany, S. R. (1993). *The motion of light in water: Sex and science fiction writing in the East Village, 1960–1965.* New York: Masquerade Books.
Delany, S. R. (1994a). *The mad man.* New York: Masquerade Books.
Delany, S. R. (1994b). *Silent interviews: On language, race, sex, science fiction and some comics.* Hanover, NH: Wesleyan University Press and University Press of New England.
Delany, S. R. (1995). Aversion/perversion/diversion. In M. Dorenkamp & R. Henke (Eds.), *Negotiating lesbian and gay subjects* (pp. 7–33). New York: Routledge.
Hart, G. (1996). Gay community oriented approaches to safer sex. In T. Rhodes & R. Hartnoll (Eds.), *Aids, drugs and prevention: Perspectives on individual and community action* (pp. 86–102). London: Routledge.
Haver, W. (1996). *The body of this death: Historicity and sociality in the time of Aids.* Stanford, CA: Stanford University Press.
Lyotard, J.-F. (1988). *The différend: Phrases in dispute* (G. Van Den Abbeele, Trans.). Minneapolis: University of Minnesota Press.
Odets, W. (1995). *In the shadow of the epidemic: Being HIV-negative in the age of AIDS.* Durham, NC: Duke University Press.
Odets, W. (1996). Why we stopped doing primary prevention for gay men in 1985. In Dangerous Bedfellows (Eds.), *Policing public sex: Queer politics and the future of AIDS activism.* Boston: South End Press.
Patton, C. (1997). *Fatal advice: How safe-sex education went wrong.* Durham, NC: Duke University Press.
Readings, B. (1996). *The university in ruins.* Cambridge, MA: Harvard University Press.
Watney, S. (1995). AIDS and the politics of queer diaspora. In M. Dorenkamp & R. Henke (Eds.), *Negotiating lesbian and gay subjects* (pp. 53–70). New York: Routledge.
Wickham, G. R. (1997). *Liberalism and cultural genocide.* Unpublished doctoral dissertation, Binghamton University, Binghamton, NY.

Chapter 19

Autobiography as a Queer Curriculum Practice

Janet L. Miller
National-Louis University

At the Bergamo curriculum theory conference[1] in October of 1991, I participated in a session where the organizers invited us to explore, autobiographically, the tensions and contradictions we experienced as women and men
working in academe. The organizers provided the materials for us to construct
writings or visual representations of our academic lives. Working autobiographically, we were invited to access ways that our daily living out of teaching,
researching, publishing, and service activities exceeds the academic frameworks that typically contain and delineate our work.

For 20 minutes, the crowd wrote, doodled, or constructed collages of
our various lives as academics. People sprawled on the floor, slouched in
chairs, or huddled over the few tables in the room. Some splayed segments
of their lives across poster board with purple, green, and yellow magic
markers. Others penned small notes on colored sheets of paper or in lined
notebooks. I scrunched down into one of those gray institutional chairs,

---

[1]The "Bergamo" conferences on curriculum theory and classroom practice have been
held every autumn since 1974, and have been sponsored by *JCT: The Journal of Curriculum
Theorizing* since 1978. Following Craig Kridel's (1996) lead, I refer to the "Bergamo"
conference rather than its more official title of the JCT Conference on Curriculum Theory
and Classroom Practice or its various locations over the years. See Kridel's section in *JCT* on
"Hermeneutic Portraits" for historical groundings of both the conference and the work of
those who have participated in its deliberations. As well, see especially chapter 4 of
Understanding Curriculum (Pinar, Reynolds, Slattery, & Taubman, 1995) for an extended
discussion of *JCT* and its conferences.

my left-handed writing supported only by the stiff-backed yellow legal pad of paper on which I hastily scribbled. When the facilitators reconvened the group, they invited us to display our representations or to read from our rough drafts. Many women and some men read or discussed vignettes filled with examples of daily lives and identities that leaked out over the edges of university tenure and promotion handbooks and spilled into classrooms, research sites, and official forms of scholarly writing. People responded to each reading or presentation with nods of recognition, murmurs, and occasional hoots of laughter.

I listened for a long while, and then suddenly decided to share my rough draft, although this was not something that I usually felt comfortable doing in a large group. I called my piece "Yellow Paper" and in it described the writing, more than 20 years ago, of my dissertation in longhand on the same kind of legal yellow writing paper that I had grabbed for this particular writing event. My theme in this free verse was the distancing of myself from my own work through the mandated use of others' words to support my dissertation thesis. And in the last part of "Yellow Paper," I spoke of not wanting to avoid or go back on my own words now and of my desires to share those words with the woman I love.

What was notable, at least to me, about this event was not that I was describing the tensions of mandated and distanced scholarly writing. Nor that I was grappling with issues of authorial authority as a possible fiction, or of women's academic words as only replicating rather than exceeding patriarchal discourses in the university. Without any preconceived intentions, I had queered an "educational" use of autobiography in this session by spontaneously declaring my new and, until then, fairly private relationship with a woman to a room full of colleagues, friends, and strangers.

I privileged that particular situation and experience in my reading of "Yellow Paper," but, at the same time, my statement did not represent a desire to enact a "modernist tale about how to claim an authentic lesbian identity" (Martindale, 1997, p. 29). I rejected such a modernist tale especially because I was exploring forms of autobiography in relation to Judith Butler's (1992) argument for "permanently unclear" identity categories:

> identity categories are never merely descriptive, but always normative, and as such, exclusionary.
> . . . [I]f feminism presupposes that "women" designates an undesignatable field of differences, one that cannot be totalized or summarized by a descriptive identity category, then the very term becomes a site of permanent openness and resignifiability. (p. 16)

I had been working in and with autobiography as a form of curriculum theorizing for a long while. And, in recent years, I had been wanting to work with autobiography in ways that defamiliarized, or queered static categories and versions of my academic, woman, teacher, researcher, lesbian selves. I wanted to use autobiography in ways that shifted autobiography in education from its modernist emphasis on producing predictable, stable, and normative identities and curricula to a consideration of "selves" and curricula as sites of "permanent openness and resignifiability."

My ongoing work in autobiography thus provided an incentive and a reason, in the conference session, to tell how my life and my love exceeded the very academic discourses, frameworks, and contexts that tried to contain them. That extensive and long-term autobiographical work also provided a backdrop against which, at that point in my life, I could queer both the subject and the forms that autobiography typically took in educational settings by pointing to the "undesignatable field of differences" within the identity categories of lesbian, woman, teacher, and researcher.

In contrast, many current uses of autobiography in education work against any notion of "permanent openness" of identity or curriculum constructions. Instead, some educators use autobiography in ways that reinforce classroom representations of a knowable, always accessible conscious self who progresses, with the help of autobiographical inquiry, from ignorance to knowledge of self, other, and "best" pedagogical and curricular practices. Such normalized versions of autobiography serve to limit and to close down rather than to create possibilities for constructing permanently open and resignifiable selves.

So, in the contexts of current prevalent constructions of autobiography in education, one could use the example of my coming out in an academic context to construct yet another modernist tale: when educators use autobiography in the classroom, we invite all kinds of closet doors to open. But do we? Here, I address what I perceive to be gaps and silences in current constructions and uses of autobiography in education that promise self-reflection and self-understanding as unmediated by language, culture, sexualities, or the unconscious. In doing so, I point to groundbreaking autobiographical work of those involved in the reconceptualization of the curriculum field that produced queer or atypical curriculum theory. And I posit some possibilities that open when autobiography is conceptualized as a *queer curriculum practice* that can help us to dis-identify with ourselves and others: "To dis-identify and to denaturalize, to make one's object un-natural is to strategically produce difference out of what was once familiar or the same" (Greene, 1996, p. 327).

Strategically producing a difference out of what was once familiar or the same about what it means to "be" a teacher or student or researcher or woman, for example, cannot happen by "telling my story" if that story repeats or reinscribes already normalized identity categories. Further, strategically producing a difference cannot happen if difference is only construed as "binary and oppositional rather than nuanced, plural, and proximate" (Greene, 1996, p. 326). Thus, addressing "self" as a "site of permanent openness and resignifiability" opens up possibilities for *queering* autobiography, for speaking and writing into existence denaturalized ways of being that are obscured or simply unthinkable when one centered, self-knowing story is substituted for another.

Autobiography as a queer curriculum practice opens possibilities for "strategically producing difference out of what was once familiar or the same" in order to make autobiographical curriculum theory's "assumptions and occlusions subject to analysis" (Greene, 1996, p. 325). Autobiography as a queer curriculum practice also can cast in new terms the ways in which we might investigate our multiple, intersecting, unpredictable, and unassimilatable identities: " 'Queer' spins the term outward along dimensions that can't be subsumed under gender and sexuality at all: the ways that race, ethnicity, post-colonial nationality criss-cross with these and other identity-constituting and identity-fracturing discourses" (Sedgwick, 1993, pp. 8–9).

"Identity-constituting" discourses of education and many of its current uses of autobiographical practices, I argue, maintain the status quo and reinscribe already known situations and identities as fixed, immutable, locked into normalized conceptions of what and who are possible.

MODERNIST AUTOBIOGRAPHICAL TALES

Autobiography as a genre of research and writing in educational research and as a method of reflective practice for teachers has become codified in recent years. And the conventions of autobiography, as they have been codified within educational practices such as teacher research, are normalizing conventions.

For example, many teacher educators, at both the undergraduate and graduate levels, encourage students to write or speak autobiographically in order to "tell their stories" as a way of examining as well as constructing their educational assumptions and practices. I presently teach in a graduate program where students conduct teacher research and are encouraged to write up the findings of that research in narrative form. Their research projects, they are told by many instructors, should "tell the story" of their research processes and resulting individual changes in their classrooms as well as in their perspectives about curriculum, research, and themselves as teachers.

But what I have found is that admonitions to "tell your story" often lead to versions of teacher research in which teachers learn about and then implement new pedagogical approaches and curriculum materials without a hitch. They lead to autobiographical accounts of how teachers were "mistaken" or "uninformed" or "ill-prepared" but now have become fully knowledgeable and enlightened about themselves, their students, and their teaching practices.

What often gets normalized in such uses of autobiography, then, is a singularity of story that a student is encouraged to tell about herself as a teacher. Such singularity closes the doors to multiple, conflicting, and even odd and abnormal—queer—stories and identities. Further, what also gets normalized is how autobiography only can be used in education to address a very narrow range and set of questions, issues, or purposes.

For example, many of the currently circulating uses of autobiography in teacher research often assume the possibility of constructing coherent and "true" portraits of whole and fully conscious selves. Or teachers at least are encouraged to work autobiographically in order to "develop" teacher selves who are always capable of fully conscious and knowledgeable actions and decisions in the classroom.

But consider what normalizing conventions of educational research, practice, and identity are reinforced when educators, consciously or unconsciously, insist on autobiography as a means to conceptualize and to work toward definitive and conclusive portraits of "developed," "reflective," and thus "effective" teachers, students, and teacher researchers. Rarely, if ever, do teacher educators encourage future or practicing teachers to address issues of sexuality, the body, the unconscious, or desire in relation to conceptions of what constitutes an "effective" or "good" teacher, for example. And what gets left out of such normalizing autobiographical practices are desires and manifestations of the unconscious that inflect all aspects of human interaction and being.

Consider too what normalizing conventions of educational inquiry and practice are reinforced when autobiography is used as means of arriving at solutions and answers to pedagogical and curricular issues and problems. And when the arrival at a solution through an autobiography is somehow seen as proof or evidence of some fully examined, accessible, and thus "accountable" teacher or student "self."

Many current uses of autobiography in educational research assume a developmental "end" product as well as possibilities of "best practice" in constructions of teacher selves, curriculum materials, and pedagogical approaches. Conventions of using autobiography in education also assume the possibility of a conclusive self-reflective examination that can illuminate "flaws" or "problems" that can be corrected in the student's educational philosophy, pedagogical approach, or constructions of curriculum.

Given rampant normalizing conceptions of school *and* of autobiography, many students and teachers find no incentive or place to explore how we are situated simultaneously in multiple and often conflicting identity constructions—some of which must be hidden in order to remain in normal school. Normalizing conventions of autobiography allow no space for exploring the possibilities that might emerge if we attempted to resist the "identity-constituting discourses" of education and, simultaneously, to create and use "identity-fracturing discourses."

Ironically, however, normalizing uses of autobiography in education also often strike a pose of inclusiveness, as if, through autobiography, all voices heretofore silenced or marginalized can now be heard. Deborah Britzman (1997) speaks of the difficulties in such versions of inclusiveness:

> In educational research it seems as though the more voices, the merrier the field becomes. And while stories of difference proliferate in education, along with the pluralistic desire to count them all, making room for diversity and making diversity a room is not the same as exploring the tangles of implication. For to explore the tangles of implication requires something more than the desire to know the other's rules and then act accordingly. One is also implicated in one's own response. Implication is not so easily acknowledged because the otherness that implicates the self is beyond rationality and consciousness. . . . The question at stake here is not so much that the voices are proliferating but that the rules of discourse and engagement cannot guarantee what they promise to deliver: the desire to know and be known without mediation and the desire to make insight from ignorance and identity. (p. 32)

When only certain stories can be told in certain ways and for certain reasons, even in the name of inclusiveness, what "tangles of implication" are refused or ignored in teachers' autobiographical examinations that assume a "self" that can "know and be known without mediation"? Rather than constituting autobiographical work in education as a means of finding, correcting, developing, or including one true and authentic self as teacher or student, I consider the possibilities that open when we conceive of autobiography as a *queer* curriculum practice.

QUEERING AUTOBIOGRAPHY IN EDUCATION

By encouraging an educator to examine disjunctures, ruptures, break-ups, and fractures in the "normal school" version of the unified life-subject and her own and others' educational practices, autobiography can function to "queer" or to make theory, practice, *and* the self *unfamiliar*. To "queer" is to denaturalize conceptions of one singular, whole, and "acceptable" educator or student "self" as well as versions of autobiography that rely on such conceptions.

Autobiography as a queering of curriculum practice can challenge educational research that normalizes the drive to sum up one's self, one's learning, and the other as directly, developmentally, and inclusively knowable and identifiable. Autobiography as a queer curriculum practice suggests a focus on a range of sexualities as well as racialized and classed identities that exceed singular and essential constructions of "student" and "teacher." Autobiography as a queer curriculum practice also compels us to consider "tangles of implication"—how we are implicated in our desires for and enactments of, as well as in our fears and revulsions toward, those identities and practices that exceed the "norm."

Further, autobiography as a queer curriculum practice can intervene in the practice of defining ourselves through already available and legitimized discourses:

> Queers participate in positioning themselves through both authoring and authorizing experience. As lesbian and gay (queer) subjects are located in an evolving discourse that preexists and constitutes them, they are, at the same time, its creative agents. Any claim to a queered perspective is therefore an embrace of a dynamic discursive position from which subjects of homosexualities can both name themselves and impact the conditions under which queer identities are constituted. (Honeychurch, 1996, pp. 342–343)

In a sense, the current rage for autobiography and narrative in education research and practice has already and always been a queer phenomenon; that is, autobiography as a form of curriculum theorizing is a queer kind of theory, theory that is not normal or typical within the academy, given the social science frameworks that still gird most theory and practice constructions in education. Autobiography denaturalizes conceptions of "appropriate" forms of educational theorizing, practice, and research by "strategically produc[ing] difference out of what was once familiar or the same" in qualitative and quantitative foci and methods of educational inquiry. Autobiography as both method and a form of curriculum theorizing certainly was regarded as not normal or typical 25 years ago, when some curriculum scholars began using autobiography as one way to reconceptualize the curriculum field.[2]

Autobiography queered curriculum theorizing in that it directly challenged mechanistic, efficient, and technologized as well as political constructions of curriculum and theory that ignored, minimized, or cast in abstractions individuals' lived experience of schools. At the same time,

---

[2]For extensive discussions as well as annotations of autobiographical curriculum theorizing within the reconceptualization, see especially chapter 10 of *Understanding Curriculum* (Pinar et al., 1995). As well, see Graham's (1991) account of the importance of Pinar and Grumet's (1976) *Toward a Poor Curriculum* in autobiographical work in education.

many theorists working with and in autobiography sought to explore its social and political potential while refusing any one version of identity or experience as sufficient for claiming the benefits of "enlightened" agency that humanistic, modernist forms of autobiographical inquiry could imply.

William Pinar and Madeleine Grumet (1976), in elaborating Pinar's *currere*, an autobiographical theory of curriculum, have increasingly drawn attention to the necessity of rendering multiple accounts of selves and school knowledge and experiences in order to "cultivate our capacity to see through the outer forms, the habitual explanation of things" (Pinar, 1988, p. 149). Those multiple accounts "splinter the dogmatism of a single tale" (Grumet, 1991, p. 72), while, at the same time, calling attention to the social and political aspects of autobiographical interpretation and analysis:

> Narratives of educational experience challenge their readers and writers to find both individuality and society, being and history and possibility in their texts. . . . On the other hand, a failure to engage in some analysis of the autobiographical texts beyond celebration and recapitulation leads to a patronizing sentimentality. It consigns the teacher's tale to myth, resonant but marginal because it is not part of the discourse that justifies real action. (Grumet, 1990, pp. 323–324)

Having participated in those initial reconceptualist forays into the complexities of autobiography as a form of educational research, what appears queer to me now is that curriculum theorizing about autobiography as method and practice has been ignored in many mainstream versions and uses of autobiography in education. Initial reconceptualist work that explored the existential, phenomenological, and psychoanalytic bases of autobiography as a form of educational inquiry led to groundbreaking disruptions of static and transparent notions of "self," "voice," and "experience," for example. But such work has not informed many current uses of autobiography in normal school.

Perhaps the queer practice of curriculum theorizing through autobiography invited too many queer stories that many educators could not or would not want to hear, stories where official school knowledge, identities, and visions of revolutionary educational practice were exceeded by heretofore unimagined or at least unarticulated constructions of students, teachers, and curricula. And perhaps autobiography as a queer curriculum practice challenged too directly the limits of a developmental and incremental notion of both learning and autobiography. As such, perhaps queered versions of autobiographical work threatened to dismantle the dominant educational narrative in which one passes from ignorance to knowledge about both the "self" and other.

But an educator who conceives of autobiography as a *queer curriculum practice* doesn't look into the mirror of self reflection and see a reinscription of her already familiar, identifiable self. She finds herself not mirrored—but in difference. In difference, she cannot simply identify with herself *or* with those she teaches. In the space she explores between self and other, nothing looks familiar, everything looks a little unnatural. To queer the use of autobiography as a curriculum practice is to produce a story of self and other with which one cannot identify. It is to recognize that there are times and places in constructing versions of teaching, research, and curriculum when making a difference requires making one's autobiography unnatural.

REFERENCES

Britzman, D. P. (1997). The tangles of implication. *International Journal of Qualitative Studies in Education, 10*(1), 31–37.

Butler, J. (1992). Contingent foundations: Feminism and the question of "postmodernism." In J. Butler & J. W. Scott (Eds.), *Feminists theorize the political* (pp. 3–21). New York: Routledge.

Graham, R. (1991). *Reading and writing the self: Autobiography in education and the curriculum.* New York: Teachers College Press.

Greene, F. L. (1996). Introducing queer theory into the undergraduate classroom: Abstractions and practical applications. *English Education, 28*, 325–339.

Grumet, M. R. (1990). Retrospective: Autobiography and the analysis of educational experience. *Cambridge Journal of Education, 20*(3), 321–326.

Grumet, M. R. (1991). The politics of personal knowledge. In C. Witherell & N. Noddings (Eds.), *Stories lives tell: Narrative and dialogue in education* (pp. 67–77). New York: Teachers College Press.

Honeychurch, K. G. (1996). Researching dissident subjectivities: Queering the grounds of theory and practice. *Harvard Educational Review, 66*, 339–355.

Kridel, C. (1996). Hermeneutic portraits: Section editor's notes. *JCT: Journal of Curriculum Theorizing, 12*(4), 41–43.

Martindale, K. (1997). *Un/popular culture: Lesbian writing after the sex wars.* Albany: SUNY Press.

Pinar, W. F. (1988). "Whole, bright, deep with understanding": Issues in qualitative research and autobiographical method. In W. F. Pinar (Ed.), *Contemporary curriculum discourses* (pp. 134–153). Scottsdale, AZ: Gorsuch Scarisbrick Publishers.

Pinar, W. F., & Grumet, M. R. (1976). *Toward a poor curriculum.* Dubuque, IA: Kendall/Hunt.

Pinar, W. F., Reynolds, W. M., Slattery, P., & Taubman, P. M. (1995). *Understanding curriculum: An introduction to the study of historical and contemporary curriculum discourses.* New York: Peter Lang.

Sedgwick, E. (1993). *Tendencies.* Durham, NC: Duke University Press.

About the Contributors

Deborah P. Britzman is an associate professor of Education, Social and Political Thought, and Women's Studies at York University in Toronto. Britzman is author of *Practice Makes Practice: A Critical Study of Learning to Teach* (SUNY Press, 1991) and *Lost Subjects, Contested Objects: Toward a Psychoanalytic Inquiry of Learning* (SUNY Press, in press).

Mary K. Bryson, plagued with a name reminiscent of cheap cosmetics, has the dubious distinction of the lowest undergraduate GPA and the shortest dissertation of any student ever to obtain a PhD.

Dennis Carlson is associate professor in the Department of Educational Leadership and director of the Center for Education and Cultural Studies at Miami University in Oxford, Ohio. He is the author of *Teachers and Crisis: Urban School reform and Teachers' Work Culture* (1992), *Making Progress: Education and Culture in New Times* (1997), and is a regular contributor to scholarly journals in education and cultural studies.

Brent Davis is assistant professor of education at York University, Toronto, Canada. His principal interests—cognitive theory and cultural studies—are focused in the areas of mathematics education and curriculum theory. He is the author of *Teaching Mathematics: Toward a Sound Alternative* (Garland, 1996).

Suzanne de Castell has five long surnames, and a title about which she tells no one. This invisible privilege is the source of her shameless dilettantism. Her PhD thesis was nearly failed by the University of London for being far, far too long.

Patrick Dilley is a doctoral candidate in higher education in the School of Education at University of Southern California. He is working on a typological history of gay college students in the United States from 1945 to the present.

Mary Aswell Doll, professor of English at Our Lady of Holy Cross College, is the author of *Beckett and Myth: An Archetypal Approach* and *To the Lighthouse and Back: Writings on Teaching and Living*. She is co-editor of *In the Shadow of the Giant: Thomas Wolfe*. She has presented at local, national, and international conferences; she has published in the *Journal of Curriculum Theorizing, Soundings, Journal of Beckett Studies, Taboo: The Journal of Education and Culture*, among others; she has published several book chapters on myth, literature, and education.

William Haver teaches Japanese intellectual history, contemporary political thought, and queer studies in the history and comparative literature departments at Binghamton University. He was written *The Body of This Death: Historicity and Sociality in the Time of AIDS* (Stanford University Press, 1996), and is currently completing a manuscript entitled "Extremity: AIDS and the Obscenity of Being."

Kenn Gardner Honeychurch is assistant professor in the Faculty of Education at the University of British Columbia in Vancouver. His professional interests include visual art, queer theory, postmodern pedagogies, research methodologies, embodied knowledge, the visual arts, and technology. He is the author of "Extending the Dialogues of Diversity: Sexuality Subjectivities and Education in the Visual Arts" in *Studies in Art Education* (1995) and "Researching Dissident Subjectivities: Queering the Grounds of Theory and Practice" in the *Harvard Educational Review* (1996).

Susanne Luhmann is a doctoral candidate in the Women's Studies Program at York University, Toronto, Canada. She is interested in the role of fantasy in reading race and sexuality. Her dissertation explores what happens when these categories become central in women's studies classrooms.

Erica Meiners is a PhD student in education at Simon Fraser University, near Burnaby, British Columbia, Canada.

Janet L. Miller is professor of education in National-Louis University's National College of Education. Since its inception in 1978, she has served as Managing Editor of *JCT: The Journal of Curriculum Theorizing*. She is the author of *Creating Spaces and Finding Voices* (SUNY Press, 1990), and the co-editor of *A Light in Dark Times: Conversations in Relation to Maxine Greene* (Teachers College Press, in press). Her research and publications focus on intersections of curriculum and feminist theories, collaborative teacher-research and issues of school reform, and autobiographical forms of postmodern educational inquiry. Elected Vice President of the American Educational Research Association, she will serve in that position for the 1997–1999 term.

Marla Morris is a PhD student in curriculum theory at Louisiana State University. A graduate of Tulane University (philosophy) and Loyola University (religious studies), she has made presentations at the Conference on Curriculum Theory and Classroom Practice and is the cultural products editor for the *Journal of Curriculum Theorizing*. She has published in the *Journal of Curriculum Theorizing and Taboo: The Journal of Culture and Education*. She teaches multiculturalism at LSU.

William F. Pinar teaches curriculum theory at Louisiana State University, where he serves as the St. Bernard Parish Alumni Endowed Professor. He has also served as the Frank Talbott Professor at the University of Virginia and the A. Lindsay O'Connor Professor of American Institutions at Colgate University (both visiting appointments); he taught at the University of Rochester from 1972 to 1985. He is the author of *Autobiography, Politics, and Sexuality* (Peter Lang, 1994), the senior author of *Understanding Curriculum* (Peter Lang, 1995), and the editor of *Curriculum: New Identities in/for the Field* (Garland, 1997).

Alice J. Pitt is an assistant professor in the faculty of education at York University, Toronto, Canada. She is interested in the implications of psychoanalytic theory for questions of pedagogy in contexts, including teacher education and feminist education, where equity and social change are the assumed and contested preoccupations for both teachers and learners. The chapter included in this volume was published in *JCT: Journal of Curriculum Theorizing*. Other work includes a chapter in *Dangerous Territories: Struggles for Difference and Equality in Education*, edited by Leslie Roman and Linda Eyre (Routledge, 1997), a recent essay with Deborah Britzman in *Theory Into Practice*. Forthcoming are essays in the *Review of Education/Pedagogy/Cultural Studies* and *The International Journal for Qualitative Studies in Education*.

Roger Platizky teaches English at Austin College in Sherman, Texas.

Nelson Rodriguez lectures in the English Department at Pennsylvania State University. The author of several articles on whiteness, he is the co-editor (with Joe Kincheloe, Shirley Steinberg and Ron Chennault) of *White Reign: Learning and Deploying Whiteness* (St. Martin's Press). He is also co-editor (with Leila Villaverde) of another book on whiteness (Peter Lang, in press). His research interests include cultural studies, critical pedagogy, and queer theory.

James T. Sears is professor of curriculum studies and higher education at the University of South Carolina. The author or editor of eight books, he serves on a variety of editorial boards, including the *Journal of Qualitative Research in Education*, the *Journal of Homosexuality*, and the

Journal of Educational Research. He resides on the sea islands near Charleston and in cyberspace at www.jtsears.com

Shirley R. Steinberg teaches at Adelphi University. She is an educational consultant and drama director. Her latest book is *Ain't We Misbehavin'? A Pedagogy of Misbehavior* (in press), and she is co-author with Joe Kincheloe of *The Stigma of Genius: Einstein and Beyond Modern Education* and *Changing Multiculturalism: New Times, New Curriculum* and *Kinderculture: The Corporate Construction of Childhood,* also with Joe Kincheloe. Along with Kincheloe and Aaron Gresson, she is also the editor of *Measured Lies: The Bell Curve Examined.* Steinberg and Kincheloe edit the journal *Taboo: The Journal of Culture and Education* and several book series. Her current research involves issues of diversity, popular culture, and curriculum.

Dennis Sumara is associate professor of education at York University, Toronto, Canada. He has published numerous articles in curriculum theory, action research, teacher education, and language arts education. He is the author of *Private Readings in Public: Schooling the Literary Imagination* (Peter Lang, 1996).

William G. Tierney is director of the Center for Higher Education Policy Analysis and professor in the School of Education at the University of Southern California. His most recent book is *Academic Outlaws: Queer Theory and Cultural Studies in the Academy* (Sage, 1997).

Rinaldo Walcott is an assistant professor in the Division of Humanities at York University, Canada. His teaching and research are in the areas of Black cultural studies and Black-Canadian and African-American literatures and cultures.

Author Index

Subject Index